PHILOSOPHERS
IN
WONDERLAND:

PHILOSOPHERS IN WONDERLAND

Philosophy and Psychical Research

Edited with an Introduction and Comments by

PETER A. FRENCH

1975
Llewellyn Publications
Saint Paul, Minnesota, 55165, U.S.A.

PHILOSOPHERS IN WONDERLAND: PHILOSOPHY AND PSYCHICAL RESEARCH. Copyright ©1975 by Peter A. French. All rights reserved. No part of this book, either in part or in whole, may be reproduced, transmitted or utilized in any form or by any means, electronic or mechanical, including photocopying, recording, or by any information storage and retrieval system, without permission in writing from the publisher, except for brief quotations embodied in critical articles and reviews. For information, address: Llewellyn Publications, Post Office Box 3383, St. Paul, Minnesota 55165. Manufactured in the United States of America.

International Standard Book Number: 0-87542-114-8
Library of Congress Catalog Card Number: 75-2318

ACKNOWLEDGMENT

No book springs forth from the presses without the assistance of many people other than the author. In this case, I owe special thanks to Peter Tritz and Martha Jo M. Onstad, who spent many hours working on the preliminary research for the book; to Professor Don Spring, who controls the funds of the Humanities Division and who loosened the purse strings; to Professor Theodore Uehling for criticisms and suggestions which have been most welcome and necessary; and to the students of Philosophy 1150 who served as willing guinea pigs in the formative stages of the book. Mr. Carl Weschcke is to be particularly commended for his courage in publishing a book in an area about which there is so little common understanding. I must express my sincerest gratitude to all of those philosophers with whom I have communicated in regard to this project. In allowing me to use their work all have been most encouraging, and some have even made revisions specifically for this volume. Finally, it is in the hope that other philosophers will carry on the investigation of the topics herein presented that this book is offered.

PREFACE

When a philosopher prepares a book primarily designed as a textbook, he generally offers some account of the value of doing philosophy and the relevance of the material in his book to the readers' attempt to understand his world. I have written such a book,[1] and I have at least two shelves of similar books in my office. Featured in books of this sort are ethical, social and political issues which the author hopes will seem very immediate to students and thereby attract them to the deeper analyses of philosophy. I have no intention of downplaying the relevance and importance of a great deal of philosophy to our everyday lives. In an age in which political intrigue, moral upheaval and social unrest predominate, the study of such philosophical issues as responsibility, obligation, justice, human rights and civil rights is not only called for, it is essential. These issues, when vaguely or poorly understood, are productive of many of the tensions of our age.

There is, however, more to philosophy than the study of the volatile issues. In fact, much of the work done in philosophy over the past 3000 years has been in the less dramatic areas of metaphysics and epistemology (theory of knowledge). These branches of the philosophical tree do not often bear the fruits of rebellion. They may fittingly be characterized as philosophy from the easy chair, not the barricade. Among the questions which one is likely to confront in the study of epistemology and metaphysics are: Is more than one space or time conceivable? What is a dream? What constitutes personal identity? What is the relationship between our linguistic practices and what we take to be the world? What is death? etc., all of which are important issues in the field of psychical research as well.

In recent years the occult, the paranormal and the world of psychical research have been rediscovered. I do not claim the sociological expertise to authoritatively say why interest in psychical research and related fields has risen to such a zenith; I have, as probably we all have, rather commonplace views on that matter. I suppose that a general dissatisfaction with organized religion plus a sense of impotence in the social and political world has led many people to a search for more than what is apparent, especially when what is apparent seems to many to be so superficial. At any rate, concern about telepathy, clairvoyance, psychokinesis, the world and powers of the dead, exorcism and other psychic phenomena has been much evidenced in a myriad of popular books, movies and television productions in the last few years. Yet in the exuberance of this contemporary concern it should not be forgotten that the study of psychic phenomena is by no means a recent endeavor, nor is philosophical interest in such phenomena and attempts to account for them a product of current fadism.

The famous Society for Psychical Research was founded in Great Britain in 1882. Among its early members were counted many prominent philosophers, including Henry Sidgwick (first president), Lewis Carroll, Gilbert Murray, Henri Bergson and William James; and through the years many other famous philosophers have joined their ranks. In this country not only has the American Society for Psychical Research been actively involved in the work of investigating purported psychic phenomena for many years, but also in North Carolina Professor J. B. Rhine some years ago founded a laboratory to study experimentally what he prefers to call "parapsychology." From Rhine's laboratory have come many statistical studies and reports on tests of persons with supposed highly developed psychic powers. It is Rhine, in fact, who coined the term "extrasensory perception"(ESP) as a convenient label under which to classify many kinds of purported psychic powers.

Despite all of this interest and activity, there exist today few books available to the student of philosophy which attempt both to decipher and to wrestle philosophically with the issues and claims of psychical research. That is not to say that there are no books by philosophers on the topic. C. D. Broad's *Lectures on Psychical Research*[2] is a weighty and extremely valuable work for those already well versed in both philosophy and psychical research. C. J. Ducasse also wrote a number of books on the subject, though again they are not specifically for the student. Psychical research and parapsychology, subjects of continuing general concern, have in fact proven to be gold mines for philosophic investigation and the vein is far from having "played-out."

I have attempted in this book to set forth a series of critical examinations into the propositions and beliefs of psychical research insofar as they are related to serious philosophical questions. Each chapter, excepting the first, should be treated as a symposium. Every attempt has been made to include the spectrum of philosophical opinion in the choice of selections, but these chapters do not provide the "last word" on the issues. That is left to the reader's critical appraisal.

A primary consideration which affected the choice of selections in this book was each author's employment of the tools and techniques of philosophical analysis as applied to the beliefs, theories and episodic accounts which characterize the Wonderland world of psychical research. The reader should be forewarned that the prevailing attitude throughout is critical and more than a bit skeptical. This book is not designed to win friends for psychical research or parapsychology. Rather, it puts into philosophical perspective those issues which lie concealed in all the talk of visitations from the dead, precognitive knowledge of the future, telepathic communication and things that go bump in the night. Unless one faces squarely these issues, the belief in paranormal occurrences and psychic powers is a hollow one, akin in many ways to a child's belief in Santa Claus and the tooth fairy. Undoubtedly many of us feel that there must be something to all of the reports of ESP, reincarnation, and the strange powers with which certain people are purportedly endowed. This book's central theme is that understanding this world of the psychical researchers necessitates an understanding of the concepts used to describe such a world. This understanding is at base philosophical.

PREFACE

A word or two might well be in order concerning how I came to have a deep interest in philosophical study of the concepts of psychical research. The answer revolves around a rather famous and bizarre probate trial in Phoenix, Arizona: the case of the will of James Kidd. During the spring and summer of 1967 the courtroom of Judge Myers was the center both of some of the most profound and the most idiotic goings on imaginable. When it was reported that a will written on an old legal size sheet of paper in barely legible hand had been discovered in the effects of one James Kidd, itinerant miner, there was little interest. After all, Kidd claimed to have had "no heirs." But when it was further revealed that Kidd had willed his earthly "fortune" to anyone who could produce a scientific proof that the soul of a human being departs the body at death, a few ears pricked and some interest in the probating of the will was aroused. It might, some groups and individual soul-searchers decided, provide a platform from which to expound one's views on these matters. Then came the bombshell. An audit of Kidd's holdings revealed that approximately $200,000 was the value of his behest. The court, as might be suspected, was inundated with claimants from everywhere. Churches, neurological institutes, mediums, psychical research organizations, individual soul-searchers, a medical school, and to no one's surprise a number of purported Kidd offspring arrived with attorneys to present their "bonafides." While the legal preliminaries were being conducted one of my colleagues on the philosophy staff at Northern Arizona University, Jere Jones,[3] suggested to the state's attorney general that some philosophical help was going to be necessary if all of the confusion of the various claims was to be removed. Hence, the philosophy staff entered the trial for the state of Arizona as a claimant. Should the monies of Kidd's estate eventually be awarded to the state, they would have gone toward the establishment of a chair in philosophical psychology. My introduction, then, to psychical research came in the form of studying the subject in preparation for the answering of interlocutory questionnaires. But the efforts of our philosophy staff were not to be successful in more ways than one. The monies were awarded to another claimant, and that other claimant was a neurological institute. We neither won, nor did we demonstrate to the satisfaction of the judge the basic intellectual, as opposed to experimental, nature of Kidd's conditions. Subsequent to the judge's ruling, however, the case was appealed and the ruling overturned. A second trial commenced, and in 1971 the Kidd behest, now valued at nearly $300,000, was granted to the American Society for Psychical Research.

What did I as a philosopher learn from the experience? In large measure, the answer is this book.

P. A. F.

NOTES

1. *Exploring Philosophy*. Cambridge and Morristown: Schenkman Co. and General Learning Press, 1970.
2. London: Routledge and Kegan Paul, 1962.
3. Now at Brooklyn College, N. Y. C.

CONTENTS

ACKNOWLEDGEMENT   V
PREFACE   VII

INTRODUCTION
"Down the Rabbit Hole"

CERTAINTY AND THE REAL CHALLENGE OF PSYCHICAL RESEARCH   3
    Peter A. French

FIRST SYMPOSIUM
"If only you'd been really with me in my dreams"

DREAMS: OPENING NOTE   23
    Peter A. French
SOME QUESTIONS ABOUT DREAMING   27
    John Hunter
THE PROBLEM OF DREAMS   44
    Roger Squires

SECOND SYMPOSIUM
"I wonder what latitude or longitude I've got to"

SPACES: OPENING NOTE   59
    Peter A. French
SPACE   61
    Immanuel Kant
SPACES AND TIMES   65
    Anthony Quinton
MULTI-SPATIAL MYTHS: KANT AND THE DREAMER   80
    Peter A. French

THIRD SYMPOSIUM
"If you knew time as well as I do"

TIME AND PRECOGNITION: OPENING NOTE	91
Peter A. French	
TIME AND TIME AGAIN	95
T. E. Wilkerson	
TIME TRAVEL	100
Hillary Putnam and J. J. C. Smart	
TIME AND APPARENT PRECOGNITION	106
H. F. Saltmarsh	
THE MYSTERY OF TIME	115
O. K. Bouwsma	

FOURTH SYMPOSIUM
"Why there's hardly enough of me left to make one *respectable person!"*

MIND AND BODY: OPENING NOTE	135
Peter A. French	
PARAPSYCHOLOGY AND DUALISM	140
Roland Walker	
MIND/BODY AND 'PSI'	154
Michael Scriven and J. G. Pratt	
MINDS AND MYSTIFICATIONS	163
A. G. N. Flew	
MATTER, MIND AND PRECOGNITION	168
A. Campbell Garnett and G. I. Mavrodes	

FIFTH SYMPOSIUM
"I can't explain myself because I'm not myself you see"

PERSONAL IDENTITY: OPENING NOTE	183
Peter A. French	
PERSONAL IDENTITY AND BODY EXCHANGE	192
John Locke	
PERSONAL IDENTITY	203
Charles Daniels	
MEMORIES, BODIES AND PERSONS	217
D. E. Cooper	

CONTENTS xiii

SIXTH SYMPOSIUM
*"Somehow it seems to fill my head with ideas—
only I don't exactly know what they are"*

ESP, P. K. AND KNOWLEDGE: OPENING NOTE	227
Peter A. French	
MIND OVER MIND AND MIND OVER MATTER	232
H. H. Price	
NORMAL COGNITION, CLAIRVOYANCE AND TELEPATHY	244
C. D. Broad	
AN ANALYSIS OF FACTUAL KNOWLEDGE	275
Peter Unger	

SEVENTH SYMPOSIUM
*"And she tried to fancy what the flame of a candle looks like
after the candle is blown out"*

MEDIUMSHIP AND SURVIVAL AFTER DEATH: OPENING NOTE	289
Peter A. French	
SURVIVAL AND THE IDEA OF "ANOTHER WORLD" AND MEDIUMSHIP AND HUMAN SURVIVAL	297
H. H. Price	
WHY I DO NOT BELIEVE IN SURVIVAL	309
E. R. Dodds	
CAN A MAN IMAGINE HIMSELF WITNESSING HIS OWN FUNERAL?	318
Peter A. French	
MYSTICISM AND THE PARADOX OF SURVIVAL	330
J. J. Clarke	

EIGHTH SYMPOSIUM
*"Why sometimes I've believed as many
as six impossible things before breakfast"*

PHILOSOPHY, SCIENCE AND PSYCHICAL RESEARCH: OPENING NOTE	345
Peter A. French	
RATIONAL ACCEPTABILITY OF THE CASE FOR PSI	347
J. B. Rhine	
SCIENCE AND THE SUPERNATURAL	355
George Price	

INTRODUCTION

CERTAINTY AND THE REAL CHALLENGE OF PSYCHICAL RESEARCH
Peter A. French

"*Down the Rabbit Hole*"

CERTAINTY AND THE REAL CHALLENGE OF PSYCHICAL RESEARCH

Peter A. French

> It would strike me as ridiculous to want to doubt the existence of Napoleon; but if someone doubted the existence of the earth 150 years ago, perhaps I should be more willing to listen, for now he is doubting our whole system of evidence. It does not strike me as if this system were more certain than a certainty within it.
>
> Wittgenstein *On Certainty*, Sec.185

We live in a world in which most things are familiar, regular, certain. We seldom seek to examine the familiar. In fact, many of our everyday certainties are beyond our powers of investigation. We would not know how or where to start in questioning them. Despite the great advancing waves and storms of twentieth century science and technology our world of beliefs and certainties remains rather placid. There are, however, those who live or at least claim to live in a world far different from our own. There are those whose "certainties" would seem to be our "impossibilities," whose sense is our nonsense. Like Alice's wonderland world their world seems to operate according to fantastic laws. Things which just can't happen regularly do happen in their world. This book is a venture down the rabbit hole into one wonderland, that of psychical research. In order to explore the wonderland of psychical research, however, we need to understand our own frame of reference. We need to know what we are certain of, what are the limits of sense. We need to remind ourselves of the character of our world of certainty.

What is it to be certain of something? In the first place, there is not just one sort of certainty. Suppose that I were to tell you that I am certain that in three days our mutual friend will be arriving in town for a visit. You ask, "What makes you certain?" I respond that I have his letter to that effect. To be certain in these circumstances is to be confident, to feel one has good grounds for believing something and that the possibility of something else occurring has been excluded. You might, of course, remind me that our friend is not very dependable, that he tends to be late or forgetful, etc. Then perhaps I would amend my claim and say something like "I'm fairly certain that he's coming," or "I'm practically certain that he will arrive when he says he will." My confidence is weakened, but not to the point of giving up on him entirely. Most of our ordinary uses of "certain" would seem to be of this type. They are expressions of confidence in regard to matters of classification, matters of fact, and matters of expectation. Let us call this sense *Certainty-1* or *C-1* for reference. One characteristic of such certainties is that they are disputable, because *being* certain that something will happen or did happen does not imply that *it is* certain that it will or did happen. I can be certain that he will arrive as promised, you can be certain that he will not arrive as promised. "He will arrive in three days" is, however, either certain or not certain. In other words, things or events being certain and people being certain are entirely different and logically not related matters.

In the case of persons, to be certain (*C-1*) is to feel certain; though, conversely, feeling certain is not always being certain. I may well feel certain that he will arrive as promised, but not be certain of it. In fact, when I say that I am certain of it I open up doors for inquisition which are not opened if I say I only feel certain. You ask, "What makes you so certain?" I must provide reasons. You might even chide, "You can't be certain of that, don't you know him any better than that?" But if I had said, "I feel certain that he will arrive," you would appear foolish if you were to retort, "You can't feel certain, don't you know him better than that?"

We also talk of *making certain* and of *making it certain*. Suppose I were to say, "I am going to make certain that he will arrive at the promised time." You would then expect that I intend to telephone him or in some way contact him in order to insure that the time is agreed upon and that all possibilities of his failing to arrive on time have been brought to his attention. If I were to say, "I am going to make it certain that he arrives on time," you would most likely expect that I am planning on escorting him or in some way insuring that nothing will prevent his arrival at the promised time.

It is important to note when analyzing *C-1* certainty that "I am certain of it" is not equivalent to "I know it." *I know* usually means something like "I have the appropriate grounds for saying this." The English philosopher J. L. Austin (1911-1960) made this point clear.[1] He wrote:

> Giving my reasons for knowing is stating how I came to be in a position to know . . . when I say 'I know' I give others my word: I give others my authority for saying that "S is P."[2]

When I say "I know that a thunder storm is coming," others have a right to inquire of me, "How do you come by such information?" or, in effect, "How do you know that?" Suppose that I were to respond, "I heard the thunder in the west; it looks like rain, and we generally get our storms from the west at this time of year." But could I have made a mistake? Perhaps it wasn't thunder that I heard at all. Could I know something and be wrong about it? What I heard was the blasting out of a roadbed for a new super highway by a construction crew working west of my place. I didn't know that! Then I should not have claimed to know that a thunder storm was coming. When I say "I know something," I have the responsibility of getting it right, but that does not mean that I cannot be wrong. Being wrong is to have something decide against the truth of my claim. I can be shown that I did not know at all (be shown evidence that blasting was going on in the west). When I say "I know," I can be mistaken, though if I was mistaken I was inappropriately using the phrase "I know."

Compare the preceding to the situation of my saying "I am certain that a thunder storm is coming." As before, I am wrong. But notice that I cannot be asked, *"How* are you certain?" Instead, I am likely to be asked, *"Why* are you certain?" Questions about knowing are *How?* questions. Questions about certainty are *Why?* questions. People may be certain about something or feel certain about something they do not know. Some religious people are certain that there is a Heaven and that they will go to their eternal reward, but it would not be appropriate to say that they know it. They believe it. In fact, I may be certain that there is no Heaven and that there are no eternal rewards. To cite a complementary example, in regard to knowing, if you know that there is a robin in the willow tree I cannot know that there is no robin in the willow tree. One of us just cannot know what he is claiming to know.

"Being certain," contrary to "knowing," is quite compatible with being wrong. One can without infelicity say one is certain where one is mistaken. No doubt no one says that he is certain while mumbling under his breath that he might be wrong. If I say, "I'm certain the storm is coming," surely I think that I know it is coming. Hence the tendency to look for equations between knowing and being certain.

Suppose that I report, "I am certain that I am now riding in a rocket ship to Mars." It is unlikely that anyone would say to me, "You are mistaken, you are here with us on Earth." No one, except in jest, would ask me, "Are you really certain?" Regarding the report of the approaching thunder storm, I was mistaken; I could be shown that I didn't know the facts. But as a response to "I am certain that I am now riding in a rocket ship to Mars," even the question "Why are you certain?" seems out of place. Let us compare this case with another: eight year old Johnny is sent to the board in his arithmetic class to complete the addition problem 10 + 12 = [?] and he writes 32 as the answer. Tim is sent to complete the same addition problem and he writes the answer 148. Johnny clearly has made a mistake. For whatever reason he has added an extra unit of tens, and it might be enough to get him to see his error if his teacher were to ask him, "Johnny, are you certain that that's the answer?" Tim, however, claims he is certain that he has the right answer, but Tim has not simply made a mistake; in fact, to argue that his answer of 148 is a mistake is to ignore Tim's problem. Tim has not slipped up on applying a rule of addition. He hasn't done anything remotely related to the problem. He does seem (only *seem*) to have the notion that when one is adding, the sum is greater than the parts; yet even that might be deceiving, for Tim could as well have written 9. Tim hasn't made a mistake in addition; he is not adding at all. As Ludwig Wittgenstein (1889-1951)[3] remarked in his *Lectures and Conversations,* "For a blunder, that's too big."

It is gratuitous to say Tim's answer is wrong: that is, when we make judgments of right and wrong, true and false, we depend upon a semi-stable ground for such judgments. Tim's answer to the addition problem as it is posed lies completely outside of the acceptable foundations of arithmetic. In order for Tim to justify his answer he would need to persuade us that some of our principles of addition would best be replaced with propositions of quite another sort—not something one would expect of an 8 year old.

It must be emphasized that Tim *feels certain* of his answer just as I *felt certain* that I was on a rocket ship to Mars. Yet one wants to say that neither Tim nor I *could be certain* of these matters. The reason for the reluctance to grant that Tim or I could *be certain* is that our certainty of the *C-1* sort is supported by another kind of certainty, *C-2*. Although certainty of the *C-1* sort is ordinarily compatible with getting it wrong, *C-2* certainty is only extraordinarily compatible with being wrong. In fact, it is so extraordinarily related to the possibility of mistake that "right" and "wrong" lose sense when applied to certainties of the *C-2* sort. *Certainty* when used in regard to *C-2* propositions is not the ordinary use of the term or at least not the common use of it. *C-2* certainty might be that sought by the great philosophers of Western tradition. Perhaps it is the certainty of Descartes (1596-1650),[4] Plato (427-347 B.C.), Leibniz (1646-1716). It is the certainty which is not compatible, at least in one important sense, with denial and doubt. Yet like *C-1*'s it is an expression of confidence and assurance; it comes veiled as common sensical fact.

"I am certain that I am alive, I am certain that I have not existed on Earth for the full span of Earth's years, I have certainly never been very far from Earth's surface." To these might be added,"I have two hands, Trees do not talk," and so on. I am certain of these rather uninformative statements, and so are you. There is a sort of communal certainty about them. We don't raise debate over them. One cannot imagine the topic for the debate society being "Trees do not talk." The English philosopher G. E. Moore (1873-1958)[5] called such common sensical statements *truisms* and maintained that when taken together they constitute the "beliefs of common sense." Moore argued, as did Thomas Reid (1710-1796)[6] and Dugald Stewart (1753-1828)[7] over a hundred years before Moore, that such statements of certainty are true, necessarily.

In a recently published collection of his last notes, Ludwig Wittgenstein contended that these so-called common sense truisms are not properly labeled "true" at all.[8] "True" could not mean what it normally does if it is used in regard to these propositions. To call them truisms is to overlook their function in our judgments of the world around us. In effect, the common sense beliefs which Moore, Reid and Stewart professed to have discovered are propositions which serve as the very basis of all of our investigative procedures. They seem to be certain in all of the *C-1* senses, but further, they cannot be doubted. They are not even open to "Why?" questions. Imagine asking anyone why he is certain that trees do not talk.

A collection of such *C-2* propositions, if Wittgenstein was right, serves as the framework of our knowledge and life. They are what he called in his *Philosophical Investigations* our "agreements in judgment." "If language is to be a means of communication there must be agreement not only in definitions but also (queer as this may sound) in judgments."[9] In Wittgenstein's terms the collection of *C-2* statements should be described as drawing the boundaries of our form-of-life. They are not suppositions for which we can amass supporting evidence. They are the very presuppositions of all of our judging, defending, reasoning, claiming to be certain *(C-1)*, investigating, knowing, etc. "I really want to say that a language-game is only possible if one trusts something (I did not say 'can trust something')."[10] *C-2* certainties are our trusted propositions. We don't have good reasons for holding them, or at least if one starts to offer reasons he soon runs out. In banker's language they are the collateral which secure our inquiries. Because they are taken to be the case other things are possible. They are, as Wittgenstein puts it, "something that lies beyond being justified or unjustified; as it were, as something animal."[11] As with *C-1* propositions, it is also inappropriate to confuse *C-2* propositions with things we know.

The propositions about which we may claim *C-2* certainty are those about which we should say, "Now, that just cannot be otherwise." *C-1's* are those propositions about which individuals can "make certain," whereas *C-2's* are "just certain." I cannot make certain that I have a body in the way that I can make certain that the noise that I hear is thunder and not the blasting of a construction crew. *C-2* propositions might best be described as *our* fundamental certainties. They are *my* certainties only insofar as I share this form-of-life. To a large extent my "making certain" and my answering "Why are you certain?" questions is dependent upon our acquiescence or tacit agreement with these fundamental certainties. They form a sort of jig-saw puzzle picture of our world view.

Like the pictures on the pieces of a jig-saw puzzle individual *C-2* propositions do not in themselves either reveal our whole world picture, nor do they always reveal themselves to be what they turn out to be in the complete picture. Nonetheless they are necessary elements in the construction of the whole, and their own sense is determinant only in respect to the whole. In effect, they get their sense from the whole even though they determine the whole in which they make sense. Once they are connected into the total picture they cannot be seen as something else. If they were to be seen differently, as for example one sees gestalt pictures—first one way, then another, our whole picture would be different. It would be chaotic. It would be Alice's wonderland world. There is a sort of mutual support between the picture as a whole and the pictures on each of the puzzle pieces. So too, there is mutual support between those propositions about which we are *C-2* certain and the hypotheses we formulate, the researches upon which we embark, the suppositions we entertain, the propositions about which we are *C-1* certain, the very things we say.

Our fundamental certainties could be described as our epistemological mythology. They tend to play roles like some kinds of game rules. Again Wittgenstein constructed a helpful metaphor. He tells us that it is as if some of our *C-1* propositions have hardened into *C-2's* so that they form a channel for those propositions which are not hardened but fluid. "The mythology may change back into a state of flux, the river-bed of thoughts may shift."[12] Wittgenstein further developed the metaphor:

> The bank of that river consists partly of hard rock, subject to no alteration or only to an imperceptible one, partly of sand, which now in one place now in another gets washed away, or deposited.[13]

Our *C-2* certainties, just like the river bank, channel our inquiry allowing us to accept one sort of judgment and demanding that we reject another sort. The constitutive rules of games permit some behavior and provide grounds for rejecting other kinds of behavior as inappropriate, as not playing the game. So too our *C-2* certainties set the boundaries of sense and mark off those enterprises we accept from those we adjudge to be half-witted or the entertainments of madmen. If I were to stop you on the street and tell you that I doubt that I have a body (remember that Descartes doubted that[14]), surely you would regard me as a fool. Imagine what it would be like to try to convince me that I do have a body. You could just pinch me or poke me or kick me while saying the sentence, "This proves you have a body." But that would not necessarily convince me that I have a body, for I might argue that no one has a body and you can't suppose those were real kicks or even real bruises. In a similar manner Tweedledum and Tweedledee "reduce" Alice to tears.

> "You know very well you're not real."
> "I *am* real!" said Alice and began to cry.
> "You won't make yourself a bit realler by crying." Tweedledee remarked ...
> "If I wasn't real," Alice said ... "I shouldn't be able to cry."
> "I hope you don't suppose those are *real* tears? Tweedledum interrupted in a tone of great contempt.

"We all have bodies," and we're not so ready to give up that. We cannot give it up without destroying all of our other judgments with it. If a skeptic asks, "How do you know you have a body?" or "How do you know trees do not talk?", one begins to feel a bit uneasy or disquieted. Consider the following short dialogue between a skeptic and an ordinary (that is, nonphilosophical) individual:

> Skeptic: "So you say you have a body?"
> Ordinary Individual: "I don't say it very often, but of course I do have a body."
> Skeptic: "How do you know? . . . How do you know you have a body?"
> O. I.: "I can do things with my hands. See, I'm raising them. I can walk using my legs. I am talking even now using my vocal cords, lungs and so on. I couldn't do all that without a body."
> Skeptic: "But how do you *know* you have a body? All you have said is that you can do things. That doesn't prove that you have a body. At best I suppose it shows that you think that you have a body or that you go about as if you have a body. Surely that's not going to count as *knowing* that you have a body."
> O. I.: (with agitation) "But what will count? What do I have to prove? What if I hit you in the face with my fist? Will that do?"
> Skeptic: "Hardly. You call that proof? And don't tell me that the blood I'll draw from your nose when I hit you back proves anything either. People don't go around proving things by fighting. Everyone knows what proofs look like anyway, say in geometry. And they don't look like that!" (waves his fist)
> O. I.: (disgruntled) "I can't deny I've got a body. I must have one!"

In regard to this dialogue, Wittgenstein's comment is apropos: "There is no judgment I could be certain of if I started doubting about that."[15] I am a fool if I sincerely doubt that I have a body because if the statement "He (in reference to me) has a body" is false, then our concepts of truth and falsity are meaningless. The skeptic's gambit is to take into the arena of knowing/proving (I know and I can prove it) what doesn't belong there. "I have a body" belongs in the arena of *C-2* certainty, where proving is not the issue. If we are *C-2* certain of X, to deny X is tantamount to collapsing the whole structure of knowledge in which the questions even of a skeptic make sense. One of the reasons the philosophy of David Hume (1711-1776)[16] is both so destructive and yet alluring is that by inappropriately asking a question of "knowledge" (a know/prove type) he seems to annihilate the very grounds for knowing or proving anything. Eliminating the *C-2* propositions from our form-of-life makes know/prove type investigations impossible. If it cannot be accepted that our foundation propositions rest on trust and all of our inquiry rests on trust, then inquiry itself cannot proceed.[17]

Our trusted *C-2* propositions, however, are not unchanging or forever fossilized in our form of life. Neither are they to be confused with the great German philosopher Immanuel Kant's (1724-1804)[18] categories of understanding, nor are Kant's categories to be viewed as stylized or capsulized versions of them. In his answer to David Hume's skepticism Kant correctly saw that knowledge is not only possible but that we have the right to claim to know a number of things. He also saw that in order for us to judge, it is necessary that there be boundaries imposed upon the use of evaluative language. And it was his view that the foundations or prerequisites of judgments could not be held open to criticism from within the system they characterize. What Kant failed to see, however, was that these requirements do not necessitate anything like universally shared categories of judgment. We should not want to say that the *C-2* certainties of our Western world view are universal or unchanging or even that they are exact. As Wittgenstein often pointed out in his *Philosophical Investigations*, exactness is not a necessary requirement of a limit or boundary.[19]

The Scottish philosopher Thomas Brown (1778-1820)[20] in his brilliant analysis of Hume's views on causation [21] voiced the opinion that our conceptions of causation and of the uniformity of nature (among other basic notions of our world view) are not to be discerned in experience. In that regard he agreed with Hume. But neither, he argued, are they simply the imaginative products of what Hume called the association of ideas. "The belief (in the uniformity of nature) is not the result of reasoning; and vain would be our toil, if we should endeavor to state some argument that originally convinces us of it." Brown added, however, "We believe the uniformity, in short, not because we can demonstrate it to others or to ourselves, but because it is impossible for us to disbelieve it." [22] Brown maintained that what we have called our *C-2* certainties are intuited beliefs and that "intuition does not stand in need of argument, but is quick and irresistible as perception itself."[23] We need not, however, attribute our *C-2* certainties to intuitions. It is adequate to say that though they may appear to be intuitions, *C-2's* are best described as limiting propositions (rules of a sort) which are embedded in our language as its very condition of use. In fact, it is that feature of their character which tends to make us think we intuit them. There is a further point made by Brown which helps to characterize our *C-2* certainties. He wrote:

> There is nothing which we can discover, as intervening in the process, between the observation and the wider belief; and therefore, whatever it may be, which the ingenuity of philosophers may strive to insert in it, we may be certain, at least, that it is not in our consciousness the supposed element is to be found.[24]

Let us attempt to list some of the *C-2* certainties which characterize our world view and against which the world of psychical research appears as sane as the Mad Hatter's tea party.

One of our *C-2's* is that events cannot have effects before they themselves have happened. Another is that causation at a considerable distance in space in the absence of intermediate causes is not possible. Should a man tell us that the match he struck in New York on the 5th of October caused the eruption of a volcano on an Icelandic island we surely would think him a comedian. There are other *C-2* certainties such as: events removed much in time (events in the past) cannot cause events in the present unless a sequence exists of other causes linking the first event to the eventual effect. English philosopher C. D. Broad (1887-1971) [25] also suggested some *C-2* certainties which he counterposed to the world of psychical research. He called his list "basic limiting principles."[26] This term, however, is not really appropriate to *C-2's*, for the class of *C-2* propositions includes far more than what might reasonably be called "principles." "I have a body, Trees do not talk, I have never been very far from the surface of the earth," etc., do not sound much like principles.

One often thinks of principles as consciously adopted rules (a principled man is one who intentionally acts consistently and strictly according to specific rules of conduct) or as methods of operation (a gasoline engine in an automobile operates according to the principle of internal combustion). There is also a widely used sense of "principle" as the fundamental source from which something proceeds. The *Oxford English Dictionary* cites as an example of such a use "Thales said that the first principle of all things was water." It might be argued that our *C-2* certainties are "principles" in this last sense in that all of our proper language use proceeds from them. This argument, however, could lead to a confusion of *C-2's* with what the contemporary linguist Noam Chomsky calls the *Depth Grammar* of our language.[27] There is also a sense in which propositions which form the basis for believing various other propositions, which "form the ground of, or are held to be essential to, a system of thought or belief," are said to be principles (for example, the principles of political economy), but here again "principle" has a formalized tone to it which should not be attached to *C-2* certainties.

Nonetheless Broad's list of "principles" helps us to see, even though they appear in stilted formal garb, some of those *C-2* propositions which are most relevant to our understanding of the world we leave behind when we are lured into the rabbit hole of psychical research. It will be helpful then to enumerate a few more *C-2's* based on Broad's list. We are *C-2* certain that mental processes in a human subject cannot directly bring about effects in the events of the physical world without the agency of the subject's body. Surely we would be suspicious of anyone who claimed to be able to move simply by thinking about them pieces of furniture in the rooms of a house many miles from where he is standing. We are certain that human beings do not have direct motive powers in regard to any natural objects other than their bodies. If a chair were to move from one corner of a room to another at just the moment someone was concentrating on moving that chair to that corner, we would search out the room for devices, wires, or riggings of some sort. Failing to find any apparent physical means of performing the feat, we would still be most unlikely to grant in any unqualified way that the feat was performed as advertised. Magic arts are fun to watch, but only because we do not really believe that the beautiful lady is being sawed in two. We would be more than a little uncomfortable if we thought that the magician was not aided by devices and illusions despite the fact that we cannot spot them.

Another of our *C-2's* would be that each of us knows what another is experiencing only by either observing the other's behavior or by being told what he is experiencing. I know that Johnny is in pain when I observe him exhibiting behavior generally associated with pain or when Johnny tells me that he is in pain. Not having observed Johnny nor heard from him nor received reliable reports about his behavior, it is inappropriate for me to say, "Johnny is in pain." If someone were to tell me that Johnny is in pain even though that person has never seen Johnny nor spoken to him nor received any communication of the normal sort (letter, telephone, call, etc.) nor received reliable accounts of Johnny's behavior from some third party, I must be most dubious as to whether Johnny is in pain. Surely I could not feel that I have any accurate information about Johnny's pain or that I know that he is in pain.

Our short list of *C-2* certainties should also include "All men are mortal" and "Death is the end of life" and "One can't experience the future in the present, one can only surmise, guess or draw inferences about the future from past data." Such inferences are licensed by another *C-2*: "The future will not be radically different from the past." It is noteworthy that this is *C-2* certain even though past experience would suggest that radical departures from behavior patterns do occur. Undoubtedly we would question the sanity of someone who claimed to be able to "see" the future as if it were going on before his eyes in the present. The statements "I know the future" and "I see the future" sound as though they mean something, but on inspection we haven't a notion what. We may understand all the words in such sentences, yet we are far from understanding them. Such an occasion is Alice's encounter with the Mad Hatter. One of their exchanges is as follows:

> "What a funny watch" she remarked. "It tells the day of the month, and doesn't tell what o'clock it is!"
> "Why should it?" muttered the Hatter.
> "Does your watch tell you what year it is?"
> "Of course not," Alice replied very readily: "but that's because it stays the same year for such a long time together."
> "Which is just the case with *mine*," said the Hatter.
> Alice felt dreadfully puzzled. The Hatter's remark seemed to her to have no sort of meaning in it, and yet it was certainly English. "I don't quite understand you," she said, as politely as she could.

If someone were sincerely to say that he knew the future, we wouldn't know how to go about convincing him that he cannot know or see that. If something we were to say to him would be such as to lead him to doubt that he knew the future we would not know how or why it had done so.[28] Of course he probably would scoff at us who must doubt his powers and say something like, "You don't know the future, but those of us who do, know what knowing the future is like; besides, you can't explain everything anyway." Then, as Wittgenstein says, "We should feel ourselves intellectually very distant from someone who said this."[29]

The power and the place of our fundamental convictions, our *C-2* certainties, in our investigating procedures and in our form-of-life as well is inestimable. Our *C-2* certainties serve as the "scaffolding of our thoughts." It was Broad's contention that they determine the grounds of normalcy. Our scientific theories and laws and our everyday theories all rest on the foundations of the certainty of our collection of these propositions.

Not too long ago the famous American parapsychologist Gardner Murphy published a book entitled *Challenge of Psychical Research*.[30] The book is an anthology of case histories and laboratory reports on various sorts of ostensible psychical phenomena interspersed with the author's commentary. It is a very informative book, but its title is misleading, for the real challenge of psychical research is not discussed.

Psychical researchers investigate the occurrence of events which are not possible.

That is a strong statement. At first it appears to be an indictment of psychical research. It is not. Instead it poses the problem of the real challenge of psychical research. The challenge is neither to psychology nor to physics. The real challenge of psychical research is to the *C-2* certainties of our form-of-life. It is a challenge to our fundamental convictions, those upon which the sciences and, in fact, what we count as a science rest. If psychical research is to accomplish anything of value, it must either clearly formulate an alternative world picture to that which is incorporated in our ordinary language or demonstrate that the phenomena it claims as its subject matter are nothing but slightly abnormal goings-on which are totally explicable when correspondingly slight alterations are made in current scientific laws (which includes perhaps changes in current psychological laws).

The latter route seems to be that recommended by parapsychologist J. B. Rhine. He identified what he calls *psi phenomena* as those occurrences that have been shown by investigation to be unexplainable wholly in terms of physical principles.[31] Rhine did not, however, make clear what he conceived "non-physical" to be. It seems to amount to "not known to be physical," that is, it necessitates a psychological explanation; but Rhine did not make it clear what he meant by "physical" and "psychological." Because he failed to give a clear account of what is non-physical other than to say that the occurrences in question are not amenable to explanation under the existing laws of physics, all we have grounds for saying is that the phenomena in question are "not known" to be physical. There is quite a difference between saying that and saying that the events studied by psychical research are non-physical.

Rhine failed to grasp the significance of the statements one would have to make when trying to describe *psi phenomena*. Such statements are not even like the descriptions of physical anomalies in the history of science.[32] Nor are they like statements describing abnormalities. Compare an account of the appearance of an apparition of the dead to an account of the birth of Siamese twins sharing one heart. The birth of Siamese twins is abnormal. It violates expectations which are sanctioned by physical law. Statements describing such births though are not senseless. We know how to deal with or at least we have built into our systems of knowledge ways of dealing with abnormality. Usually the way of dealing with apparent abnormal occurrences is to show that the violated natural laws are not actually violated by the occurrence. In the case of the abnormal birth of Siamese twins sharing one heart we might explain that such an event could be expected to occur with a low probability consistent with genetic laws. In some instances the apparent abnormal occurrences might be such that it would force us to alter our accepted physical laws or at least admit a number of exceptions to such laws. The point is, however, that the reports of apparent abnormalities are not sufficiently shocking to elicit such a reaction as, "If that's true, then I know nothing at all." They pose a challenge to our conception only of the laws of nature.[33]

The accounts given of psychical phenomena, e.g. the appearance of an apparition of a dead relative, are, however, different in kind from those given of abnormalities. After reading many such accounts (see symposiums), one wants to say, "If that's true, how can I be certain of anything anymore?" It is as though something that we had thought to have excluded intrudes, the unwelcome guest at a party. The laws of nature are not as much threatened as is the very ground on which the formulation of those laws makes sense. If, for example, J. W. Dunne did have precognitive knowledge,[34] if he could move forward in time, "out of sync" with the rest of us, then our concept of time seems itself threatened.

This is far more than just a matter of saying, "Alright, what I took to be certain is not so; it was just one way of looking at the world." It cannot be that, because to say that is to say, "I cannot be certain." Take away certainty and inquiry loses its point. Dispute disappears when certainty disappears. Consider this last point. One cannot dispute what is *C-2* certain, but one could not dispute anything if nothing were *C-2* certain. The disputes of science, mathematics and philosophy only take place where there is agreement on *C-2* certainties. Should two scientists not substantially share a set of *C-2* certainties, they could not dispute. Their attempts at arguments would be what in informal logic are called "talking at cross purposes."

The seismic effect of apparent psychical phenomena is not appreciated if those phenomena are classed as abnormal goings-on, and Rhine was entirely confused when he claimed that psi-phenomena are a normal part of nature.[35] To borrow a term (and to some degree the account of it) from C. D. Broad,[36] apparent psychical phenomena must be classed as *paranormal*. Let us then define *paranormal events* as those events the accounts of which must include sentences which are strictly nonsensical. These sentences cannot be true or false statements because they violate the grounds of our judging truth and falsity.

If psychical research is the study of apparently paranormal phenomena, and if admittedly such phenomena are not explainable by application of any of the usual methods in our form-of-life, what justification is there for such an endeavor, and why ought philosophers be interested in it? Haven't we just written the whole business off as nonsensical?

The study of nonsense and its production is not itself nonsensical; often it is illuminating. It can reveal to us much of the sensible. Wittgenstein proffered the exhortation that philosophers study grammatical jokes.[37] Psychical research might be seen as a collection of rather better than ordinary grammatical jokes. Also we have maintained that our certainties, even of the *C-2* variety, are not permanent fixtures. They do change, not like Latin American governments, but nonetheless, as the metaphor of the river and its bed suggests, there is shifting; and sometimes a meander forges out a new channel. It is not usually dramatic; it is a slow process. Yet the nonsense of today's psychical research might well be the certainty of tomorrow's psychology and even eventually the certainty of our common linguistic heritage.

Such a remote possibility, however, is hardly a good reason for studying psychical research from a philosophical point of view. Instead, the study of nonsense of this sort is itself edifying. The propositions of psychical research, those which purportedly describe and explain such ostensible phenomena as telephathy, clairvoyance, psycho-kinesis, astral projection and mediumistic communication appear to be quite sensible on first reading. They sound plausible, even to the point of being alluring to those of us who claim to be normally sensible people. In this regard they are very like many of the propositions one encounters in the history of philosophy such as: "I know when I'm in pain; Meaning is an act; A thing is identical with itself; I can only know another is thinking, feeling, etc. by analogy to myself." The nonsense here is not evident: it is "disguised." The task of a philosopher, as conceived by Wittgenstein, is the "uncovering of one or another piece of plain nonsense and of bumps that the understanding has got by running its head up against the limits of language."[38] The philosopher's aim is to discover how to "pass from a piece of disguised nonsense to something that is patent nonsense."[39] But the philosopher does more than merely follow the consequences of disguised nonsense until it becomes obvious nonsense. Nonsense, to adopt a phrase from the contemporary American philosopher George Pitcher, can be used "like a vaccine that cures us of itself."[40] What better source to turn to for the raw material of philosophy than one about which so much has been written and into which so many supposed investigations have been launched?

It is also the case that in the attempt to expose nonsense and thereby to come to understand sense, a fruitful technique—again one developed by Wittgenstein—is the attempt to describe worlds in which the *C-2* certainties are different from our own.

> If anyone believes that certain concepts are absolutely the correct ones, and that having different ones would mean not realizing something that we realize—then let him imagine certain very general facts of nature to be different from what we are used to, and the formation of concepts different from the usual ones will become intelligible to him. (*P. I.* p. 230)

The world of psychical research is an already conceived one (or at least it purports to be one) in which "certain very general facts of nature" are radically different from our own. But to appreciate its philosophical value one must become its captive. Like Alice in wonderland one must be taken in to feel the full impact of such nonsense. The philosophical examination of psychical research is then the study of the function (use and meaning) of the propositions of psychical research, a study which necessarily involves trying to function in the world of psychical research.

We shall then embark upon both an entertaining and profitable adventure in a world where people will tell you that it is certain[41] that some people can know the future by directly experiencing it in the present, that events in the minds of some people can cause physical events in the absence of direct bodily influence, that men are immortal, that people can communicate without using any of the recognized channels for so doing, that there is more than one space, etc.

It would be wise as we begin this investigation to remind ourselves of another remark of Wittgenstein:

> The philosopher is the man who has to cure himself of many sicknesses of the understanding before he can arrive at the notions of the sound human understanding.

To this he adds:

> If in the midst of life we are in death, so in sanity we are surrounded by madness.[42]

NOTES

1. J.L. Austin was one of the most important figures in the Oxford school of ordinary language philosophy. His major papers are collected in *Philosophical Papers* (1961). His work on sensation and related topics is found in *Sense and Sensibilia* (1964), and his very influential discussion of language is found in *How to Do Things with Words* (1962). Austin was basically interested in drawing out the fine distinctions which are operative in our way of using words. Much of his writing is a summary of his meticulous research into word usage. One of the values of his work is the revealing to other philosophers the ordinary usage of language from which they, to his way of thinking, depart only at the risk of saying something nonsensical. Austin's research into linguistic usage led him to the development of his theory of speech acts, one of the most provocative notions in contemporary philosophy.

2. *Philosophical Papers*, (Oxford, 1961, 1970), pp. 81, 99.

3. Ludwig Wittgenstein, perhaps more than any other philosopher, has been the generating spirit of nearly a century of Anglo-American thought. He wrote *Tractatus Logico-Philosophicus* (1922), which emphasized that the central task of philosophy is the clarification of language use, making propositions clear. In his later works, *Blue and Brown Books* (1958), *Philosophical Investigations* (1953), *Zettel* (1966) and *On Certainty* (1969) a far freer picture of language using than that necessitated by the strict application of logic in the Tractatus predominated. It is characteristic of the later Wittgenstein that he emphasized the multi-uses of language and the relationship between contexts and language use (language-games). Philosophy, as the later Wittgenstein pictured it, does not discover new

data; it clarifies by careful description.

4. "The first rule was never to accept anything as true unless I recognized it to be certainly and evidently such: that is, carefully to avoid all precipitation and prejudgment and to include nothing in my conclusions unless it presented itself so clearly and distinctly to my mind that there was no reason or occasion to doubt it."

Descartes, *Discourse on Method*, Second Part, 1637.

"Since reason already convinces me that I should abstain from the belief in things which are not entirely certain and indubitable no less carefully than from the belief in those which appear to me to be manifestly false, it will be enough to make me reject them all if I can find in each some ground for doubt."

Descartes, First Meditation, *The Meditations Concerning First Philosophy*, 1641.

5. G.E. Moore is responsible, in large measure, for the analytical bent of Twentieth Century Anglo-American philosophy. Moore is often classed as a defender of common sense against the views of idealism. His principal works include *Principia Ethica* (1903) and *Philosophical Studies* (1922). Moore insisted that there are usually good reasons for using language in the common sensical way and that when attention is paid to such usage many apparent philosophical puzzles are cleared up.

6. Reid's principal work is entitled *Essays on the Intellectual Powers of Man* (1785). He also wrote *Essays on the Active Powers of the Human Mind* (1788). Reid was the leader of the Scottish school of common sense philosophy which predominated on the British Isles in the latter part of the Eighteenth Century.

7. Stewart was a follower of Reid. His major works include *Elements of the Philosophy of the Human Mind* (1792) and *The Philosophy of the Active and Moral Powers of Man* (1828). Stewart hoped to transform the "science of mind" into a Baconion investigation. Reid referred to intuitive convictions as "the principles of common sense." Stewart called them "the fundamental laws of human belief," but his descriptions of them were not too different from Reid's accounts. Stewart argued that these "laws of human belief" carry with them the tacit consent of mankind; they cannot be denied without giving evidence of insanity.

8. *On Certainty* (Oxford, 1969). Hereafter referred to simply as *O.C.*)

9. *Philosophical Investigations* (Oxford, 1953) Sec. 242. (Hereafter referred to simply as *P.I.*)

10. *O.C.* Sec. 509.

11. *O.C.* Sec. 359.

12. *O.C.* Sec. 97.

13. *O.C.* Sec. 99.

14. "... and let us think that perhaps our hands and our whole body are not such as we see them." Descartes, *First Meditation*.

15. *O.C.* Sec. 490.

16. Hume was an empiricist. He argued that all knowledge comes from impressions and ideas which are copies of impressions or the results of the association of other ideas. We do not have general ideas but only ideas of particular things which we can consider collectively by the use of general terms. Such notions as the uniformity of nature, causality and even the self are constructions of habit and imagination and are not seen or demonstrable in experience. Hume argues that we have good reasons for skepticism because there is inadequate evidence to support most of our beliefs. Hume, however, finds that in practice we must believe those very things about which he had raised skeptical doubts. Hume's philosophy has been a major influence on contemporary philosophy, and many historians of philosophy rank his works as the best in the English language. Hume's major works were: *The Treatise of Human Nature* (1737), *Dialogues Concerning Natural Religion* (1779) and *Enquiry Concerning the Principles of Morals* (1751).

17. Albert Einstein wrote: "Certain it is that a conviction akin to religious feeling, of rationality or intelligibility of the world, lies behind all scientific work of a higher

order." *Essays in Science*, (New York, 1934), p. 11.

And Norbert Wiener maintained in his *The Human Use of Human Beings* (Garden City, 1954) that faith is a necessity for science. (pp. 187-193).

18. Kant must be considered one of the greatest philosophers in the Western tradition. Kant attempted to meet Hume's skepticism by establishing the possibility of metaphysics. Kant saw the necessity of universal and necessary truths which cannot be derived from experience, or knowledge would have no basis. Kant's work is far too vast to capsulize, and it would be an injustice to try to do so. His major works include: *The Critique of Pure Reason* (1781), *The Critique of Practical Reason* (1788), *Prologomena to Any Future Metaphysics* (1783) and *The Critique of Judgment* (1790).

19. *P.I.* Secs. 68, 71, 76, 79, 99, 163, and 499.

20. Brown opposed much of the Eighteenth Century Scottish common-sense traditions of Reid and Stewart, though he did share with them the appeal to intuitive truths. Brown was a precursor of the analytic movement in 20th century philosophy. He was a tireless analyst of what he took to be disguised notions. Brown united empirical analysis with the principle that the authority by which we invoke such notions as the uniformity of nature is intuitive certainty. Brown's principal works were: *Inquiry Into the Relation of Cause and Effect* (1818) and *Lectures on the Philosophy of the Human Mind* (1820).

21. *Inquiry Into the Relation of Cause and Effect* (Edinburgh, 1818) Part Fourth.

22. *Ibid.*, p. 304.

23. *Ibid.*, pp. 313-314.

24. *Ibid.*, p. 316.

25. Broad has written extensively in many areas of philosophy. Of concern to us is his work on the issues of psychical research. His most important work in that area is *Lectures on Psychical Research* (London, 1962). It is perhaps the most detailed and sympathetic account of the subject and its ramifications.

26. C.D. Broad, *Lectures on Psychical Research* (London, 1962), Introduction.

27. Noam Chomsky argues that underlying our use of language is a grammar that is only revealed after one has passed from consideration of surface syntactical structures to a consideration of transformational rules. Implicit in Chomsky's view is the belief that the depth grammars of the various languages are essentially similar and hence that all language using depends ultimately on certain innate grammatical structures. See his *Syntactic Structures* (1959), *Aspects of the Theory of Syntax* (1965) and also *Cartesian Linquistics*.

28. See *O.C.* Sec. 257.

29. *O.C.* Sec. 108.

30. (New York, 1961).

31. Note Rhine and J.G. Pratt's account of psi phenomena in their *Parapsychology* (Springfield, Ill., 1957) Chapter 1.

32. For a useful account of what is involved when anomalies occur in science see T.S. Kuhn, *The Structure of Scientific Revolution* (Chicago, 1962).

33. It is of note that the laws of physics are perhaps best described as inaccurate and for good reason. See M. Scriven "The Key Property of Physical Laws - Innaccuracy" in Feigl and Maxwell *Current Issues in the Philosophy of Science*, (1961), pp. 91-101.

34. See appendix.

35. Rhine and Pratt, *op. cit.*, p. 12.

36. Broad, *op. cit.*

37. *P.I.* Sec. 111.

38. *P.I.* Sec. 119.

39. *P.I.* Sec. 464.

40. "Wittgenstein, Nonsense and Lewis Carroll," in K.T. Fann, *Ludwig Wittgenstein* (New York, 1967), p. 315.

41. Psychical researchers, at least those related to the famous societies both in England and the U.S.A., would argue that they are themselves skeptical of the purported phenomena they investigate. The Society for Psychical Research, in fact, claims to have no bias at all. It is undeniably the case, however, that in the attempts of Society members from Myers to H.H. Price to explain the phenomena of their investigations the philosophically interesting substitutions of alternative world views have occurred.

42. *Remarks on The Foundations of Mathematics*, Part IV, Sec. 53.

FIRST SYMPOSIUM

DREAMS: OPENING NOTE
Peter A. French

SOME QUESTIONS ABOUT DREAMING
John Hunter

THE PROBLEM OF DREAMS
Roger Squires

"If only you'd been really with me in my dreams"

DREAMS: OPENING NOTE

Peter A. French

Accounts of dream experiences comprise a major portion of the sporadical cases studied by psychical researchers. Note for example the following cases from the files of the Society for Psychical Research:

Mrs. D. wrote to Dr. Hodgson:

June 22nd, 1899

In reply to your letter of the 20th to Mr. Davis, relating to our "dreams," I will relate my experiences as perfectly as possible.

The first sensation I remember in my dream was of finding myself sinking in a pool, a large pool, or pond of water by the roadside, and of throwing up my arms above the water and trying to scream for help, and just as I felt my hand grasped by someone, I could not tell by whom, to help me, Mr. Davis spoke and I awoke.

I sometimes have unpleasant dreams and make a slight sound, when he always wakens me, but we both thought it remarkable when on this occasion we found that there was perfect coincidence in the time, even to a second, and almost perfect coincidence in the subject matter of our dreams.

June 18th, 1899

Noticing your address in the N.Y. *Sunday Journal* of even date, I write to tell you of an instance of telepathy in which, as an additional straw, your Society may find interest.

In the summer of '97, one night while sleeping I dreamed that I was in an old, abandoned and ruined saw-mill, which was built on timbers out over a river. The plank floor was gone except for now and then a plank, and the water, about eight feet below, looked black, stagnant and slimy. There were just enough planks and timbers left to cause a "creepy," shadowy darkness to prevail below. There were two ladies came to look at the place, and being afraid to trust the planks for footing, I took one on each arm, and was proceeding out to the further end of the ruin, over the water to where the old saw was, when something white glimmering in the water below through the dusk attracted my attention, and I saw it to be the face of my wife, . . . Mrs. D., just showing above the water, with her large eyes looking into mine, but without a motion or sound. I immediately jumped into the water and caught her round the shoulders and neck to support her, and at that instant was roused from sleep by a smothered cry from Mrs. D. at my side. Intuitively I knew how matters were and asked her (after shaking her to awaken her) what she had dreamed to frighten her.

She said that she was dreaming that she was in the water drowning and was trying to reach up her arms to help herself, and cried out as I heard her . . . .

The purported phenomena of astral projection or astral wandering (out-of-body experiences) also are most often described as occurring during sleep. It is therefore essential to an attempt to understand many of the accounts of psychic phenomena to first come to some understanding of the concept of dreaming. Dreams are not, however, unproblematical from a philosophical point of view. Issues which often puzzle philosophers are the question of the reality of dreams and whether dreams are conscious experiences.[1] Do dreams belong in the catalogue of a person's experiences? If so, then the door is opened to a serious consideration of dream episodes, nocturnal adventures, as real and thereby appropriate subjects of scientific and perhaps historical interest.

There are, however, a number of reasons for not holding the view that dreams are experiences, not the least of which is to be found in the everyday way we talk about our dreams. Generally we preface the telling of our dreams with the expression "In my dream . . ." or "Last night while dreaming . . .," which seems to indicate that we do not take what follows to be legitimate reports of our experiences or events in our biographies. Few people take seriously the things they report having done in their dreams and still fewer yet expect to meet with the consequences of their dream-behavior at any future time, even in the next night's dream. Nonetheless, there remains a nagging suspicion that there is more to dreams than mere entertainment or the telling of breakfast table stories or the fantasizing of a repressed *id*. It is difficult to ignore the fact that such a suspicion dates back as far as recorded history.

We begin this philosophical expedition into the psychical researcher's Wonderland with a symposium on the nature of dreams. At least in the case of dreams we all have a notion, albeit often a muddled one, of the subject of our inquiry. Almost no one claims never to have dreamed.

> So she sat on, with closed eyes, and half believed herself in Wonderland, though she knew she had but to open them again, and all would change to dull reality . . . .

NOTES

1. Rene Descartes wrote: Nevertheless, I must remember that I am a man, and that consequently I am accustomed to sleep and in my dreams to imagine the same things that lunatics imagine when awake, or sometimes things which are even less plausible. How many times has it occurred that "the quiet of" the night made me dream "of my usual habits": that I was here, clothed "in a dressing gown," and sitting by the fire, although I was in fact lying undressed in bed! It seems apparent to me now, that I am not looking at this paper with my eyes closed, that this head that I shake is not drugged with sleep, that it is with design and deliberate intent that I stretch out this hand and perceive it. What happens in sleep seems not at all as clear and as distinct as all this. But I am speaking as though I never recall having been misled, while asleep, by similar illusions! When I consider these matters carefully, I realize so clearly that there are no conclusive indications by which waking life can be distinguished from sleep that I am quite astonished, and my bewilderment is such that it is almost able to convince me that I am sleeping. (*Meditations*, trans. by Laurence J. Lafleur, New York: Bobbs-Merrill, Liberal Arts Press, 1960, pp. 76-77)

And G.E. Moore wrote: . . . even in sleep, so long as we dream we are performing acts of consciousness. (*Some Main Problems of Philosophy*, London: Allen and Unwin, 1953, p. 4)

In *Human Knowledge*, Bertrand Russell maintained: What, in dreams, we see and hear, we do in fact see and hear, though, owing to the unusual context, what we see and hear gives rise to false beliefs. Similarly, what we remember in dreams we do really remember; that is to say, the experience called "remembering" does occur. (London: Allen and Unwin, 1948, pp. 214-15)

SOME QUESTIONS ABOUT DREAMING

John Hunter

1. *Is it possible that we do not experience anything when we dream, but that something happens in our brains when we sleep, and when we awake it seems to us that we have had the experiences that we call dreams?*

The above possibility is of course counter-intuitive, because we have the very strongest conviction that in dreams we do have experiences, broadly resembling waking experiences, of people and places, of conversations, of doing things and having things happen to us. But is it not possible that we are not in fact conscious of these things at the time the dream is supposed to have occurred, but that what then happened was a certain activity of our nervous system such that, had we been conscious, it would have resulted in our having the experiences that it seems to us on waking that we had? According to this supposition, it is not the case that *nothing* happened as we slept, but that what did happen was not what later seems to us to have happened, but rather the neurological correlate that such experiences would have had, had they been conscious; and that in remembering or seeming to remember dreams, the same sort of neurological mechanism is at work that enables us to remember waking experiences: the neurological correlate leaves traces of some kind which later in some way are responsible for our recollections; and as long as the neurological correlate occurs, it is not necessary to our remembering (or seeming to remember) that there should have been any experience of which it was the correlate.

This conjecture is stated in very general terms, and includes no sophistication as to how exactly the nervous system operates in these regards, but this should not be an objection. It is extremely unlikely to make any difference to the discussion we are embarking on whether the nervous system works this way or that. *A priori* one would think that the only discoveries in this area that would bear on our discussion would be either *(a)* that we remember by "storing" the shapes, colors, sounds, etc., that we experience in just the form in which they are experienced, or *(b)* that the nervous system is not involved in memory, but that (perhaps) spiritual substance does the job quite independently of our bodies. But given only that the nervous system is indispensable, our question does arise.

A thesis of the above kind would seem to square well enough with various reasonable assumptions, if not known facts:

(i) It seems reasonable to suppose that there is some correlate in our nervous

Reprinted from *Mind*, Vol. 80 (1971). Used by permission of the editor and Basil Blackwell, publisher.

system of every experience we have, that this correlate is causally responsible for our experiences and that the mechanism by which we remember an experience is not one of somehow storing the experience itself, but of somehow storing the neurological correlate of it.

(ii) It seems reasonable to suppose that if the neurological correlate of an experience occurs, it will not be necessary to the functioning of the recollective machinery that the phenomenological correlate should have occurred, just as, if electrical impulses in an amplifier can cause the impression of someone singing, then although normally a singer is necessary to provide the input, it will be theoretically possible to deliver the output without the aid of a vocalist.

(iii) It is reasonable to believe that one has to be conscious in order to experience anything, and that since in sleep one is not conscious, no experience occurs: there is no phenomenological correlate.

(iv) One is easily able on this supposition, to account for the fact that we seem to *recall* dreams: something (namely the neurological correlate) did occur while we slept; and it is by virtue of the functioning of the same mechanisms as normally operate in remembering that we have the impression that we dreamt.

(v) One is easily able to account for the fact that dreams are at least roughly datable by the occurrence during sleep of such behavior as smiling, frowning, muttering, etc.: something did happen at that juncture, and it is quite believable that we should acquire a disposition to react directly to the neurological correlate of an experience, in the same way that we would have reacted to the experience itself.

(vi) One might with this thesis also be able to explain some bizarre features of dreams. A young man dreams of a delightful flirtatious conversation with a girl, who however looks like Joseph Stalin. These things, one feels just will not go together into a possible experience, but it is quite possible that the neurological correlates of the two things should occur at the same time.

In spite of these considerations I find that I cannot believe this theory about dreams. I suspect that my reasons I give may be only a justification of what I (do not) believe on instinct, but I do offer the following counter-arguments:

(i) It is somewhat surprising, if this theory is true, that we do not remember things that happen around us when we sleep, such as conversations that occur in our neighborhood. It is at least possible that when a sound is made near us, the neurological correlate of our hearing a sound occurs, but just does not, as one might put it, "reach consciousness"; and if it does occur, one would expect on this theory that it would sometimes be remembered upon waking. It is of course an empirical question just where the neurological activity stops, and if it were found to stop just at the eardrums then this point would turn out to be worthless. But not only might it stop there, there is a presumption that it does not in the fact that teaching can be done with microphones under our pillows while we sleep. This phenomenon seems to count in another way as evidence against the thesis: people *absorb* what is fed to them during sleep, but it does not appear to them later that they have *heard* what they thereby acquire, the way it seems to us later that we have experienced the content of a dream. They do not know where it came from.

(ii) It seems probable *a priori* that there would be some neurological feed-back from our actually being conscious of something, so that there would be different traces, or whatever, from the same neurological process when it did and when it did not have a phenomenological counterpart, and that this difference would show in the way it appeared to us when we remembered it. This might explain why it is that when a person has been fed information while asleep, though he absorbs it, he has no impression as to how he acquired it.

(iii) In the cases where one can be persuaded that something one might otherwise have been inclined to suppose to be an experience is not in fact—in the case of meaning what one says, for example, or of intending—it is not simply the arguments that are convincing, but the arguments clear away the prejudice that prevents one from seeing that in fact that is just how one remembers many cases of meaning something or intending something. You find that after all you *remember* no experience in these cases, or no experience that you would care to call "meaning" or "intending." But no matter how strongly I am tempted by the arguments supporting the above thesis about dreams I cannot rid myself of the impression that I do remember dreams as experiences.

(iv) We react to dreams: they are delightful, disturbing, terrifying. They are that way, not merely now when we remember them (perhaps hardly at all when we remember them), but at the time: people smile as they dream, or go rigid with fright. But while it is natural and typical of people to react in these ways to such experiences as chatting with a delightful person or being chased by tigers, it is not so comprehensible that they should react to the neurological correlates of these experiences. People could no doubt so develop that the occurrence of the neurological correlate gave rise directly to the reaction. Even if it is tigers themselves that are terrifying and conversations themselves that are delightful, and we originally react to *them*, those reactions could set up a secondary pattern of such a kind that whenever the nervous system is in the state it is in when we perceive a tiger, it moves directly to the state it is in when we are terrified. But this is surely an enormous hypothesis, in view of the tremendous complexity of the nervous system, the many different conditions of it that would be involved in seeing tigers of different sizes, shapes and postures, and the slight neurological difference between seeing a real and seeing a paper tiger, which does not terrify.

Moreover if a secondary pattern of this kind were set up there would be a problem as to whether it would no longer be the case that we were in the ordinary way afraid of tigers, or whether we would be *doubly* afraid when we saw a tiger, first because the beast was there, and second because our nervous system was in one of those states that leads directly to fear; and as to whether we could distinguish between the fear inspired by the tiger and that begotten by the condition of the nervous system. Would the latter be relieved entirely by turning our back on the beast so that the nervous system was no longer in one of its fear-begetting conditions?

(v) It seems to be the case that we can remember dreams in words, that is that the things we say about a dream can be our first recollection of it. It is comparatively easy to understand our being able to do this if we suppose that we did have experiences such as we upon waking describe. After all, we have learned language partly as a way of talking about things of just that general kind, people, tigers, long avenues of trees, etc; so that the word "tiger" now comes immediately to the lips when we see a tiger. We do not have to *judge* it to be a tiger, a feat some people think we could not do while asleep. But we have not learned to recognize neurological conditions as the counterparts of being chased by tigers, and if we had, it would be odd that we should report the occurrence of these conditions as "seeing a tiger," rather than as what they are: being in the neurological condition appropriate to seeing a tiger.

These counter-arguments, I believe, will account for all but one of the considerations advanced in support of the thesis that dreams only seem to be experiences. In general those considerations were intended to show that the known facts or reasonable suppositions about dreaming could be adequately accounted for in terms of neurological correlates, and that even if the common sense view of dreaming also accounted for these facts and suppositions, the neurological correlate thesis was preferable because it did not require us to say that we could have experiences when we are not conscious. The counter-argument so far makes it moderately clear that the neurological correlate thesis does not account for the known facts or reasonable suppositions, while the common sense view does; but there still remains the final and supposedly crucial consideration that the common sense view requires us to say that it is possible to have experiences when we are not conscious. How much of a difficulty is this?

I suggest it is no difficulty at all. It is of course true that we cannot smell, see, hear or even imagine things when we are not conscious; and we might carelessly generalize from this to the conclusion that we can experience *nothing* when not conscious. But surely if we asked any careful person whether this generalization would hold, a moment's reflection would suggest the case of dreaming as a strong and obvious counter-instance. At that intuitive level of argument, the case of dreaming is just as good evidence against the thesis as the cases of seeing, hearing, etc., are in support of it. As far as I can see there will be no considerations of a more abstract kind that bear on the question. If not being conscious is just not being accessible to external stimuli, then *of course* we will not be able to see, hear, etc.; but if dreaming does not require external stimuli then there will be no conceptual impossibility about having dream experiences while not conscious.

Perhaps if we think of being conscious as a matter of shining the lights on the internal stage, that being as it were the condition on which stage persons or props of any kind will be perceptible, then of course dream persons and props will not be perceptible *either,* when "the lights are off." But this is just a roundabout way of making the generalization that we concluded was unwarranted. If we must entertain such a picture, we will simply have to amend it in such a way as to allow for the possibility of dream experiences while "the lights are off," for example by saying that dream tigers and forests are self-illuminating.

2. *Does the concept of error apply to our recollections of dreams?*

There are two distinct claims that one might be inclined to make as to the application of the concept of error to dreams: (i) that in the case of dreams, whenever we really seem to remember something, then something of that kind did in fact occur in our dream: seeming to remember is infallible; and (ii) that we cannot either get it right or get it wrong; it simply seems to us that something happened, and that is the end of it. What is interesting is not, cannot be, whether we got it right, but only that it should so seem to us. Let me first make a few general observations about these possible claims, and then discuss each in turn.

Clearly the issue we have just been discussing will have important bearings on either claim: it would for example be very difficult to see how a dream recollection could be *right* unless it was in line with what had actually happened, and therefore an infallibility thesis would seem to require that we do experience dreams, although of course the converse does not hold. The thesis that we do experience dreams would in no way entail that our recollections of them could not be in error. There might, however, be a strong sense in which we could get it right if the neurological correlate of what we seemed to remember occuring did occur. But even under these auspices, and even in some future time when neurological correlates, if there are such things, may be mappable, for practical purposes saying that a person was not wrong about his dream recollections would only be tantamount to saying that there is a special kind of current human fancy that is not imagining or whimsy or pretense but—what would we say?—comes from deep down.

The thesis that dream recollections can be neither right nor wrong would on the other hand at least be strongly implied by the thesis that dreams are not experienced at the time they are thought to have occurred. It is at least not obvious, however, whether the converse of this holds. One would certainly be much inclined to say that if a dream experience of a certain description did occur, then whether or not we ever *know it*, our dream recollections are in fact right or wrong, accurate or inaccurate. But there is perhaps an equally strong inclination to say that if there is absolutely no way of knowing whether our dream recollections are accurate, then it makes no sense to claim accuracy for them, or inaccuracy either.

It is extremely easy to confuse the two theses we are now considering, since one way of expressing the view that the concept of error does not apply is to say that one's dream recollections cannot be wrong; but from this it appears to follow that they are necessarily right; and that is another way of saying that they are infallible. But what one means in saying that they cannot be wrong is not that they are always right, but that it makes no sense to say that they are wrong, or right either. We can see the absurdity of the inference to infallibility very clearly if instead of saying that dream recollections cannot be wrong, we say that they cannot be right. This is an equally good way of expressing the thesis that the concept of error does not apply; but proceeding in the same way that we proceeded from the "cannot be wrong" way of expressing it, we would arrive at the conclusion that dream recollections are necessarily erroneous.

That is of course only the beginning of the possibilities of confusion: it is equally difficult to keep separate the kinds of considerations that are relevant in assessing the two theses.

I will first make some brief remarks about the infallibility thesis, and then at greater length consider the view that dream recollections can be neither right nor wrong.

2(a). *Are our memories of dreams infallible?*

There seems to be very little to recommend this supposition, except perhaps as a disguised form of its sophisticated cousin, the thesis that dream recollections can be neither right nor wrong. We would *treat* dream recollections the same way on either theory, that is we would not ask whether they were correct, but treat the fact that a person does believe he had a certain dream as the important thing; and the difference would be that our reason for not inquiring whether the dream occurred would in one case be that it made no sense, while in the other case it would be that we did not or would not doubt that it did occur.

This refusal to doubt could not however be justified in any way, and could only be treated as an article of faith. If one were struck by the fact that we have no other means of access to dreams than our present recollections of them, and if one were worried about the possibility that we might be radically wrong, either about what happened or about whether anything happened, and would have no way of detecting such error, one might wish to lay it down that we simply do not make mistakes about dreams, that whatever really seems to us to have happened did happen.

One could not however say that such a principle was a discovery based for example, on the fact that it had never been found to fail that a person actually had dreamt what it seemed to him that he had, or on the fact that the special brain cells used for remembering dreams are not liable to malfunctions the way the cells used for other kinds of remembering are. Either of these grounds for the infallibility thesis would have to rest on just what we are supposed not to have: access to what happens in dreams independent of what it now seems to us that we dreamt. Even if we found that there were special brain cells used in remembering dreams and that they were peculiarly well formed, we would still need to test their output against their input to determine whether their admirable form was such as to deliver recollections unerringly.

2(b). *Does it make sense to wonder whether a person has remembered a dream correctly?*

Since to do otherwise would, monumental sophistication aside, settle the question without more ado, in this part of the discussion I shall assume that dream experiences do occur during sleep, and simply ask whether, for whatever reason, we must ignore this fact in dealing with dream recollections.

I shall also assume that we are able easily enough or often enough to distinguish cases of story-telling or spoofing from genuine cases of dream recollection. But we will see later that there is a certain problem about this.

One way of making out a case for the view that it makes no sense is to draw up a comparison between ordinary remembering and the recollection of dreams, with a view to showing that in the latter case we have none of the aids to remembering, or checks on remembering, that are available in the former case, and that therefore there can be no substance to a claim that we have got it right about a dream.

In the first place it is obvious that in the case of dreams there is available none of such supporting evidence as photographs, letters, maps, the testimony of other people, etc., as is available in support of other claims to remember.

Secondly, although the amount of such evidence varies in individual cases down to nil, there is another important type of consideration available for ordinary remembering and not for dreams, namely what we might call relational clues: I remember that he spoke of his children's problems but cannot right away remember what he said, but I can remind myself by reviewing what I know of their problems or by finding out what their problems are; I remember that someone made a certain remark but cannot remember whether it was Mr. A or Mr. B, but if I know or find out that Mr. A is too witless to say such a thing while Mr. B is not, I may have some confidence that it was the latter; I seem to remember a train of events in a certain sequence, but on the other hand I know that it is extremely unlikely that those events should occur in that sequence, while quite likely that they should occur in a different order, and I conclude that that is how it must have been; or a conversation as I first remember it would not make sense or would not make the kind of sense I remember it did make, but with certain revisions would make that kind of sense, etc. These clues are not available in the case of dreams. A man, even if he is identified as someone one knows, will not necessarily or even likely speak of his children's problems when, in real life, he has none; persons encountered in dreams do not generally have sufficiently well-defined personalities to enable one to conclude anything as to what they would or would not say: there are few if any limits or even faint probabilities as to the sequence in which dream events will occur; dream conversations do not have to make sense or to make nonsense either. And so on I think for any sorts of relational clues one might suggest.

Thirdly, with ordinary remembering one can sometimes remember more fully or more exactly just by intensity of concentration. One perhaps tries to think of absolutely nothing else and then suddenly it comes clear. But this process brings it about that we get it right only if for example another person then says "Yes of course! How stupid of us not to remember that!", or if our spectacles do turn out to be just where we suddenly remembered leaving them, etc. But in the case of dreams there is never this grounding of the recollections that in this way seem to come clear, and therefore there is no difference between getting it right, and its merely appearing differently to us after having tried hard to remember.

This comparison might be taken to show either one of two things: either that remembering dreams is so radically unlike ordinary remembering that none of the things on the basis of which the concept of error applies to ordinary remembering holds in the case of dreams, and therefore the concept of error cannot apply; or merely that remembering dreams is very different from ordinary remembering, and therefore questions of truth or accuracy are ever so much more murky and uncertain in the case of dreams. I wish to defend the latter view. To keep my arguments separate I will number them.

(i) We said that in the case of ordinary remembering but not in the case of dreams, there was available to us such evidence as photographs, documents, the testimony of other people, etc. This is generally true; but it is true neither that we always take advantage of such evidence, nor that in every case there is any of it available. One does not have to reach for weird or out of the way cases where there is no such evidence available: There is no possible evidence of the pacing around I have done this afternoon in my room, of the rabbit I saw from my window this morning dancing the Charleston, or of any number of the things that we see or do in the course of a day; yet we remember many of them, and have no doubt that they occurred.

To take a more classic philosophical case, let us consider a conversation at which no one was present but myself and my dying friend. We say he was dying in order to eliminate any later testimony of his as to the course of the conversation; and to eliminate "relational clues" we will suppose that he was somewhat delirious, did not reminisce about his past or mention his family or friends, spoke in a way very uncharacteristic of his normal personality, and directed me to a buried treasure which on no interpretation of his instructions was discoverable. On the principles governing the above claim about the recollection of dreams, I think one would have to say that it would make no sense to suppose that I remembered this conversation correctly; yet while I might have some difficulty remembering some parts of such a conversation, and while no one could have any grounds for affirming that I got any of it right, it is monstrous to say that the question whether I got it right makes no sense—if this implies, as I think it does, that "I don't know whether to believe him or not." "I believe him" and "I don't believe him" are equally absurd reactions to my account of the conversation.

To this someone might reply that although in a case like this there is in fact no available evidence, still it is the kind of case in which there might have been witnesses, or tape recordings or relational clues. We know what it would be like to verify it, even if we cannot in fact do so. But I am not clear what difference this fact would make, if it were a fact; nor do I know what to make of the idea of someone else being present at a conversation at which no one else was present.

In this connection the following consideration may not be altogether fanciful: it might be suggested that we *train* our memories, and that they *become* reliable, through repeated experiences of being corrected about our recollections, and through the establishment of the habit of connecting the thing to be remembered in various ways with other things in the world. The result of this training, it might be suggested, is a certain presumption of reliability even in cases, such as the death-bed scene, where there is little or no possibility of corroboration. But, this line of argument might proceed, no such training is possible in the case of remembering dreams, both because our recollections of them never stand to be corrected, and because there is no way of connecting them with other things in our world. Hence while it is acceptable to say that in some cases of ordinary remembering we simply remember, it is not acceptable in the case of remembering dreams, because there can be no established presumption of reliability in this case.

Surely, however, this is an argument that can cut both ways. If the reliability of my memory for conversations has been built up through conversations with my wife, can this reliability carry over into the case of conversations with strangers? If it cannot, then there would be very little general presumption of reliability of anyone's memory, since so many of the matters we are called upon to remember are not matters of which we have long experience; while if it does, then it is difficult to see why it should not equally carry over to one's recollection of dreams. It is not after all as if dreams were radically unlike other experiences. The constituents of dreams: people, buildings, animals, etc., though they may be related to one another in weird ways, are generally speaking all items of which we do have waking experience, and are just the kind of things concerning which, on this supposition, our memory becomes reliable.

(ii) The claim that the concept of error does not apply would be a good deal more believable if we told of our dreams with an untroubled mind, so to speak: spontaneously, easily and with no sense of trying to remember, despairing of remembering, wondering whether we have missed something, no sudden realization that we have been omitting an important feature of the dream. But that is not how it is. We try to remember dreams in just the frame of mind that we try to remember anything else, regarding the concept of error as applying, although unable to use most of the tactics and devices that are useful in other kinds of remembering.

(iii) It is of some importance that those tactics that I called relational clues are not such as to show us what happened, but only such as to help us remember; if I remember that he spoke of his children's problems, but can not remember what he said, then a review of those problems will not show me what he said, but only put me on the road to remembering what he said; and it may turn out that what at last I remember is utterly surprising in view of what I know about those children. As far as the relational clues are concerned, the recollection has to be self-supporting, and to this extent is in no stronger position than the recollection of dreams.

(iv) Although there is not evidence of the alternative-record kind, photographs, recordings, the testimony of other witnesses, etc., as to what a person dreamt, it is not the case that we can never be certain what a person dreamt. Consider these cases:

(a) There is an automobile accident and when the news of it first breaks my friend is visibly shaken by it, because he says he dreamt just last night that there would be an accident at that place, involving those persons. He goes on to describe some of the details of the dream; and upon visiting the accident scene is utterly appalled to find it all to be just as he had dreamt. In such a case we would surely be as certain as we are of most things, that he did have that dream, especially if in general we knew him not to be a practical joker or a person with a macabre imagination.

(b) If I had a drug which, within a short time after a person took it, during which time he did not sleep, made it seem to him that he had had a certain dream last night, I would be as sure as I am of anything that he did not have that dream, and that it only seemed to him that he did.

(v) We might in general be inclined to say that all we are certain of is that it really does seem to a person that he has dreamt: as to the dream itself we cannot ask. But

(*a*) the above two cases seem to count against this view. In the case of the man who dreamt of the automobile accident, what everything convinces us of is not that it really seemed to him that he had that dream, but that he did have it. The drug case is even clearer: we are at the same time convinced that it really did seem to him that he dreamt, and that he did not dream. And

(*b*) we perhaps take it too much for granted that its seeming to a person that he dreamt is the clear notion, and his having dreamt is the dark one. The seeming, we may feel, is something present and examinable, it is right here in our laboratory, while the dreaming is not only now lost in the mists of the past, it would not be accessible even if it were now present.

But it may appear just the other way around if we ask ourselves under what conditions outside philosophy one would say that it really seemed to a person that he had dreamt. We would say it when we had reason to doubt that he did dream, or knew for a fact that he did not, and therefore the cases would be rare in which there was a justification for saying it. In the ordinary case, what we become convinced of is not that it seems to a person that he dreamt, but that he did dream.

Here one might of course be inclined to reply that while we regard ourselves as, and talk as if we were, reaching conclusions as to what people dreamt, or whether they dreamt, still the evidence we have is all evidence as to whether it seems to them that they dreamt, and therefore that is what we are really concluding; but since it is not useful in practice to make any distinction between this and the dreaming itself, we say that we become convinced that he did dream.

But while much of the evidence is of that kind, that is not peculiar to dream recollections, but is typical of all remembering. Some of the evidence has to do with the dream itself. It is for example evidence against a man's having had a terrifying dream if he was observed to sleep peacefully during all the time when he regards himself as having so dreamt; and in our drug example, the fact that he did not sleep at any appropriate time is even stronger evidence. But since we seldom have occasion to mount a watch on a person while he sleeps, the following case may be more interesting: a young man tells a dream to a young woman he admires, which is suggestive, charming, flattering, but somehow not believable as a dream. We think that either dreams do not run that way or it would be a fantastic coincidence if he had happened to have a dream that served his romantic purposes so admirably. We therefore do not believe that he so dreamt, *and from this conclude that it does not really seem to him that he did.* We could strengthen the example by supposing that he was a very good actor, and went through all the agonies of trying to remember, sketching it dimly at first, filling in details, making revisions, pausing in rapt concentration, experiencing sudden flashes of recollection, etc., so that all the evidence would point to its really seeming to him that he had dreamt. But in spite of this we conclude that it does not so seem, on the grounds that he did not so dream.

3. *Can dream recollections involving the identity of persons, places, buildings, etc. be correct or incorrect?*

As an alternative to the very general thesis we have just considered regarding the applicability of the concept of error to dreams, one might put forward a number of special theses, one of which we will now consider, and another of which will be examined later on. Whether these special theses might cumulatively be equivalent to or support the general thesis I will not consider.

If I say I dreamt that I had a conversation with Ryle, or that University College was on fire, it seems incontestable that it makes no sense to ask whether it was really Ryle, or really University College. A person would be making an ass of himself if he said it could not be Ryle, because Ryle is in Oxford and I am in California, or because he had asked Ryle, and he had no recollection of it; and it would be equally foolish, if one knew Ryle to be travelling in California or to be egregiously absent-minded about conversations, to say that it might have been he. Does this show that the concept of error does not apply to recollections involving identity?

I think it does not; it only brings out something about the *concept* of dreaming. I said I *dreamt* it, and this *means* that no real conversation occurred, that it would be senseless to see if Ryle himself would confirm its occurrence, or to enquire whether he and I were geographically close enough for it to be possible. It does not touch the question of whether I might have misremembered my dream: of whether (*a*) the person with whom I chatted looked or talked like Ryle, or (*b*) of whether, regardless of what he looked like or said, in my dream I *took* him to be Ryle.

3(a). *Can one misremember the appearance of (for example) a person in a dream?*

This I think is just a particular case of the general question discussed in Section 2, and it should be moderately clear now, (i) that if we do not initially remember the appearance of someone of whom we have dreamt, it makes sense to try to remember it. We will see later that we can not assume that a person in a dream has any appearance; but this I think adds a further dimension to what we may try to remember. We may try to remember whether the person we chatted with "had any appearance," and if so, what? (ii) We may initially remember something one way, but then have it strike us that we were wrong, and that the dream actually was quite different in various ways. I remember that I had a conversation in a dream with Ryle, and initially I am inclined to say that he looked like Ryle; but then it strikes me that while I took the person I spoke with to be Ryle, it was in fact a large middle-aged woman who sat nursing a child as we talked. That is possible; and hence it is possible that, conscious of the false assumptions I make as to the contents of my dreams, I should very often ask myself whether I have got it right.

Perhaps, however, the person who claims that it makes no sense to suppose that we may have misremembered a dream is less interested in this stage of the proceedings than he is in the point at which it does seem to us that it was in fact (*e.g.*) a middle-aged woman nursing a baby. He might say that when we remember that we had a conversation with Ryle, it is not so much that we remember that the person looked like Ryle as that we assume he did; that the only *remembering* of the appearance of the person comes when it strikes us that it was in fact a middle-aged woman; and that at that point we can not ask whether we might be wrong.

If this distinction between assuming and remembering is essential to the claim that we cannot misremember what we ultimately seem to remember, I think it would be very difficult to make it stick. It of course seems very clear in the case in which it suddenly dawns upon us that we have been wrong: then we perhaps see clearly that we were just assuming that the person resembled Ryle in appearance. But in the ordinary case in which there is no dawning of new realization we would not distinguish between assuming and remembering. Assuming does not have a phenomenological character such that by careful examination of ourselves when we are assuming we can discover that that is what we are doing. It only takes on a character, perhaps of foolishness, *after* we have discovered that we were merely assuming something.

"Really remembering" similarly seems to have a special character only in the case in which it dawns on us that we have been making a mistake: there is a clarity and excitement about it that is not otherwise present. But not all cases of remembering are of the sudden dawning kind, and there are no special marks of remembering in the common run of cases.

Moreover it does not seem impossible that a sudden dawning should in turn be subject to correction. It strikes me that the person I took in my dream to be Ryle in fact bore a resemblance to Miss Anscombe, but wait: perhaps that was not the same dream. I had other dreams last night, in at least one of which I remember Miss Anscombe figuring; and I also know myself to relish the contemplation of the very strange things that can occur in dreams. Perhaps the combination of these factors resulted in its falsely seeming to me that I took a middle-aged woman to be Ryle.

Here the fact that one may have almost no resources with which to answer such questions may become the key consideration. But I do not think that this should deter us from saying that the questions make sense. In the first place, while we cannot have a high degree of confidence as to the answers, we are not always absolutely without resources. I may in a case like the above remember quite a few of the details of the other dream in which an Anscombe-like figure appeared, and may also remember an Anscombe-like figure saying things which I do not remember as being part of that episode but which could be part of the conversation-with-Ryle episode. The supposition that there were two Anscombe-episodes may be reinforced by a recollection of having awoken briefly and mused on the fact that I was having so many dreams involving an Anscombe-like figure. Or when I put myself the question whether I am merely driven by my fascination with the weirdness of dreams to say that this dream had this weird feature, it may seem to me in this case simply untrue. None of these is of course a weighty consideration, but neither are they worthless.

Secondly I think we are too much inclined to take a case like this in which doubts abound as the test case, and to judge every case of dream recollection by it. One certainly can find cases in which there is nothing certain or even moderately probable. But that does not show that doubts abound in all cases.

One can raise the same doubts as to waking experiences, and once raised they will not likely be resolved. But in many cases we would treat these doubts as being academic, and simply would not in fact doubt. Consider for example the case mentioned earlier of the man who dreamt of the automobile accident.

3(b). *Can we misremember whom we took a person in a dream to be?*

There are several quite persuasive considerations that might be advanced in support of an affirmative answer to this question:

(i) In a dream it is not on the basis of a person's appearance that we take him to be so-and-so. We do not size him up and judge him to be so-and-so, nor do we know right off that he is so-and-so, but one's regarding him as being so-and-so and the figure he cuts in the dream are as it were independent constituents. I can take a person to be Ryle although he looks like Miss Anscombe, and although it would be quite impossible for me to behold an Anscombe-like figure and say "I know him (her?), he's (she's?) Ryle." And in the same way it is not on the basis of what people say or do in dreams that we take them to be a certain person. A dream figure could be talking like Hegel or dancing the Watusi and still be taken by me to be Ryle. Therefore a large body of possible evidence as to whom a dream character was taken to be fails to operate in dreams the way it might in waking experience.

(ii) This point is further reinforced by the fact that a dream person need not have any characteristics: dreams are sometimes like beforehand rehearsals of conversations we are going to have, for example, with a prospective employer, where we do not always imagine any face or figure playing the part of the other person. We just suppose that there is someone there, and do not fuss about what he looks or sounds like.

(iii) Our taking a dream person to be so-and-so need not itself have been an event or series of events in the dream. We need not have thought "It's Ryle," or addressed him by name or referred to him by name in speaking to any other person figuring in the dream. Our taking him to be Ryle may come to a head only in our saying upon waking that we did. There therefore seems not necessarily or even generally to be any dream phenomenon here to be either remembered or misremembered.

(iv) It is not absurd to regard dreaming as being at least importantly like imagining, that is, to think that in dreams we do something like illustrating a story with pictures, and that sometimes the wires get crossed so that we produce all the wrong illustrations, but the same crossing of wires results in its seeming to us as we dream that we are illustrating appropriately. If I set out to imagine Iris Murdoch and produce a likeness of Elizabeth II, one cannot say that I have not imagined Miss Murdoch, but only that I have done a very bad job of it. My setting out to imagine her makes it her that I imagine no matter how ineptly I do so. Similarly it is not the case that I do not regard a dream person as being Ryle if the illustration of him that I produce is Anscombe-like. In this way *regardings* are not falsifiable.

I described these considerations as very persuasive, and I am by no means certain that the conclusion they are supposed to support is erroneous. But I will offer one or two points that I think might at least lead one to doubt it.

(i) The fact that the person taken to be so-and-so need not resemble that person either in appearance or in behavior does not seem to me to show that it can never be a relevant consideration whether there is such a resemblance. Might this not depend on among other things the dreamer? If he was very much given to having the mixed-up sort of dreams we have been describing, then it would be no evidence at all; but if his dreams ran heavily to being coherent in this regard, then the fact that a particular dream had this kind of strangeness might justifiably lead him to doubt whether he had taken an Anscombe-like person to be Ryle. Such a doubt need not itself be unsettleable. Perhaps on further reflection he will recall that he in fact had two dreams, and will be able to spell out to himself in some way how he has run them together.

(ii) The fact that taking someone to be so-and-so need not at the time of taking consist of anything, *i.e.* need not be an action or an event and in that way a normal object of remembering or misremembering does not seem conclusive as to whether it is possible to misremember it. It was after all *at the time* that I took him to be so-and-so. If I say I had a dream about Ryle, I do not *now* judge from my recollection of his appearance or of the things he said that that was who it was. Indeed were that all I had to go on, I could not say that I had a dream about Ryle, but only someone very Ryle-like. Dream persons, no matter how like real persons, cannot *be* those persons. I *remember* that I took him to be Ryle. Might I be wrong about this? Suppose that on thinking further about the dream I seem to remember someone saying Wisdom will be here soon, and then someone having arrived to whom I spoke, and that he is the one I now seem to remember as Ryle, and I do not remember any surprise that although Wisdom was expected, Ryle came, and further I am in general apt to become muddled about English philosophers, and upon considering these facts the conviction that I took him to be Ryle fades: might it not then be quite doubtful whether I had taken him to be Ryle? Of course none of these considerations is weighty: the shift of identities is just the sort of thing that in dreams is taken to be a matter of course. In such a case I could hardly become satisfied that I had in fact taken him to be Wisdom. But the point is that a reasonable doubt now exists as to whom I took him to be, and this is what is not supposed to be possible in the case of dream recollections.

4. *Does it make sense to try to remember more of a dream than one initially recalls?*

In the daytime world, if one is talking to someone, there is someone there; it is either man, woman or child; if a woman, she is dressed in a certain way, is either pretty or plain, has either one facial expression or another at any given juncture in the conversation; she is sitting, standing, lying down, walking, running or dancing; the conversation occurs either indoors or outdoors, and if indoors, in a room that is large or small, elegantly or plainly furnished, a sitting room or a bedroom, etc. While there may be many circumstances of a daytime conversation that were either not visible to a participant in it, or not noticed by him, we know *a priori* that there is an answer to such questions as whether it was man, woman, or child, whether the conversation occurred indoors or outdoors, etc., and therefore it makes sense to urge a person to try to remember such particulars.

But it is different in the case of dreams, where we can have conversations with persons who are neither male nor female, neither blond nor redheaded, neither formally nor casually dressed, neither standing nor sitting, neither indoors nor outdoors. We can even, without it striking us as in the least marvelous where the other voice comes from, have conversations in which the other person simply has no physical presence. It therefore makes no sense to say to the dreamer, or for the dreamer to say to himself, "Come now. She must have been young or old, pretty or plain, seated or standing, and it must have occurred either in the daytime or at night, either indoors or outdoors. Do try to remember." The person who says this is pressing a logical mistake on us. It is even a mistake, I think, when one remembers in a dream having been charmed by a room or annoyed by a facial expression, to assume that it must have been by certain recollectable characteristics of the room that one was charmed, or by the actual occurrence of a facial expression in the dream that one was annoyed, and so try to remember it. It is possible in dreams to have these reactions without there being anything in the dream to which one is reacting.

We do not need to agree that dreams are such queer things as this for this point to be valid: if we *are* in a room and there *is* a human figure there with whom we are chatting, but his face is averted when he makes some particular remark, it makes no sense to wonder whether he was smiling or not. This is not because, although he definitely either was or was not smiling, we could never find out which it was because we did not see it and there is no one we could ask. It is because characters in dreams have no life but the life that shows in the dream. In this they are like characters in plays or novels. It is not to be assumed that Peter and Charlotte either did or did not meet again after the end of the story, and it makes no sense to puzzle over which way it was.

It is not that dream persons have at most only front sides. A dream person is not faceless when his back is turned, and if he says he turned away to hide a smile we would not disbelieve him or not on general principles. We might have a dream in which the unseen parts of people were non-existent; but that would be a novel sort of dream and would be reported with special fascination. In it this curious feature would show for example when people leaned against a wall, or had to turn their backs to you to retrieve a wallet from a hip pocket. Normally, however, a dream, like a story, is about people like us, with all their parts there all the time. But while having a face is part of what it is to be a person, having some particular expression is not, and therefore if we imagine a person with his back turned, he *of course* has a face, but it is absurd to wonder whether he is smiling.

One could say: dreams do not have depth. There is no more to be discovered about a dream than we did experience. But this is not the same as saying that there is not more to be remembered about a dream than we do remember.

Or we could put it this way: it is a mistake to try to remember a facial expression on the assumption that everyone at all times wears some expression or other, but not a mistake to try to remember it if one has some specific reason for thinking that it figured in the dream, for example remembering having been charmed or vexed by it, but not right off remembering what it was.

I said above that one *can* in a dream have the experience of being charmed by a face without the experience of the face itself, and this might seem to imply that remembering being charmed is not a reason for trying to remember the expression. But we would not want to lay it down *a priori* either that the expression that pleased you was not actually there, or that if you could not immediately remember it, it was not there. These are surely empirical questions, albeit peculiarly murky ones. One tries to remember, and then perhaps *remembers* that it was "not there." If one tries and fails to remember an expression, one can not conclude that there is nothing to be remembered, but only that one cannot remember. What would show that there was nothing to be remembered would be one's remembering that there was nothing.

5. *Is there any justification, practical or otherwise, for raising questions about the correctness of dream recollections?*

In the ordinary course of events, other people virtually never and we ourselves hardly ever raise questions about the correctness of our dream recollections, and I would not want the strenuousness of my defense of the possibility of doing so to suggest in any way that we do or ought to engage extensively in such inquiries. We find accounts of dreams entertaining, intriguing or terrifying, and we envy or pity people for the dreams they have; but generally we would no more inquire whether they do have them than we would inquire whether a person who says he would have liked to stay longer *would* have liked to stay longer.

Similarly if someone says he dreamt last night of being chased by a tiger, it is somehow off color to ask whether he could feel the wind on his face as he ran, whether he perspired much, how he decided it was a tiger. These questions are not asked in a normal conversation, and this shows us something of some interest about the telling of dreams, namely that as with the reporting of other incidents, we do not ask questions about the facts which do not affect the *drama* of the tale.

There are indeed circumstances in which we conclude that a person did not have the dream he purports to have had, but is only saying so to make conversation, to flatter, or to display his attitude toward something or someone; and then we play it differently with him. But *(a)* even there, we would not generally contest whether he had the dream, and *(b)* this is a different case from the one in which we take it that a person is not pretending, is telling the dream as he remembers it, but in which there might be a question as to whether he misremembers it.

We would not generally have any grounds, in the latter kind of case, for suspecting error, for suspecting that the conversation with Ryle that I remember might in fact have been a conversation with Plato, or with nobody in particular. We do not yet know that in certain phases of the moon Ryle does not appear in dreams, while Plato does, or that California is rather too far from England to permit a resident of California to dream of a resident of England. Nor could we for example suspect that it was not Ryle because I had him saying things that Ryle would never say; or inquire particularly whether it was Ryle because of the importance, *e.g.* for the interpretation of *The Concept of Mind,* of his having said what I had him saying.

In these and perhaps other ways it can be seen to be generally an idle suspicion that I might be wrong. But only generally so: we can imagine people, psychiatrists, perhaps, with a more extensive knowledge of the ins and outs of dreams and of the consequences of the fact that I dreamt this exactly, rather than that, having very good reasons for inquiring more particularly as to what one dreamt.

It is sometimes said that what matters about dreams is only that it should now seem to the dreamer that he so dreamt. But there is no reason why it should not also matter whether he did so dream—why different inferences could not be drawn from the fact that it falsely seems to a person that he had a certain dream, than can be drawn from the fact that he did have it. Might there not be a class of psychological abnormalities whose symptoms were tendencies to misremember dreams in certain ways?

6. *Have these questions been about dreams, or about the concept of dreaming?*

In many ways it may look as if we have been investigating the *phenomenon* of dreaming, rather than the concept. We have noted various things about dreams in the course of the discussion, such as that it is possible in dreams to take a person to be Peter who looks like Mary, that people may say things in dreams they would never say in real life, that it is possible for dreams to occur neither indoors nor outdoors, possible to have a conversation with a person whose hair is neither long nor short, brown nor blonde, etc. But although we do note these things about dreams, our problem is not whether these observations are correct: we take them to be obvious. Our interest is in such questions about the *concept* of dreams as whether it is a mistake to assume that a person in a dream had some facial expression or other at every moment in which he figured in the dream.

You might think that anyway we answer these questions by reflecting on how dreams *are:* by recalling that one can have dream conversations with faceless or otherwise indeterminate persons; and therefore there is no distinction between the concept and the phenomenology.

But it will be found I think that the key conclusions arrived at in this paper rest on no other difference between dreams and waking experience than that the former are dreams, *i.e.* are not real. It may be that in a dream Ryle would say things that Ryle would never say; but even if the Ryle of my dreams is very life-like, his having made any particular remark is no evidence as to how *The Concept of Mind* should be interpreted, *just because it is a dream.* Similarly it may be that we can have conversations in dreams with faceless or figureless persons, but in the most life-like dream it makes no sense to wonder whether a person whose back is turned is smiling, not because we find it to be the case in dreams that persons whose backs are turned have no facial expression (if persons in the same dream so situated as to be able to see these people's faces so assured us, it would make no sense to *believe* them), but just because they are dream figures, and as such, without being regarded as in the least weird in the way dream figures can be weird, are not to be thought of as having any depth, any characteristics that do not show. If Ryle behaves strangely one day, one may wonder whether it is because he has a splitting headache. But if the man in my dreams behaves just the same way, one may not wonder this. Except perhaps *in the dream.*

That it makes no sense to ask such questions is not something we discover about dreams, but something we bring to dreams. We can quite imagine a race who thought they lived in one world by day and another by night, and that although the night world had some special features, such as discontinuity and want of coherence, it was in general of the same logical kind as the day world. The couple of whose romance they dreamt last night either got married after the dream ended, or they did not; the man glimpsed on a far hilltop was either admiring the view, or he was not, etc. We can imagine them finding it deeply regrettable how many unanswered questions their night life left them, and that some of them would spend endless hours trying to fit together the pieces, and to devise ways of further exploring the night world. We would laugh at them for believing in such a world, but if it came down to a hard argument there would be nothing about dreams themselves to which we could draw their attention and which would show or even suggest that they were wrong. If we ever convinced them it would not be by parading facts about dreams, but by parading such principles as Occam's razor. But of course it would be unlikely that such people would be very partial to that principle.

THE PROBLEM OF DREAMS

Roger Squires

1. The scientific study of sleep has recently been stimulated by comparisons between people and advanced computers, whose normal activities need to be suspended periodically for reprogramming. I quote from a popular account by Dr. Christopher Evans, which appeared in the *Sunday Times* during 1969:

> Sleep is of course the state in which the brain-computer is "off-line," during which time the vast mass of existing programmes are sorted, outdated ones revised in the light of recent experiences and useless ones or the remnants of modified ones cleared and eliminated. These processes take place for a substantial part of the night, but because the brain is "off-line" and consciousness suppressed, we are mostly not aware of them. However, if for some reason our sleep is disturbed or when we wake in the morning, as the conscious mind "comes to" it catches the programme operations at work, and for a moment has no way of knowing whether the events are internal or external in origin. It sets to work therefore to try to make sense of the programme or fragments thereof that are being run through, and the result is what we call a dream—though we should presumably call it an *interrupted* dream

The first sentence expresses an exciting suggestion about the function of brain activity in sleep. It is comparable to what biologists tell us about other parts of the body; for example, that the liver eliminates waste materials and that the heart pumps blood through the organism. There is no reason to suppose that the liver and the heart need internal or external supervisors. Similarly, Evans does not mean that an unconscious mind is at the controls during sleep, sorting and filing in the same kind of way as a human programmer. This would be self-defeating, since any operator skilled enough to do this would need a memory and intellect comparable to that which these sleeping processes make possible for their owners. The unconscious mind would need to go to sleep during the day shift!

Again, when Evans says the conscious mind "comes to" and catches the program operations at work he does not suppose that there is an operator in the head of the person waking up, who seeks to make sense of what is happening in there like a scientist trapped in his own computer. Granted, the anthropomorphic descriptions, "comes to," "has no way of knowing whether," "sets to work to make sense," make this primitive way of construing the matter a very natural one. But the amazing complication of the brain should not tempt us back to animistic models properly discarded by anatomists and physiologists concerned with the function of other parts of the person. It is better to avoid the word "mind" here, which is itself a product of the old animism.

Once again, Evans would not wish his talk of the mind to be interpreted as a reference to the person, who is still asleep. It is not McX or Ann Other who finds the neural machinery still ticking over, tries to use it in the familiar waking way and strives to make sense of the odd results of so doing. People are not equipped to observe their own brains, let alone operate them. They are therefore not puzzled by the results of operating with them inappropriately. Because this kind of suggestion can be ruled out, it is fair to interpret what Evans says as being a functional description, figuratively expressed in personal terms, as if the activities described were intentional.

I hope I shall be forgiven for suggesting that this kind of view should be interpreted in something like the following way:

> Neurophysiological processes occur in sleep with a function analogous to what happens to a computer when it is "off-line." For instance, such processes are essential to the efficient use of old information. Sometimes, other brain processes begin which are typical of what happens in the brain when its possessor is awake. The function of these processes is, perhaps, to enable the person to react to his sensory input, to recognize things. When the "waking" processes operate in sleep before the "sleeping" processes have concluded in the normal way, this changes the brain in such a way that when the person wakes up he may seem to remember events which did not occur.

The invention and testing of such suggestions is, of course, no ambition of mine.

My footnote is merely that such theories about neurophysiological mechanisms would not, if established, support popular assumptions about waking impressions. The cerebral processes typical of Rapid Eye Movement phase sleep are not what we (men in the street) call "dreaming." We are equally unaware of the cerebral process which inappropriately switches on when our sleep is disturbed. So we (the men in the street) would not call this an "interrupted dream." It may well be true, on the other hand, that such interruptions *explain* or *cause* what we commonly call "remembering a dream." But this neurophysiology by no means shows that what we thus refer to as a dream occurs in the night, or at all. It does not show that our waking impressions are memories but rather the opposite.

Metaphorical language about the working of the brain, especially when it says that the mind knows this or does that, encourages the animistic thought that the brain needs a controller. Since it works at night, it is easy to suppose that the controller is still a person, wearing a different nightcap (the same mind, only subconscious); that the sleeping person (or his mind) is nevertheless alive to what is happening to him. This fits the traditional assumption that waking impressions are memories of what happened in sleep. But remove the metaphors, the mind, the awareness in sleep, and this pseudo-scientific support from popular accounts of neurophysiological mechanisms evaporates.

This is not a criticism of scientific suggestions such as those advanced by Evans. It is a caveat about how they are described and interpreted. That they do not support what I shall claim to be mistaken popular assumptions in no way diminishes, and may increase, their interest and importance.

2. It is almost universally believed that dreams occur during sleep and that people are capable of recalling them when they wake up. In his excellent book *Dreaming* (Routledge and Kegan Paul, 1959), Norman Malcolm, following some hints of Wittgenstein, bravely rejects this popular view as senseless. He thinks that our ordinary use of the word "dream" is perfectly in order and therefore cannot be based on any such view. I agree with the criticisms of this position expressed by Hilary Putnam in "Dreaming and Depth Grammar" (*Analytical Philosophy*, 1st series, ed. R. J. Butler, 1962). The popular view is not nonsense and is integral to the meaning of "dreaming." Unlike Putnam, however, I shall argue that we are not aware of the interesting things that happen to us while asleep and that, though we often appear to recall strange events after waking up, we in fact remember nothing of what has happened to us in sleep. Ordinary talk of dreams may not be in order.

The uncompromising version of my claim would be that people simply don't dream. But we could insist that dreams are simply what people appear to recall in the morning. My claim would then be that dreams do not occur in the night and that there are no "unremembered" dreams. Alternatively, we could insist that dreaming is the sleeping activity which is responsible for a person's waking impressions. My claim would then be that a person is unaware of his dreams. Our use of the word "dream" may depend on how we resolve the issue of whether we are contemporaneously aware of what happens to us in sleep, so in discussing it we should probably tread softly on dreams.

It is tempting to argue, as Malcolm does, that there is an inconsistency in claiming *both* that someone is asleep *and* that he is alive to what is going on. If waking impressions were memories, would we not have to cancel the claim that a person had been asleep? This short way seems too short. Perhaps it is part of the meaning of being asleep that the sleeper should not recognize things in his everyday environment. It is harder to maintain that he cannot be aware of anything, even in special ways. Again, perhaps someone cannot be said both to act in certain ways and be asleep. It is harder to maintain that he cannot act at all, perhaps by making internal movements of which we are presently ignorant. Such things should not be ruled out before investigation.

It is my contention that they should be ruled out *after* investigation. The rejection does not, I hope, depend on any special "theory" about meaning, evidence or criteria. There just don't seem to be good reasons for treating waking impressions as memories. The arguments against this depend on what is urged in its favor.

3. The ability to relate strange adventures when awakened has been correlated with characteristic Rapid Eye Movement phases of sleep. In such REM phases,

heart rate, breathing and blood pressure are irregular and brain waves show a distinctive pattern. What appears certain is that something happens in sleep which determines the occurrence and possibly the nature of a person's waking impressions. But it is a long stride from this to the conclusion that a person is even dimly aware of what is happening in sleep and that he awakes with confused impressions of what was happening.

Admittedly the occurrence of eye movements in sleep would suggest in isolation that the sleeper is watching something. But there is good reason to think that he isn't, in that nothing is moving about in front of him and his eyes are closed. Scenes painted inside his eyelids would be too close to be visible. Possibly he is watching something with another sense, an inner eye. But why should movements of his "outer" eye be evidence that he is watching something with a totally different sense?

When rhesus monkeys were trained to respond only to images on a screen by pressing a bar they also made this movement during REM sleep. This was widely taken to confirm the hypothesis that dormant monkeys see images which they cannot distinguish from screen images. Yet we know there is no ordinary screen or image. And the monkeys are not usually fooled by something very different. Moreover, they have their eyes shut.

No doubt it is possible that one day brain surgeons should unearth minute objects or physiologists exhibit phenomena in the brain which are detected by an inner-directed scanning mechanism and which are to the observer indistinguishable from things detected by the eyes in daytime. But it seems to me that superficial similarities between sleeping and waking behavior are totally insufficient to support such speculative hypotheses. Indeed, insofar as neurophysiological studies have revealed no inner screen or inner eye it may be reasonable to suppose them disconfirmed in the same way as one disproves the thought that a dormant bar-pressing monkey is responding to a screen in his cage.

4. It is sometimes said that the observation of what happens in sleep confirms the evidence of waking impressions. What sort of evidence is this? if McX is under the impression that he saw a dragon, this is a reason for thinking that he did. There are no dragons. So it is perhaps a reason for thinking that he saw something like a dragon, such as a bulldozer or a statue. If McX has been dozing, not bulldozing, this can also be ruled out. McX had his eyes closed. Perhaps his inner eyes were open. But how can his false impression that he observed one type of event in the ordinary way be evidence that he witnessed another type of event in a totally different way? It is a matter of experience that people sometimes mistake bulldozers for animals. It is not a matter of experience that people mistake internal objects for animals.

It may be replied that someone who wakes up under the impression that he has been fighting dragons does not usually believe that any ordinary events occurred in his sleep. His impression is of special status events scanned in an unusual way. If his memory is usually reliable, why can't we accept these impressions as the best kind of evidence for special status events? It is doubtful if this reply is adequate because the awakened sleeper's reasons for putting his claims in terms of special status events are of a negative kind. He knows there are no dragons and that he is prone to have false impressions after sleeping. In short, it appears that he has no more reason than the rest of us for taking his impressions of not-seen non-dragons as recollections of the denizens of his skull as revealed by a mysterious mode of consciousness.

The attraction of the inner event account is that it offers an explanation of our waking impressions as recollections of our night life. The alternative, it may seem, is to leave our impressions unexplained. But unless there is independent confirmation of the framework in which an explanation operates, it is an intellectual encumbrance. Consider these events or images, postulated to explain waking impressions. Are they "trained to spend their nights in dancing"? Can we happily leave it to neurophysiologists (who, so far as I know, have not stumbled upon such things in their researches) to explain the nature of these internal things and the manner in which we perceive them? Perhaps we should leave researchers to explain our waking impressions, dropping the nocturnal intermediaries. Perhaps we should resist the temptation to explain and admit that the usual inferences from a person's being under a certain impression break down in those special cases where he has just been asleep.

5. It is well known that there is a connection between some things which happen to the sleeper and his apparent memories upon awakening. Suppose the room is very hot, his alarm-clock goes off without waking him up and someone sprinkles water on his face. When he finally wakes up he may be under the impression that during a hot spell the house caught fire, that fire-engines with bells ringing raced to the scene, and that they fought the fire with water hoses. It is tempting to suppose that the sleeper's apparent memories of fire bells and hoses are genuine memories of his alarm-clock and the water on his face. If some of his apparent recollections are genuine recollections of what happened to him in sleep, is there not some reason for thinking that all his impressions are impressions of what happened in sleep, though this may be hidden to other observers?

But does the sleeper remember the alarm-clock ringing? Compare a waking incident. Someone working in his office sees a dark cloud issue from a distant building and later hears a bell ringing. Arriving home, he announces that there has been a fire but the fire engines were soon at the scene. Now suppose that the "smoke" was a cloud of locusts and the "fire bells" were produced by someone ringing a handbell. Though the office worker does not remember fires and fire engines he obviously remembers *something,* the dark cloud and the bell ringing. By virtue of the facts that the dark cloud was a swarm of locusts and the bell was a handbell, we could also say that he remembers the locusts and the handbell.

Can we find a corresponding something which the awakened sleeper, with his false impressions of fire engines, undoubtedly remembers? When he wakes up he does not know, nor is he under the impression, that his room was hot, that the alarm went off and so forth. He does not even *seem* to remember these things. Perhaps, though, he at least heard a ringing noise, which he mistook for a fire engine, but which was in fact the alarm-clock. Certainly if you ask him he will say he is under the impression that he heard a ringing noise. But we need to establish that it was the same ringing noise as that made by the alarm-clock. So we ask him to identify the noise. He says, "Oh, the one made by the fire engine." That won't do, so we ask him when and where the noise was. "It came from the street," he replies, "a few minutes after the fire." This won't do either, because he is only identifying it within an admittedly false story.

If he has no independent way of picking out the noise, and he does not appear to have, then there is no way to establish whether "it" was or was not identical with the noise made by the clock. It is no escape that the person himself may wake up to find the alarm ringing or notice that it must have been ringing in his sleep. Now he can identify a noise alright, that made by the clock. But he is unable to identify it as the noise he seemed to have heard in sleep, for the same reason that outsiders could not make this identification.

There is no evidence that the sleeper, assailed by fire, air and water, identified anything in the way that the office worker identified the dark cloud and the bell. This is a reason for denying that he was aware of what happened to him in sleep or that he remembers what happened to him or that his waking impressions are impressions of those events.

6. "Surely it is not a coincidence that a person's waking impressions are of rain or fire hoses after water has been sprinkled on him in sleep. He simply must be remembering what happened. He probably felt the water on his face and misinterpreted it." It is not in question that there is a connection between sleeping events and waking impressions. The sprinkled water has an effect on the sleeper which may make a difference to his later impressions and actions. The physiological explanation of how the water "registers" may well be analogous to what happens when someone feels water on his face. If this is what is meant by saying that the sleeper must have been aware of what happened, there is no need to disagree.

Environmental influence in sleep is partly similar to the phenomenon of "subliminal advertising." By flashing images on the screen during a film, for instance, it is apparently possible to shape the later actions of the audience, even though the images passed so quickly that the audience was not aware of them either at the time or in retrospect. While admitting that this is a correct description, one is nevertheless inclined to say, "It couldn't be a coincidence that they all bought Snibbo later. They must have been aware of the images after all, and been persuaded by them." Probably the phrase "subconsciously aware" would be used here. It is also the natural way of describing the sleeper, that he is subconsciously aware of water on his face and subconsciously misinterprets it as a fire hose.

The claim that the audience must have seen the images (though it didn't) or that the sleeper must have been aware of the water on his face (though he wasn't) can be taken in two ways. It may mean that the images and the water affected their victims by a similar mechanism to that which would have operated had they actually seen the images or felt the water. This vague physiological claim is very likely true. On the other hand it may mean that, despite appearances, the members of the audience did see the images, that the sleeper actually identified the water on his face. This seems to be false.

7. The point may still be pressed that there is a sense in which the sleeper

subconsciously remembers some of the things which happened to him in sleep. Is this not a reason for thinking that his other apparent memories are genuine, if subconscious, recollections of other things which occurred in sleep? It may soon be possible to account for waking impressions in detail by reference to neural activity during REM phases. We may be able to produce apparent memories upon awakening by stimulating the sleeper's brain. Surely this would confirm the view that our waking impressions are subconscious memories of brain activity, which we were subconsciously aware of in the night? I shall argue that this would be an illegitimate extension of subconscious memory.

What makes it attractive to describe the sleeper as subconsciously aware of the water on his face is not just the causal connection between this occurrence and his later reports. A wet face is something we are usually aware of and, if we had restricted information, it would be understandable if we attributed it to rain or even fire-hoses. This suggests that it is by virtue of the physiological machinery which equips us to feel water when awake that the water can have effects on us in sleep and also that it is because of our proneness to interpret and misinterpret what we feel that the water makes a difference to our later impressions. These vague claims *may* be expressed by saying that the sleeper subconsciously misinterprets or misremembers the water which fell on him.

We are not usually aware of brain activity, however. It is not identified by the way it looks and feels, as water often is. No one knows what neural processes look, sound or feel like. Therefore, if it is found that whenever certain neural processes are initiated in someone's brain he wakes up and tells a story of dragons, there is still no reason to claim that he subconsciously misinterprets the neural process. For there is no way to tell whether it is understandable to mistake a neural process for a dragon or anything else. Since we do not know what it would be like for a person to be aware of his brain activity (except with the aid of elaborate equipment), a mere causal connection between that activity and some later propensities of the person concerned is an insufficient reason for talking of subconscious perception, awareness, misinterpretation or remembering.

8. If we reject the view that someone asleep monitors special status events or engages in internal adventures, an attractive alternative beckons. This is that the sleeper at least thinks that he sees and does things. He suffers total hallucination or delusion. For example, he may suppose that tigers are after him or be under the impression that he is slaying a dragon. On this view, he is completely mistaken about the existence of what he imagines and about the nature of his own actions. So we are apparently freed from the search for miniature dragons, inner scanners, or even appropriate sleeping actions.

I think the idea of a total hallucination or delusion is self-defeating. To attribute a false belief or mistaken impression to someone is to interpret something he did or would have done. It is not just to say that he did, or would have done, certain actions, but to explain those actions as appropriate to some non-existent state of affairs. The content of a false belief, *what* is falsely supposed, is a description of that situation which, if it obtained, would have rendered intelligible the person's actions or dispositions (including, of course, what he said or would have said). For example, suppose Macbeth's eyes focus in mid-air, he mutters something about a dagger and gropes forward with his hand. Nothing in the hall explains these mysterious things. But if there *were* a dagger in the air, their pattern would be immediately obvious. The content of his belief is what would make these actions intelligible, namely, the existence of a dagger in front of him. By virtue of the fact that there is no dagger before him, his belief is a mistaken one.

Now if a person is to be *totally* mistaken, it cannot be true of him that he performs a successful action. For this would imply that he is not mistaken about something, that he knows what he is doing, if only in a limited way. Equally, it can hardly be true of him that he *would* act in certain ways, for this would imply a capacity for successful action, which would involve some correct, if inoperative, beliefs on his part. (It may be true of him that he would act in certain ways if he were not deluded, but this capability is explicitly not what the attribution of delusion is intended to explain.) I conclude that if there is anything (some action or disposition) for the attribution of false belief to explain, the hallucination or delusion cannot be total. Where the capacity for action is lacking, the apparatus of delusion or hallucination gets no grip.

A promising objection to the above argument runs as follows. To attribute beliefs to a person all that is needed is that he should *try* to perform actions, not that he should succeed. Not even successful limb-movements need to be carried out, for the person may be paralyzed. It seems to me, however, that the attempt, no less than the deed, confounds the attribution of total illusion. The paralyzed man who tries to move his arm, for example, believes he can move it, he wants to move it and would if he could. We can hardly ascribe these beliefs and intentions as an explanation of, or on the basis of, his "pure tryings," since if we are justified in attributing attempts to him at all it thereby follows that he has already certain beliefs and intentions. So we come back to the point that the subject of such claims must be capable of action and not totally mistaken.

If we cannot ultimately settle on something a person did or would have done there can be no grounds for attributing a mistake or false impression to him.

Consider, again, the hallucinated Macbeth. He is not aware of a dagger or of something like a dagger or of a picture of a dagger, since there is no such thing. Nor is he aware of the activity of his heat-oppressed brain which is doubtless causing his confusion. But he is aware, on the other hand, that he is in the hall of his palace, that he intends to murder Duncan and that he is groping about in the air. On the basis of such correct beliefs we can attribute mistakes to him. Now if he were "totally hallucinated," we should presumably have to replace all his correct beliefs. It seems to me that he would not then be aware of anything, though his cerebral activity may be at a peak. If the brain activity plays havoc with his later reports, this is an insufficient reason for saying that he was deluded or mistaken at the time of its occurrence. (If he had been capable of false claims at the time of course he could not have been "totally hallucinated.")

9. Those who talk of sleeping hallucinations, delusions, mistakes,

misinterpretations or false impressions, tacitly assume that a person is capable of acting in sleep. It is well known that elaborate activity does occur in sleep, but it appears that it is not remembered.

"The sleep-walkers appeared to be aware of their environment but indifferent to it. Their eyes were open, expressions blank, and movements somewhat rigid ... if spoken to, the subjects answered monosyllabically as if annoyed ... There was complete amnesia for the incidents when they awakened." (Jacobson, Kales, Lehmann Zweizig in *Scientific American*, July 1965.) Such activity does not occur in REM phases but in "deep" sleep when the brain is apparently least active. Since there is no connection with waking impressions, I shall not discuss whether these "automatic pilot" activities, such as sleep-walking and sleep-talking, are properly described as deliberate acts, expressing their executor's awareness or misapprehensions.

The minimal limb-movements, erratic eye-switching and related phenomena that occur in those phases of sleep during or after which the interrupted sleeper is most liable to "tell a dream" do not even appear to be actions of the sleeper. Though slightly similar to things which would be appropriate to certain familiar situations, they are much more obviously dissimilar. For example, eye movements are appropriate when a person is looking for something, but not when he has his eyes closed. If it is said that the sleeper does not know his eyes are closed, this makes it difficult to maintain that he *does* know his eyes are moving, presumably a prerequisite for regarding these movements as under his control, as exhibitions of his aims and mistaken assumptions.

Similarly, suppose Kipper's leg jerked. The suggestion is that Kipper jerked his leg. Why should he do that, rocking peacefully in his hammock? "Perhaps he thinks he is playing football." Why doesn't he do all the other things pertinent to playing football? "Perhaps most of his other impulses are inhibited by sleep." Then Kipper must get very frustrated, though he doesn't show it! "Perhaps he does not know he is 'switched off,' does not realize that he is not playing football." Do you still wish to maintain that he does realize that his leg jerked? It is possible that such things should turn out to be actions. My point is that such evidence as we have renders the possibility remote.

10. There is a world of difference between seeming to remember that a tiger chased you and remembering that a tiger seemed to chase you or recalling that it seemed as if a tiger was chasing you. The hallucination or delusion view of dreams is that a person remembers things that seemed to happen. Evidence is needed, over and above the waking impressions themselves, to establish that he does not merely seem to recall nocturnal adventures.

Consider some undoubted instances of recalling a mistaken impression. Suppose McX walks into a mirror under the impression that it is a doorway between two rooms. His action is explicable by reference to a state of affairs which does not obtain. He may remember the whole incident, including stepping forward and smashing the glass. As a result of the impact, however, he may only recollect walking towards the mirror when told to circulate or being surprised that there were so many guests at the party, or saying to himself, "I'll go through that door into the other room." He remembers being under a false impression even in these cases because he recalls doing something which was, whether he knows it or not, to be explained as appropriate to an imagined situation. This is a sufficient qualification for the description, "recalls being under the mistaken impression," though not a necessary one. McX may only remember things he would have done. For instance, he may remember that he would have pointed to the mirror for the way out. Provided the explanation of what he would have done lies in specifying the imagined situation, he still remembers being under the false impression. But if he does not recollect what he did, or would have done, at the party, he does not recall being under any impression.

The question is whether someone who has been asleep remembers anything he did or would have done while asleep. He does not remember the neurophysiological activities that occur when he is awake. There is no reason to suppose he remembers them after he has been asleep. He does not know how to jiggle his brain cells or fire his nerves. He does not remember that his oculomotor system was periodically innervated, that his pulse rate soared or that his breathing was irregular, any more than that his brain waves roared and his basic skin resistance increased. Does he remember anything he would have done in sleep? Suppose Pewter has the impression that a tiger chased him. If he had had that impression in the night presumably he would have jumped out of bed, locked the door and telephoned the police. But he does not recall that he would have done this, because his impression was of being, not in the bedroom but in the jungle, when such actions would have been inappropriate. Nor does he remember what he would have done if he had not been asleep. For he does not remember being asleep. I see no reason to suppose that he knows what he would have done while still asleep.

11. It may be thought that the sleeper remembers trying to do things in sleep. If a person was completely tied up or paralyzed, that the appropriate nerves fired when he was asked to move his arm would be excellence evidence that he tried to move it. Now motor impulses are similarly cut off in sleep. Yet we may find that those nerves fire which would have produced limb-movements. Does this not show that attempts are made to move? It may be suggested that it is this trying which is later misreported as, for example, "running away from a tiger."

I shall argue that even if the neurophysiological evidence were thus favorable it would be insufficient to warrant this conclusion. If someone remembers doing something it does not follow that he remembers how he did it. He may remember winning a game of chess, for example, without remembering anything he did in order to win. Similarly, if someone falsely but sincerely claims to remember doing something, it does not follow that he remembers trying to do that thing, even if it is an undisputed fact that he did try to do it.

Suppose Jennings attempts an anagram one morning by eating fish for breakfast and gazing into a crystal ball, intoning the letters one by one. He fails. That afternoon he claims to remember, or is inclined to think he remembers, having solved the anagram in the morning. It by no means follows that he at least remembers trying to solve it, even though he obviously did try to solve it. When we ask him further questions, we may find that he has no recollection of any steps he took or even of any steps he contemplated or would have taken. If this is so, we should deny that he recalls trying to solve the anagram.

Is the case not like this for waking reports? People appear to remember doing various things, not attempting to do them. When they do appear to remember trying to do something, what they appear to recall bears no resemblance to the recondite neurophysiological phenomena which might tempt a researcher to suppose that the sleeper is trying to make bodily movements. A person may tell that he tried to escape from a tiger by running or climbing a tree. No one appears to recall that he fired his nerves or what he would have done if his motor impulses had not been cut off. Even if he did try to do such things in sleep, there would be no reason to suppose that he remembered or misremembered this after he woke up.

Our imaginary researcher has the idea that the sleeper does what he can to act out his later narratives, but that all that happens is that his nerves fire, the usual sequel being blocked by some physiological barrier. On the face of it, this is no better than the idea that he was able to keep still all night only with an effort, since he would have run amok if he had not cut off his motor impulses! Of course, it is assumed that the nerve-firing is under control, but not the blocking mechanism. Evidence is needed for this question-begging approach. In particular, that the person is wholly oblivious to the failure of his spectacularly abortive "attempts" makes it doubtful whether they were attempts at all.

The analogy with someone who cannot move because he is tied up is misleading. The bound person is thwarted and knows it. We, and he, know that he would move if he could for all kinds of reasons. And he would know whether or not he had succeeded in achieving these further ends. Pewter asleep does not realize his limbs won't move. If they did move, there is no reason to suppose that he would have succeeded in anything or even known that they had moved (unless he woke up). There are no grounds for ascribing aims or purposes to Pewter. Does he want to shoot a tiger? One needs to be awake to shoot at tigers. But if we try to help him by waking him up he is much more likely to shoot at us.

The upshot is that the sleeper does not remember what happened to him in sleep. He may be told what happened or surmise it from his general knowledge of such cases. But this cannot make legal tender of his counterfeit waking impressions. These would only be evidence for actions, or propensities to act, in sleep if they could be correlated with them. But there seem to be no independent reasons for holding that people can do things during REM phases. Therefore, there are no good reasons for holding that they think things then, that they suffer delusions, have hallucinations or fall under false impressions.

12. "Surely it is no coincidence that Pewter became restless in sleep and burbled about tigers, that perspiration broke out on his brow in the last REM phase before he woke up and seemed to remember being chased by a tiger. He must have been reacting at the time to what he recalled later."

We need to distinguish the traditional belief that apparent memories after sleep are genuine memories, from scientific hypotheses which are prompted by the similarity between our state when we remember and when we merely seem to remember. Probably the cerebral states of the persons recalling and apparently recalling are in some respects the same. In view of the correlation between REM phases and apparent memories, it seems likely that the parts, features or aspects of the brain which are involved in ordinary remembering are also affected in some way during the REM phase. Probably the sleeping processes which produce these cerebral changes also produce the externally obvious sleeping reactions, such as those ascribed to Pewter. If such a scientific story were confirmed, the correlation between some sleeping reactions and waking impressions would not, of course, be coincidental.

Suppose that, as a by-product of some cerebral function in sleep, electro-chemical changes occur which are very like those that normally enable us to remember what has been going on. There may be associated reactions. For example, if someone sees another aim a blow at him, no doubt his brain registers vital changes which enable him to duck away or parry it. If similar brain changes occurred in sleep there could be a related effect. It may be that the reaction of the person who is awake is something he learned, something under his control. Then his corresponding sleeping reaction would be what it is because of the person's deliberate waking reactions. This would provide a ground for talking of the sleeper's subconscious reactions, of his acting in sleep as if he were awake. For similar physiological reasons, we saw that it may be tempting to say that sleepers sometimes subconsciously perceive such things as water on their faces.

Because workers in the field and their interpreters take it for granted that waking impressions are genuine memories, they may present physiological accounts of the genesis and mechanism of apparent memories as if they were evidence for the traditional view. "We have shown that it is no coincidence that Peter blanched and cried 'Wolf' in sleep," they proclaim correctly. But then it is tempting to conclude, incorrectly, that his later story of wolves was a memory after all.

13. Here is a similar example where the results of scientific investigation have probably been misrepresented. The events of a fairy tale occur when the story says they occur and not at all. You can either say the ghost appeared to Hamlet in the early morning or that the events related never happened. The same is true of the tales people tell after sleeping. If these are not recollections, it is silly to press the question when the events really occurred. On the other hand, this would be sensible if the popular accounts were correct. Therefore, the discovery that if someone wakes up during or after an REM phase he may have quasi-memories, but that before an REM phase he never will, is widely taken to show when the apparently remembered events occurred.

Macbeth appears to see a dagger three feet in front of him when there is no dagger, or anything like a dagger, in that position. Where is the dagger Macbeth thinks he sees? That it appears to him to be three feet away is the only sensible kind of answer. Now suppose we discover that when a shield is put between Macbeth and where he places the dagger, he no longer appears to see a dagger. This does not establish that the imagined dagger is really somewhere beyond the shield, that it now has a real as well as an apparent position or that its apparent position has been confirmed! It shows something about the conditions under which Macbeth has the hallucination. The spatial position of the apparently seen dagger is analogous to the temporal position of apparently remembered events. The causal evidence about REM phases no more confers a time upon the supposed events than the (postulated) causal evidence would confer a place upon the hallucinated dagger. The correlation with REM phases helps to establish some conditions under which a person will seem to remember taking part in strange adventures.

14. It is often said that what we remember upon awakening are "experiences" which occurred in sleep. The first difficulty is that, in normal usage, someone who recalls the experience of running away from a lion is someone who ran away from a lion. So it is sometimes said that what occurs in sleep is an experience exactly like being chased by a lion except that there was no animal involved and the sleeper did not run away. As if the experience can be described without saying anything at all about what actually happened.

The trouble is that it is not obvious that anything has been described. Something occurs, which is exactly like being chased by a lion, except that . . . it is nothing like it? And I have something in my pocket which is just like a florin except that it's nothing like a British silvery coin twice the value of a shilling! (This rejection is dogmatic, but I cannot at present find an interpretation of the technical word "experience" which makes it plausible to say that a person's waking impressions are recollections of his experiences.)

If to describe an experience is to say nothing about what there is "out there," but to talk of internal film shows, experiences should be rejected for the excellent reason that nothing like that goes on in the head. If to describe an experience is to describe what goes on in the head, only some scientists are partially qualified to describe them. If to describe an experience is to say what someone thinks or supposes rather than what he did, we have seen that there is no reason to suppose that a person has experiences in sleep or that people commonly even seem to remember experiences.

Unfortunately, the protean word "experience" enables some accounts to be stated in elusive ways. For example, experiences are said to be like moving pictures in that they are regularly mistaken for tigers and lions: yet they are not in the head or outside it. They are observed with an inner eye: yet they are nowhere to be seen. Even the inner eye is often said to be the eye of the mind, rather than of the person. It seems to me that such riders deserve disqualification from the scientific stakes. Just as the addition that souls are insubstantial renders safe but useless the claim that they wander in sleep, so the appeal to experiences which are non-spatial and apprehended by a mental eye gains immunity from disconfirmation at the expense of its explanatory force.

15. But in the dark hours of the morning, when the perfumes of the night are in one's nostrils or the flesh creeps at the thought of terrors past, how absurd it seems to deny that something is remembered! It is the magic of this primitive certainty that sustains the scotched myths; not laboratory evidence, reflection on unusual occurrences or even grammatical illusions. In the cold light of day, perhaps we should also wake up to the fact that this spell-binding certainty only shows what it shows: that we sometimes wake up with apparent memories. But can the rest be dogmatism about slumber? Have we been dreaming?

SECOND SYMPOSIUM

SPACES: OPENING NOTE
    Peter A. French

SPACE
    Immanuel Kant

SPACES AND TIMES
    Anthony Quinton

MULTI-SPATIAL MYTHS: KANT AND THE DREAMER
    Peter A. French

"I wonder what latitude or longitude I've got to"

SPACES: OPENING NOTE

Peter A. French

Astral wanderers, dreamers, dream objects and the spirits of the dead are said by many psychical researchers to exist in a space, contemporaneous with and in some cases overlapping the space of our public physical world. Note the following from Muldoon and Carrington's famous *The Projection of the Astral Body:*

> There is a *dream world*. When you are dreaming you are not really in the same world as when you are conscious—in the physical—although the two worlds merge into one another. While dreaming, you really are in the astral plane, and usually your astral body is in the zone of quietude. The distance of separation has nothing to do with it; once detached—whether slightly or remotely—you are in the astral plane.

Such a claim amounts to the proposition that there exist, or at least it is conceivable that there exist, more than one space or that "space" as we generally understand the term does not refer to anything real, but is the name of a relationship among things.[1] Our usual way of looking at the world, however, is to conceive of space as unitary. There is only one Space. No doubt most of us would admit that space can be divided into this space and that, a space for the new boat and a space on the side of the page for jotting down notes; but we do not pluralize space in the sense that we do not allow the various ways we talk of spaces to lead us to the belief that there exist a number of spaces of which the familiar space around us is but one. On the other hand, however, our public space has not the space to accommodate the queer creatures of our dreams nor the spirits that allegedly converse with humans at seances.

The topic of this symposium, then, is Spaces. Are we bound to view space as unitary? Is everything that is real in public, physical space? What do we mean by the word "space"? Surely these are not new problems for philosophers, especially for metaphysicians, but their relevance to our understanding of purported psychic and occult experiences has not in the past been made sufficiently evident. Serious thought needs to be given to the philosophical implications of alternative spatial conceptions and what sort of view of the world they entail if an explanation of psychic phenomena is thought to depend upon the theory that there exist spaces other than public physical space.

For example, if things can be said to have legitimate existance in spaces other than normal public space, terms which serve in our perceptual language as indicators of confused or deceptive perceptions, terms such as "hallucination, mirage, apparition," etc., might have entirely different meanings. What is an hallucination in one space might be all too real in another. Then there is the question of how spaces may be transcended, as when it is reported that someone had breakfast at home and moments later witnessed strange ritualistic happenings in another space. Must it be the case that human beings exist in or over a number of contemporaneous spaces in order to make intelligible those experiences which are the subject of the parapsychologist's research? Or do we exist in one space which is, on occasion, transcended by creatures of another space?

NOTES

1. Compare the following remarks by famous philosophers on the nature of space:
Aristotle: "For the parts of a solid occupy a certain space, and these have a common boundary; it follows that the parts of space also, which are occupied by the parts of the solid, have the same common boundary as the parts of the solid. Thus, not only time, but space also, is a continuous quantity, for its parts have a common boundary." (*Categories*, 5a, 8-14)
Descartes: "A space, or intrinsic place, does not differ in actuality from the body that occupies it; the difference lies simply in our ordinary ways of thinking. In reality the extension in length, breadth, and depth that constitutes the space is absolutely the same as that which constitutes the body." (*Principles of Philosophy*, Part II, X)
Leibniz: "I hold space to be something merely relative, as time is; that I hold it to be an order of coexistence as time is an order of successions. For space denotes, in terms of possibility, an order of things which exist at the same time, considered as existing together; without inquiring into their manner of existing. And when many things are seen together, one perceives that order of things among themselves." (*The Leibniz-Clarke Correspondences*, ed. by H.G. Alexander, Manchester University Press, 1956, Third Paper)

SPACE

Immanuel Kant

Metaphysical Exposition of [The Conception of Space]

By means of the external sense (a property of the mind), we represent to ourselves objects as without us, and these all in space. Therein alone are their shape, dimensions, and relations to each other determined or determinable. The internal sense, by means of which the mind contemplates itself or its internal state, gives, indeed, no intuition of the soul as an object; yet there is nevertheless a determinate form, under which alone the contemplation of our internal state is possible, so that all which relates to the inward determinations of the mind is represented in relations of time. Of time we cannot have any external intuition, any more than we can have an internal intuition of space. What then are time and space? Are they real existences? Or, are they merely relations or determinations of things, such, however, as would equally belong to these things in themselves, though they should never become objects of intuition; or, are they such as belong only to the form of intuition, and consequently to the subjective constitution of the mind, without which these predicates of time and space could not be attached to any object? In order to become informed on these points, we shall first give an exposition of the conception of space. By exposition, I mean the clear, though not detailed, representation of that which belongs to a conception; and an exposition is metaphysical when it contains that which represents the conception as given *a priori*.

1. Space is not a conception which has been derived from outward experiences. For, in order that certain sensations may relate to something without me (that is, to something which occupies a different part of space from that in which I am); in like manner, in order that I may represent them not merely as without, of, and near to each other, but also in separate places, the representation of space must already exist as a foundation. Consequently, the representation of space cannot be borrowed from the relations of external phenomena through experience; but, on the contrary, this external experience is itself only possible through the said antecedent representation.

2. Space then is a necessary representation *a priori*, which serves for the foundation of all external intuitions. We never can imagine or make a representation to ourselves of the non-existence of space, though we may easily enough think that no objects are found in it. It must, therefore, be considered as the condition of the possibility of phenomena, and by no means as a determination dependent on them, and is a representation *a priori*, which necessarily supplies the basis for external phenomena.

This selection is extracted from "The Transcendental Aesthetic," *Critique of Pure Reason,* translated by J. M. D. Meiklejohn, London, 1854.

3. Space is no discursive, or as we say, general conception of the relations of things, but a pure intuition. For, in the first place, we can only represent to ourselves one space, and, when we talk of diverse spaces, we mean only parts of one and the same space. Moreover, these parts cannot antecede this one all-embracing space, as the component parts from which the aggregate can be made up, but can be cogitated only as existing in it. Space is essentially one, and multiplicity in it, consequently the general notion of spaces, of this or that space, depends solely upon limitations. Hence it follows that an *a priori* intuition (which is not empirical) lies at the root of all our conceptions of space. Thus, moreover, the principles of geometry—for example, that "in a triangle, two sides together are greater than the third," are never deduced from general conceptions of line and triangle, but from intuition, and this *a priori*, with apodeictic certainty.

4. Space is represented as an infinite given quantity. Now every conception must indeed be considered as a representation which is contained in an infinite multitude of different possible representations, which, therefore, comprises these under itself; but no conception, as such, can be so conceived, as if it contained within itself an infinite multitude of representations. Nevertheless, space is so conceived of, for all parts of space are equally capable of being produced to infinity. Consequently, the original representation of space is an intuition *a priori*, and not a conception.

Transcendental Exposition of the Conception of Space

By a transcendental exposition, I mean the explanation of a conception, as a principle whence can be discerned the possibility of other synthetical *a priori* cognitions. For this purpose, it is requisite, firstly, that such cognitions do really flow from the given conception; and, secondly, that the said cognitions are only possible under the presupposition of a given mode of explaining this conception.

Geometry is a science which determines the properties of space synthetically, and yet *a priori*. What, then, must be our representation of space, in order that such a cognition of it may be possible? It must be originally intuition, for from a mere conception, no propositions can be deduced which go out beyond the conception, and yet this happens in geometry. But this intuition must be found in the mind *a priori*, that is, before any perception of objects, consequently must be pure, not empirical, intuition. For geometrical principles are always apodeictic, that is, united with the consciousness of their necessity, as: "Space has only three dimensions." But propositions of this kind cannot be empirical judgments, nor conclusions from them. Now, how can an external intuition anterior to objects themselves, and in which our conception of objects can be determined *a priori*, exist in the human mind? Obviously not otherwise than in so far as it has its seat in the subject only, as the *formal* capacity of the subject's being affected by objects, and thereby of obtaining immediate representation, that is, intuition; consequently, only as the *form of the external sense* in general.

Thus it is only by means of our explanation that the possibility of geometry, as a synthetical science *a priori* becomes comprehensible. Every mode of explanation which does not show us this possibility, although in appearance it may be similar to ours, can with the utmost certainty be distinguished from it by these marks.

Conclusions from the Foregoing Conceptions

(a) Space does not represent any property of objects as things in themselves, nor does it represent them in their relations to each other; in other words, space does not represent to us any determination of objects such as attaches to the objects themselves, and would remain, even though all subjective conditions of the intuition were abstracted. For neither absolute nor relative determinations of objects can be intuited prior to the existence of the things to which they belong, and therefore not *a priori*.

(b) Space is nothing else than the form of all phenomena of the external sense, that is, the subjective condition of the sensibility, under which alone external intuition is possible. Now, because the receptivity or capacity of the subject to be affected by objects necessarily antecedes all intuitions of these objects, it is easily understood how the form of all phenomena can be given in the mind previous to all actual perceptions, therefore *a priori*, and how it, as a pure intuition, in which all objects must be determined, can contain principles of the relations of these objects prior to all experience.

It is therefore from the human point of view only that we can speak of space, extended objects, etc. If we depart from the subjective condition, under which alone we can obtain external intuition, or, in other words, by means of which we are affected by objects, the representation of space has no meaning whatsoever. This predicate is only applicable to things in so far as they appear to us, that is, are objects of sensibility. The constant form of this receptivity, which we call sensibility, is a necessary condition of all relations in which objects can be intuited as existing without us, and when abstraction of these objects is made, is a pure intuition, to which we give the name of space. It is clear that we cannot make the special conditions of sensibility into conditions of the possibility of things, but only of the possibility of their existence as far as they are phenomena. And so we may correctly say that space contains all which can appear to us externally, but not all things considered as things in themselves, be they intuited or not, or by whatsoever subject one will. As to the intuitions of other thinking beings, we cannot judge whether they are or are not bound by the same conditions which limit our own intuition, and which for us are universally valid. If we join the limitation of a judgment to the conception of the subject, then the judgment will possess unconditioned validity. For example, the proposition, "All objects are beside each other in space," is valid only under the limitation that these things are taken as objects of our sensuous intuition. But if I join the condition to the conception and say, "All things, as external phenomena, are beside each other in space," then the rule is valid universally, and without any limitation. Our expositions, consequently, teach the *reality* (i.e., the objective validity) of space in regard of all which can be presented to us externally as object, and at the same time also the *ideality* of space in regard to objects when they are considered by means of reason as things in themselves, that is, without reference to the constitution of our sensability. We maintain, therefore, the *empirical reality* of space in regard to all possible external experience, although we must admit its *transcendental ideality*; in other words, that it is nothing, so soon as we withdraw the condition upon which the possibility of all experience depends and look upon space as something that belongs to things in themselves.

But, with the exception of space, there is no representation, subjective and referring to something external to us, which could be called objective *a priori*. For there are no other subjective representations from which we can deduce synthetical propositions *a priori*, as we can from the intuition of space. Therefore, to speak accurately, no ideality whatever belongs to these, although they agree in this respect with the representation of space, that they belong merely to the subjective nature of the mode of sensuous perception; such a mode, for example, as that of sight, of hearing, and of feeling, by means of the sensations of color, sound, and heat, but which, because they are only sensations and not intuitions, do not of themselves give us the cognition of any object; least of all, an *a priori* cognition. My purpose, in the above remark, is merely this: to guard any one against illustrating the asserted ideality of space by examples quite insufficient, for example, by color, taste, etc.; for these must be contemplated not as properties of things, but only as changes in the subject, changes which may be different in different men. For, in such a case, that which is originally a mere phenomenon, a rose, for example, is taken by the empirical understanding for a thing in itself, though to every different eye, in respect of its color, it may appear different. On the contrary, the transcendental conception of phenomena in space is a critical admonition, that, in general, nothing which is intuited in space is a thing in itself, and that space is not a form which belongs as a property to things; but that objects are quite unknown to us in themselves, and what we call outward objects, are nothing else but mere representations of our sensibility, whose form is space, but whose real correlate, the thing in itself, is not known by means of these representations, nor ever can be, but respecting which, in experience, no inquiry is ever made.

SPACES AND TIMES

Anthony Quinton

We are accustomed to thinking of space and time as particulars or individuals—even if we should hesitate to describe them as things or objects or substances. We say "space has three dimensions," "material things occupy space," "the debris has disappeared into space" and we talk in a comparable fashion about time. Not only do we think of space and time as individuals but, in many connections at any rate, we think of them as *unique* individuals. When we talk about spaces and times in the plural, when we say "fill up the spaces on the form," "it could go in the space between the lamp and the door," "there were peaceful times in the early years of their marriage," we think of these multiple spaces and times as parts of the unique all-encompassing space and the unique all-encompassing time. Kant believed that we could not help thinking of them in this way. We do, at any rate, in fact think like this and it is this conviction that I want to examine. What, I shall ask first of all, does the belief that space and time are unique individuals come to? Secondly, is the belief in either case true? Finally, if it is true in either case, is it necessarily true or is it simply a matter of fact?

1

What, to start with, does it mean to say that space is a unique individual? We could say instead that all real things are contained in one and the same space. Two things are in the same space if they are spatially connected, if there is a route connecting them, if each lies at some definite distance and in some definite direction from the other. The relation of spatial connection is clearly symmetrical. If I know the route leading from A to B, I must also know the route leading from B to A. It is also transitive. Given the route from A to B and the route from B to C the route from A to C is unequivocally determined. Now it does not follow from these properties of the relation of spatial connection that everything is in one and the same space, that everything is spatially connected to everything else. What does follow is that if A and B are spatially connected then everything spatially connected to A is spatially connected to B and vice versa. Spatial connection is anologous in form to identity in color, which is also symmetrical and transitive. Provided that A and B are identical in color everything identical in color with A is identical in color with B. But there are, of course, many distinct colors and so many pairs of things which, while identical in color with some things, are not identical in color with each other. So

This essay is reprinted from *Philosophy*, Vol. 38 (1962) 130-147. Used with the permission of the editor and Anthony M. Quinton.

far, then, it is an open possibility that spatial things should be arranged in spatially connected groups—just as colored things can be arranged in color-identical groups—all of whose members were spatially connected to each other but none of whose members were spatially connected to any of the members of any other group. To say that everything is in one space is simply to deny this possibility and to assert that all things are spatially connected. Naturally this assertion applies only to things that are in some sense spatial, things to which spatial predicates can intelligibly be ascribed. But this qualification does not affect the situation. The unity of space is not involved in the conception of a spatial thing. To say that a thing is spatial is to say either or both of the following: (a) that it is extended, that its parts are spatially connected to one another and (b) that it is spatially related, that it is spatially connected to something distinct from itself. It does not follow from either of these or from both of them taken together that it is spatially connected to everything. It does not follow, then, from the mere conception of a spatial thing that space is a unique individual. So far the formal possibility of a plurality of spaces remains open.

The same thing holds for time, as can easily be shown. Let us call two events temporally connected if there is a time-interval between them or if they are simultaneous. This relation, like that of spatial connection, is clearly symmetrical and transitive. So it allows for self-contained and exclusive groups of temporally connected events. Nor does the unity of time follow from the conception of a temporal thing or event. A temporal thing is something that occupies a lapse of time, that has temporally connected parts or phases and/or is something that is temporally connected to something else. From neither of these conditions does it follow that a temporal thing is temporally connected to everything.

But although the unity of space and the unity of time are not formally deducible from the concepts of spatial and temporal connection or the concepts of spatial and temporal things we do appear to believe that space and time are unities. Our direct information about the spatial and temporal connection of things is comparatively local. We observe the spatial disposition of things—the tree beside the barn, the mountain on the other side of the river—and we observe their temporal succession—the egg-white turning into a meringue, the bruise following the blow. Cartographers and chronologists piece these facts together in a single system of spatial and temporal positions. Provided that they can be answered at all, questions as to where things are or were and when they happened can always, it seems, be answered in terms of a system of positional references in which all positions are connected. As things are if a thing cannot be found a home in this unitary system of positions we conclude that there is no such thing.

The belief in the existence of one all-embracing space and one all-embracing time has not gone unchallenged. Bradley, in his determination to show the merely apparent character of space and time, addresses himself to the question at various points in his writings.[1] He argues that the unity of space and time is not only no necessity but that it is not even a fact. Why, he asks, should we take time as one succession and not as a multitude of series which are altogether temporally disconnected and separate although the members of each such series are temporally related to one another? In support of this proposal he draws attention to the relation between events in dreams and stories. In these imaginings events occur that are indisputable temporal entities since they are temporally related to other events in the same imagining. Yet these events cannot be located in the framework of public or historical time. Bradley rejects the suggestion that they should be dated by the time of their appearance in the mental history of the imaginer which can, we may assume, be located in ordinary public time. His argument is characteristically summary: it would be absurd, he says, to date the events of a novel by the date of its publication. The point he is making can be more persuasively developed. We can understand having good reason for saying that a dream lasted for thirty seconds or less of the dreamer's mental history while the content of the dream occupied a much greater tract of time. Here the events of the dream and the process of dreaming it are at least in the same order though the intervals between the things ordered are different. But we could also have reason for saying that the things I dreamt about on Monday were subsequent to the events I dreamed about on Tuesday. For on Monday I might have dreamt about myself as I am now and on Tuesday about myself as a child at school. Similarly it is quite possible for novelists to think up and for novel-readers to read what would naturally be called the later part of a story before the earlier part. Isherwood's *The Memorial* and Fitzgerald's *Tender Is The Night* are familiar examples of the latter possibility. Bradley goes on to suggest that even if all the events of which I am aware do fit into one all-inclusive temporal scheme it does not follow that there could not be events entirely unrelated to my time-series. But this is an empty proposal since he does not suggest any circumstances in which we could have any reason to think that there were such series. He attempts to dispose of the unity of space in a more cursory way. At first glance the order of extension seems to be one whole. But if we reflect we can see that extension is manifested in dreams: the trapeze I dream that I am swinging on is an obviously spatial thing but it is connected by no spatial route whatever to the familiar spatial contents of the common world.

Bradley's arguments for plurality all derive from the spaces and times of imagination. But since Russell's first works on the theory of knowledge we have become familiar with another source for arguments of the same kind—the spaces and times of sensation. My visual sense-data are extended, spatial entities, occupying positions and spatially interrelated to other things in the space of my momentary visual field. To the extent that my sense-data are veridical and have been obtained under normal conditions of observation they will at least correspond to the contents of common, public space. But they are not located in it. For I am the only person in the world who is even tempted to suppose that they are to be found there. And I need not give way to this temptation. If I look at a mountain and then close my eyes I do not suppose that anything at all has happened in the part of public space that is occupied by the mountain. To the extent that my sense-data are not veridical they do not usually even correspond to anything in public space. At best they have some sort of causal determinant within it. To take an example whose existence at least is uncontentious: my after-image is plainly a spatial thing, it occupies at any one moment a definite position in my visual field, but it has no real location in the public world.

There is a short but not entirely convincing answer to Bradley's arguments from the spaces and times of imagination. It could be said that imaginary objects and events, the contents of our dreams and fantasies, are nowhere at all. The contents of our imaginings are simply unreal. They can raise no problems of spatial and temporal location because they just do not exist. But to this it could be replied that although the trapeze I dreamed about last night has never hung in any actual, publicly observable circus tent, there really was something, a private entity, an image or dream-element, of which I was aware shortly before I woke up this morning. The remarks I produce at the breakfast table are not free and spontaneous creations, mere playing with words. I make earnest efforts to get my descriptions right, to leave nothing out, to set out the events dreamed of in the exact order in which I dreamt them. Bradley's argument can only be countered in this way if one is prepared to adopt a theory of dreaming like Professor Malcolm's which takes them to be no more than the utterance of sentences which, though just like the sentences we use to give genuine descriptions of our past experience, are not in fact being used for this purpose and are not intended to be understood as if they were. If this is accepted we do not have to worry about the spatial and temporal character of whatever it is that the report of a dream describes because such reports do not describe anything.

The most straightforward way of bringing out the implausibility of this theory is phenomenological: one has only to point to the experienced difference between making a story up out of one's head and reporting a dream or an earlier product of the imagination. There are two sides to the activities of the imagination: the story and the experience. The story is the words, written or spoken, in which a dream is reported or a piece of fiction is told. The experience is the body of images or private elements that the dreamer was aware of while he was dreaming, that the novelist was aware of while he was working out his book and that the reader is no doubt intermittently aware of as he reads. Only if we can eliminate the experience, by regarding it, for example, as no more than the disposition to produce a story, can Bradley's argument be summarily disposed of. Even if we do eliminate experience from our account of imagination there is still the spatial and temporal character of sensation to be dealt with. Bradley's argument for a plurality of spaces and times can be said to rest, then, on the spatial and temporal character of private experience—of images, dreams and sense-impressions. In private experience we are aware of things that are spatially extended and temporally enduring. These things are spatial and temporal in virtue both of the spatial and temporal relations between their parts and of the fact that they are spatially and temporally related to other spatial and temporal things. The dream-trapeze has ropes stretching away above the bar and the whole thing hovers above the sawdust surface of the dream arena. If we cannot show private experience to be the disposition to speak in a peculiar way we must either accommodate its contents in the unitary space and time of the common world or concede Bradley's point—that there is in fact a plurality of spaces and times.

We should perhaps reconsider this first alternative that Bradley so rapidly brushed aside. Can the tiger I am now picturing in my mind's eye be accommodated in public space? It cannot be accommodated at the place at which it looks as if it were. In the first place it may not look as if it were anywhere in particular. The background against which I am now experiencing it may be too dim and vague to provide any clue to location or it may be entirely unfamiliar. In these circumstances there can be no such activity as trying to find out where it is imagined to be. All I can do is to imagine it to be definitely somewhere, perhaps on the steps of the Albert Memorial and thus against a definite background located in public space. But in doing this I have not so much found out where it was as moved it there or, should one say, imagined another, no doubt very similar, tiger to be there. The situation is no better if the tiger does definitely look as if it were at some known and familiar place. For even if I dream of a tiger on the steps of the Albert Memorial, the real steps of the real Albert Memorial are not occupied by the tiger I am aware of in my dream. I can perfectly well have such a dream and accept reliable testimony that no tiger has been seen anywhere near the place I dreamt of. Even if, by some wild chance, there was an escaped tiger on the actual steps at the moment I was having my dream, we do not have to say that it is the very tiger I was dreaming of, however close the similarity. If my dreams turned out to be consistently correct representations of what was currently going on in the places I was dreaming about we might come to regard them as visions or cases of long-distance perception. But in that case they would no longer be dreams and it is characteristic of dreams that they do not exhibit any reliably attested correspondence of this kind.

The only other alternative is to locate the dreamed-of or imagined tiger at the place where I am, as, for example, quite literally, in my head. But this is an obviously hopeless maneuver. When I dream of tigers there generally are no tigers anywhere near where I am, my head is not large enough to contain tigers, the possible pattern of electrical activity in my brain associated with dreaming of tigers is not identifiable with the tigers I dream of since I know that I have dreamt of tigers but the electrical activity is an unstable compound of hearsay and guesswork. We cannot literally identify the places *in* my experience with the places *of* my experience.

2

Is the same thing true of time? Earlier, developing a rather sketchy argument of Bradley's, I suggested that the lapse of time someone dreams of might be much greater than the interval between the time at which he began to dream of it and the time at which he stopped doing so and I also suggested that one could dream of events happening in an order opposite to that of the events of dreaming of them. It might seem that these suggestions could be resisted. Could we not say that the estimate of time made in the dream is just a mistaken one, that the dreamed-of fall from the top of the building and the dreamed-of splash into the river are really only a fifteenth of a second apart even though they seemed in the dream to be separated by an interval of several seconds or even minutes? Again if I dream on Monday of taking off bandages to find my wound almost healed and on Tuesday of receiving the wound with a great deal of associated connecting tissue to link the two dreams together am I not compelled to say that the time in the dreams is in reverse order to the time of dreaming them? The wound I dream of on Tuesday could be said to be a new wound in the same place, if we felt compelled to link the two dreams together. In the first example the determination to identify the time of the dream with the time of dreaming is rather gratuitous. The correlation of dreams with their manifestations in the public world is tentative and infrequent. My audible cry of "help" does not have to be taken as simultaneous with my dreaming of a fall from the building nor my visible shudder with the splash. In most cases there is nothing even to suggest to us that the time of the events dreamed of is anything but what it appears to be. In the second example the situation is not so clear. In the first place the temporal propriety being defended is of a more fundamental kind. The topology of time-order is more sacred than the geometry of time-intervals. All the same it would seem unreasonable to deny that there was a difference between the time of the dream and the time of dreaming it if on a series of twelve nights one dreamt and remembered in precise detail a series of occurrences whose content could only be naturally arranged in exactly the reverse order to that in which they were dreamed. My general conclusion, so far, then is that we do have reason for admitting the existence of a plurality of experiential spaces over and above the space of the common world and that we could have reason for a similar admission about experiential times. There is no obvious contradiction in saying that there is such a plurality and, given the implausibility of strictly verbal accounts of private experience, better reason for saying that they do exist than that they do not. However if we consider the character of these experiential spaces and times more closely it will appear that they are so different from physical space and time that the concession we have made to Bradley's line of thought involves only a small modification of the common conviction of spatial and temporal unity.

3

There are two fundamental differences between physical and experiential space and time. Where the physical is vast and systematic, the experiential is small and fragmentary; where the physical is public, the experiential is private. These are not exactly contingent features even though comprehensiveness and publicity could vary in degree. Consider the space of dreams. There is ordinarily no ground for saying that the space of Monday night's dream has anything to do, or is any way connected, with the space of Tuesday night's dream. We often have several spatially disconnected dreams in one night. And in the course of one more or less continuous dream it is only the comparatively momentary spatial relationships of the dreamed-of things, the spatial relationships revealed in a temporal cross-section of the whole dream, that are at all definite. First I am on the trapeze. Below me I see a familiar face. Shortly afterwards my friend and I are seated side by side in a boat. Such continuity as there is is provided by the familiar face but it is not sufficient to establish any spatial relation between the trapeze and the boat. Many dreams are more coherent than this, of course, but it would seem that the constructibility of non-momentary spaces, spaces that endure as the scenes of comparatively protracted change, is the exception rather than the normal case in the experiential realm. We do have dreams where temporally successive incidents occur against a fairly definite and persisting background and there can be enough correspondence between the spatial contents of two quite distinct dreams for it to be reasonable to regard both as relating to one and the same spatial order. But as things are this is about as much in the way of system and coherence as our dreams ordinarily yield. It is plain that the same thing holds for our imaginings which, being so much more interrupted, so much more exposed to the solicitations of the external world, are perhaps even less coherent than dreams. It is also to some extent true of our sensations which only become coherent as a result of a good deal of suppression and filling-in. Privacy is as obvious a feature of the experiential realm as fragmentariness or incoherence. Nobody, as things are, can tell what our dreams or imaginings are unless we tell them. In the case of sensations reliable inferences can be made on the basis of well-established correlations between sense-experience and the condition and environment of the observer. If such correlations were available for inference to the other domains of experience they would have to rest in the end on the admissions of observers. We can imagine circumstances in which the correspondence between the dreams of two or more people was so extensive as to lead us to say that they were dreaming the same dream, especially if in the event of some marginal disagreement between two corresponding dreamers one of them subsequently admitted that he was mistaken. If there were many more blind people than there are, the remarks of the sighted about clouds and sunsets might well appear to be the by-products of a widely-shared dream. This is not altogether unfamiliar ground. The raptures of mysticism and musical appreciation incite, in rather different ways, just such a response among the less respectful of the uninitiated. Only if the correspondence becomes general enough to count as normal can dreaming come to be accounted as observation.

These differences between physical and experiential space and time are substantial enough as things are for the thesis that space and time are unitary to survive Bradley's arguments almost intact. Instead of saying that there is only one space and only one time the defender of unity must say that there is only one space and only one time that is coherent or public or both. Coherent and/or public space and time are, he might say, the only real space and time. Other spatial and temporal entities are fragmentary and private, a sort of ontological litter to be bundled into the wastepaper basket of the imaginary. He could argue that we only count those things as real that can be fitted into the one coherent and public space and time, that such locatability is a criterion of being real. For what is a dream or a fantasy or an illusion of the senses but an experience that fails to fit into the unitary spatio-temporal scheme? From this it follows that Descartes' hypothesis that perhaps everything is a dream is illegitimate. It cannot be significantly affirmed since to call a tract of experience a dream is to say that it fails to conform to the standard of coherence and publicity exhibited by the greater part of our experience. So to say that all our experience is a dream is to say that none of it comes up to the standard of most of it, a straight self-contradiction. Here is one case, at any rate, where the paradigm-case argument works. It does not entirely dispose of the Cartesian hypothesis. A man might have acquired a standard of coherence from somewhere else, perhaps a religious experience, though this would not show that the present distinction between waking and dreaming was improper, only that it should be differently named. More important is the fact that even if life hitherto cannot all have been a dream it does follow that the whole structure will not come to pieces in the next few minutes, that from then on none of our experience will attain the standard we have come to expect and all will be as incoherent as what we have hitherto regarded as dreams.

4

The position we have arrived at, then, is that even if it is not true that absolutely everything can be located in one space and one time, everything real, provided that it is spatial and temporal at all, can be so located. If the suggestion that such locatability is a criterion of being real is correct, it follows that the thesis of unity in its revised form is a necessary truth. Now this is essentially the opinion of Kant.[2] Space and time, he said, are not discursive or general concepts of the relations of things in general but pure intuitions. In other words they are not universals but particulars and unique particulars at that. His argument is that we can only conceive limited spaces and times as parts of one all-inclusive space and one all-inclusive time. These unique particulars are not literally composed of perceptually observed spatial extents and temporal durations, are not constructions from these extents and durations as elements, because they are somehow presupposed by these elements.

The logical status of arguments from conceivability is always insecure and in this type of case especially so, for we are concerned with a very primordial feature of our experience. Our habits of thinking about space and time are so early acquired and so deeply ingrained that their extreme familiarity can easily look like logical indispensability. It is clear anyway that we do in fact take all real spatial extents and temporal durations to be parts of the one space and the one time. But Kant is claiming more than this and to assess his claim we must ask whether we are compelled to think in this way. We can even concede that on our present interpretation of "real" the statement "everything real is in one space and in one time" is analytic. The question still remains whether there are any conceivable circumstances in which it would be reasonable to modify this interpretation. For it can be maintained that there are, in a sense, degrees of analyticity. That we have a certain concept at all can often be explained by referring to facts which might not have obtained. With any one concept there may be a number of such explanatory facts which can be arranged in some order of importance. The essentials of the concept would remain if some of the less important facts did not obtain and if, therefore, the conventions that depend on them did not exist. Let us take a very simple example, that of brotherhood. Our existing concept of brotherhood is determined by facts of biology and sociology. Men are borne by women, as a result of sexual intercourse between those women and other men, and pass the helpless years of infancy in a group commonly led, protected and provided for by their parents. Now imagine a society in which women were elaborately promiscuous or which all conception came about through artificial insemination by anonymous donors. Suppose also that the family group consisted of the mother and her children alone. In these circumstances we should presumably count children of the same mother as brothers and the statement "all brothers have both parents in common" would be no longer analytic but contingent and false. It is too narrow to describe this situation as one in which we should use the word "brother" to mean what we now mean by "maternal half-brother." For what is really important about the concept of brotherhood, that it relates persons who share both a biological inheritance and certain fundamental loyalties and affections, is still retained by the revised concept. Now suppose that children were taken from their mothers at birth and raised in institutions. Even here there might be some point in having the concept if the institutions in which children were brought up had something of the emotional structure of the ordinary human family as it now exists.

Let us look at a more complicated and perhaps more philosophically interesting example considered by Professor Ayer, which concerns the privacy of pain.[3] As things are, the causal conditions of pain are commonly found in the body of the sufferer. If I am in pain it is not usually the case that anyone near me has a similar affliction and I cannot generally get rid of the pain by moving about. Now suppose that circumstances were different, that everyone whose body is in a certain region of space during a certain period of time feels a pain of much the same sort, that the intensity of this pain uniformly diminishes as they move away from a determinable point in the region and that it disappears altogether when they are at a certain distance, roughly agreed upon by all, beyond this central point. In these circumstances, Ayer suggests, we might well cease to think of pains, as we now do, as being private and might come to accord them much the same sort of status as we now give to material things. "Look out," we might say to a man walking in a certain direction, "there's a pain there"; and we might say this with good reason even if there were at the time no one in the region in question and therefore no one suffering the pain. If this were to come about people might cease to speak of "my pain" and "your pain" and there would be no question that different people could feel the very same pain. In other words the statement "no one but me can feel the pain I am feeling" would no longer be analytic. The same thing would happen to the statement "all pains are felt by somebody."

It would still, of course, be open to philosophers to talk about pain-data and they might well be encouraged to do so if there were perceptible differences of sensitivity between people or if some people felt pain in places where nobody else did. They would have the same reasons for talking about pain-data and pain-hallucinations as they now have for talking about sense-data and hallucinations of the senses. Ayer's supposition reveals the contingencies on which our current convictions about the concept of pain rest. If it came true it would be reasonable to alter these conventions and to regard many statements as synthetically true or false which we now regard as analytic or contradictory. The essentials of the concept have not been tampered with; under his supposition there are still experiences which people generally and instinctively dislike having.

Can we construct a myth that will reveal the ultimately conventional character of the Kantian thesis that real space and time are unitary? Do our current convictions about the unity of space and time rest in the end on contingencies which we can conceive as ceasing to obtain? I believe that there is an important asymmetry in this respect between space and time and I shall argue that a coherent multi-spatial myth can be envisaged but not a coherent multi-temporal one. So I shall begin with space.

5

Now suppose that your dream-life underwent a remarkable change. Suppose that on going to bed at home and falling asleep you found yourself to all appearances waking up in a hut raised on poles at the edge of a lake. A dusky woman, whom you realize to be your wife, tells you to go out and catch some fish. The dream continues with the apparent length of an ordinary human day, replete with an appropriate and causally coherent variety of tropical incident. At last you climb up the rope ladder to your hut and fall asleep. At once you find yourself awaking at home, to the world of normal responsibilities and expectations. The next night life by the side of the tropical lake continues in a coherent and natural way from the point at which it left off. Your wife says "You were very restless last night. What were you dreaming about?" and you find yourself giving her a condensed version of your English day. And so it goes on. Injuries given in England leave scars in England, insults given at the lakeside complicate lakeside personal relations. One day in England, after a heavy lunch, you fall asleep in your armchair and dream of yourself, or find yourself, waking up in the middle of the night beside the lake. Things get too much for you at the lakeside, your wife has departed with all the cooking-pots and you suspect that she is urging the villagers to sacrifice you to the moon. So you fall on your fish-spear and from that moment on your English slumbers are disturbed no more than in the old pre-lakeside days.

There are some loose ends in this story but I think they can be tidied up. What, first of all, about your lakeside life before the dream began? Either the lakesiders will have to put up with the fact that you have lost your memory, and we can leave it open whether they are in a position to fill in the blank for you or not, or you might find "memories" of your earlier lakeside career spontaneously cropping up. The most immediately digestible possibility is perhaps a version of the latter in which your lakeside past gradually comes back to you after an initial period of total amnesia. But complete loss of memory is the easiest to handle. Next, how are the facts that you are awake sixteen hours and asleep eight hours in each environment to be reconciled? How can sixteen hours of England be crammed into eight hours of lake and vice versa? Well, why not? As long as there is some period of sleep in each day in each place there is room for the waking day in the other place. We often say, after all, that dreams seem to take much longer than they actually do. The same principle could be applied to our alternative worlds. To make the thing fairly precise we could correlate hours in England with hours by the lakeside, on the basis of nocturnal mumblings and movements, so that midnight to eight a.m. in England is eight a.m. to midnight at the lake and vice versa. This would have mildly embarrassing consequences but not contradictory ones. If I stay up till 4 a.m. in England I cannot wake up beside the lake until 4 in the afternoon. If an alarm clock wakes me two hours early in England, i.e. at 6 a.m., then I shall find myself dropping irresistibly off at eight p.m. by the lake. One embarrassment is common to both hypotheses: if in either place I stay up all night I must sleep all through the day in the other. Some of these embarrassments can be avoided by supposing that the lakeside day is normally eight hours long and the lakeside night sixteen hours long. To imagine such a comatose manner of life is perhaps easier than having to put up with the embarrassments of rigid correlation.

Now if this whole state of affairs came about it would not be very unreasonable to say that we lived in two worlds. So far it may seem that only one of the properties of physical space as we understand it has been added to the space of dreams, namely its coherence. But it only takes a small addition to equip it with publicity, an addition already implicit in the fable as I have told it. For I am not alone at the lakeside, there is my wife and the moon-worshiping villagers, whose statements and behavior may confirm all the spatial beliefs I form at the lakeside, with the usual minor exceptions. It might be argued that this sort of publicity is bogus, that it is only dream-publicity. But as it stands this is just prejudice. At the lakeside, on my hypothesis, we have just as good reason to take our spatial beliefs as publicly confirmed as we have in England. However, a less questionable type of publicity can be provided if we suppose that the dreams of everyone in England reveal coherent order of events in our mythical lake district and let everyone have one and only one correlated lake-dweller whose waking experiences are his dreams. (In this case we should have to correlate the clocks of England and the lakeside, either by the rather embarrassing proposal of elastic time-intervals or by that of the eight-hour lakeside day. For otherwise I could drop off at the lakeside on Monday, wake up before you go to sleep and tell you a whole lot of things about Tuesday in England before, from your point of view, they had happened.) There are various ways in which we can suppose that people who know one another in England could come to recognize one another at the lakeside, for example, by the drawing of self-portraits from memory or by agreeing, in England, to meet at some lakeside landmark.

I shall not pursue the hypothesis of a dream that is public in this strong sense since it becomes imaginatively too cumbrous, though not, I think, self-contradictory. One special difficulty is that in such circumstances some measure of causal interpenetration by the two worlds would be natural. Even if physical causation cannot, *ex hypothesi*, operate from one region into the other, psychological causation presumably would. The injury I do you at the lakeside may be revenged not there but in England. I think, in fact, that my original one-man hypothesis is sufficient for the purpose in hand. But we can publicize this a bit further without going all the way to publicity in the strong sense. It might, for instance, be the case that everyone's dream-life was coherent but that no one person's dream-life corresponded with anyone else's. In this case everyone would inhabit two real spaces, one common to all and one peculiar to each. This residual asymmetry can, of course, be eliminated by requiring that the same be true of all the lakesiders. On this supposition the worlds we have some reason to believe in fray off into infinity. Each of my lakeside acquaintances has his other life, in which he comes across people, each of whom has his and so on. But this infinity does not seem to be a vicious one.

It might be said that if this myth were realized we should either have to say that the dream-place was somewhere in ordinary physical space or else that it was still only a dream. Both of these alternatives can be effectively disputed. Suppose that I am in a position to institute the most thorough geographical investigations and however protractedly and carefully these are pursued they fail to reveal anywhere on earth like my lake. But could we not then say that it must be on some other planet? We could but it would be gratuitous to do so. There could well be no positive reason whatever, beyond our fondness for the Kantian thesis, for saying that the lake is located somewhere in ordinary physical space and there are, in the circumstances envisaged, good reasons for denying its location there. Still suppose we do find a place, in New Guinea let us say, exactly like the lakeside. I, the dreamer, lead the expedition into the village, brandishing trade goods. Friendly relations having been established with the elders of the place, we are led to the longhouse to meet the populace and there, to my amazement, is the face I have often seen in my dreams while bending over the pools at the lake's edge in pursuit of fish. Now if the owner of this face is fast asleep and cannot be woken up until I go to sleep this village and the place of my dreams can be identified. But suppose he is wide awake and we get into conversation. He turns out to have coherent dreams about my life in England and in fact to have dreamt last night of my progress towards the village on the preceding day, just as I dreamt last night of what he was doing the day before. The natural conclusion will be that we are connected by a kind of delayed cross-telepathy and that what the Kantian insists are still only dreams are at any rate in the same order of reality as dreams. If, then, we do find what is to all intents and purposes the place of my dreams, the Kantian's dilemma—either in the one real space or just a dream—does apply. But if we do not there is no reason to insist upon it.

If, failing to find the scene of my coherent dream in ordinary physical space, we insist that it is, then, only a dream we are neglecting the point of marking off the real from the imaginary. Why, as things are, do we have this ontological wastepaper basket for the imaginary? Because, approximately, there are some experiences that we do not have to bother about afterwards, that we do not, looking back on them, need to take seriously. Dream-events, where they have consequences at all, do not have serious consequences. If I dream of cutting somebody's throat my subsequent dreams will in all probability be entirely unrelated to him and to my act. Even if they are, when I am haled into court I am as likely to be given a bunch of flowers as a death-sentence. But beside the lake there is a place for prudence, forethought and accurate recollection. It is an order of events in which I am a genuine agent. There is every reason there for me to take careful note and make deliberate use of my experience. Reality, I am suggesting, then, is that part of our total experience which it is possible and prudent to take seriously. It is, of course, because I am ultimately interpreting reality in this way that I can envisage dispensing with locatability in one physical space and time as a criterion of it. My conclusion so far, then, is that it is a contingent matter that the experience we can and prudently should take seriously can all be assigned to one space. Kant's unity of space is not an unalterable necessity of thought.

6

Let us turn finally to the case of time. Can an analogous myth be constructed here? Can we conceive of living in two distinct orders of spatial extension? The lakeside story did present some peculiar temporal features, in some of its versions a sort of time-stretching, but at least the proprieties of temporal order were respected. And, with the eight-hour day, it was possible to do without time-stretching. Another avoidable difficulty was the temporal status of the events "remembered" by me at the lakeside after I have started, *nel mezzo del cammin*, consciously living there. Here again temporal order is all right. The trouble arises about the correlation of my "remembered" twelfth birthday and initiation ceremony at the lakeside with events in my English life. However this is not a serious problem. Either we can say the date of my initiation in English terms is unknown, apart from being before such-and-such a date on which my lakeside experiences started or we can extrapolate with the help of rules of correlation we have established in the directly experienced parts of my lakeside life. Our multi-spatial myths are not, then, also multi-temporal myths.

So for a multi-temporal myth we must begin again from the beginning. What we are in search of, in general terms, is this: two groups of orderly and coherent experiences where the members of each group are temporarily connected but no member of either group has any temporal relation to any member of the other. Such a search seems doomed from the start. How can these experiences be my experiences unless they constitute a single temporal series? This will become clearer if we consider some examples of possible multi-temporal myths.

Consider first the myth that results from a small complication of the original myth about England and the lakeside. Suppose that my memories become, so to speak, disconnected, that I can remember the relative temporal situation of English events and the relative temporal situation of lakeside events but not the temporal relations of any English events to any lakeside event. I can remember that I got on the bus after I had spoken to Jones about our favorite television program. I can remember taking part in the fertility rite after setting the fish-traps. What I cannot temember is whether getting on the bus occurred before or after setting the fish-traps. The trouble with this obstacle to unitary dating is that it is too easily circumvented. At the beginning of day 1 in England I write down in order all the lakeside events I can remember. On day 2 in England I cannot remember whether the events of day 1 follow or preceded the lakeside events in the list. But the list will be there to settle the matter and I can, of course, remember when I compiled it.

A desperate shift that might suggest itself at this point is the supposition that

I cannot remember lakeside events at all when I am in England nor English events while I am at the lakeside. But this is self-destroying. For unless I have memories of one series of events while experiencing the other there can be no reason for saying that I am involved in both of them, that both are experienced by one and the same person. *Ex hypothesi* the lakeside can have no physical, observable traces in England, so my memories of it in England are the only reason there can be for me, in England, to think that the lakeside exists.

Another line of approach requires us to suppose that the experience of dreaming coherently about the lakeside is general or at least widespread. It might be thought that we could all pass in and out of the coherent dream-world, or the alternative reality, at different times. But suppose the salient events of the day for two people in England are kipper for breakfast and steak for lunch, while the salient event for the approximately corresponding day at the lakeside is a distant volcanic eruption. The two people breakfast together in England, so their kipper-eating is simultaneous. After breakfast one of them drops off and witnesses the volcanic eruption. He awakes for lunch and over their simultaneous steaks tells his partner about the eruption. After lunch the second man falls asleep and witnesses the eruption for himself. At first glance this might seem to suggest that the eruption cannot be fitted at all into the English time-sequence. But on reflection it is clear that we can fit "the eruption" in only too well. For it happened, to A, before their simultaneous lunch and, to B, after it. What happens before an event, happens before everything that happens after that event. Therefore the eruption happened before itself. The only consistent conclusion from the data is that two eruptions took place and for each of these there is a perfectly unequivocal position in the English time-series.

The moral of these unsuccessful attempts to construct a multi-temporal myth is the same in each case. Any event that is memorable by me can be fitted in to the single time-sequence of my experience. Any event that is not memorable by me is not an experience of mine. This second proposition is not equivalent to a Lockean account of personal identity which holds my experiences to be all those experiences that I can remember. For the memorability to which it refers is memorability in principle not in practice. All that is required for an experience to be mine is that I should be logically capable of remembering it. But from the fact that, at a given time, I am logically capable of remembering a certain experience, it follows that the experience is temporally antecedent to the given time, the time of my current experience, and so is in the same time, the same framework of temporal relations, as it is. Thus if an experience is mine it is memorable and if it is memorable it is temporally connected to my present state. The question we are raising—is it conceivable that we should inhabit more than one time—answers itself. For what it asks is: could my experience be of such a kind that the events in it could not be arranged in a single temporal sequence? And it seems unintelligible to speak of a collection of events as constituting the experience of one person unless its members form a single temporal sequence. This view of the concept of a person's experience is supported by another consideration. It is possible to imagine that our experience might not be spatial. As Mr. Strawson has shown, if our experience were all auditory, although it might contain features and differentiations which could be used as clues to spatial position with the aid of correlations with the deliverances of other senses, these features would have no spatial import on their own.[4] On the other hand it is not possible to imagine an experience that is not temporal. We should, of course, have no sense of the passage of time unless our experience exhibited change. But an unchanging experience is no more intelligible than a non-temporal one. An experience of one unvarying sound, or even of an unvarying mixture of sounds, would not be an experience at all. A high, thin, metaphysical whistle sounding in one's mind's ear from birth to death would be in principle undetectable, like the impression of the self that Hume rummaged unsuccessfully around in his consciousness for.

I conclude, then, that we can at least conceive circumstances in which we should have good reason to say that we knew of real things located in two quite distinct spaces. But we cannot conceive of such a state of affairs in the case of time. Our conception of experience is essentially temporal in a way in which it is not essentially spatial.

NOTES

1. F.H. Bradley, *Appearance and Reality*, chapter 18, pp. 186-9.
2. *Critique of Pure Reason*, A25, B39.
3. A.J. Ayer, *The Problem of Knowledge*, chapter V, section iii, pp. 228-9.
4. P.F. Strawson, *Individuals*, chapter 2.

MULTI-SPATIAL MYTHS: KANT AND THE DREAMER

Peter A. French

Kant's position in "The Transcendental Aesthetic" is that space is a pure "form of sensibility" (of outer sense), that it is not a condition of things in (by) themselves, but of the appearances of things to the mind in perceiving, and that it is the subjective condition of the immediate awareness of things in the manifold. Space is an individual and not a concept. It is "a unique individual." It seems to me that this is an expression of the rather normal way most of us think of space. In fact, I suspect that a case might well be made that Kant's analysis of space (and time) amounts to an analysis of the ordinary use of those terms. Talk of spaces—"Fill in the blank spaces on the card, Hang the painting in the space between the door and the window, We drove across the wide-open spaces"—generally does not imply a plurality of spaces. There appears to be a common belief in a single all-encompassing space. I would expect that the ordinary man (the non-professional metaphysician) faced with the question, "How many spaces are there?" would respond that "Really, there is only one space."

Kant's doctrine of space (and time), which Russell calls the most important part of the *Critique*, is basically an attempt to solve the problem of perception, the problem of objects. By claiming that we can "represent to ourselves only one space; and if we speak of diverse spaces we mean thereby only parts of one and the same unique space,"[1] Kant is explicitly ruling out the intelligibility of multi-spatial myths and related perceptual theories, i.e. some forms of the representative theory.[2] I shall examine certain recent attempts to formulate multi-spatial myths (Quinton's in particular, but also Smythies' and Price's), which, if they were more than superficially intelligible, would force us to reconsider our belief (Kant's) that space is a "unique individual" and, secondly, would throw into question the basic theory of perception of The Aesthetic.

Attempts to formulate multi-spatial myths are surely nothing new. Bradley had argued against the unitary space and time doctrine in *Appearance and Reality*, Chapter 18. His arguments were based on examples taken from dreams and literature. He claimed that extension is not only manifested in the physical space of waking life but that it is also to be found in dreams. The objects in dreams (and novels, etc.) are described in spatial language but are in no way connected to the familiar spatial objects of the physical world.[3] Bradley's conclusion was that there are non-related spaces which accommodate these objects.

Reprinted from *The Southern Journal of Philosophy*, Vol. XI, No. 3, (1973) 167 ff. Used with the permission of the editor.

Russell introduced a multi-spatial (and temporal) myth when he talked of the spaces and times of sensation.[4] He referred to the extension and position and spatial interrelatedness of things in the space of momentary visual fields. Russell claimed that in so far as my sense data are veridical they will correspond to the contents of public space, but are nowhere to be found in public space. Therefore we are not tempted to think anything has happened to objects in public space when we no long have them in view. Non-veridical sense-data do not correspond to anything in public space. They cease to exist when they ceast to exist for the "observer." Quinton gives a rather uncomplicated version of the distinction Russell may have had in mind. "My after-image is plainly a spatial thing, it occupies at any one moment a definite position in my visual field, but it has no real location in the public world."[5] For Russell, the postulation of private spaces interestingly enough led him to problem of other minds, a problem which he "solved" not so much by analogy as by an appeal to the consistency of the belief in other minds with established knowledge: that it systematizes a vast body of facts, and that it "extends our knowledge of the sensible world by testimony." His account is rather less than convincing. The very knowledge cited by Russell as vindication of the belief in other minds is dependent upon those other minds for confirmation. There is still no convincingly demonstrable reason to reject solipsism. That Kant was never trapped into these problems is perhaps traceable to the unitary space doctrine.

What Kant intended by the "space as a unique individual" doctrine needs to be clarified before examining Quinton's criticism of it. Space (and time) is said by Kant to be a pure intuition. It is a particular. By that he means that space is a "form of sensibility" and not a conception derived from experience. In Kant's terminology a conception is always a combination of the parts which had come before it. But Kant argues that the "parts of space" can be thought of only in terms of the whole. They are limitations of the whole and belong within it. We cannot conceive of a part of space or a "space of . . ." before the form of space in general. If space is not a concept, then for Kant it must be an intuition (the whole precedes the parts in intuitions), and if it is an intuition it is by definition a single individual.

There are major difficulties involved here due to the fact that "form of sensibility" is at best vague. How Kant intended it to be understood is open to at least two interpretations: 1.) "a linguistic convention for discussing our visual experience"[6] and 2.) a psychological theory to explain the spatial character of perception or perceptual data. The former, had it been Kant's intent, would have created no major difficulties for multi-spatial mythmakers or representative perceptual theorists. Briefly, Kant might have meant that when I make the claim, "I saw a bear," the perception always, by convention, refers to some object in some spatial coordinates or other. That is, perceptual talk presupposes spatial terminology. "I saw a bear." Where? Over there"; but not, it might be suspected, "I saw a bear. Where? In my dream." (The status of "I *saw* a bear in my dream" shall, however, be considered in some detail later.) On interpretation (1) Kant might have, by appeal to convention, argued that "I saw a bear in my dream" is not a report of perceptual experience, "in my dream" not being legitimately substitutable for "over there."

The majority of commentators, however, take interpretation (2) to be closer to Kant's view of a "form of sensibility." This position is that there is a psychological apparatus at work in human perception which makes most of our experience of the world spatial. As Weldon puts it, Kant's claim is always that "We can distinguish between the form and the matter of what we perceive."[7] When we say that we see something, we are receiving impressions, sensations, and our minds are imposing a form or structure upon them. Sensations are the matter, space and time are the forms of our sensibility.

The first and second arguments on space establish the non-empirical and *a priori* nature of the "form." It must be subjective, and the third and fourth arguments (in B) are intended to prove it also must be an intuition and not a concept. The result of Kant's analysis then is the claim that we not only do, but must, perceive by means of this psychological apparatus and that all real spatial extents must be thought of in these terms. Put differently, all that is real is, analytically, in one space (and one time). It is this latter claim, or a similar one, that of the *a priori* nature of the unitary space doctrine, that Quinton attacks. He argues that the Kantian thesis on space is at best conventional, if not altogether contrary to fact.

Quinton puts the problem in this form. "Do our current convictions about the unity of space and time rest in the end on contingencies which we can conceive as ceasing to obtain?"[8] He attempts an account of a multi-spatial myth as an answer to the question. He asks one to suppose that his dreams underwent such a change that upon going home to bed and falling asleep he found himself awakening in a hut raised on poles at the edge of a lake. He participates in family, social, and other relationships during a typical day by the lake. Then he climbs a ladder into the hut, falls asleep, and awakens at home to the world of normal responsibilities and relationships. Each night his life by the lake continues in coherent and natural ways from the point at which he left off the previous night. If his lakeside wife asks why he slept restlessly he responds with an account of his normal non-lakeside day (in the form of recounting a dream), and vice versa. Concerning temporal sequences, Quinton points out that it need only be assumed that the lakeside day is normally only eight hours long with sixteen hour nights, thereby fitting both sequences into our normal 24 hour day.

Quinton concludes that if such a supposed state of affairs did come about it would not be unreasonable to claim that the dreamer lived in two worlds in two different spaces. The only apparent addition to dream space which Quinton claims to have made is that of coherence. This is, of course, a major alteration of what we normally take to be dreams. Kant, in the Second Analogy, depends strongly on the chaotic nature of dreams for his proof of causality. I think, however, that the problem of objects in dreams, even for Kant, is more important to the argument. Where is the lake of the dream world? Quinton replies:

> There could well be no positive reason whatever, beyond our fondness for

> the Kantian thesis, for saying that the lake is located somewhere in ordinary physical space and there are, in the circumstances envisaged, good reasons for denying its location there.[9]

Surely it is unlikely that we could search the world over to locate the lake, but this, as Quinton fails to grasp, is due to our commitment to the Kantian doctrine, not because we (tacitly) accept a multi-spatial myth.

Quinton's myth depends on a number of considerations and definitions, most of which completely corrupt the notion of dreaming. A simply and somewhat popular current reply to Quinton is that "the objects and events" of our dreams are nowhere at all, that dreams (nocturnal adventures) do not exist. Malcolm[10] and Bouwsma[11] maintain that dreams are not something one experiences but are dispositions to tell certain stories at the breakfast table. The descriptions we give of our dreams are not genuine descriptions of past experience, and we do not really intend them to be so construed. Taken to the extreme, this position, however, seems to ignore evidence from psychological and common experience. Nonetheless, I think that Kant would be inclined to take a position not too dissimilar from Malcolm's in regard to whether or not dreams can be counted as experiences.

The phrase "in my dream" creates the problem. On cursory analysis we might expect that "in my dream" is like "in my house," a place with physical spatial-temporal coordinates. But are dreams places such that I can meet persons, be affected by objects, etc., in them? When we say, "In my dream I ran from a bear," do we mean "Nowhere did I run from a bear"? That was not the dream reporter's intention, but certainly "in my dream" does not designate a place like Denver, Colorado. MacDonald[12] is led to call dreams a state of mind (similar to "a state of anger, a state of madness, What a state he is in!" but, "a state of delusion"?) rather than anything spatial because of the difficulty in applying the language of physical space to the locating of objects in dreams. Surely the expression "it is only a dream" has appropriate usage different from "it is only a village." Quinton's account of the coherent dream world, however, forces him to assert that often the expression "it is only a dream" confuses the point of "marking off the real from the imaginary." One wonders when it would be appropriate to utter the expression or what it might mean to anyone who uttered it.

Returning to one of the basic questions of The Aesthetic: what does it mean when one says, "I saw ... a bear"? For Kant, the object is given to us by sensibility and "the mind is affected in a certain way," yielding, through the forms of space and time, an intuition which is thought through the understanding, producing the concept. Kant's claim is that we cannot apprehend data outside of a spatial-temporal context. The "bear" is not perceived as a thing in (by) itself, but is an "appearance" given to our sensibility. The term "sensibility" is problematic in the *Critique*. Kant's use of it should not be confused with that of the Phenomenologists or with Plato's world of appearances. Appearances for Kant are never illusory (B69-70). Kantian appearances are not like empirical appearings. Graham Bird comments:

> The term appearance must be understood to cover things that are spatial, and distinct from us, as well as things that are "in us" and mere modifications of the mind, belonging to inner sense, such as sensations.[13]

In other words, Kant uses "appearances" to refer to anything given to the sense. Appearances are not sensations or things by themselves and they are not ideas. One might say that "appearance" is the aspect of an object which can become an intuition, all other aspects being unknowable. "Appearances" are not representations of the things by themselves.

There is a need to distinguish between Kant's use of perceptual words, even though the *Critique* is not as consistent in usage as one would hope. *Vorstellung* (representation) is a blanket term (an umbrella word) which refers to anything "present to the mind when it thinks." It is, in simple English, an idea. *Erscheinung*, on the other hand, is generally translated as "appearance" but *Erscheinungen* can be said to have insides and outsides, to be solid or liquid, to obey mechanical laws. Things by themselves, of course, are not in space or time, whereas appearances can be talked of in spatial and temporal language. But "appearances" are not sense data. *Erscheinung* and *Vorstellung* are distinct. What then is the object of perception? Weldon tells us that Kant did not have enough epistemological words to draw the distinctions within perceiving which would be necessary "to expound his concept of the 'object of perception.'" Nonetheless, I think that Kant tends to identify the object of perception with the thing as it appears to normal observers: phenomenon. B 69-70, III makes clear that the object of perception is the *Erscheinung* and that the unitary space doctrine serves to distinguish appearances from illusions. The bear that I see is the object as it looks to me under normal conditions in space and time. It is not the illusion of a bear nor the creation of a representative mechanism (such as a television picture of a bear).

What then is meant when one says, "I saw a bear by the lake in my dream"? The dreamer is not claiming to have been in two places at once. He is not claiming to be reporting events which occurred outside of his bedroom. Or is he? According to Quinton, the dreamer's lakeside life is not a deception. Though it is not difficult to imagine circumstances, in spite of Quinton's account, in which utter confusion would plague his dreamer's days (and nights). Those who dream usually are not worried about the accuracy of their dream accounts or about spatial statements they make about their dreamworlds. Such a concern would suggest that the dreamer is in need of psychiatric help. Quinton, however, maintains: "I am not alone at the lakeside, there is my wife and the moon-worshiping villagers, whose statement and behavior may confirm all the spatial beliefs I form at the lakeside, with the usual minor exceptions."[14] This is most odd, for surely whatever spatial beliefs the dreamer formulates he does not formulate them while dreaming and at the so-called place (the lakeside) of his dream. The fact that I formulated a unified field theory in my dream last night does not entail that I did formulate or could formulate such a theory. The grammar of dreaming is violated when one cannot make normal distinctions between dream and waking life. Furthermore, if I am not alone at the lakeside, if my dream wife and the dream moon-worshiping tribe are not just objects in my dream but persons capable of confirming my statements about spatial objects, my memories, etc., then the sense of calling this a dream is totally lost. If dreamed persons are, in fact, persons then perhaps my son's dreamed monsters are, in fact, monsters, and "It was only a dream" would be less than comforting. I would surely appear apprehensive as I said it to him, looking around yet realizing I was looking in the wrong place for his monsters, that I was systematically incapable of looking in the right place. Better for him not to dream, better for him not to sleep at all.

Certainly the ordinary man's view of dreams is to regard them as interesting and/or annoying diversions and to attribute no reality to the objects which may appear in them. If Quinton's dreamer were to have killed a neighbor by the lake, then awakened, it is most unlikely that his conscience would be bothered or that he would seek out the services of a lawyer. "Oh, it was only a dream" is not equivalent to saying, "Oh, it took place in another space." It didn't on the ordinary view, and, I think, on Kant's view as well, take place at all.

Quinton wants to define "reality" in terms of the seriousness with which one can take either imaged or sensed experience. He therefore talks of "objects of awareness" in spatial relationships which cannot possibly be found in a unitary space. H. H. Price expresses the same view as follows:

> Mental images, including dream images, are in a space of their own. They do have spatial properties ... they have spatial relations to one another. But they have no spatial relation to objects in the physical world.[15]

But as previously suggested, this notion of "spatial objects" seems quite out of the ordinary indeed. By appeal to common usage and experience it is abundantly clear that "spatial object" has no place in talk of dreams and that Kant must have held a similar notion. The point quite simply is that dreams are not usually taken to be genuine experiences in which objects occur, and further unlike Quinton's dream myth, dreams are not understood to be coherent. In fact, it is doubtful given Quinton's account that the dreamer would feel comfortable prefacing any of his narratives with the phrase "In my dream ..." or "I dreamed ..." In trying to use dreams to make his point about multi-spatial myths, he has only succeeded in doing away with dreaming as we understand it. In effect, the account Quinton gives of his coherent multi-spatial life is unintelligible if there is no use for the expressions of dreaming.

Kant's epistemological system rules out objects in dreams and therefore dreams as sensible experiences (which is not to say that dreams do not occur). The Second Analogy, though admittedly dealing with time and not space, provides ample evidence of Kant's view on the matter.

Kant makes the following comments in the Second Analogy:

> I.) Let us suppose that there is nothing antecedent to an event, upon

which it must follow according to rule. All succession of perception would then be only in the apprehension, that is, would be merely subjective, and would never enable us to determine objectively which perceptions are those that really precede and which are those that follow. We should then have only a play of representations, relating to no object . . .

II.) That is something merely subjective, determining no object; and may not, therefore be regarded as knowledge of any object, not even of an object in the (field of) appearance . . .

III.) I render my subjective synthesis of apprehension objective only by reference to a rule in accordance with which the appearances in their succession, that is, as they happen, are determined by the preceding state. The experience of an event (i.e. of anything as happening) is itself possible only on this assumption . . .

IV.) That something happens is, therefore, a perception which belongs to a possible experience. This experience becomes actual when I regard the appearance as . . . an object that can always be found in the connection of perceptions in accordance with a rule.

V.) If this synthesis is a synthesis of apprehension of the manifold of a given appearance, the order is determined in the object or, to speak more correctly, is an order of successive synthesis that determines an object. In accordance with this something must necessarily precede . . . something else must necessarily follow . . . were I to posit the antecedent and the event were not to follow necessarily thereupon, I should have to regard the succession as a merely subjective play of my fancy; and if I still represented it to myself as something objective, I should have to call it a mere dream.

I have numbered these passages for easy reference. I realize that they are not part of the same argument. I, II, and III come from what Kemp Smith calls the "Third Proof"; IV comes from the "Fourth Proof," and V from the "Sixth Proof." I do not intend to represent this arrangement as an argument. I do, however, think that the end result of these comments must be that Kant cannot consider dreams to be experiences, simply for the reason that objects, "appearances," are not and cannot be found in them. In the Second Analogy proofs of causality are his aim, and the unitary time doctrine is essential to those proofs. It seems further, however, that the unitary space doctrine is equally necessary and is assumed, or Kant would not be able to treat dreams as he does and would instead be committed to a causal theory in which causality says nothing about space and in which events in one space may be said to produce effects in other spatially unrelated worlds.[16]

Kant's analysis of so-called dream objects (image objects) as presented in I-V is a relatively uncomplicated solution to multi-spatial problems, one with which, I take it, the ordinary man would agree, and one which answers Quinton's criticisms of the unitary space doctrine, I think, decisively. Kant's account revolves around the necessity that there be "appearances" to objectify knowledge. If a succession of perceptions does not fit a rule (causality) it can be said to be only a product of apprehension (used in the Leibnizean sense); that is, that it is only subjective and thereby cannot aid in our attempts to determine perceptions that actually precede others from those that only follow others. Simply, in the phenomenal world object A may be the cause of B, and we can agree upon this. On the other hand, dream or subjective "perceptions" have no objective referent. We cannot then distinguish their mere succession from real causality. If Kant were to have allowed causality within dreams, then he would have been forced back into Hume's psychological causal theory. In dreams we might say that "perception A" followed "perception B," but without an objective appearance we are in no position, as Hume rightly contended, to say that B precedes A in a causal relationship. If Kant is to save the scientific notion of causality, then he must distinguish those dream "perceptions" from perceptions in the normal sense, and he does so in terms of objects. Dream or subjective successions are only a play of representations relating to no objects.

II makes clear that if the representations of dreams as described determine no object, then they cannot be regarded as knowledge, have no place in the field of appearances. Without the causal rule (as shown in I) the experience of an event is impossible. An event has duration, A precedes B, etc. by rule. The dream as a "succession of representations" which merely follow each other cannot be considered an event, and thereby (III) something happening is impossible. IV makes clear that only if I can regard the appearance as an object always found in the connection of my perception in accord with the causal rule, as I cannot in the case of subjective representations, can knowledge of something happening be actual.

A dream then for Kant (and the rest of us) is representing (mis-representing) something subjective which has no object as being objective. The telling of dreams prefaced by "In my dream ..." or "Last night while dreaming ..." reveals our normal attitude toward these supposed nocturnal adventures. Telling dreams is not a legitimate case of reporting because there is no possibility of getting it wrong or that "getting it wrong" would ever have the significance of, for example, getting a newspaper report of a political assassination wrong.

Quinton's multi-spatial myth fails to show the Kantian thesis to be conventional. Even if we were to have the coherent dreams of a life beside the lake, the effect of those representations on the unitary space doctrine can only be in terms of our telling those dreams while awake in normal life. Part of what it is like to tells dreams is to make the Kantian distinctions I have stressed. There is no reason to equate the mere assumption of coherence with a causal rule. The so-called things of our dream-life, though describable in the language of objects, are not objective, and our waking life and our normal use of spatial and perceptual expressions make this clear to us.

NOTES

1. Immanuel Kant, *Critique of Pure Reason*, trans. Norman Kemp Smith (New York: St. Martin's Press, 1929), A25.

2. For example: J.R. Smythies, *Brain and Mind*, "The Representative Theory of Perception" (London: Routledge and Kegan Paul, 1965), pp. 241-257.

3. This point is central to Price's attempt to make intelligible the survival hypothesis. See H.H. Price, "Survival and the Idea of 'Another World'" reprinted in *Brain and Mind*.

4. Russell, *Our Knowledge of the External World*, Lecture III (New York: New American Library, 1929, 1956).

5. Anthony Quinton, "Spaces and Times," *Philosophy*, 37, 1962, p. 133.

6. T.D. Weldon, *Kant's Critique of Pure Reason* (Oxford: Clarendon Press, 1958), p. 110.

7. *Ibid.*

8. Quinton, *op. cit.*, pp. 140-1

9. *Ibid.*, p. 143.

10. Norman Malcolm, *Dreaming* (New York: Humanities Press, 1959).

11. O.K. Bouwsma, *Philosophical Essays* (Lincoln: University of Nebraska Press, 1965).

12. Margaret MacDonald, "Sleeping and Waking," *Essays in Philosophical Psychology*, Donald Gustafson, ed. (Garden City: Doubleday and Company, Inc., 1964), p. 252.

13. Graham Bird, *Kant's Theory of Knowledge* (New York: The Humanities Press, 1962), p. 51.

14. Quinton, *op. cit.*, p. 142.

15. Price, *op. cit.*, p. 12.

16. Smythies illustrates such a causal theory with an example of a television screen revealing what is going on elsewhere. However, he appears to be little concerned with the electronic transmission and reception of a TV picture which do not certainly necessitate a multi-spatial myth. I doubt that he could say anything about the circumstances in which we receive a poor picture on a portable set, but upon moving the set closer to the transmitter the picture becomes clear and distinct.

THIRD SYMPOSIUM

TIME AND PRECOGNITION: OPENING NOTE
Peter A. French

TIME AND TIME AGAIN
T. E. Wilkerson

TIME TRAVEL
Hillary Putnam and J. J. C. Smart

TIME AND APPARENT PRECOGNITION
H. F. Saltmarsh

THE MYSTERY OF TIME
O. K. Bouwsma

"If you knew time as well as I do"

TIME AND PRECOGNITION: OPENING NOTE

Peter A. French

In many ways the concept of time has been more intriguing than that of space. Our science fiction, from that of H. G. Wells to Kurt Vonnegut, abounds in accounts of time travelers. In *The Time Machine* H. G. Wells has his time traveler argue:

> There are really four dimensions, three which we call the three planes of Space, and a fourth, Time. There is, however, a tendency to draw an unreal distinction between the former three dimensions and the latter, because it happens that our consciousness moves intermittently in one direction along the latter from the beginning to the end of our lives.
> ... *There is no difference between Time and any of the three dimensions of Space except that our consciousness moves along it* ... You are wrong to say that we cannot move about in Time. For instance, if I am recalling an incident very vividly I go back to the instant of its occurrence: I become absent-minded, as you say. I jump back for a moment. Of course we have no means of staying back for any length of Time, any more than a savage or an animal has of staying six feet above the ground. But a civilized

man is better off than a savage in this respect. He can go up against gravitation in a balloon, and why should he not hope that ultimately he may be able to stop or accelerate his drift along the Time-Dimension, or even turn about and travel the other way?

There has always been a keen interest in exploring the possibilities of going either backward or forward in time. The future is one of the great mysteries we all seek to solve.

Although "time" obviously has its scientific uses, basically it is a philosophical concept. Our thinking about time is in general influenced by a very pervasive picture: what appears as a C-2 certainty that time flows from the past to the future. There are major difficulties with the picture of flowing time,[1] but there is no denying its power in our patterns of thinking about temporal matters.

It is no doubt due to that power that purported cases of precognition strike us on the whole as highly dubious. After all, someone claiming to have had a precognitive experience is claiming to have experienced something of the future, which is inconsistent with the picture of flowing time and therefore unintelligible. Nonetheless, ostensible cases of precognition continue to be reported. Among the most dramatic are those claimed by J. W. Dunne in his *An Experiment with Time*, one example of which follows:

> I was staying at the Hotel Scholastika on the borders of the Aachensee, in Austria. I dreamed one night that I was walking down a sort of pathway between two fields, separated from the latter by high iron railings, eight or nine feet high, on each side of the path. My attention was suddenly attracted to a horse in the field on my left. It had apparently gone mad, and was tearing about, kicking and plunging in a most frenzied fashion. I cast a hasty glance backwards and forwards along the railings to see if there were any openings by which the animal could get out. Satisfied that there were none, I continued on my way. A few moments later I heard hoofs thundering behind me. Glancing back I saw, to my dismay, that the brute had somehow got out after all, and was coming full tilt after me down the pathway. It was a full-fledged nightmare—and I ran like a hare. Ahead of me the path ended at the foot of a flight of wooden steps rising upward. I was striving frantically to reach these when I awoke.
>
> Next day I went fishing with my brother down the little river which runs out of the Aachensee. It was wet-fly work, and I was industriously flogging the water when my brother called out: "Look at that horse!" Glancing across the river, I saw the scene of my dream. But, though right in essentials, it was absolutely unlike in minor details. The two fields with the fenced-off pathway running between them were there. The horse was there, behaving just as it had done in the dream. The wooden steps at the end of the pathway were there (they led up to a bridge crossing the river). But the fences were wooden and small—not more than four or five feet high—and the fields were ordinary small fields, whereas those in the dream had been park-like expanses. Moreover, the horse was a small beast, and not

the rampaging great monster of the dream—though its behaviour was equally alarming. Finally, it was in the wrong field, the field which would have been on my right, had I been walking, as in the dream, down the path towards the bridge. I began to tell my brother about the dream, but broke off because the beast was behaving so very oddly that I wanted to make sure that it could not escape. As in the dream, I ran my eye critically along the railings. As in the dream, I could see no gap, or even gate, in them anywhere. Satisfied, I said, "At any rate, *this* horse cannot get out," and recommenced fishing. But my brother interrupted me by calling "Look out!" Glancing up again, I saw that there was no dodging fate. The beast *had*, inexplicably, just as in the dream, got out (probably it had jumped the fence), and, just as in the dream, it was thundering down the path towards the wooden steps. It swerved past these and plunged into the river, coming straight towards us. We both picked up stones, ran thirty yards or so back from the bank, and faced about. The end was tame, for on emerging from the water on our side, the animal merely looked at us, snorted, and galloped off down a road.

This symposium offers a number of theories of time, some of which suggest the possibility of movement in time. We must remember, however, that the psychical researcher's notion of precognition is not consistent with our general intuitions about time. Consequently, alternative temporal pictures must be offered and argued to support any account of precognitive or retrocognitive experience. It might be wise to keep in mind the following comments by Gardner Murphy from *The Challenge of Psychical Research* (page 155):

Telepathy and clairvoyance together are *certainly* easier to cope with than precognition, since the time dimension is involved in the latter. To make contact with that which does not yet exist is, for many, a contradiction in terms, a philosophical paradox, an outrage; or even may be held to come under the category of "impossibility" in a way which is not quite true of telepathy or clairvoyance ... how one might cut through the future into a situation not yet existent ... remain(s) a problem for philosophy ... Philosophical difficulties remain, and the experimental evidence can certainly not be regarded as settling the issue conclusively.

NOTES

1. C.D. Broad remarks:
Let us begin with the attempt to represent temporal becoming by means of motion. Here we are supposed to have a series of event-particles related by the relation of earlier and later. This may be represented by a straight line, which may be uniformly shaded if the process is to be qualitatively uniform, or may be colored with a continuously variable shade from one end to the other if the process is to be one of continuous qualitative change. The characteristic of presentness is then supposed to move along this series of event-particles, in the direction from earlier to later, as the

light from a policeman's bullseye might move along a row of palings.

The following fatal objections can at once be raised. (i) If anything moves, it must move with some determinate velocity. It will always be sensible to ask "How fast does it move?" even if we have no means of answering the question. Now this is equivalent to asking "How great a distance will it have traversed in unit time-lapse?" But here the series along which presentness is supposed to move is temporal and not spatial. In it "distance" is time-lapse. So the question becomes "How great a time-lapse will presentness have traversed in unit time-lapse?" And this question seems to be meaningless.

(ii) Consider any event-particle in the series. At a certain moment this acquires presentness and then loses it again without delay. Before that moment it was future, afterwards it is past. Now the acquisition and the loss of presentness by this event-particle is itself an event-particle of the second order, which happens to the first-order event-particle. Therefore every first-order event-particle has a history of indefinite length; and, at a certain stage of this there is one outstanding second-order event-particle; viz., the acquisition and the immediately subsequent loss of presentness. Yet, by definition, the first-order event-particle which we have been considering has no duration, and therefore can have no history, in the time-series along which presentness is supposed to move.

The two considerations which I have just mentioned would seem to make the following conclusion inevitable. If there is any sense in talking of presentness moving along a series of events, related by the relation of earlier-and-later, we must postulate a second time-dimension in addition to that in which the series is spread out. *Examination of McTaggart's Philosophy*, Vol. II, Part I, Chapter XXXV, Cambridge: Cambridge University. Press, 1938.

TIME AND TIME AGAIN

T. E. Wilkerson

". . . and he arranged it all. It's done me the world of good, I can tell you. And that's why I said that yesterday was *both* yesterday and two years ago."

"Well, it still sounds nonsense to me. I told you H. G. Wells would do you no good."

"It's perfectly true. I dare say you can't see it, because you're one of the many unfortunate people who only experience *one* temporal dimension. But it doesn't follow, nor is it true, that there is *only* one. You're very like the people in Flatland who refused, in spite of the evidence, to believe that there was a third spatial dimension. Let me show you how it works in terms of a simple diagram. After all, I've had two years since yesterday to work it out! On the

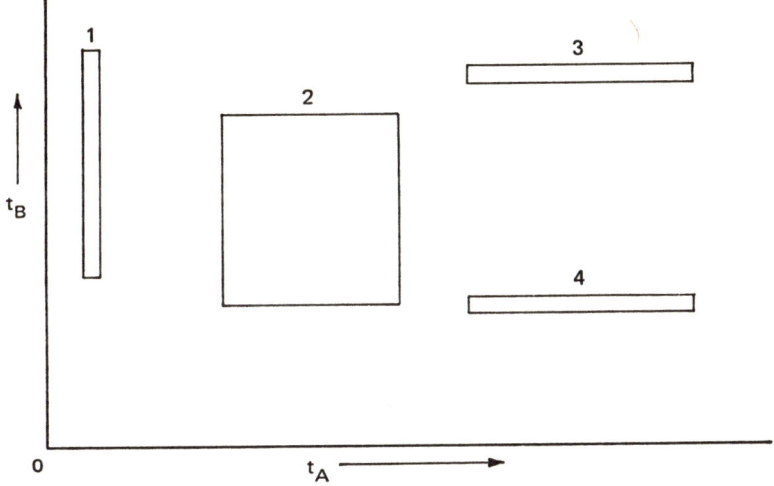

horizontal axis we measure the temporal dimension that you are acquainted with—t_A. I'm trying to convince you that there is (or at the very least there *could* be) a second temporal dimension, t_B, which is at temporal right-angles, so to speak, to t_A. In a straightforward sense two temporal dimensions yield two event-dimensions as well, and I've thrown in a few schematic events to make the diagram more interesting. (I've used very simple geometrical shapes, but there's no reason why they shouldn't be more complicated.) Some events, as you can see (e.g. 1), may take longer in B-time than in A-time; some (e.g. 2) may take about the same time in each; some (e.g. 3) may take longer in A-time than in

---

This selection is reprinted from *Philosophy*, Vol. 48, No. 184 (1973), 173 ff. Used by permission of the editor and T. E. Wilkerson.

B-time; two events (e.g. 3 and 4) may coincide in A-time, but not in B-time, and so on. Just as a ship can travel three thousand miles east without moving more than a few miles north, so I've been "travelling" about in B-time quite a lot, while only "travelling" twenty-four hours in A-time."

"I'll forgive you your spatial metaphors, because I suppose they offer the most easily understood way of telling your ridiculous fairy-story. But, metaphorical or not, the story flies in the face of all the best empiricist principles about time. For example, if you're to talk of *any* dimension of time, you have to have a way of measuring it. Times (including B-time) logically require clocks: you can't just dignify your fantasy into a story about a second temporal dimension, unless it refers somewhere to a B-clock as well as what you would call our ordinary A-clocks."

"Certainly—and I see no problem. Just as our concept of A-time is irretrievably connected with our having A-clocks, that is, fairly enduring things which change A-constantly and A-regularly, as it were, so our concept of B-time is connected with our having fairly enduring things which change B-constantly and B-regularly. It is clearly possible to have A-clocks (heavenly bodies moving relatively to one another in an A-regular way); by parity of reasoning it is possible to have B-clocks (some objects changing B-regularly in some fairly obvious way)."

"There is a second problem—which, you probably remember, was raised in recent discussion of the claim that there might be two times, temporally unrelated. That claim is not your claim, but the problem, one of identity, is the same. Suppose a caterpillar changes into a chrysalis and then into a butterfly in about six months. Presumably the changes can take place in either A-time or B-time. If our caterpillar is at O on your diagram, it can presumably change into a butterfly in six B-months, even though only five A-minutes have elapsed. Clearly, it can't effect the same change in five A-minutes: so we are left in the absurd position of having to say that five A-minutes after the point of origin, O, the caterpillar is *both* a caterpillar *and* a butterfly. Similarly with human beings: a man may spend three score B-years and ten, passing from birth to death, while only five A-minutes have elapsed. We have to admit the absurd possibility that a man is *both* an old man *and* a baby five A-minutes after his birth. The only alternative, which is even more grotesque, is to abondon all our criteria of identity completely."

"I don't see that we have to adopt either alternative. We need merely to point out that changes do take time, and specify how much of *which* time they take. For example, changes from caterpillar to butterfly take six *A-months* from baby to old man threescore *A-years* and ten. The changes that take place over the B-months and B-years obviously must keep in step with the changes over the A-years, if criteria of identity are to be preserved. Within those limits, there is no danger of anything being both a man and a baby, or both a caterpillar and a butterfly; and within those limits the rate of A-change and rate of B-change may vary somewhat. (You may well find that caterpillars *can* change into butterflies in five B-minutes, or that men have been known to take five hundred B-years to pass from babyhood to old age.) All these restrictions on temporal rearrangement are surely no different in principle from restrictions on spatial rearrangement—for example, two material objects which have occupied a place at different times cannot re-occupy it at the same time."

"Well, let me move to a more fundamental objection altogether—That it is difficult to see what grounds we could have for believing there was a second temporal dimension at all. If we return to the people of Flatland for a moment, you'll remember that they had very good grounds for believing that there was a third spatial dimension. For example, whenever a three-dimensional sphere passed through their two-dimensional Flatland, they observed the appearance of a spot, which grew steadily to a circle, contracted to a spot, and disappeared. This curious phenomenon made their science very messy as long as they held on to their two-dimensional geometry, but the assumption that there was a third dimension simplified things considerably. Now, to get back to the question at issue, it's not good enough for you to say that the fairy-story about B-time is logically consistent: you'll have to offer a reason for our wanting to tell the story in the first place."

"That's a fair request, and the answer is a bit complicated. Let's take another version of the simple diagram I used before. Now, *if* there is a second temporal dimension, B-time, there might well be a number of people, like myself, who have had the opportunity to "travel" in B-time as well as in A-time. Suppose

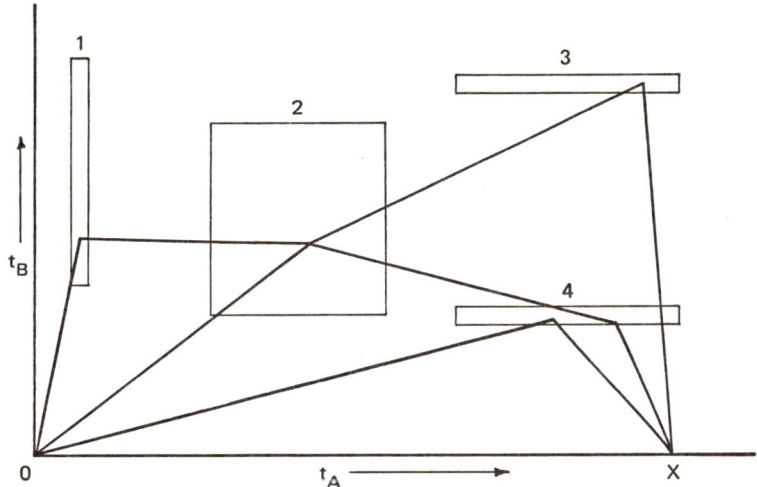

they have met at a point of origin O, and meet again at X, which is A-later than O, but at the same B-time as O. And suppose they make various claims about their experiences since they last met at O. Clearly, these temporal "movements" will not have been the same, just as people's spatial movements are not the same. That is, they will have taken different temporal "paths" from O to X, as in the diagram. One person may have witnessed events 1, 2, 3 and 4 between O and X; another 2, 3 and 4; another, 2 and 4; another, perhaps, only event 4. Their stories are obviously very different. If they are told sincerely, and if the differences cannot be explained in terms of spatial geometry, it becomes plausible to explain them in terms of temporal geometry. When we have a fairly large number of such stories, it is a comparatively simple matter of temporal geometry, first, to show that there are various events, happening (or having happened) in two quite different temporal dimensions and, secondly, to plot precisely "where" they are. The exercise is in principle the same as that of plotting the spatial geometry of a certain area, on the basis of a series of detailed reports by people who have rambled over the area from a fixed starting-point to a fixed finishing-point.

"There is one possible complication: to do the job properly we would need a reliable *third* clock (over and above the A-clocks and B-clocks) to measure what might be called experiential time—that is, to measure the "length" of each temporal "path," We have pedometers to measure how far people walk; and the pedometer measurement will be quite separate from, say, the measurement of longitude and measurement of latitude. Similarly it would be convenient to have, not merely A-clocks, and B-clocks, to give us the "longitude" and "latitude" of time, but also some temporal analogue of the pedometer. Psychological clocks are notoriously inaccurate, and the obvious substitute, a heartbeat-clock, is not much better. Obviously, without a precise third clock the temporal geometry of A- and B- time would not be very precise.

"Perhaps there's another snag. Although I had two (heartbeat-) years to think about it, I never worked out the mechanism of choice with respect to B-time. That is, although we can move about all dimensions of space of our own free-will, I don't understand yet how we can choose to move about B-time. Still, I suppose we can't *choose* to move about in A-time either, so I shouldn't complain. Anyway, when you've got the hang of it, it's very exciting being in *two* temporal dimensions. For example, one of the great things about B-time (as you can see from the second diagram) is that, whereas you can only "move" in *one* A-temporal direction, you can move in either B-temporal direction."

"And doesn't that demonstrate conclusively the absurdity of the whole fantasy? For doesn't it mean that all the people who had "set out" from O into the B-future might decide to "come back" into the B-past, and "arrive back" at their starting-point? And doesn't *that* mean that they would be experiencing an event (at O) *both* for the first time *and* for the second time? Wouldn't they *both* remember the event (the second time round) and *not* remember it (the first time round)? To put it mildly, that would put our notion of memory, and therefore, of course, our notion of personal identity, very sadly out of joint."

"Yes, but there is apparently one restriction: whatever exotic things you can do in the B-dimension, you have to make *some* constant A-progress, however small. That is, you can never experience the same event twice, or rather the same phase of the same event twice, because at least some A-time will have elapsed between the two experiences."

"'Well, you're welcome to your fantasy: at the very least, I don't see that it is of great interest until you produce a very large number of people retailing similar fantasies."

"On the contrary, I think it *ought* to be of interest, even to someone as sceptical as yourself. Even from a sceptical point of view the "fantasy" as you call it, is an interesting way of drawing attention to certain important connections between, say, time and measurement, or between time and the identity of things, especially the identity of people. And I, as one of the less sceptical, will continue to look back on the adventure as a great holiday. As I said, that travel agent fixed it all up—although I didn't like him very much at first, I must say. Mediterranean type, by the look of him—a name something like "Chronos," I think it was. I'll let you have his card—."

TIME TRAVEL

Hillary Putnam and J. J. C. Smart

Hillary Putnam: I believe that an attempt to describe in ordinary language what time travel would be like can easily lead to absurdities and even downright contradictions. But if one has a mathematical technique of representing all the phenomena subsumed under some particular notion of "time travel," then it is easy to work out a way of speaking, and even a way of thinking, corresponding to the mathematical technique. A mathematical technique for representing at least one set of occurrences that might be meant by the term "time travel" already exists. This is the technique of *world lines* and Minkowski space-time diagrams. Thus, suppose, for example, that a time traveler—we'll call him Oscar Smith—and his apparatus have world lines as shown in the diagram on page 101.

From the diagram we can at once read off what an observer sees at various times. At t_0, for example, he sees Oscar Smith not yet a time traveler. At time t_1 he still sees Oscar Smith at place A but also he sees something else at place B. At place B he sees, namely, an event of "creation"—not "particle-antiparticle creation," but the creation of two macro-objects which separate. One of these macro-objects is easily described. It is simply an older Oscar Smith, or an individual resembling in all possible ways an older version of Oscar Smith, together with the apparatus of a time machine. The world-line diagram shows that the older Oscar—let's call him Oscar$_3$ —leaves his time machine. The other object that was created in the same event is a somewhat peculiar object. It is a system consisting of a third Oscar Smith, or, more precisely, of a body like that of Oscar Smith, seated in a time machine. But this system consisting of the Oscar Smith body and the time machine is a very exceptional physical system. If we take a moving picture of this physical system during its entire period of existence, we will find that if that movie is played backwards then the events in it are all normal. In short, this is a system running backward in time—entropy in the system is decreasing instead of increasing, cigarette butts are growing into whole cigarettes, the Oscar Smith body is emitting noises that resemble speech sounds played backward, and so forth. This system that is running backward in time continues to exist until the time t_2, when it merges with Oscar Smith, and we see annihilation—not "particle-antiparticle annihilation," but the annihilation of the real Oscar Smith and the running-backward system. During a certain period of time, there are three Oscar Smiths: Oscar Smith$_1$, Oscar Smith$_3$, and the Oscar Smith who is living backward in time (Oscar Smith$_2$, we shall call him). We can even predict subjective phenomena from the world-line diagram. We can say, for example, what sort of memories Oscar Smith$_3$ has at the

---

This selection is extracted from "It Ain't Necessarily So," *Journal of Philosophy*, Vol. 59 (1962), 665 ff. Used by permission of the *Journal of Philosophy* and Hilary Putnam.

moment of his "creation." He has, namely, all the memories that someone would have if he had all the experiences of Oscar₁ up to the moment of his annihilation and then all the experiences shown as occurring to the living-backward Oscar, Oscar₂, on a movie film, provided the movie film is reversed so that these experiences are shown as happening in the normal order. I have no doubt whatsoever as to how any reasonable scientist would describe these events, if they actually transpired. He would interpret them in terms of the world-line diagram; i.e., he would say: "There are not really three Oscar Smiths; there is only one Oscar Smith. The Oscar Smith you call Oscar Smith₁ lives forward in time until the time t_2; at t_2 his world line for some reason bends backward in time, and he lives backward in time from t_2 back to the time t_1. At t_1 he starts living forward in time again and continues living forward in time for the rest of his life."

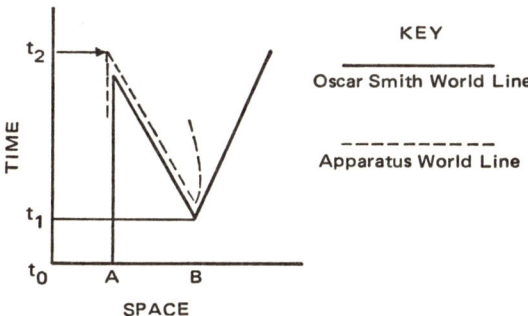

I remember having a discussion concerning time travel with a philosopher friend a number of years ago. I told him the story I have just told you. My friend's view, in a nutshell, was that time travel was a conceptual impossibility. The phenomena I described can, of course, be imagined; but they are correctly described in the way I first described them; i.e., Oscar Smith₁, lives until t_2 at which time he collides with the strange system. When the two systems merge, they are both annihilated. At the time t_1 this strange physical system was created, as was also another individual very much resembling Oscar Smith₁, but with an entirely fictitious set of memories including, incidentally, memories of Oscar Smith₁'s existence up to the time t_2.

Let us ask ourselves what makes us so sure that there is here a consistently imaginable set of circumstances to be described. The answer is that it is the mathematical representation, i.e., the world-line diagram itself, that gives us this assurance. Similarly, in the case of space with variable curvature, near the sun, the only thing that makes us sure that there is a consistently imaginable set of phenomena to be described is their representation in terms of the mathematics of non-Euclidean geometry.

The present case also exhibits *dis*analogies to the geometric case. In the geometric case we could not go on using language in the old way—if to preserve Euclidean geometry is to go on using language in the old way—without finding ourselves committed to ghost places and ghost paths. In the present case, we can go on using language in the old way—if my friend's way of describing the situation *is* the one which corresponds to "using language in the old way"—without having to countenance any ghost entities. But there are a host of difficulties which make us doubt whether to speak in this way is to go on using language without any change of usage or meaning. First of all, consider the sort of system that a physicist would describe as a "human being living backward in time." The same system would be described by my friend not as a *person* at all, but as a human *body* going through a rather nauseating succession of physical states. Thus, on my friend's account, $Oscar_2$ is not a person at all, and $Oscar_1$ and $Oscar_3$ are two quite different persons. $Oscar_1$ is a person who had a normal life up to the time t_2 when something very abnormal happened to him, *namely, he vanished,* and $Oscar_3$ is a person who had a normal life from the time t_1 on, but who came into existence in a very abnormal way: *he appeared out of thin air.* Consider now the legal problems that might arise and whose resolution might depend on whether we accepted the physicist's account or the account of my friend. Suppose $Oscar_1$ murders someone but is not apprehended before the time at which he vanishes. Can we or can we not punish $Oscar_3$ for $Oscar_1$'s crime? On the physicist's account, $Oscar_3$ *is* $Oscar_1$, only grown older, and can hence be held responsible for all the actions of $Oscar_1$. On my friend's account, $Oscar_3$ is only a person under the unfortunate delusion that he is $Oscar_1$ grown older, and should be treated with appropriate kindness rather than punishment. And, of course, no one is responsible for $Oscar_2$'s actions on this view, since they are not really *actions* at all. And if $Oscar_1$'s wife lives with $Oscar_3$ after t_2, she is guilty of unlawful cohabitation, while if she lives with $Oscar_3$ prior to t_2, she is guilty of adultery. In such a case, to go into court and tell the story as my friend would tell it would be to use language in a most *extraordinary* way.

J. J. C. Smart: In his discussion Hilary Putnam has given an interesting defense of the conceptual possibility of time travel. Of course a lot depends on what might be meant by "time travel," and it is worthwhile inquiring whether the sort of thing that Putnam understands by "time travel" is the sort of thing that H. G. Wells,[1] for example, meant by the term. I wish to try to get clear as to senses in which time travel is and is not a conceptual possibility. My purpose is of course not to indulge in science fiction but to attain greater clarity about the notions of space and time.

As I have remarked elsewhere,[2] there are two importantly different senses of the term "space." In the first place we often use the word "space" in the sense of a *continuant.* Here the word "space" goes with our ordinary tensed language of the permanent and the changing. In this sense we can say that a region of space has or has not remained occupied or that its curvature has remained the same or has altered. Space in this sense is like a star, a table, or an animal in that it can change or stay the same. In the second place there is the mathematical sense of the word "space," in which space is not a continuant and must be spoken of tenselessly. It is in this tenseless or mathematical sense of the word "space" that Minkowski space-time is a space. So also is a three-dimensional cross section of space-time a space in this second sense. Quite clearly neither space-time nor an instantaneous cross section of space-time can be said either to change or to stay the same. When we say in our ordinary language of the permanent in change that a region of a space has changed, we can express the same fact in the tenseless language of space-time by saying that one region of space-time is different from another.

The distinction between the "continuant" sense of the word "space" and the "tenseless" or "mathematical" sense of the word is important in understanding the concept of travel. For to travel is to move from one point of space to another in the *continuant* sense of the word "space." A space-ship that travels from a star S to a star T is described in the space-time language as lying along a world line that intersects the world lines of S and T. Bodies that do not move relative to one another are represented by parallel world lines in the space-time diagram, whereas relative motion is represented by the relative inclinations of world lines. It is clear therefore that we cannot represent motion *through* space-time. To do so would be illegitimately to treat space-time as if it were a space in the continuant sense. Motion is rate of change of space with respect to time, and so we cannot have motion through time or through space-time. As Schlick has put it, "time is already represented within the model and cannot be introduced again from outside."[3]

Now it seems to me that it is this illegitimate notion of movement through time or through space-time that is to be found in H. G. Wells's story. It will be remembered that Wells's time traveler is in a machine which remains always at approximately the same point on the Earth's surface, and he travels up and down the Earth's world line. This is certainly a conceptual impossiblity, for the reasons stated at the end of the last paragraph. Similar absurdities sometimes occur (fortunately inessentially) in some works on physics. We hear of signals being propagated through space-time. The Feynman theory of pair production and pair annihilation is sometimes described as claiming that a positron is an electron "traveling backwards in time." (Does an electron travel *forward* in time? Of course not!) However, it is easy to translate this sort of talk aseptically. Instead of talking of a signal being propagated from the space-time point A to the space-time point B, we can say that the signal lies along the line AB. The Feynman theory can be stated in terms of zig-zag and bent-back world lines.

Putnam's case of "time travel" avoids the above confusions. Whether his case is to be described as one of *travel* is another matter. If Putnam's time traveler travels into the past, then we are all time travelers, traveling into the future. This, however, is to revert to the absurd notion of traveling through time, a movement up or down our own world line. Putnam's account avoids this sort of nonsense. His conception is roughly that of an N-shaped world line. In the diagram on p. 101 of his discussion we find that the "time traveler," Oscar Smith, lives for a time in the normal way and then gets into an apparatus which has the peculiar property that thermodynamic processes within it run the other way (toward entropy decrease instead of increase) from that in which they run in the surrounding universe. At the instant Oscar Smith gets into the machine the machine and he cease to exist, but the machine, with an older and "backwards" Oscar Smith, has existed for some time past. (This is not all the story, and I refer the reader to Putnam's own account.) Is all this a conceptual possibility? It seems inconsistent with thermodynamics, for what happens at the boundary between the region in which entropy increases and that in which entropy decreases? If there is an inconsistency with thermodynamics does this make Putnam's case a conceptual impossibility? Or is it a conceptual impossibility if it is inconsistent with a geometry? Or with logic? It seems clear that Putnam does not wish to draw a sharp line between, say, the case of thermodynamics and that of logic, and that his position is that *nothing* is in any absolute way a conceptual impossibility, except possibly some violations of trivial analytic truths, such as married bachelors. In a relativized sense of "conceptual possibility" (relative to thermodynamics), one might question whether Putnam's case is a conceptual possibility. In any case I do not wish to quarrel over thermodynamics. Nor do I wish to go into the question of the physical possibility of the "creation" and "annihilation" of his Oscar Smith. I shall grant the conceptual possibility of his example, though I should wish to characterize it in a less misleading way than as "travel."

Donald Williams has trenchantly criticized the notions of passage, of time flow, and of our journey through time.[4] In passing, he produces a neat argument against the possibility of time travel: time travel involves the contradiction that "five minutes from now, for example, I may be a hundred years from now."[5] Williams's argument is certainly cogent against the notion of time travel that we find in H. G. Wells's story. In a footnote Williams makes this clear by quoting from the epilogue to *The Time Machine*: "He may even now—if I may use the phrase—be wandering on some plesiosaurus-haunted oolitic coral reef, or beside the lonely saline seas of the Triassic Age."[6] Well's interpolation, "if I may use the phrase," is evidence of his own uneasiness about the consistency of his story.

Though Williams's argument is a just objection to H. G. Wells's concept, a sophisticated defender of time travel might seek to get round it by drawing attention to a possible ambiguity in phrases like "five minutes from now" and "a hundred years from now." It is a contradiction that someone should be both five minutes from now and a hundred years from now if these times are measured with respect to the same coordinate axes. There is no contradiction at all in supposing that something that is five minutes from now relative to the system of axes K is a hundred years from now relative to the system of axes K'. This is a commonplace of the theory of relativity. If we can use this fact to avoid Williams's objection, perhaps we can develop a notion, different indeed from Wells's, which it would be natural to characterize as one of "time travel."

If I am shot off in a rocket ship at very nearly the speed of light, while you remain behind, then my time axis is inclined at very nearly half a right angle to yours. (I am supposing that we choose our space and time units so that the velocity of light is unity.) If my velocity is sufficiently great, an event five years hence on my time axis can be simultaneous (according to you) with one a hundred years hence on your time axis. If I am shot off sufficiently fast to a remote part of space and there turned round and shot back again (we shall here neglect the physiological effects on me of all this acceleration and deceleration!) I may get back to earth still in middle age and yet able to converse with the generation of a hundred years hence. Suppose AB is part of the world line of the Earth. I leave the Earth at point-instant A, am shot off to a remote region at high velocity, and am turned round on my homeward journey at point-instant C. I return to the Earth at point-instant B. The distance AB gives the time between

A and B as measured on the earth. The time I have lived through is given by the length of the bent world line ACB. Because of the fact that the geometry of space-time is rather different from Euclid's, the distance ACB is very much *less* than AB. This is why the space traveler can return still young to find his contemporaries all long since dead.

Should we call this "time travel"? Perhaps we can, for it would be a method of experiencing the middle of the twenty-first century, which would otherwise be out of our reach. On the other hand we might feel more inclined to describe it simply as very rapid space travel! Moreover, fast rockets will not enable us to experience past ages. However, if our fast rocket has existed in the past within a Putnam "reversed-entropy" apparatus and if there has been within it a backwards and "older" me, then by combining the fast-rocket method with the Putnam method I can live a hundred years ago and yet be only a few years "older." Putnam's story will therefore almost give sense to the notion of visiting remotely past ages. . . . It should also be noted that the above relativistic ideas will not help to make sense of H. G. Wells's story, since Wells's time traveler remains throughout in the same region on the Earth.

Suppose that it is agreed that I did not exist a hundred years ago. It is then a contradiction to suppose that I can make a machine that will take me to a hundred years ago. Quite clearly no time machine can make it be that I both did and did not exist a hundred years ago. Putnam's Oscar Smith lives at t_2 and "visits" an earlier time t_1. This is because a reversed entropic Oscar Smith in fact lives at t_1. If someone says that by means of a time machine we could visit times at which we did not or will not exist, we can convict him of patent absurdity. Putnam's story is free from this particular error, as indeed is that of H. G. Wells. Nevertheless, since we did not in fact live in the Triassic age, only a time machine that allowed us to commit the absurdity of both living in the Triassic age and not living in it would be of much use to would-be observers of the lonely prehistoric seas, and such a machine is patently impossible.

To conclude. We may concede the conceptual possibility of Putnam's case and of certain others more or less distantly related to it. There is an objection to calling such cases "time travel," since ordinarily by "travel" we mean change of *space* with respect to *time,* but if this objection is waived we can concede the conceptual possibility of time travel. Nevertheless there are concepts of time travel, such as that in H. G. Wells's story, which are demonstrably absurd.

NOTES

1. H.G. Wells, *The Time Machine, The Wonderful Visit, And Other Stories* (London: T. Fisher Unwin Ltd., 1924).
2. "Spatializing Time," *Mind*, 64 (1955): 239-241.
3. M. Schlick, *Philosophy of Nature*, translated by A. von Zeppelin (New York: Philosophical Library, 1949), p. 48.
4. *Journal of Philosophy*, 48, 15 (July 19, 1951): 457-472.
5. *Ibid.*, p. 463.
6. H.G. Wells, *op. cit.*, p. 117.

TIME AND APPARENT PRECOGNITION

H. F. Saltmarsh

There are two sides to the question of precognition. First, how we can come to know a future event, and second, the mode in which the future can be held to exist.

In putting forward my suggested hypothesis I do not for a moment suppose that it is a complete explanation or even that it represents how things actually happen. It is merely a suggestion of a possible mode of looking at the phenomena based on an analogy with an established psychological doctrine.

It is clear that the crux of the whole thing is *time*.

We must distinguish between two sorts of time, or rather between two different conceptions of it, viz. the mathematician's and physicist's time and psychological time. the former is admittedly an abstraction; it consists of point-instants having no magnitude but only temporal position; it has no more real existence than the mathematical point or line.

Psychological time is time as experienced.

Strictly speaking, of course, time is never actually experienced. What is really the object of experience is change, i.e., events taking place. Time is an abstraction from change.

With mathematician's time we have no concern. Its proper place is in physical science, and in its proper place it acts as a well behaved abstraction should act. Its conduct is not, perhaps quite so faultless as is that of some other mathematical abstractions, but that is no concern of ours. Unfortunately the mathematician's concept of time has to some extent influenced our ordinary ideas, and these should, of course, be formed solely on our experience, i.e., psychological time. . . .

We must distinguish between two different types of experience of change; first, that of an event actually taking place before our eyes as it were, and second, that of an event having taken place. In the first the experience is direct and immediate, as when we actually see an object move or change in some way; in the second we infer change by comparing our immediate perception with our memory of another perception of the same object.

For example, look at a watch; you see the second hand actually move, the hour hand appears to be stationary; but if you look again in half an hour's time, you infer that the hour hand was moving because you see that it has changed its place.

We look at the watch in what we call our present.

Now if we perceive an event actually occurring, that present must have some duration. Were it a mathematical point-instant having no dimension, change could not occur within it. There is no room inside a point.

Perception, whatever else it may be, involves a state of consciousness, and a state of consciousness must possess some duration.... That our present moment has a definite duration is pretty generally accepted by psychologists. It is known as the doctrine of the specious present....

If I talk of an event as being in the past or in the future, I require some "present" in reference to which that event is past or future. Now the only present of which I have any experience embraces a slab of duration. All the parts of it are present. I can, in imagination, cut it up into slices, and one slice may precede another, but it is quite an arbitrary matter which slice I take as the actual, or as I prefer to call it, the fictitious present. If I wish to call one particular slice past and another future, I must place my fictitious present somewhere between them. But what grounds can I have for selecting the slice which is to be my present moment? The whole idea of a fictitious present is due, in my opinion, to the influence of that abstraction, mathematician's time.

Moreover, unless the slice of duration which I select as my fictitious present has no magnitude, i.e., is a point-instant, the question of past and future within its limits applies just as much to it as to the whole of the specious present. Yet point-instants never enter into my experience; they are abstractions and exist only qua abstraction.

It may be objected that an event occupying a certain duration can be cut up into any number of slices and that each particular slice will occupy its own particular slice of duration and no other. Further, that there is no limit to the number of slices into which we can cut it up.

It is true that we can do so in imagination, yet even so we never arrive at a slice having no duration.

It is a form of the old paradox of the flying arrow. The paradox arises only when we deal with abstractions, viz., a mathematical point on the arrow, a mathematical point in space and a mathematical point-instant in time. If we abstain from abstraction even in only one respect, say we consider the arrow as a whole, the paradox vanishes....

There is, of course, a mode in which I may reasonably speak of events as being past or future; my specious present covers a comparatively short length of duration, and events which are located outside of it are either past or future from its point of view. Also suppose that I have a specious present extending from t to t', and another person has one from T to t to t' to T', then from my point of view events in the period T to t in the other man's present would be past and those in t' to T' would be future.

There is a further point to be considered. All the events occupying the specious present are not presented with equal clearness. This may be represented in a diagram. Let the horizontal line represent duration and the vertical

FIG. 1

coordinate the degree of clearness of presentation. Then we should get a curve which would represent the consciousness during the specious present. It might take the form A (Fig. 1), in which case an event located near to t' would be presented with a smaller degree of clearness than one situated midway between t and t'. In all succeeding diagrams t is to be understood as being towards the past and t' towards the future.

As the specious presents succeed one another the clearness of presentation in each will grow to a maximum and then gradually decrease to zero; the succession of specious presents would, in reality, be due to the fact that every event which is perceived is perceived throughout a finite time with continually varying degrees of clearness which eventually diminishes to zero. . . .

The diagram in Figure 1 represents a single specious present. The actual fact is, of course, that there is a succession of specious presents, either as a continuous change, i.e., one merging into another by infinitesimal degrees, or else a discontinuous series. I do not attempt to decide which of these two alternatives is correct. To do so would involve the discussion of some of the most recondite and difficult problems of metaphysics. However, a decision on the point is fortunately not required for the present purpose, but as it is impossible to represent continuous change in diagrams, I shall, in what follows, show the series of specious presents as discontinuous, with the proviso that it is only to be taken as a symbolic representation for the sake of convenience, and not as implying any acceptance of the view that they are really discontinuous.

There is, however, one point on which I must insist, viz., that if it be a discontinuous series, the succeeding terms overlap to some extent. This is, I think, in accordance with experience. The representation in diagram of the series of specious presents will therefore take somewhat the form suggested in Figure 2.

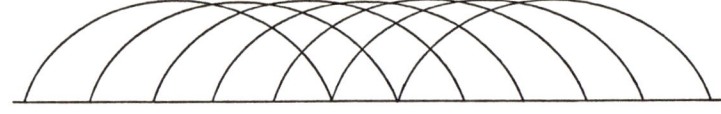

FIG. 2

I can now state my tentative theory of supernormal precognition. I suggest that the specious present of the subliminal mind is of longer duration than that of the supraliminal, so that some events which are in the present of the subliminal would appear to be either past or future from the point of view of the supraliminal.

Dr. C. D. Broad, to whose generous help and criticism I owe a great debt, which I hereby acknowledge, has pointed out to me that this is an inadequate statement of my theory, and has very kindly supplied the following accurate account.

"There is a one-to-one correlation between the series of supraliminal specious presents in a given mind and a series of subliminal specious presents in the same mind. Any term of the latter series overlaps in time the corresponding term of the former, extending further backwards into the past and further forwards into the future than the corresponding supraliminal specious present."

(I wish to make it absolutely clear that the assistance which Dr. Broad has so kindly given me does not imply that he endorses my suggestion or is at all prepared to accept my tentative theory.) This theory may be represented in diagram as in Figure 3.

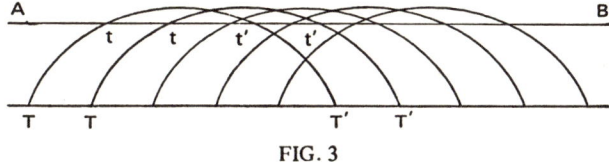

FIG. 3

The line A-B represents the threshold between the supraliminal and the subliminal, the supraliminal specious present from t to t' has a corresponding subliminal specious present which extends from T to T'. Similarly, the succeeding specious present t, t', corresponds with the subliminal T, T'....

The contents of the supraliminal and subliminal minds, in so far as they are presented events, may be shown as in Figure 4. Here $x_1, x_2, x_4, x_7, x_8, x_9, x_{10}$

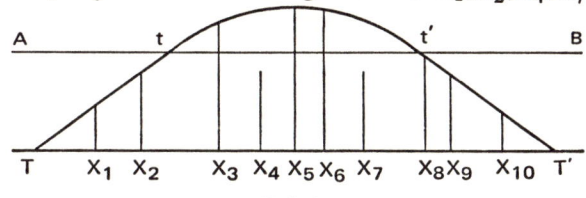

FIG. 4

are presented to the subliminal only, x_3, x_5, x_6 are presented to the supraliminal. We may say, therefore, that for the supraliminal mind x_3, x_5, x_6, are present events, x_1 and x_2 are past, x_8, x_9 and x_{10} future. For the subliminal all the events from x_1 to x_{10} are present. I have in this diagram shown only one specious present, as it would have made it too confusing to have shown all the overlapping curves, but it is easy to see how it would look if they were filled in.

There is one point which must be mentioned, viz., that it is possible that an event, say x_8, which was presented only to the subliminal in one specious present, might reach the supraliminal in a succeeding one.

Let us now see how we can represent a supernormal precognition, and for this purpose we will assume a fictitious case. At twelve noon, that is to say within the specious present of my supraliminal mind in which the striking of noon by my clock is presented to me, I have a supernormal precognition of an event which happens at 6 p.m. on the same day. The first diagram is shown in Figure 5. Here

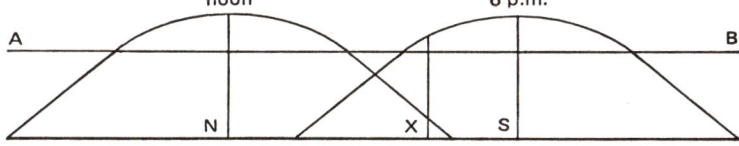

FIG. 5

the first curve shows the specious present in which the striking of noon is presented. This is represented by the line from N. The second curve is the specious present in which the striking of 6 p.m. is presented, or would be presented if the spatial conditions are favorable. In the first curve the event x is present to the subliminal only, for obviously while that curve is in being the second has not yet occurred. But in the second specious present, viz., that at 6 p.m., x is presented to the supraliminal. That is to say, it is experienced in the normal way.

Now my hypothesis suggests that the subliminal presentation of x in the first curve is somehow or other transmitted to the part of the curve above the line A, B. This might be represented as in Figure 6. I show only the first curve, as this diagram represents the state of affairs at noon. The dotted line represents the

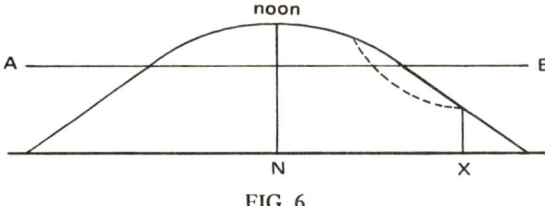

FIG. 6

supernormal transmission of the subliminal presentation of x through the threshold to the supraliminal. When 6 p.m. arrives x is normally presented in the specious present at that moment, and this brings about the verification of the precognition.

All, therefore, that is required for my hypothesis to account for a supernormal precognition is that the specious present of the subliminal should extend sufficiently to cover the actual event, and that there should be a means of transmission to the supraliminal. That which is a precognition for the supraliminal is only a cognition for the subliminal.

Stated thus, these may not seem to be very extravagant demands for an hypothesis designed to account for so bizarre and puzzling a phenomenon as supernormal precognition. We know that the specious presents of the individual vary in length under the influence of fatigue, drugs, and probably concentration of attention. Moreover, it is likely that different individuals normally have specious presents of different lengths. It seems, therefore, not a very great leap to suppose that the supraliminal mind should differ from the subliminal in a similar way, but to a greater extent.

As regards the second requirement, viz., means of transmission through the threshold, we are in a similar position. That is to say, all we need to postulate is an extension of a process which we already know to exist. It is generally admitted that passage through the threshold does to some extent occur normally, as for example, in dreams, the mechanism employed frequently includes the use of symbolism; moreover there is ample evidence of supernormal transmission; e.g., in the cases of hyper-aesthesia. This is usually accompanied by, or occurs during, states of dissociation. It may not be correct to say that the subliminal perception itself is transmitted, though in some cases this appears to be so. It would, perhaps, be better to restrict ourselves to the statement that the knowledge acquired by the subliminal perception is conveyed to the supraliminal.

In these non-precognitive cases of transmission through the threshold the events concerned lie in that portion of the subliminal specious present which coincides with that of the supraliminal. The diagram in Figure 7 will make this clear. The events, subliminal perception of which may be transmitted to the

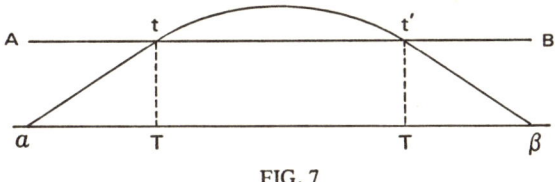

FIG. 7

supraliminal, lie between t and T'.

All that is required, therefore, for my hypothesis is that we should deny to these events any special privilege in the matter of passage through the threshold. All the events lying between A and B are *present* to the subliminal. Is there any obvious reason why a certain section of them should possess any special privilege simply from the fact of their position relative to the supraliminal specious present? . . .

We have a little evidence to guide us in this matter of the length of the subliminal specious present. Precognitions of events weeks or even months ahead are fairly common. We have several quite good cases which stretch over years. Now if the conscious contact which the subliminal mind makes with the future can extend for a period of years, there seems to be no particular reason why it should not extend indefinitely. If the length of the contact is limited at all, I feel that it must be comparable in length with that of the supraliminal mind, i.e., the normal specious present. . . .

I suggest, then, that we must revise our ordinary ideas of the nature of time, however difficult may be the task and however unsatisfying the result. That this is no novel demand the history of metaphysical thought since Kant clearly shows, and those who are familiar with MacTaggart's great work, *The Nature of Existence*, will already be prepared, if not to accept it, at least to regard it as within the sphere of reasonable discussion.

Briefly, my own personal ideas on the subject, for what they are worth, are as follows: I accept MacTaggart's view of the unreality of time and change in so far as sequences of completely determined events are concerned, but I hold, in disagreement with him, that there are non-determined events, such as events arising from free will, which exhibit true change and therefore are subject to true time. But in all sequences of events, whether subject to true time or not, there is temporal order or location; that is to say, if A causes B, and B causes C, B will always lie between A and C. In other words, A is and always was and will be earlier than B, and C is, was and will be later. This conception of temporal location must be accepted as a fundamental feature of experience and held along with, but quite distinct from the conception of true time. That it is a difficult conception to grasp and hold, I freely admit, but it seems to me to be necessitated by the facts, and mere difficulty of conception is, or should be, no bar. . . .

It might seem at first sight that my theory implies that a future event, meaning thereby an event which does not yet exist, can exercise a causative influence on the present. This is obviously impossible, for non-existence cannot exercise a causative influence. But my suggestion is that the event which is the object of a precognition is not future in this sense; it already exists in the present of the subliminal. It is future only in the sense that it is temporally located later than events which are in the present of the supraliminal.

We must now turn to the other side of the matter.

I have suggested that the fact that precognitions occur shows that the subliminal mind is in conscious contact with a section of duration lying ahead of the normal specious present; that is to say, what we ordinarily call the future.

If this be so, the future exists now in some sense. Can we form any idea of the manner in which it exists?

I have already argued, unless we can show that all future events whatsoever are theoretically capable of being subjects of precognition, we cannot claim that the few scattered cases of which we have evidence prove the theory of universal determination.

But our inability to prove a fact certainly does not justify us in denying it. If all events are completely determined, that is to say, if free will is an illusion, then in my opinion, MacTaggart is right in denying reality to time. All events are coexistent in reality. We call one event past and another future simply because of their temporal location with regard to another event which we call present, and our reason for selecting that particular event is that it is included within our specious present. That is to say, it is presented to my consciousness with sufficient clearness to pass the threshold dividing the subliminal from the supraliminal. Now obviously, clearness of presentation is a completely non-temporal feature, so that it is really a very poor sort of reason, when one comes to think of it, for fixing the present moment.

I do not for a moment suppose that this theory of the unreality of time in determined sequences will be acceptable to everyone, but the matter can be considered apart from any theories. We say that an event happens and that it happens in the present. Well, then, what is it that happens when a completely determined event happens? Being completely determined by events and conditions which already exist, and thus being incapable of being changed in any way, its actual happening seems to be reduced to the level of a mere formality. The happening adds nothing to it. It is true that it may be presented in my supraliminal specious present while it is happening, provided that conditions for observation are favorable. But if this be the only difference between present, past and future, when no observer is available, happening is reduced to a mere formal possibility of being observed. I admit that these considerations are not conclusive, because the formal possibility may depend in part upon a real time relation. The nature of time can be investigated only by metaphysical examination. . . .

The view which I would like to suggest may be pictured somewhat as follows: Imagine a bundle of wires or threads all running roughly parallel to each other. You are looking at the bundle through a narrow slit across its length so that you can see only a short section at any one time. The slit moves along in the general direction in which the wires run.

Not only can you see through the slit, but you can also touch the wires through it. Some of the wires are flexible and elastic, others rigid and immovable. You are able, therefore, to exercise a limited control over their arrangement and relative positions.

The wires that are capable of being moved have this peculiar property, that after the slit has passed over them they become rigid, so that the whole bundle astern of the slit is fixed and immovable.

The edges of the slit are not sharply cut, but have fringes, so that your vision is clearest about the center and diminishes in clearness at the edge.

The bundle of wires represents a strand of history, the slit the specious present of the observer. The screen in which the slit occurs is the threshold between the supraliminal and the subliminal. Those wires which are rigid throughout their whole length are those events over which we are not able to exercise an influence by the interposition of our free will; they are completely determined. The flexible wires are those which we can affect by free will; they are not completely flexible and elastic and can only be moved to a certain extent, thus symbolizing the limitations of our power over them.

To make the picture complete, a further complication must be introduced. The eye which looks through the slit is, of course, the eye of the supraliminal, but somehow or other the subliminal mind is on the other side of the screen all the time and is in conscious contact with the wires. If my earlier suggestion be accepted, this conscious contact is effected, not by means of the ordinary senses, but by an undifferentiated faculty of knowing.

But leaving this aside for the moment, let us try to imagine what happens when the position of one of the wires is altered by the exercise of a free-will act operating through the slit.

The arrangement of that part of the wires which is seen through the slit is disturbed; astern of the slit they are all frozen into rigidity, so no effect is produced; but ahead the whole length of the wire touched is moved, so that the disturbance stretches indefinitely in that direction.

Thus an action in the present immediately modifies the entire future. If we suppose that there are forces of attraction and repulsion between the wires, the slight movement of one of them occasioned by the free-will act operating on the small section covered by the slit may bring about an upsetting of the equilibrium at any part lying ahead, and thus cause profound and far-reaching changes.

Suppose that I move my chair. In its original position it was in certain spatial and gravitational relations with the rest of the universe. By moving it I have changed these relations. The relations are reciprocal. My chair stands in a certain spatial relation with, let us say, a particular electron on Sirius; the electron has a reciprocal relation with my chair. To describe that electron completely, all its relations must be included; they are part of the conditions which determine its present and future existence. I move my chair, thereby altering some of these relations and with them the conditions which determine the present and future existence of an electron on Sirius. The entire universe is changed by my free-will act; its future is modified; it can never be the same again.

We may say then that the future is completely determined by the present, but is not inexorably fixed.

I cannot see that the ontological difficulties raised by regarding the future as determined yet plastic are any greater than those which arise from the ordinary view which we take of the present; that is to say, as existent yet subject to modification by free will. That there are difficulties I do not deny, but then ontology is always difficult.

We must look, then, on to the future as existing but as being subject to change, so that at the present moment the future, say this time next week, is so and so, call it A.B.C., but in half an hour's time it may be different, say D.E.F., having been changed by some free-will act which I have performed in the meantime.

If I were now to experience a visual precognition of an event a week ahead I should get a picture of A.B.C., but in half an hour should the precognition occur, it would be a picture of D.E.F.

I have one case which illustrates this rather well. It is a warning case. The visual precognition included the detail of the coachman falling from a box and crushing in his hat on the pavement. All the events occurred as foreseen up to a certain point when, owing to the interposition of Lady Z in calling to the policeman, the course is altered. So far as one can see, had not Lady Z interposed, things would have happened exactly as in the dream.

Although I quote this case as an illustration, I am by no means sure that it is a true example. In the first place it is somewhat doubtful whether Lady Z's action in calling to the policeman was really a free will action. I am inclined to regard it as impulsive and determined. Moreover, it might be suggested that the detail of crushing in the hat was an embellishment to the story given by the precognition, an added detail, that is to say, derived from the dream factory itself, and not from outside....

We may say, therefore, that the future exists now in the sense that it is determined by the present. Yet it is not immutably fixed, but subject to modifications which are themselves determined by actions taking place in the current present.

My theory is that the deepest stratum of the subliminal mind is in permanent conscious contact with this ever-changing future and that precognitions occur when, for some reason which we do not understand, the knowledge acquired by the subliminal of events lying ahead of the supraliminal specious present is somehow transmitted through the threshold; such knowledge, can, of course, be only of the future as it then is, or, in other words, as it then is determined to be by the present. It will have been observed that I have been using terms which imply the reality of time, whereas I have admitted my adherence to the opposite view. But when doing so I particularly limited my remarks to completely determined sequences, while now we are discussing non-determined events. Although I agree with MacTaggart that time is unreal as regards determined sequences, I hold that it is real, or rather I ought to say that change is real, for time is only the common element abstracted from change....

THE MYSTERY OF TIME

O. K. Bouwsma

I

Once upon a space there was a man who laid linoleum, a fantastical fellow, who did not believe in clocks. He would get up from the floor, his measuring foot in hand, and stare at the clock, laying down his measure in this direction and that, round about the clock. Sometimes he would move his hand through the air in the neighborhood of the clock as though he were trying to feel something, a current or stream. "Nothing there," he would mutter as he returned to his linoleum on the floor, patting the linoleum, pleased to rest his hand on something tangible. He'd go on taking measurements and at intervals he would caress his measuring stick and would talk to it. A few minutes later he would look up at the clock, almost angrily. The clock went on ticking. At times he'd clench his fist. Whole mornings he would pass in this way, making love to his foot-rule and fighting the clock. He would speak scornfully of everything pertaining to the clock, calling it an imposter. "Time," he would say, "time, seconds, minutes, hours, days, knights and their ladies. Bah!" He was grim. Then he'd look at his ruler. "Tell me, tell me, how many inches in an hour?" And he'd look at the clock and come down hard on the next nail in the linoleum.

There have, of course, been other strange encounters with clocks and watches. In the inventory which the Lilliputians made of what they found in the pockets of Gulliver is the following note: "Out of the right fob hung a great silver chain, with a wonderful kind of engine at the bottom. We directed him to draw out whatever was fastened to that chain; which appeared to be a globe, half silver, and half some transparent metal: for on the transparent side we saw certain strange figures circularly drawn, and thought we could touch them, till we found our fingers stopped by that lucid substance. He put this engine to our ears, which made an incessant noise like that of a watermill, and we conjecture it is either some unknown animal, or the god that he worships; but we are more inclined to the latter opinion, because he assures us (if we understood him right, for he expressed himself very imperfectly) that he seldom does anything without consulting it: he called it his oracle, and said it pointed out the time for every action of his life." Later the Emperor "was amazed at the continual noise it made, and the motion of the minute hand, which he could easily discern; for their sight is much more acute than ours; and asked the opinions of his learned men about him, which were various and remote, as the reader may well imagine

---

This selection is extracted from *Philosophical Essays,* University of Nebraska Press (1965), 99-127. Copyright by the University of Nebraska Press and reprinted with its permission.

without my repeating; although indeed I could not very perfectly understand them." But my only point now is to point out that the man who laid linoleum is not the first to have been mystified by a watch or clock. Besides I'm not through telling about him.

Of course, this man was not simply curious. He was quite disturbed. It was no joke. All his life he had been familiar with clocks. They had had ever so many times together until this "antic disposition" took hold of him. And so it was on the day of which I was speaking. In the evening he visited his friend the clockmaker, seated in the midst of his clock-works, taking tictation and tightening short-hands. He entered the clock-shop, glanced hurriedly about with both ears, and sat down. Not much was said at first. This was a clock-shop and two hundred clocks stared down at him. Pendulumonium! At eight o'clock the whole clock-works began to move, bells rang out from tiny clock-steeples, roosters crowed on tiny perches, cuckoos clock-cooed from tiny balconies, and eight assorted insects flew past a waiting bird as she gobbled up the hours. On the face of one trick clock, the minute hand was extended from the face of the clock, its fingers outspread with the end of the thumb resting on the tip of what seemed to be a nose raised in the center. Fortunately he did not see this. But he did see and hear too much. He could bear it no longer. Most absurd thing! "Ach," he cried, getting up from his chair, "Your clocks! Your clocks! What do they mean, your clocks?" and he gave a short kick in the direction of the case set in order with clocks before him. The clocks went on ticking, tick, tick, not heeding.

"Come," he said, with marvelous self-control, "I see your clocks. Now show me time, not ages, not aeons, but just one minute, and then I'll believe in your clocks." And he handed him his foot-rule. The clock-maker smiled, embarrassed, and glanced at his clocks. Plainly he felt responsible, but he returned the foot-rule. "I'm in earnest," his friend continued. "Today I fought your clock. I threw my hammer at it. And missed. Look!" And he got down on his hands and knees and measured the long side of the linoleum in the clock-makers's shop. "There," he said. "I measured the linoleum. Here's my foot-rule. You saw how I laid it down, laid it down, again and again, and counted to twelve. There are twelve feet on this side. You see the linoleum and you see the foot-rule. Now, then, as I have just shown you, so now you show me twelve minutes of time. Twelve feet of linoleum, twelve minutes of time! If, for instance, you got down on your knees with the clock in your hand and measured the linoleum, and counted thirty-six minutes of linoleum, then, I should understand how you were using the clock and what you were measuring. Or if you rolled your clock from one edge of the linoleum to the other, and you counted the rolls, that too would suit me. There might be circular foot-rules. But how do you manage to get down on your hands and knees or whatever you do, and so hold time down flat, and pull it straight so that you can get your measurement? Linoleum, five minutes flat."

He was in dead earnest. The clock-maker rubbed the bristles of his chin and tried not to be afraid. He looked about him and looked into the faces of his clocks. There was no help there. In his desperation he picked up a clock and was about to get down on his knees with the clock in his measuring hand, when another of his clocks rang off and a cuckoo stepped out and cocked its little head in his direction. The clock-maker, crouched as he was on one knee, looked up and burst out laughing. He set the clock back on the shelf. The layer of linoleum did not smile. He looked grimly at the cuckoo still cocking its head and the whole hickory-dickory-dock shebang. Dumb clocks! And he thought of that man who had made the largest machine in the world, which could do nothing, which also could not measure linoleum. He frowned and he got the notion that clocks were designed to make fun of laying linoleum, as though laying linoleum consisted of nothing but raising two hands and counting up to twelve. He was getting angry. "Listen," said the clock-maker, "the clock isn't used in that way and time isn't like an edge of the linoleum. There are other forms of measure. You can't pour linoleum into a cup nor squeeze it out of an eye-dropper. Ten drops of linoleum! Trying to explain to someone what a twelve-foot length of linoleum is like, by showing him how an eye-dropper works—well, that won't do any good. You don't talk about pounds, ounces, and pence in giving a man change for a kilocycle. There are all sorts of measures." He paused. Then he brightened. "Did you ever read this line in Black: 'Can wisdom be put in a silver-rod or love in a golden-bowl?' You just try it." He felt that he was doing pretty well. He was rising in his own estimation and began to feel airy. "And here is a line from such another: 'I have measured out my life in coffee-spoons.'" Then he switched. "Ah," he said. "I think I can explain clocks to you. Do you know the hour-glass and the sun dial?" But it was too late. His friend was not listening. Ever since the idea of pouring linoleum and the idea of the eye-dropper had been mentioned, he was pre-occupied. He was talking to himself, asking: What is time? and pausing, and then going on: What is water? He was trying to get the hang of his own question and when he thought of water he felt much better. If only he could meet time, as he could meet water, dipping his delighting fingers into it, then he might yet be a friend of clocks. He got up, musing, waved his hand to the clock-maker, and then, looking about him, he waved to the clock too. "Good," he said, "If I can manage to figure time in liters, I'll shake hands with all of you," and he made a gesture as though he were about to shake hands with a clock. They all ticked back at him, speeding up their tempo, and fidgeting with their hands. At least so it seemed to him. "Keep quiet," he shouted, and a chorus of clocks shouted back to him: "We keep time." He rushed out.

He walked. As he passed the town-hall, he looked up at the great wheel in the tower. It began striking the hour and boomed down at him. He winced at every stroke, covered his ears, and walked faster. He hurried to his friend, an expert in water-meters. His friend saw him coming. "Good!" he said to himself. "We'll play a game of bridge," an excellent game, by the way, for people so much occupied with water. They greeted each other, but it was soon evident that there was to be no game of bridge. His visitor began at once: "Listen, listen," he cried. "Will you show me the workings of your water-meter?" He gave no explanation and his friend asked no question. "Well," he said, and he showed him a model meter encased in glass, all its secrets open, its outsides transparent. His visitor studied it carefully, saw where the water runs into the water-meter and out again, and he read the chasing figures, 1, 2, 3, 4, . . . , and he saw that all was wet as it should be. It ticked like a clock and this especially pleased him. "Ah," he said, "I'm on the right track. I see the water and I see the measure-chamber, gulping and spilling measures of water, as the water flows. And there are the numbers." Satisfaction warmed his face. "Wonderful! Wonderful! Forty gallons, so many cubic feet of water, have run through the chamber while I watched the number goose-trot through the opening. Water plain as linoleum!" He felt thoroughly relaxed. This is what he wanted to see. Now for the clock. "If only I had a transparent clock, then I should see time flow as now I saw the water in this meter flow. Time meter! Time flows. Time like a river. " 'Time, like an everflowing stream.' " The more he saw and the more he said, the more he felt assured.

The water-meter master watched his friend curiously, but understood neither his excitement nor his words. He realized that there was some concern about a clock and about time, and he glanced at the old grandfather pendu-slumbering in the corner. Nothing striking about that! He was glad in any case that his water-meter had been useful. "What's the matter?" he asked. "Has your clock stopped?" His friend looked at him troubled. "Clock stopped? Clock stopped? Was it going somewhere?" And he looked serious. "No, indeed. My foot-rule is clogged. Can't tell time on your water-meter." He sniffed. Obviously he was not going to explain. The other shook his head, slipped a cover over the water-meter, and drew out his watch. He handed it over to his friend, who looked at it, turning it over carefully, then he glanced in the direction of the water-meter. Then he returned it without a word. A minute or two later he said: "I must be going." And he left.

So the friend of linoleum went home. He walked up the stairs, trying to make a noise like a clock, ticking, just to work up his sympathies, hoping in this way to understand the clock. When he got to his room, he walked straight to the clock and sat down on the bed to examine it. He turned it upside down, and turned it round and round. He shook it and squeezed it. He noticed the knobs and keys on the back-side of it. He was taking time seriously, almost anxiously. He looked for an opening to discover where time comes in and he found one at the top just under the bell, and he held his hand over it, but the clock went on ticking and he felt no time on his hand. He shook the clock again, hoping to catch a few seconds seeping through the seams from the inside, but he saw only a fine spray of dust sifting down on the table. He was, however, in no mood to take time for that or that for time—though he was at first startled to see it, was for a moment hopeful. "Ah!" he exclaimed. But then he knew. Finally he decided to take the clock apart, to get a look inside. "Clocks keep time. Well, we'll see." And so, poor fellow, he undid the clock. He was not a bit surprised. The insides of the clock were not even wet. There was not a sparkle of temporal dew even in the spring. He sighed. He gathered the debris of his clock in his hands and laid it on a chair. And he could not imagine how time, had there really been some, could have escaped him. He had been so careful.

But this was not the end of his perplexity. He went on trying to puzzle out how the clock could be measuring something. In his most meticulous fashion he would say: "Well, perhaps the clock does measure something. Per hand from six to twelve is six units of the push of the turn of the index-thumb against the key that winds the spring that unwinds against the cog that moves with the wheel that goes tick." And then he would write this down and snuggle up to it, it was so reasonable. "So one o'clock is so much of the push of the index-thumb against the key spent in the progress of the hand from some point in the circumference of the face to another point in the circumference of the same face, semi-ambi-dextrous to the center." And so too the hour-glass measures sand. On other days he would review what he had said before. "Is push time? But why, then, does a man, when he looks at his watch, run for a bus?" And he would hold his head. And then he would come up with another theory. "Time," he would say, "is invisible, an invisible water, and it flows through clocks and is gulped and spilled in upsy-downsy containers, ticken upwards and ticken downwards, as the invisible flows," And this is right too, for is not time invisible? What a comfort in comparison with time linoleum is, so simple—and visible, too! And water, too. But his speculation was not always so gentle. There were times when he suspected clock-makers of a grand conspiracy, obviously, for profit, imposing their machines upon all the people and teaching them a language to go with it, and calling their watches and clocks time-pieces. And the people had now been taken for some generations, so that though people knew very well what the insides of a clock are like, one seldom heard of anyone doing as he had done, investigating a clock to find out whether there was anything in it. "Time is an illusion, a mere appearance," he would say, "engineered by people who are giving us the works." He thought it un-American too.

II

In the preceding section, I have presented the simple case of a man who does not know what time is. It is obvious enough that he approaches the clock with the foot-rule, expecting to discover something vaguely like linoleum, and that later he approaches it with the expectation that it, the clock, works like a water-meter, and that something vaguely like water runs through the clock. Knowing what time is would in this case be something like feeling the drift of time against the surface or against the edge of one's foot-rule or like feeling something soft as a baby's breath in the palm of one's hand as one shakes the clock over it. Time tipping the edge of a foot-rule, time on one's hands! The explanation is, I think, also obvious. This man knows to begin with that we measure linoleum, water, and time. How much linoleum? How much water? How much time? He also knows how to measure linoleum, and discovers how to measure water. He understands the use of the foot-rule and also the use of the water-meter. Now, then, he tries to understand the clock and the use of the clock in terms of the foot-rule and the water-meter and their use. It is this comparison which leads to the idea of something like linoleum, and something like water, and it is something like linoleum and something like water that he looks for in the neighborhood of the clock. Finding nothing, he is troubled and says that he does not know what time is.

I have noticed in this explanation that we measure linoleum, water, and time. This means that there is an extensive parallel in the language of these. We use numbers in respect to each, and, of course, there are units. In measuring we do some things that are similar. We read off numbers on the foot-rule, on the face of the clock, on the face of the water-meter, and, of course, we add, subtract, etc. Naturally it doesn't follow that one can answer such questions as: How many square feet of linoleum in one hour? or how much water in five minutes? If someone insisted that he did not know what an hour is because he could not say how many square feet of linoleum there are in an hour, then, in any case, you would see what it was that he did not know. And so with how much water in five minutes. Now what I have noticed here is a relatively uninteresting illustration of the way in which the language of time is intertwined with the language of quite different contexts. This intertwining of the language gives rise to something like the experience one may have when a familiar street in one neighborhood leads one without one's being aware into a neighborhood which is of a quite different character. From the village into the Italian section, from this busy square into a street of quiet houses and gardens. A different world! This may be entertaining. It may also be quite confusing and distressing. "I'm lost. Where am I?" So too with the language of time. Stepping, as it were, on one word and pressing it hard, loosing it from its present context, one may suddenly find oneself stepping along in a different context, scarcely knowing where one is, and then thoroughly confusing neighborhoods. In the city the view of one bit of street by which one came into the different neighborhood may mislead one into supposing he hasn't left the other neighborhood at all and so he may continue to try to find his way within this neighborhood as he well might in the other. This is dizzying. It may be like trying to find your way in a strange house, in the middle of the night, when you are not enough awake to realize you are not at home. So you blink and bump your head.

In what immediately follows I am going to present an heterogeneous grouping of fragments of the intertwining of the language of time with the language or languages of other things. There will be nothing systematic about this. There will be fragments, sentences or phrases, which will be like short streets connecting neighborhoods. There will be others in which I enter the adjacent neighborhood. The point of this will be to provide further illustration of that aspect of language which, when taken in a certain absentminded way, may give one's head a permanent whirl, or when taken in a certain well-lit mindedness, may give one a ride not unlike that one gets in a fun-house.

Notice the variety and color: Once upon a time. He's behind time but four steps ahead of Jones. A long time ago. There's been a mix-up in time. A time interval. Can you tell time? I wouldn't if I could. Time is mean. Mean-time. The clock is striking the hour. Savagery in the belfry. Time passed. So did the milk-man. The time is up. Night fell. No wonder, it's so dark! In a twinkling. In the shake of a lamb's tail. Shorter than the shake of a puppy's tail. The turn of the century. The turn of the screw. The turn of a phrase. It will soon be time. What was it before? A month of Sundays. Five minutes late. Which five minutes? Times overlap. It seams so. He lives in the past. He dies in the future. Time is money. What's money? Money is groceries. Time is groceries. Right now. Wrong hereafter. Relativity of time and morals. On the hour. Shove over about five minutes. The crowded years. Squeeze in a little time. Time slips away. Between the hours of four and six. Ah! There you are! A stitch in time. A gap in the years. Time heals all things. Remove the stitches. The fulness of time. The fulness of skirts. Time takes its toll. Toll pays for highways. "Time hath a wallet at her back." Nevermore. Nevertheless. Always the same. The day is shot. "Who killed cock-robin?" Not yet? No, yet. Pause for a second. The second is late. No duel without a second. No duo without a second. Take your time. Why does he get a larger piece? Down the corridors of time. Electric light and running water for the first fifty years. "Looking backwards." A time capsule. Chrono-Belcher. A secure tomorrow. Yesterday teetering on the verge of 12 p.m. The future "in a retrospective arrangement." The past teaches us. The lessons of the past. "There, that will teach you to keep your hands out of the fire." The past teaching all hands present to mind future fires. The best time of the year. The dancing hours. Compline hour. The hour of decision. Tossed coin. All heads saying, "Tails." Time to eat. Chronic gluttony. Stuffing yourself, gobbler. Fat as a tick. Spare a tidbit, just a tasty interval. Time consuming. Just a minute for dessert. Time to turn over a new leaf. From the palm in my hand to the tree taking leaf in the spring.

And now I should like to nimble-numble at a few of these. *"Once upon a time."* Indeed! Twice below a certain space we met. In the subway. You said: "Have you the time?" And I said: "I have fifty years." You pouted. It was about time you, a pout about. *"He's behind time."* What a pity! He can never catch up. Time cannot be overtaken. No overtaking. And he with his future always just a jiffy ahead of him, and he crying, "Halt! Halt!" *"A long time ago."* A far country. Go back in time some place, and live in those other people's presents. Go to bed in 1953 and get up in time to buy corn from Joseph in Egypt. "Is your name Benjamin?" "No, no, sir. I did not steal your silver-cup. I have just dreamed in from the U.S.A." He would not understand. "You are under arrest. You are an anachronist. When do you come from? How did you get out of your century?" Meeting Caesar there too, asking Joseph for a few husks and a bucket of ashes to celebrate the Ides of Kislev. "What language do you speak?" "Dico the Roman language," he says in his very best Egyptian which is English. "It was once going to be the most up-to-date, by jabberers, before the future returned." Joseph goes on filling sacks as though time had been renewed and tomorrow was still to come. "There's been a mix-up in time." Tangles in tense. A tense wood. Was issing and will and soon wassing. Ex post factos ante factoring. Eternal recurrence in a jumble. What are your whenabouts? *"The clock is striking the hour."* A careless hour, loitering on the way to ten o'clock. Came in with chiming morning face, like snail, unwillingly to gong. Ten strokes on his pendulum. Doing time.

There are good times, corking good times, uncorking good times. ("A barrel of fun," "a barrel of monkeys.") There are bad times, perfect times, dandy times, nice times, high old times, hard times, grand times, gay times, sad times, rotten times, times that are out of joint. There's railroad time, Greenwich time, five-o'clock shadow on the sun-dial, exact time. We have, we make, we spend, we gain, we buy, we save, we sell, we put in, we waste, we while away ("wit a whittle whittle stick"). We give, we fill, we take out, we steal, we shorten, we squeeze out, we spare, we stretch, we lengthen, we cut, we halve, we keep, we hoard, we get, we take, we seize, we use, we watch, we pick up, we lack, we find, we need, we divide, we lose, we fritter away, we kill, we beat, we invest. What? Time. Time is money. Put time in the bank. Invest weekly. He, taking up his gun, said: "I'm going out to kill time." She shuddered. Expert marksman. Catching time on the wing. But time flies. Time runs, time flows, time creeps ("Tomorrow and tomorrow and tomorrow ... to the last syllable ..."), time never stops, time marches on (clopperty, clopperty, clop). Time waits for no man always at the same speed, twenty-fours every so many minutes.

Time is pressing. With a mangle, alas! ("And at my back I always hear.") Time withers. (Wrong. "Time cannot wither nor custom stale.") Time corrupts. The prey of time, the ravages of time. The prisoners of time. ("Stone walls ... nor iron bars ..." but ...) One solid hour. Packed with thrills. Room for only one more bubble. Time is a blabber. Time will tell. A lost week-end. Found in the middle of no-when, a tiny island surrounded by something like water. Free time. "The gift of another day." The space of one week. How to compute the area of one week with two unknowables. My time is yours. I have a second. Let's split. A split second. Sounds like a cocoa-nut. Nothing inside. A light-year. A dark hour. Sign of the times: Neon, jitters, robins, whirring, falling leaves, squirrels hiding nuts. Working against time. ("Give me a lever long enough and a fulcrum strong enough ..." and I'll stop everything.) Time hangs heavy. Ripe bananas. Seize the moment. By the scruff of the nick of time. A time-piece. "Slab of eternity." A chip off the old block universe. Times without number. Times with number: three times three. In a trice. In a tricecycle, over and over and over. He came in on time. Time is faster than a horse.

The time is coming. (Have you had word? Travel plans.) The time is near. ("I can hear the whistle blowing.") The time is here. (Bring out the red carpet.) The time is going. (All aboard!) The time is gone. (Disappearing in the shadows.) Yesterday is but a shadow of its former self. You'd scarcely know it was the same day. So changed. Been through something. Do you remember the time? Indeed. I'd recognize it anywhere. Is it long since? My last haircut. Travel by memory. Make it in no time at all. See the world from a howdah decked out by your own "imagicnation." A week's work. Six working days, everybody else sitting around. Five-day week. Seventy-some in a year. The first day of the week fell on a Sunday. That's why Sunday walks bowed. Many happy returns of the day. Recurrence to suit wishes. Same day last year this year. Eat the same cake, burn the same candle at the other end. In one year and out of the other. A full day, brimming over, spilled. My time is exhausted. Breathless. Can't stand the pace. A blue Monday, a white Christmas, a black day in our history, "the violet hour," "rosy-fingered dawn," a golden age, the faded past, a green morning, dark ages, the mauve decade, a gray day, a pretty soon, a handsome present, a bright future. Time in assorted colors. Velvet night. What color is Tuesday? Tuesday is fat and florid.

There's no time like the present. There are no apples like the apples of my eye. There's no space like here. "There's no place like home." Never postpone today. Postpone tomorrow. When? Tomorrow. But I may not have the time. That's just the time to postpone. A sentence of five years. Parse it. An exercise for logicians who live a thousand years. A compound proposition. For ever and a day. A baker's dozen. A billion years. The story of the rocks. "Once upon a glacial morning, before the sun rose; there was no sun...." The crucible of time. Hot. Rag-time.

A man on his way lost time. His watch also lost time. A double loss! Time lost cannot be recovered. Like spilled milk. Sop it up. Ten minutes in a wet towel. "Little Sheba." Another man found time, but not the time the other man lost. Ten minutes as good as new, unused, second-hand. Second-hand time goes faster. He also found one dime and he found some things impossible. When he said that he had found some things impossible people would not believe him. They said no one could find things impossible, that there are no impossible things. Time, they allowed, was possible, and when they asked him where he found time, he said time was up and wouldn't say another word. They figured that what is up must come down and so they waited. Time would find them out. They winced at the thought. Then the man who found time turned, elbowing his way through time, he was virtually in time, and said to the man who had lost time, "My time is yours," and so finder shared with loser, the ten minutes he had found, breaking it into two five-minute time-pieces. They tick-talked to one another until time ran out of them. Surprised, they both exclaimed, "Where has the time gone?" One answered, "South, for the winter," but the other answered: "No, time is up again. It was high time, you know. It went past like that." And he pretended that he was a bird. "Of course," said the other, "Time flies, have you never heard of the mosquito fleet? But will time return?" "No," said the other. "Time is no homing pigeon." And they were very sad, as they both stood, looking up, watching time flapping its wings in the avisphere.

These are "the fragments I have shared" in order to prepare myself for what I propose to do in the next section. These fragments, you may remember, I intended as further illustration of the intertwining of the language of time with the language or languages of other things. Obviously this intertwining may be exploited sportingly. My interest is in the fact that there is this intertwining. And my interest comes about in this way. There are cases in which this intertwining has serious consequences, and in which it is difficult to see both what the intertwining in a particular case is, and that the serious consequences do arise from such intertwining. The serious consequence I have in mind is that a man should say, "I do not know what time is."

III

In this section I want to study a second case of the man who does not know what time is, this case a bona-fide one, a case with which I have wrestled. The case is expressed in the following long sentence: "The great mystery of Time, were there no other; the illimitable, silent, never-resting thing called Time, rolling, rushing on, swift, silent, like an all-embracing oceantide, on which we and all the universe swim like exhalations, like apparitions which are and then are not; this is forever very literally a miracle; a thing to strike us dumb,—for we have no word to speak about it." "The great mystery of Time." I propose now to try to understand just what it is that is the mystery of time by way of certain other mysteries. Time is not the only mystery. There is the mystery of the sea and there is the mystery of the sky and stars. There are, of course, minor mysteries such as the mystery of caves and of deep places. And man too, it is said, is a mystery, the greatest mystery of all. For the present I wish to consider the mystery of the sea and that of the sky and stars. I am no doubt led to these in particular by the language in which the mystery of time is expressed. I turn first to the mystery of the sea.

Consider, then, some thoughtful man in the days of Columbus or some days before Columbus, as he looks out to the west from some high rock on the shore of the great ocean. He ponders that endless expanse of water, water, water, and more water, on and on, water, wave upon wave, never-ending. Is there another shore? A shoreless sea! His eyes find no relief. There is only water. He stomps with his foot on the rock, with a relish for terra firma. He turns his gaze upon the hills behind him, his eyes resting there, a refuge from the terrors of endlessness. "Are there hills like these there?" and he fixes his eyes steadily on the west. He imagines himself winged like a bird, in flight over the water, arriving at another shore, strange peoples, palm trees, rich meadows, a better land, who knows? "Giants, perhaps, with walrus mustaches. And clusters of grapes borne between two upon a staff." This is not the first time he has stood upon this rock and mused upon the lands that are far away, washed by the water at his feet. There has been talk too, hushed and wonder-full with friends, and even some levity. "Come, let's get into my little boat and we'll find the other shore." All for smile's sake. They knew and he knew that they would not venture out in any boat, big or little. Another shore? Might not their boat suddenly be carried by the strong waters, tumbling into the abyss, far away from mama and the kitchen stove? Leviathan is no house-cat. And even were the sea set in a saucer and all were well in quiet weather, might not some storm carry them all over the edge like spilled coffee to spatter the floor of the fundament? And so the sea teased them but they did not dare to attempt to pluck out the heart of its mystery. "Three wise men of Gotham!" One man did, of course. And, whether in unquiet desperation (furious at the infinite) or in quiet confidence, he set sail to set his eyes to rest upon that other who-knows-whether shore. On Columbus day! "There is another shore." And he looked back, following the line of the wake of his boat, and he thought of that rock on that other other shore.

Here, then is a simple case of mystery. Is there another shore? Are there people there? (Is Mars inhabited? No, not yet. But there is a little clover growing out of the rocks.) There are questions, and wistfulness, and a certain helplessness. "We'll never find out." (What's at the end of the rainbow?) And then some brave sailor dares to face the terrors, and returns with a few gay feathers and an olive leaf and a piece of wampum. And that is the end of the mystery.

This is, however, by no means all of the mystery of the sea. Imagine the sea under a pale moon with clouds. Mystery has its own sky. "I should never have made the sun, but I should have made the moon. The sun is too bright." The moon is for vague and sweet wonder, the sea and waves in soft light and shadow. And things under the sea! The lost Atlantis, the submerged cathedral, Davy Jones' locker, lost ships, mermaids, and pirates' gold. "So is this great and wide sea, wherein are things creeping, innumerable, both small and great beasts." The sea is deep and is dark and wide, and swarms with tiny lights, the lanterns of little fishes. Oh! for a walk in that dark deep on the ocean floor to see the strange creatures like living gold and silver, treasures of the sea. The whale's home. "As we have seen, God came upon him in the whale, and swallowed him down to the living gulfs of doom, and with swift slantings tore him along 'into the midst of the seas,' where the eddying depths sucked him ten fathoms down, and 'the weeds were wrapped about his head' and all the watery world of woe bowled over him." "Ten fathoms down... the watery world of woe." And there are storms at sea and darkness and fog and rain and a thousand ships tossing under the stars. The Ancient Mariner, The Flying Dutchman, the man without a country, Captain Carlson on the broken ship!

And now notice this echo of the sentence which I quoted above: "The great mystery of the Sea, were there no other: the illimitable, noisy, never-resting thing we call The Sea, rolling, rushing on, swift, noisy, an all-embracing ocean, on which we and all the earth swim like exhalations, like apparitions which are and then are not; this is forever, literally a miracle; a thing to strike us dumb,—for we have no word to speak about it."

This, I think, will not do. But I should like to notice the divergence in the following elaboration, engaging still the language in which the original sentence goes on about time. Imagine this mediation: "The great mystery of the sea, were there no other," and he, the man on the rock, shakes his head slowly, sighs, and looks out upon the water. And he thinks of the stars. "The illimitable." He begins counting the waves for as far as he can see. He gives up, and looks out beyond the last wave he counted. "Noisy." The waves break upon the shore. "Listen! You hear the grating roar." "Never-resting thing we call the sea." "Sophocles long ago heard it on the Aegean." Not one drop of water in all this expanse is still, nor has ever been. "Endlessly rocking," as water falls rise, and water-rises fall, rocking water. "Rolling, rushing on, swift." His eyes catch one line of surf cresting one high wave and they follow its rising tumult, faster, faster, as it pursues the wave before it, swifter, swifter, till it dashes in foam upon the shore. He shouts "Stay! Stay!" and braces himself as with his eyes to halt the wild seahorses, which rise and leap over his command. Testing his power! (King Canute went home pretty well soaked.) Tide waits and waves wait for no man, nor for any man's word or eye. "An all-embracing ocean." Three-fourths of the earth's surface is water and all the land is an island, floating on that all-encompassing sea. "On which" we and all that is on the earth and all that land, swim like flotsam and then some, like "mire and dirt" cast up by the troubled sea. Our land rests at anchor at the mercy of impervious, reckless water, sustained and shaken by an incontinent sea into whose depths, at the stir of one wild shudder, any windy day, it may fall down, down, down, whales scampering, itself to be dissolved, water to water. "This is forever very literally a miracle: a thing to strike us dumb, for we have no word to speak about it."

Now I should like to comment on this. I tried in the first place to represent the mystery of the sea, its overwhelming extent, its depths and darkness, the lore of history and story, the great beasts and shining little fishes, strange, unknown to man. The sea is full of mystery. My intention was to see whether I could, having had a glimpse of the mystery of the sea, write about that mystery in the words in which the sentence goes on about the mystery of time. Time is illimitable. Well, so is the sea of overwhelming extent. For the purposes of wonder it is large enough. "Silent?" No, not silent, but, then, perhaps noise has its own mystery. "Never-resting?" Indeed! the sea never rests. "Rolling, rushing, swift?" Yes, sometimes more spectacularly even than time. "An all-embracing ocean-tide?" You could say so. There's water all around us. And we and the universe exhalations, apparitions, swimming? No. And this in any case does not enter into the mystery of the sea. And now if we say that time like the sea is very big and very restless, "mighty like a whale," is time's mystery further like the mystery of the sea? The sentence takes no account of the light of the moon shining pale on time, no account of lost cities, lost ships, lore of history and story, submerged in time. Where are they now? at the bottom of the sea of time. It takes no account of "things creeping, innumerable," "of small and great beasts" hidden in the folds of time, time stretched out like a curtain. So far, then, I think we can say that comparing the mystery of time to the mystery of the sea helps on the whole chiefly to see that they are not similar, that one cannot understand the mystery of time in this way. Tentatively, let us say that both time and the sea are of marvelous extent and that both are restless.

There is another mystery, the mystery of sky and stars. Mystery is, of course, bound up with the unknown, with wonder. The mystery of the sea is articulate, but the mystery of sky and stars is relatively inarticulate. There are no such questions as: Is there another shore? If I go straight up, will I bump my head? The question, in any case, hasn't the right tone. The sky is not strewn with lost ships, with pirates' gold, with a lost Atlantis. If on occasion a great church were suddenly whirled off the earth into space and we saw it disappearing in the direction of a far star, intact, not a brick out of place, and if men now and then were caught in a draught, waved good-bye from a cloud, and we saw them ride off for a spree among the stars, or if we now and then saw or thought we saw in faintest outline the inter-stellar caravans moving swiftly, red and green lights flashing, before and after landing, then we should have something more like the mystery of the sea. Even such a question as: Is Mars inhabited? hasn't the right atmosphere, is generally unconnected with the mystery of the sky and stars. Wonder in this case is vague wonder. The sky and stars are too far away, and they have not swallowed, and have not hidden in their depths, treasure and the burnished lore of history and story. So Our wonder has little substance. We do not look steadfastly at some star and ask: And are they singing a hymn in that church, high notes bouncing off the points of neighboring stars? Will Jonathan, who flew away yesterday, sift down a spray of star-dust to show Stella he hasn't forgotten?

Still, there is wonder.
Consider the verses:

> Twinkle, twinkle, little star!
> How I wonder what you are!
> Up above the world so high
> Like a diamond in the sky.

Little stars are cherished shining in the wonder of children and children's wonder twinkles in the winkles of the star.

And now this from a man who did not write nursery rhymes: "Two things there are fill the mind with ever new and increasing admiration and awe, the oftener and more steadily we reflect on them: the starry heavens above and the moral law within." "The more steadily we reflect on them!" Did Kant on his walk one day look into the sky and at one bright star and say: "How I wonder what you are!" I suppose not. He looked into "The starry heavens above," and reflected. And what were his words? Did he say: "And behold the height of the stars, how high they are," or "When I consider thy heavens, the work of they fingers, the moon and stars which thou hast ordained, what is man that thou art mindful of him?" Only, I take it, as we connect the stars with man, for instance, or with God, is there any richness in this mystery of the stars. St. Augustine's feeling, not only towards the heavens, but also towards the earth and sea is expressed in the following passage:

> And what is this? I asked the earth; and it answered, "I am not He." And whatsoever are therein made the same confession. I asked the sea and the deeps, and the creeping things that live and they replied, "We are not thy God; seek higher than we." I asked the breezy air, and the universal air with its inhabitants answered, "Anaximenes was deceived, I am not God." I asked the heavens, sun, moon, and stars: "Neither," say they, "are we the God whom thou seekest." And I answered unto all those things which stand about the door of my flesh: "Ye have told me concerning my God that ye are not He; tell me something about Him." And with a loud voice they exclaimed, "He made us." My questioning was my observing of them; and their beauty was their reply.

The mystery of the stars is, I take it, something special, bathed in a religious light. There are descriptions of the heavens which are, however, quite different. Notice:

> This most excellent canopy, the air, look you; this brave o'erhanging firmament, this majestical roof fretted with golden fire—why it appears no other thing 'to me than a foul and pestilent congregation of vapors.

And this:

> And that inverted bowl they call the sky
> whereunder crawling cooped we live and die,
> Lift not your hands to It for help for it
> As impotently moves as you and I.

And this:

> A wise man
> watching the stars pass across the sky,
> Remarked:
> In the upper air the fireflies move more slowly.
> *Amy Lowell*

And in these the note of mystery is gone.

Apart from the religious overtones, however, some men have spoken of the mystery of the heavens in a different vein, almost literally of that mystery as a form of consternation. It comes, I think, to something like this. There are forms of picture-puzzle arrangements of black dots, for instance, on a white background, and the puzzler is invited to make out the picture of an old man brushing his shoes or of a bear with his head in a jar. If he cannot make it out, then, of course, the arrangement remains a mystery. Now, then, it is supposed that if the stars were arranged all over the blue himmels in a network of squares, then there would be no mystery. No one would then be fascinated by the stars. It might in that case be very monotonous and anyone who suggested that the stars should be redistributed as if scattered out of a pepper-pot might be acclaimed as a fine architect of the new heavens. Nevertheless this deep-seated hankering for a pattern has this consequence, that when men now do look into the star-lit skies they are overwhelmed and baffled as by a puzzle which exceeds their capacities. They do, of course, find what relief they can in the big and little dipper and the lady in a chair, the arrow and the little fox and so on. The aim however is one picture and it is the frustration involved here which is expressed in the idea of the mystery. The fascination remains, even after one has given up. A variant of this idea is that when one looks into the sky he is tempted straightway to count them, this, perhaps, being one way of arranging them. But he cannot. Hence, the following comment of Burke:

> The number is certainly the cause. The apparent disorder augments the grandeur, for the appearance of care is highly contrary to our idea of magnificence. Besides the stars lie in such apparent confusion as makes it impossible on ordinary occasion to reckon them. This gives them the advantage of a certain infinity.

So it is in various ways the overspreading "heaven-tree of stars," the everlasting chandelier in the ceiling of the world feeds our wonder.

And now reflect: "The great mystery of the Heavens, were there no other; the illimitable, silent, never-resting thing called the Heavens, rolling, rushing on, swift, silent, like an all-embracing ocean-tide on which we and all the universe swim like exhalations, like apparitions which are and then are not; this is forever very literally a miracle; a thing to strike us dumb,— for we have no word to speak about it." Will this do?

I am trying to understand "the mystery of Time," meaning by this that I am trying to understand the man who speaks of such mystery. The clues to understanding him may be such other mysteries as we are acquainted with, and, of course, what he goes on to say. It is in this way that I came to remind myself of the mysteries of sea and sky. The language in which the author of the sentence writes of the mystery certainly encourages this. We have already seen that this may throw some light upon the mystery. Time is "an all-embracing ocean-tide." Strange sea! If one could paddle with one's feet on the bank of time as one can paddle on the bank of the sea, then, surely, a part of time would be laid. As it is, we know that we do paddle with our feet in the stream of time, but we cannot feel it. No one stubs his toe there against the current. As for what I have noted of the mystery of the heavens and stars, there is even less that is useful in understanding "the mystery of time." There is nevertheless something else which may be described as the mystery of the heavens which may be useful and which is analogous to the idea of "the strange sea." I should like to return to this, but before I do so, I want to study more closely the "description" of time in the sentence about the mystery.

It is clear that no one has come to think of time as like the sea or like the sky, by having seen both time and the sea or sky, as one might have come to think of the sky as like the sea. For we do see both sea and sky. But, then, the question is as to how we do come to think of time as like the sea. The answer is, I take it, simple enough. The same types of sentence which serve us in discussing time or in remarks about (?) time, serve us also in describing the sea. It is this similarity which gives rise to the illusion that time is a sea.

The sentences that I want to notice are these:

> *Time is illimitable.*
> *Time is silent.*
> *Time never rests.*
> *Time rolls, rushes on.*
> *Time is all-embracing.*

I propose with respect to each of these sentences, first of all to explain briefly the use of the sentence, and then to go on to show how by assimilating the meaning of the sentence to somewhat parallel sentences about the sea, we come up with the stirring meta-mystery of time. My explanation of the use of these sentences will very likely be incomplete and may be incorrect. My intention, however, is to exhibit the character of that use, sufficiently to distinguish its use from the analogous sentences about the sea.

Time is illimitable. What does this mean? Briefly, this means that for such expressions as "The first hour," "the last hour," "the beginning of time," "the end of time," we have, save in certain contexts such as "the first hour of the day," "during the last hour," no use. This involves further that we also have no use for such sentences as "there is no first hour" and "there is no last hour." We may all recollect how St. Augustine wrestled with this.

The temptation, however, to try to understand this in a different way is exceedingly strong. "If the roving thought of anyone should wander through the images of by-gone times," then one may go on as follows. Beyond the present moment, there is a next, and a next and a next. Tomorrow is coming, and next week, and January and 1955. And then? Then another decade, another century. And the same thing will be the case if you look behind you over this present moment's shoulder. There is the moment before and so on and on. There is yesterday and last week and September and 1953. And then? Then the forties, and 1900. And, of course, you can go on indefinitely, tearing the leaves off old calendars and making new ones. A shoreless sea! Isn't this how it is at sea when you stand high and look over the water, the sea before you, wave upon wave, dimming into the waters of tomorrow and the waters of yesterday? Is not every man a Flying Dutchman until the sea of time swallows him? There is no shore, no harbor. Time is illimitable.

Time is silent. This is a remarkable detail, and is emphasized by repetition in the sentence quoted at the beginning of this part of the essay. Consider. Time passes. Listen! You could hear a pin drop. "Like a thief in the night." (Time is a thief. It steals your youth away. "Gather ye rosebuds while ye may." "Time, you old gypsy man!") Time passes. There's not a squeak. Helmholtz could not have heard it. The highest fidelity cannot capture it. On cat's paws! Keep your ear to space, catch an echo as time bangs against the earth's axis, a faint throbbing. The sea is not silent. As the waves pound one another, they roar; but time hasn't even a tiny cry. It is also true, of course, that time is not blue, does not smell of fish, and tastes neither salty nor of lemonade. Why, then, is a special point made of this, that time is silent? Well, I take it that if one has already got an impression of time as like the sea, and one has in mind too its restlessness and its rolling, then the silence of such a sea intensifies the mystery. Imagine a sea, a turbulent sea, silent as a picture. Is not that a strange sea?

I need, perhaps, not remark that, apart from conversations between two men, neither of whom knows what time is, the sentence: "Time is silent," has no point. Neither is space sour.

Time never rests. It's never an hour for more than sixty minutes. That's how it is with now, too. Now always comes in at the same time, now, that is, and moves on. Guests may stay on, but four o'clock leaves on schedule. Tomorrow is coming, moves in, moves on, is gone, joins yesterday. It will never come by this way again. Time does not stand still. Nor does tomorrow come in, move out and then rest. It keeps on going and every day it's further away. There is no siesta, no rest, for time. Time marches on. Time waits for nobody. "Sun, stand thou still upon Gibeon; and thou moon, in the valley of Ajalon," was not spoken to Time. Time goes on, unwearied, what endurance! unwearying, without a break. Perpetual motion. Nothing can keep time back. Time is irresistible. Put your foot out on the last of Monday to halt Tuesday, and Tuesday runs, subtly rilling, over and through your foot. Get your foot wedged in between 4:59 and 5:01 and see it carried away, disappearing in the mists of last week. King Canute, throwing time back, buckets full of today hitting him full in the face as he tries to make tomorrow stand still. Too much pressure. Build a wall to keep the future out of this year. Make a lunge, telescoping time, jamming 4000 years into a 1000-year space. The engineering feat of the milleniums. The latest advances in Chronodamnamics. Working against time. Hopeless! Time rolls, rushes on, pushed on by the wave of the future. Against the sea you can build a wall. The sea has a bed. It does not rest but can rest. But time has no bed. Its waves are dashed against no shore. There is no shore. The past recedes every day another day. The future advances every day another day. This is, shall we say, an eternal fact, as old as calendars.

So, in this case, there never will be a Columbus who will set sail to explore and to discover the shore from which the future starts out. The future, no matter how far into tomorroworroworrow he will have advanced, will already be on its way. Time will not be caught napping.

Time is all-embracing. Everything is in time. When is four o'clock? In time. When did Socrates live? In time. When will you keep still? In time. How can time hold so much? Time is very big. The fishes are in the water. The ships are in the sea. The stars are in the sky. The birds are in the air. And all things, fishes and water, and birds and air, and stars and sky are in time. Time is immense. Without water fish cannot swim. Without air birds cannot fly. Without sky the stars cannot shine. The water carries the fish, the air carries the birds. The sky carries the stars. Water, air, and sky are buoyant. And water and air and sky are themselves buoyant, buoyed, in buoyantest time. Time is all embracing, all-embuoyant. And if, now, everything is in time, is time also in all things? Are not all things time-embracing? Mutual love! it is so. Time permeates all things. Lift the tiny scales of little fishes, time is there. Examine the entrails of birds, time is there. Tiresias knew. And in the hottest regions of the stars, time is there. In the drop of water, in the breath of air, in a patch of sky, time is there. Time permeates all things. And now we can also understand the words: "on which we and all the universe swim." For as fish swim in the water and birds swim in the air and the stars swim in the sky, so all swimming in the water and all swimming in the air and all swimming in the sky are swimmings in time, the sea, air, sky, of time. Time is a sea, an air, a sky.

And now, I think that we are near to plucking out the heart of the mystery of time. But we are still to explain the rest of that part of the sentence which begins: "on which we and all the universe swim." It goes on: "like exhalations, like apparitions which are and then are not." Time's exhalation, apparitions of time! For this purpose I should like to quote the following sentences from Sir Isaac Newton, from which it will, I think, be clear that the mystery of time is twin to the mystery of the aether.

> But to proceed to the hypothesis: It is to be supposed therein, that there is an aetherial medium, much of the same constitution with air, but far rarer,

subtler, and more strongly elastic. . . . But it is not to be supposed that this medium is one uniform matter, but composed partly of the main phlegmatic body of aether, partly of other various aetherial spirits, much after the manner that air is compounded of the phlegmatic body of air, intermixed with various vapours and exhalations. For the electric and magnetic effuvia, and the gravitation principle seem to argue such variety. Perhaps the whole frame of nature may be nothing but various contextures of some certain aetherial spirits or vapours, condensed as it were by precipitation, much after that manner that vapours are condensed into water, or exhalations into grosser substances, though not so easily condensable; and after condensation wrought into various forms, at first by the immediate hand of the creator, and ever since by the power of nature, which by virtue of the command, increase and multiply, became a complete imitation of the copy set by the Protoplast. Thus, perhaps, may things be originated from aether.

So the aether too is an all-embracing sea or atmosphere, a medium like air, and to it are related "vapours and exhalations," as to time are related exhalations and apparitions. "Thus, perhaps, may all things be originated from aether," as on time, "we and all the universe swim, like exhalations, like apparitions." And now as there is a mystery of the aether so too there is a mystery of time. For the aether, though much like air, is "rarer, subtler, and more strongly elastic," and whereas one can paddle in the water with one's feet, and one can hold out one's hand in a breeze, the aether goes right through one's foot and hand. One can catch neither touch nor sight of it. Besides it is silent. Also there are the mysteries of vapors and exhalations, of precipitation and condensation. And so the mystery of time is analogous. Is not time also "rarer, subtler" and perhaps "more strongly elastic" than air, and, perhaps, even than aether? It is difficult, perhaps, to say whether the mystery of time in the sentence quoted is the same as the mystery of aether or whether it is the mystery of a medium even rarer and subtler than aether of which the aether itself is an exhalation, a gross form. On the latter assumption there is this order of media: water, air, aether, time. In any case, the following sentence is not an unreasonable parody: "The great mystery of Aether, were there no other; the illimitable, silent, never-resting thing called aether" (notwithstanding its phlegmatism), "rolling, rushing on, swift" (these words show the traces of the analogy with the sea, but wind also rushes), "silent, like an all-embracing ocean-tide, on which we and all the universe swim like exhalations, like apparitions which are and then are not; this is forever literally a miracle; a thing to strike us dumb, for we have no word to speak about it."

So we can understand this case of a man who does not know what time is, as like that of the man who does not know what aether is. He is like one who breathes deeply to take one big breath of time, hoping to get wind of it in this way. And he would like to know how out of so much time and a trowel to make a star.

There, now I think I know what it is that this man who does not know what time is, does not know. He also did not get the drift.

FOURTH SYMPOSIUM

MIND AND BODY: OPENING NOTE
Peter A. French

PARAPSYCHOLOGY AND DUALISM
Roland Walker

MIND/BODY AND 'PSI'
Michael Scriven and J. G. Pratt

MINDS AND MYSTIFICATIONS
A. G. N. Flew

MATTER, MIND AND PRECOGNITION
A. Campbell Garnett and G. I. Mavrodes

"Why there is hardly enough of me left to make one respectable person!"

MIND AND BODY: OPENING NOTE

Peter A. French

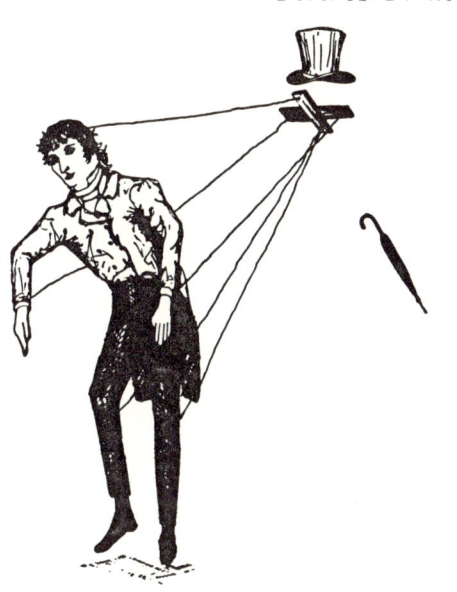

The mind-body problem is one of the oldest in our intellectual history and has probably led to the expense of more printers' ink than any other philosophical issue. Briefly, the problem is one of definition and exposition. First it is concerned with the definition of a man, and secondly it involves the attempt to work out the implications of various definitions of man. Generally there have been two basic kinds of answers to the question, "What sort of entity is a man?" The majority of contemporary thinkers seem to have opted for some form of materialist monism, the view that man is not a composite entity but is essentially a physical entity. Nonetheless, there has been a strong and vocal philosophical tradition dating at least from Plato which has maintained that descriptions and/or explanations of human behavior are in certain cases incomplete if they are composed only of sentences about physical entities. It is argued that no account of man is adequate which does not include reference to a non-physical entity, usually called a mind, but sometimes, a soul, and its peculiar mental workings, e.g. thinking, intending, imagining, etc.[1] The mind-body problem has usually then been posed as the question, What is the relationship between a man's mind and his body?

The general assumption on which the dualist view rests is that men have, or more accurately men *are*, minds, totally non-physical entities, and that they also *have*, but are not, bodies. Exactly what is involved in the concept of a non-physical entity is, however, far from obvious; and how that entity operates in conjunction with a physical entity is equally uncertain. Difficulties inherent in this concept of mind as well as the difficulties involved in the attempt to explain the relationship between mental activity and physical activity[2] have contributed to dualism's lack of popularity in the present day. Purported evidences of psychical powers and phenomena, however, seem, at least on certain interpretations of their import, to suggest strongly that man has capacities which cannot solely be attributed to the workings of a physical entity. Note, for example, the remarks of J. B. Rhine:

> When we find that ESP transcends distance and time and that PK transcends distance and mass relations, there is no doubt we come upon a clean break with the physical tradition in the science of living beings. Here is something that is not of the physical universe; it is extraphysical.[3]

In another article Rhine writes:

> The ESP and PK experiments introduce a radically different type of evidence which opposes this trend toward a wholly physical interpretation of man. For ESP, as has long been established, does not fit into a physical mode of description. It is not subject to decline with the square of the distance. It is independent of angles and barriers, and even of the dimension of time. And the PK work, as far as it has gone, confirms this evidence. It shows that the mental system has a determinative influence which produces registrable effects without any conceivable physical intermediation. These effects reveal the stamp of intelligent purpose and do so in a way that is nonetheless physically a cause-effect phenomenon. A type of lawfulness peculiar to mind and contrary to physics is increasingly evident in the ESP and PK researchers.[4]

Of course many dedicated psychical researchers do not agree with Rhine's account and instead argue that a purely physicalist explanation of the facts of ESP will one day be forthcoming. Regardless of such opinion, however, Rhine's view that parapsychology provides evidence which makes more likely the correctness of the dualist view of man's nature has attracted many philosophers. Consequently, although it surely cannot be considered the main or sole reason a confirmed dualist might set forth in support of his views, the "evidence" of psychical research has played an exemplifying role in the anti-monistic writings of such philosophers as C. D. Broad, H. H. Price, C. J. Ducasse and H. D. Lewis.

Dualism and especially that form of dualism, interactionism, which pervades our popular literature and lies firmly embedded in our ordinary usage of language, is first and foremost a philosophical theory, thus evidence of the "scientific" sort is not straightforwardly relevant to deciding upon its merits as a theory of man's nature. Ludwig Wittgenstein remarked on the peculiar character of philosophical problems:

> It was true to say that our considerations could not be scientific ones. It was not of any possible interest to us to find out empirically "that, contrary to our preconceived ideas, it is possible to think such and such"—whatever that may mean ... description gets its light, that is to say its purpose, from the philosophical problems. These are, of course, not empirical problems: they are solved, rather, by looking into the workings of our language, and that in such a way as to make us recognize those workings: *in despite of* an urge to misunderstand them. The problems are solved, not by giving new information, but by arranging what we have always known. Philosophy is a battle against the bewitchment of our intelligence by means of language.[5]

This symposium is a philosophical investigation of the dualist theory and its relationship to the subject matter of parapsychology.

NOTES

1. Rene Descartes wrote: Because I know certainly that I exist, and that meanwhile I do not remark that any other thing necessarily pertains to my nature or essence, excepting that I am a thinking thing, I rightly conclude that my essence consists solely in the fact that I am a thinking thing (or a substance whose whole essence or nature is to think.) And although possibly (or rather certainly, as I shall say in a moment) I possess a body with which I am very intimately conjoined, yet because, on the one side, I have a clear and distinct idea of myself inasmuch as I am only a thinking and unextended thing, and as, on the other, I possess a distinct idea of body, inasmuch as it is only an extended and unthinking thing, it is certain that this I (that is to say, my soul by which I am what I am), is entirely and absolutely distinct from my body, and can exist without it (*Meditations*, 1641).

2. Gilbert Ryle has called dualism the myth of the Ghost in the Machine. See *The Concept of Mind*, London: Hutchison, 1948, chapter 1.

And John Passmore writes: Mind and body are supposed to differ not only in properties, as an explosion differs from a lighted match, but in ontological status; the conditions which have to be fulfilled by a mind in order to exist, on the traditional theory, are entirely different from those which have to be fulfilled by a physical object. To assert that a physical body exists is to say that something is going on at a particular time in a particular place, something which is describable in principle by physical laws. To say that a mind exists is to say that at a particular time, but not in a particular place, something is happening which is describable only by spiritual laws, e.g., by teleological as distinct from efficient causality. Then the difficulty can be put thus: it has to be granted that in some sense the mind influences the body and vice versa. But the only force the mind has at its disposal is spiritual force, the power of rational persuasion; and the only thing that can move it is a purpose. On the other side, a body has no force at its disposal except material force and nothing can influence it except mechanical pressure. This means that bodies cannot appeal to minds to act; they can only push; and minds cannot influence bodies by putting purposes before them, because bodies are not susceptible to this sort of influence. So there is no possible way in which one could influence the other. We cannot nominate any particular place—whether it be the pineal gland or the synapse—where mind interacts with body, because mind is no more in that place, nor next to it, than anywhere else. Yet if once we say that mind itself is spatial, subject to physical force, capable of exercising physical force, and so on, the supposed ontological contrast breaks down (*Philosophical Reasoning,* New York: Basic Books, 1961, p. 54).

3. "Parapsychology and Dualism," *Journal of Parapsychology*, Vol. 9, 1945, p. 226.

4. "ESP, PK and the Survival Hypothesis," *Journal of Parapsychology*, Vol. 7, 1943, pp. 224-226.

5. *P. I.*, sec. 109.

PARAPSYCHOLOGY AND DUALISM

Roland Walker

This is primarily a reaffirmation of faith in the mechanistic hypothesis as a firm base for the exploration of reality. The need for such reaffirmation may be doubted when the faith has almost become dogma to the great majority of scientists, including the embryologists and psychologists to whom vitalism or dualism might be most persuasive. However, when phenomena, such as those of "extrasensory perception," lead to dualistic formulations like those of J. B. Rhine, it is time to reexamine assumptions and their consequences.

Mechanism and Dualism

The idea of mechanism is here meant to include the full range of integrated causality. It is not dreamed that we will soon be able to interpret all of biology in terms of the chemistry of the periodic table. The concept of emergence has been fruitful: there are levels of integration whose complexity demands laws that are not inherent in the nature of molecules or neurons, yet must depend on the simpler or more fundamental laws.

When the idea of emergent evolution was relatively fresh, it may have seemed to be something different. To some of the embattled vitalists or mechanists of the time, it may have seemed a neuter; and some vitalists may even have thought of it as an ally against the cruder forms of mechanism. Now that the lines of dispute have been revised, most of the present generation are glad to accept the idea of emergence as a necessary refinement of the mechanistic concept. Even though laws of a complex system may not be directly inferred from molecular behavior, as soon as a firm relationship is empirically established between the laws of different levels, they then become part of the web of causality.

The mechanistic hypothesis, then, extrapolates this trend of increasing integration in our understanding: nature is one and continuous; laws when adequately refined will be generally applicable at their own levels; one may expect to relate the various levels of the scientific system, approaching the state where understanding of causal relationships will form a continuous fabric. This hypothesis specifically excludes dualism. There is no need for extraphysical entities when the fabric of causality is closely woven. Occam's razor removes the nap.

In the wider sense, science is the search for integration—for the unification of the present and future islands of scientific activity. Just as in the individual experiment a single result has little meaning until brought into a pattern with

This selection is reprinted from *The Scientific Monthly*, Vol. 79 (July, 1954), 1-9. Used by permission of the editors of *Science*.

others, so in the larger area of science, even when empirical relationships at a given level are well formulated, we feel that any "explanation" is incomplete until it relates to an already consolidated body of knowledge. But the razor of William of Occam (which trims away unnecessary postulates) must be used with discretion; while taking off the fuzz, it may cut the fabric of reality. Though the smoothest formulation is not necessarily the truest, the razor has been useful in reducing science to a closely woven discipline. However, if a dualist does not want a unified discipline he may decline use of the razor.

Unresolved differences in a scientific or philosophic controversy may depend on the choice of axioms, on the selection and weighting of "facts" to be considered, on the logic, and on relative satisfaction with alternative conclusions. Faith in axioms may determine conclusions, or vice versa, with equal logic. Since the differences between mechanism and dualism seem to be axiomatic, the emphasis in this discussion will be on the logic of some interpretations from data gathered by parapsychologists.

Parapsychology

The phenomena under investigation in the field of parapsychology ("psi phenomena") include both "extrasensory perception" (ESP, which includes both telepathy and clairvoyance) and "psychokinesis" (PK, a subject's influence on a physical system without any known intermediate physical energy). Also involved in some ESP is precognition or some other warping of the normally understood time sequence in causality. Some of these phenomena have been part of literature and folklore through the centuries, and there have been attempts to gather and authenticate records. To the individual, a premonition of the death of a loved one, with circumstantial details later realized, may be utterly convincing. However, such anecdotal cases are seldom convincing to the scientific skeptic who considers the chances of such reports as compared with the numbers of vivid dreams unfulfilled and forgotten. For this reason, parapsychologists have built an imposing structure of experimental attack on the questions of the reality and nature of psi phenomena. Under the prod of skepticism, there have been refinements in technique, in experimental design, and in statistical treatment; and experiments are still being repeated and extended.

One of the largest series of experiments uses cards with special symbols: a pack of 25 with five each of five different symbols. The subject tries to specify the symbols when the faces are not visible. With an expectation of five correct "guesses" in 25 any statistical excess of correct answers may be considered as due to the influence of extrasensory perception. The statistical excess is generally small so that large numbers of runs are necessary for statistical assurance. This thin margin has, however, given cumulative assurance satisfying to many skeptical critics.

Comparable experiments in psychokinesis may involve attempts to influence the fall of dice by will. Here, there have been precautions to neutralize any possible bias of the dice by rotating the choice of target face and precautions that "will" cannot be read into mechanical skills, even though subconscious. This has meant that the subject is removed from contact with the rolling mechanism.

Experimental design has had to avoid confusion of will between the experimenter or recorder and the subject. Again a statistical margin of success has been repeatedly reported.

In both ESP and PK experiments, there has been cross-analysis of the results from many points of view. One startling result from reanalysis of ESP experiments is that, sometimes, when statistical success is low with respect to the target cards the same series may show high statistical "success" with respect to the card preceding or following the target. Subjects differ in psi capacity, and individuals fluctuate in capacity. Since no quantitative analysis of the whole population for psi capacity is being attempted, it is fair enough that study of the nature of the phenomena should be concentrated on favorable subjects.

Meaning and Interpretation

J. B. Rhine, the leader of the school of para-psychology in this country, is an enthusiast. He has been indefatigable in experiment, in organizing the activities of others, in bringing to bear as many converging lines of evidence as possible on the problems of the field, and finally in interpreting the results and publicizing them against great inertia or resistance on the part of the scientific public. Because the work of his school is the best known in this country, and because of the wide publicity for his interpretations and attempts to give philosophic meaning to these experiments, it seems well to examine some of his arguments.

Since the immediate question is on logic and philosophy, experimental design and statistics will not be closely examined here. Although some careful skeptics are still not satisfied with some of the experiments, for the present it is assumed that under adequate experimental control, there is a considerable body of valid phenomena of the kind outlined in the preceding section and referred to by Rhine's school as psi phenomena. It is also assumed that some of the spontaneous pheomena of this kind are beyond coincidence. Without some faith in these assumptions, examination of the derived logic and philosophy would be irrelevant. With this limited goal it seems appropriate to consider Rhine's *The Reach of the Mind* and a few of his editorials in the *Journal of Parapsychology* rather than the original experimental reports.[1] *The Reach of the Mind* summarizes many experiments, and we will here accept the first conclusions. though not necessarily the further interpretations.

Words may lead us astray by changing meaning unexpectedly. Let us go to the standard glossary in the *Journal of Parapsychology:* "ESP (extrasensory perception): Response to an external event not presented to any known sense."[2] So far, good! This is defined in terms of the unknown, not the unknowable. But Rhine repeatedly emphasizes his dissatisfaction with such weak definitions. "Extrasensory perception in human beings is not *merely* perception ... that is not yet accounted for on sensory grounds. It is more than a negatively defined phenomenon."[3]

An editorial by Rhine appeals for cooperation by zoologists in extending the study of psi phenomena to animals.[4] On first reading, the introductory paragraphs seem to be a fair statement of a job that needs doing, and there is presented a good sample of the many unexplained areas of animal behavior. such as direction-finding in migration and homing. This field has been partly worked by von Frisch,[5] Griffin,[6] Matthews,[7] and many others, but if parapsychologists can suggest fruitful extensions of experiments, so much the better. However, the elegant experiments of von Frisch with bees and of Griffin with bats have extended our understanding of the *senses* beyond what was conceived before and have, thereby, reduced the scope of the unknowable. Surely parapsychologists would give due honor to such experiments, but apparently this appeal for cooperation is motivated by interest in the areas of unknown causation; here the multiplication of unsuccessful attempts to implicate the senses may "prove" the existence of psi in animals.

A recurrent confusion is epitomized by "the fact that psi is extrasensory";[8] or again, "...we find behavior that can be accounted for by nothing else that is *known and experimentally verified* except extrasensory perception.... It is the only *known* principle that is adequate."[9] If we start with the definition "... not presented to any known sense" and then consider the experiments (cards are "read" without sight, hearing, touch, and so forth), and if the success is statistically better than chance, then this is ESP according to the definition, and a fact; fair enough. But many such little facts add up to a big fact or principle, and now "psi" changes from a label for unknown factors concerned in a class of phenomena to a principle, to a metaphysical entity. And at the same time, the term *extrasensory* has changed its meaning: it is not merely that the sense mechanism is unknown, but that there is no sense mechanism (which does not appear fron the experiments); and by faith that there is no causal relationship in the usual physical sense we have proved that psi is extraphysical. A large part of the doubtful philosophic superstructure of parapsychology is built over this gap between the words and the experiments from which they should have taken their meaning. Rhine also says:

> ... if it should turn out that psi is a general property of living organisms ... this would identify an extraphysical function with life itself. Since psi offers the one scientific challenge thus far presented to the physicalistic theory of the organism, the substantiation of this hypothesis would at least open the way for the possibility of an extrasomatic element in the personality that might survive organic death.[10]

This yearning for evidence of immortality is expressed again and again, together with faith in the demonstrability of free will by means of psi.

Rhine has repeatedly stressed that extrasensory perception is not *merely* perception that is not yet accounted for on sensory grounds. "One positive identifying characteristic of ESP is the familiar fact that ESP in man is an unconscious function . . . and sensory perception conscious."[11] This criterion seems doubtful, for there are some sensory modalities that make very poor contact with consciousness. The kinesthetic and equilibratory functions in man are weakly transmitted to consciousness but are highly effective reflexively. And in sleep and anesthesia, some integrated response to sensation persists after unconsciousness. A possible quibble, on whether these sensations are "perceived," is irrelevant here, for Rhine has insisted on the unconsciousness of extrasensory *perception*. Besides, he asks for studies of psi in animals. He suggests that, although we cannot verify consciousness in animals, we should *expect* to find ESP in lower orders of living things as a presensory mode of orientation. Why should we expect, and how could we know?

For further identification of psi phenomena in animals (beyond the failure of proof of sensory mediation), Rhine suggests a constellation of peculiarities in human psi experiments with parallels in work on orientation of rats and mice: (i) extreme elusiveness (only marginal deviation from chance); (ii) best effects with a limited number of trials per day (pitch of motivation); (iii) some animals are without the ability, high-scoring animals being rare; (iv) a change of trend after a certain number of trials; (v) a consistent avoiding reaction in some mice and rats (that is, less than chance score); (vi) a tendency for a high rate of success at the start, followed by a drop.[12] He puts forward these similarities as merely suggestive, but surely a compounding of elusiveness with fluctuation and variability does not give greater assurance of a common nature of the underlying factor. Since every one of these items is a divergence from the "ideal" of high scores, this almost sounds like "things unequal to the same thing are equal to each other." Are such marginal functions in mice and men to be the foundation stones of assurance of immortality?

Homing in Pigeons

Before we leave the question of psi phenomena in animals, it may be of interest to discuss briefly one biological problem, such as homing in pigeons, where there is as yet no sure explanation of the mechanisms, and where there is active traffic both in experiments and hypotheses. It has long been known that specially bred and trained homing pigeons tend to return to their lofts from considerable distances, beyond the range of familiar landmarks. Is random or systematic search enough to account for the success, or do one or more specific sensory mechanisms (known or unknown) give initial orientation toward the home loft? To these possibilities, parapsychologists add the suggestion of extrasensory perception, meaning in this case real orientation but without sensory mechanism, known or unknown.

In the case of homing pigeons, the statistics of time and distance, as well as the observed tendency to initial orientation, imply more than mere search for the loft. Matthews has recently shown that, although over-all success in homing increases with age and training, the capacity for initial orientation is full-blown after minimal training and, so, is apparently innate.[13] Hypotheses of visual or kinesthetic recording of the out-journey have seemed inadequate, since the orienting tendency was not influenced by carrying pigeons in darkened cages or rotating drums.[14]

Yeagley suggested that homing might be directed toward the loft coordinates in a grid formed by lines of equal vertical components of magnetic force crossing lines of latitude; and when pigeons trained to home to State College, Pa., were released in Nebraska, they tended to fly toward Kearney, Nebr., which has coordinates equivalent to those of State College. Though no receptor is known for weak magnetic fields, Yeagley seemed to get disorientation by fixing magnets to the pigeons' wings.[15]

Matthews and others, however, have got contrary results.[16] For the latitude component of Yeagley's hypothesis, Ising had already suggested that the inner ear might interpret the Coriolis effect of the earth's rotation.[17] However, both vertical and horizontal components of this effect are so very slight, as compared with gravity or with other inertial forces incident to flight, that both Matthews and Griffin have discounted this hypothesis on theoretical grounds.[18]

Beecher has tried to interpret a "gyrocompass" effect from the action of Coriolis forces of the semicircular canals, but his interpretation is based on two misconceptions: that the inertia effects work in an independent *semi*circular canal (ignoring the full-circle communication through the utriculus); and that the horizontal component of the Coriolis effect in the Northern Hemisphere is always to the east (instead of to the right, whatever the direction of horizontal motion).[19]

Some form of sun navigation has long been suspected, since pigeons do not home at night and are disoriented by heavy overcast. The standard conditions of pigeon racing involve training along one compass line and racing from an extension of the same line. This might suggest a fairly simple sun-angle clue, especially if releases are at the same time of day. Kramer and St. Paul, after training pigeons along a single line, concluded from the off-line test, in which most pigeons preferred the training direction to the actual loft bearing, that there was a direction sense.[20] Though under these conditions the pigeons might have been trained to a relatively simple sun angle, to the neglect of their other abilities, Yeagley had already pointed out the necessity of around-the-compass training to develop homing to definite coordinates.[21]

Matthews has recently reexamined this problem and by the statistics of orientation from the release point, he has shown that more than simple sun angle is involved.[22] There was significant orientation from releases off the training line at times of day other than those of training releases; and also when pigeons had been kept from view of the sun until the minute of release. Matthews' hypothesis is that, from the small arc of sun movement during the minutes of orientation, the pigeon extrapolates the curve to its highest point (south, local noon); that this noon altitude is compared with home noon altitude to give latitude difference; and that the difference in azimuth at noon (or a direct time difference) gives longitude difference. Matthews got confirmation by keeping birds from view of the sun for 6 days before the September equinox, when sun altitude was changing most rapidly.[23] At the time of release, this dislocation of the sun from its remembered position induced a corresponding error in orientation. And when physiological time was thrown off by several days of irregular periods of artificial light, temperature change, and feeding, he reduced the pigeons' orientation to random. After careful discussion of the difficulties, Matthews concludes that visual acuity, angle measurement, and time sense are probably adequate for this hypothesis, which is otherwise well supported by his experiments.

Even though sun navigation, according to Matthews' hypothesis, seems the best present explanation of much of the pigeon's orientation capacity, such navigation may be supplemented or submerged under special training conditions; it is supplemented for homing by local pilotage to recognized landmarks; and it is obviously inapplicable to the orientation of night-migrant species. Really, the alternative hypotheses of pigeon orientation have not been excluded but merely made highly improbable: we are unwilling to believe that kinesthetic recording of the out-journey can take account of as many irregular movements as have been superposed. Though the results of experiments with magnets are equivocal, the logic of "disproof," if magnets should not disturb orientation, would depend on disbelief that a small background magnetic effect could be read through gross experimental fluctuations. So also our experience of sense-organ thresholds makes us doubt whether the inner ear could get Coriolis compass clues not overwhelmed by gravitational and chance inertial effects. Finally, however, though Matthews' hypothesis of sun navigation seems to be well supported experimentally, it rests on assumptions of fine measurements of angles and time which, before the event, most of us would have ruled out as equally improbable.

Into this flux of ideas, extrasensory perception is introduced as a possible explanation for direction-finding. Pratt now proposes an experiment to test ESP: instead of training from a fixed loft, one might train pigeons from a mobile loft with three habitual stations, perhaps 10 miles apart at the points of a triangle.[24] The experimental flights would determine whether the pigeons could choose the direction of the new station to which the loft had been moved. This proposal has the real merit of going beyond the usual assumption and asking a testable question: Is homing really to the "remembered" space coordinates, or is there something about the loft *per se* that is perceived when out of visual (?) range? One who is tradition-bound might doubt, before the event, whether the answer would be in the latter sense. If there is such homing to a new location (and there are equivalent anecdotes of dogs "psi-trailing" their masters), there will really be something to think about. To the mechanist, this would leave a lot to be explained; to a dualistic parapsychologist ESP would be the explanation —Q.E.D.

Therein lies one major point of this discussion. If the difference between mechanism and dualism is essentially in choice of axioms, what consequences are likely to follow from the two attitudes? If Pratt should perform this experiment and get striking results consonant with his ESP hypothesis, probably he or other parapsychologists would repeat and extend the experiments. Such further investigation would be partly for self-assurance, and to confirm the results against skeptical criticism, and partly to define the conditions and limits of the phenomena, but would hardly be to look for the explanation. The "explanation" is already there. A mechanist confronted by such results would feel that he lacked an explanation. He would hope to design further experiments, especially to test the nature of the causal relationship between the loft (abstracted from a constant location) and the pigeon's behavior. Explanation should relate to some known physical or physiological systems. If imagination should fail, or the tests prove inconclusive, or time or energy run out, the problem would be filed with unfinished business. A mechanist would not think that, because the file is labeled, he may write Q.E.D. One may propose as virtues in science (however poorly realized) the continued tension of search, and the constant remembrance of the gaps between evidence and interpretation and of the gaps between proved relationships and the other areas of knowledge. Q.E.D. is a punctuation point for mathematics and logic rather than a goal of the material sciences. It is a symbol for tension relaxed, a scientific nirvana.

Extraphysical Functions

Rhine discusses not merely "extrasensory" perception but also "extraphysical" relationships between the external world and the extracerebral mind. Again, we seem to find that the word *extraphysical* is used to blow hot or cold at will. We find clear statements of dualism, later vaguely qualified, and apparently ending with "relative dualism." Against the challenge of materialism he says:

> The real issue, however, is not merely one of whether or not psi phenomena can be explained by *physical* principles. It is rather a question of whether man is a relatively simple, one-system creature or whether he has the much greater complexity attaching to a combination of two different systems of lawful operations.[25]

This is qualified:

> The kind of absolute dualism that drove psychology into the arms of physics is concededly not defensible. . . . Fears of absolute pluralism should not blind the scholar to distinctions that are matters of experimental observation. . . . Rather, observations should lead back from the phenomena to the underlying causal nexus in some deeper-lying substratum where the basis of unification can be discovered. Thus faith in the integrety of the universe may be restored for those who are worried about it.[26]

This sop to the feelings of the mechanists is just pushing the same problem one step further back if the substratum is below the level of physical causality. This substratum becomes the mystical entity if it is not observable; if it becomes part of the fabric of causality, the concept of "physical" may be extended.

The term *energy* is used with vague or fluctuating meaning. Besides the known physical energies, there is according to Rhine, a psychic energy that does not affect the senses and does not produce effects directly related to time, space, and mass. "There is to our knowledge, however, nothing but a psi phenomenon that appears to defy all these criteria of physical operation and at the same time displays intelligent purposes in the process."[27]

What is meant by the independence of psi from space-time-mass? In each bit of evidence offered, we see, not a logical exclusion of the physical influence, but a failure to explain such influence. In telepathic experiments, almost equally good results have been recorded with the agent and percipient in adjacent rooms or separated by the Atlantic; in physical experiments, any influence should fall off with distance; ergo, this experiment shows ESP to be independent of distance (space) and, so non-physical.

With respect to independence of mass relationships, psychokinetic experiments are cited.[28] In experiments with large and small dice of the same material, there was often no significant difference, but in one series there was higher success with larger dice: "just the opposite of what one might expect from a physical theory." Likewise with dice of equal volume, higher success was obtained with those of greater density (metal versus wood). And in both of these series, it is suggested that the difference may be due to preference on the part of the subjects. But here *are* physical differences related to the results, yet the results are dismissed because they are contrary to a naive, *a priori* concept of the unknown physical system. Both here and in long-distance ESP, if we do not know what physical forces are working, or how, is it fair to say that, if they were working, it must be by the simplest system imaginable; and if this first hypothesis does not work, that the system is extraphysical? We might recall some of the children's paradoxes, such as the downward jet of air through a hollow cone which lifts a ball into the throat of the cone; unless one knows how the forces are channeled, it is unsafe to draw large conclusions.

Rhine says that the physics of tomorrow is a pointless speculation; that the parapsychology of tomorrow may add further to the difficulties of a physical explanation; that we must think in terms of present knowledge, both in physics and in parapsychology.[29] No! There would have been slow scientific advance if we had not sought explanations for phenomena uninterpretable at the time. When Rhine says that "Every conceivable counterexplanation has been considered and found inapplicable to the findings,"[30] we must take exception. If we accept the pattern of phenomena labeled ESP and PK, we must continue to look for mechanisms and so hope to augment the physics of tomorrow and enlarge the scope of the conceivable.

Mind and Brain

Since parapsychology developed in relation to questions of human personality, the most obvious context of dualism here is the mind-brain relationship. Rhine has stressed this as a fundamental problem: "It is this higher stratum of the personality dominating through intelligent volition the receptor effector levels of life that is the *terra propria* of psychology, a domain that stands clear of physiology."[31] Most of the logic of his "relative dualism" is based on the supposed demonstration that the psi phenomena are extrasensory and extraphysical, meaning again not "have not yet been explained," but "will never be explained in terms of the senses or of physics."

Certainly there is at present no agreement among neurologists or philosophers on whether the mind is something beyond the functional and subjective aspects of the brain (or better, of the body). This may be clearly seen in a series of BBC broadcast talks on *The Physical Basis of Mind*, an attempt to summarize knowledge and express convictions for the lay public.[32] Both the neurologists and the philosophers, all considering about the same range of evidence (differently evaluated), show the full range from mechanism to dualism. Sir Charles Sherrington and Viscount Samuel reiterate most explicitly the Aristotelian query of how the mind is attached to the body; a dichotomy is assumed. Even Penfield, a neurosurgeon, after making an elegant, brief mechanistic interpretation of the brain's activity, concludes: "...something else finds its dwelling-place between the sensory complex and the motor mechanism ... there is a switchboard operator as well as a switchboard."[33] This final twist is given no support beyond a patient's subjective feeling that the movements induced by electric stimulation of his motor cortex are not by his will. Some of the neurologists make mechanistic exposition of their data without discussing the philosophy, but others have specifically indicated the semantic pitfalls. Zuckerman says: "If mind is conceived of as something which interacts with body—or as some parallel manifestation to body—the scientist may be misled into trying to solve problems which may prove unreal."[34]

A stimulating symposium on *Cerebral Mechanisms in Behavior* is less for the lay public than shoptalk between neurologists and psychologists trying to come to common terms.[35] As with most shoptalk, the philosophy is in the background, but it seems clear that these men are talking with a common faith in causality. One is impressed by the energy and eagerness of attack on a series of problems that go far beyond the older anatomy and simple reflex physiology. Some of these problems are definitely in the field of "mind" and at a level beyond the artificial simplification that once made reflex physiology almost irrelevant to psychology. This field has matured greatly in the last quarter-century; another century may still further justify the mechanistic hypothesis.

It is clear that modern physiology is revising the anatomical pattern with respect to which the ultimate question may be asked. Certainly the brain by itself is not enough. Even by old tradition, we say that under the guillotine a man loses his head, not his body. The personality is a function of the whole organism. If many of the obvious nervous correlates of mental activity seem to be concentrated in the head, and if the cerebral cortex of man seems to be at the top of a hierarchy, we still cannot consider the cortex as independent of its sensory input or its motor discharge patterns. Many of these motor patterns are already functioning on a genetic or conditioned basis at a subcortical, even spinal, level. Their spontaneous, repetitive, or sequential nature depends on feedback by reverberating circuits, and these patterns are then modulated by cortical activity. Sperry has suggested that a motor approach to the mind-brain problem may be more fruitful than the traditional sense-centered approach to perception: operational adjustment is more significant than impressed sensory patterns, and conscious unity means that the brain becomes adjusted to deal with the perceived object as a unit.[36]

When Rhine suggests that only by research can we find whether the cerebrocentric or psychocentric view is correct, we may assent. In the meantime our thinking will be guided by something less than complete proof. Rhine seems to derive conviction from his experiments and from philosophic deductions based on ambiguous words. On the other side, though equally without logical proof, there is much of human dignity in the valedictory of C. J. Herrick after a lifetime of research, *A Neurologist Makes Up His Mind:*

> ... this mind is something that I have made ... it is an active part of me, something that I am doing.... My conscious motives, what I want, what I work for, and my ideas about it, are actually caused by previous events.... But my mind is not something ... detachable from my body.... The biologist as biologist cannot be a dualist.... All nature as he knows it is an orderly unit, and anything outside of this integrated ... system ... is unnatural and therefore out of reach by the method of natural science.... For as Dr. Cannon has graphically shown, there is a wisdom of the body and, as I maintain, there is no other kind of wisdom.[37]

Free Will

Closely related to the concept of mind is the problem of free will, and here Rhine has met (or made) a paradox. He concludes that there is evidence for precognition (psi phenomena are thus independent of time as well as of space and mass). In the present preliminary state of experimentation, the range of accuracy of precognition is not yet known. He sees that if it were 100-percent accurate, and if everyone had full precognition, then events must be completely predetermined; there could be no free will. But limited precognition is made into an argument for free will:

> Half of the social toxicity of the cerebrocentric view of man lies in the fact that it allows no true volitional freedom ... the ESP and PK experiments show that the mind has freedom from physical law. In fact these researches offer the only clear-cut evidence available that can help in the solution of the problem of ethical freedom. They give an experimental basis for a satisfactory 'freedom ratio' or latitude of self-regulation enjoyed by the mind.[38]

This is a circular argument. It is clear that Rhine considers free will as urgently desirable, socially. But what is this socially desirable free will? Surely not merely an ability to perceive at a distance or in the future, or to exert influence without known physical intermediation; and these are all that the experiments seem to show. But too much precognition would be the gift of Cassandra, and since that would be repugnant and unthinkable, we must accept the evidence for a satisfactory freedom ratio.

E. W. Sinnott, in *Cell and Psyche: The Biology of Purpose,* develops a thesis:

> ... that biological organization (concerned with organic development and physiological activity) and psychical activity (concerned with behavior and thus leading to mind) *are fundamentally the same thing.* To talk about 'mind' in a bean plant ... is more defensible than trying to place an arbitrary point on the evolutionary scale where mind, in some mysterious manner, made its appearance.[39]

Not only mind, but purpose too is continuous throughout the evolutionary scale; purpose is a special aspect of self-regulating systems. "Homeostasis ... is the satisfaction of our most basic desires."[40] Minnaert extends this idea to astronomy: a star also is a homeostatic system; no entelechy is needed for the maintenance of equilibrium, since existing systems are those that have historically established such equilibria; explanations must be sought in cosmogony or phylogeny.[41] Minnaert, like Sinnott, stresses organization as a basic concept, but he extends it beyond living systems.

Sinnott feels that he has sidetracked the mind-body dualism by showing mind and body to be two aspects of one problem, and that the real issue of freedom is the question of what it is that sets up self-regulating systems and, thus, creates purposes. The interrelated philosophic problems, if sidetracked, are temporarily left where most modern mechanists could not object. But somehow the meaning of free will is blurred if we say that we and beans are free to circumvent, if we can, any obstructions to our mechanistically determined purposes (inborn, conditioned, or more subtly come by). We are free to desire what we must desire. After this essentially mechanistic analysis Sinnott ends up with some poetic aspirations and a statement of preference for an aggressive idealism over the usual materialistic position. It is hard to see the relationship between this and his preceding analysis. It almost seems as though he and Rhine had arrived at a similar "relative dualism" by very different routes. Rhine, incidentally has used Sinnott's hypothesis of biological continuity of mind and purpose to suggest a wider field for psi phenomena.[42] Again we may wonder whether he is really careful of the distinction between psi phenomena and psi as a mystical non-physical principle. Is he willing to assimilate the psi concept to the mechanistic analysis of Sinnott and Minnaert?

Scientific Recognition

Rhine is distressed at the reluctance of scientists in various fields to recognize the work of parapsychologists. Besides the inertia or ignorance or lack of interest, there has been active opposition. As with any controversial subject, experiments have been criticized, the statistics brought into question and there have even been imputations of bias. If the results seemed valid, there were still some who sulked and went back to *a priori* denial or, as in the present case, criticized the logic of the conclusions. All this has seemed to Rhine to be an irrational, unscientific defense of entrenched prejudice. This question is again timely in the light of a survey whose results have recently been published by Warner[43] and discussed by Rhine.[44]

The questionnaire on psychological opinion of ESP was addressed to a good sample of Fellows of the American Psychological Association and was similar to one sent to psychologists 14 years before. The distribution of answers, too, was surprisingly similar to that for the previous questionnaire: about three-quarters still consider ESP either a remote possibility or merely an unknown. However, the answers indicating acceptance of ESP as an established fact or a likely possibility rose from 8 percent to 16 percent, while those considering it an impossibility dropped from 14 to 10 percent. This seems to Rhine a thin return for 14 years of effort. He is particularly disturbed that in each survey about 20 percent of the respondents admit to basing their opinions on purely *a priori* grounds. Actually 32 percent have put in an *a priori* objection, but this merely accentuates the point.

Rhine tries to analyze possible reasons for the psychologists' reluctance. Perhaps they are just not good scientists for not looking at the evidence? Perhaps the parapsychologists have been impolitic in overzealous claims for the significance of their work? Neither of these, nor the two together, can account for the whole situation.

> Psychology cannot accept ESP and still hold to a physicalistic philosophy of man.... Psychology's difficulty over ESP is concerned not with the evidence—neither its amount nor its quality—but with its implication for his philosophy.[45]

One may agree so far, and yet reject the next step in which he implies that the doubters let their philosophic position determine whether or not empirical findings are acceptable. It becomes pertinent to reexamine the questionnaire. The key questions are in the form: "In your opinion, is 'extrasensory perception' a likely possibility?" and so forth. If the question is thus nakedly put, without definition or qualification, how is the respondent to know whether he is asked to judge ESP phenomena or the philosophic doctrine erected thereon? The statistics of the answers become meaningless. Indeed, it is clear from the written-in comments, of which Warner gives a sample, that several have consciously wrestled with that problem before committing themselves to any answer. Some have accepted the empirical findings but have rejected the term *extrasensory perception* as a prejudiced interpretation. In spite of these comments, Rhine seems to ignore their significance.

Undoubtedly, there are many "scientists" with closed minds. And it is likely true that prejudice in academic departments and scientific journals has made less easy the investigation of parapsychological problems and their publication. But many whom Rhine suspects of prejudice may be glad to examine the evidence while reserving judgment on the interpretations. If neurophysiologists or students of sensory perception or of animal behavior see the opportunities in this field, they may well help to bridge the gap. But if they are persuaded that no bridge should be found, why should they try? Although cooperation by neurophysiologists might be good, Rhine has a more urgent interest in the study of psi phenomena: *"what other scientific basis is there for challenging materialism?"* [his italics].[46]

In the field of parapsychology, there is much still to be explained. There are problems with human interest, with dramatic overtones, and with fundamental questions for psychology, physiology, and physics. Not only Rhine and his colleagues but many others are pursuing this important work. Assuming that the experimental findings have demonstrated some valid patterns of phenomena, it becomes important that their meaning be understood. Here it seems that Rhine's enthusiasm has led to too free derivation of consequences from the experiments.

The focus of attention in this article has been on these interpretations rather than on the experiments. It will be agreed that in parapsychology, as in all of science, much is still unknown; concerning the unknowable, we may not agree. Given time and effort, we have faith that, without resort to mystical entities, what is now unknown may be woven, thread by thread, into the fabric of scientific understanding.[47]

NOTES

1. (New York: William Sloane Associates, 1947).
2. Vol. 16 (1952): 300.
3. Vol. 15 (1950): 244.
4. *Ibid.*
5. K. v. Frisch, *Bees: Their Vision, Chemical Senses, and Language* (Ithaca: Cornell University Press, 1950).
6. D. R. Griffin, *American Scientist*, Vol. 41 (1953): 209.
7. G. V. T. Matthews, *Journal of Experimental Biology*, Vol. 28 (1951): 508; Vol. 30 (1953): 243.
8. Vol. 15: 230.
9. *Ibid.*, p. 247.
10. *Ibid.*, p. 231.
11. *Ibid.*, p. 244.
12. L. Vogelberg and F. Kruger, *Z. Tierpsychol.*, Vol. 8 (1951): 293; W. Newhouse, *Z. Tierpsychol.*, Vol. 7 (1950): 380.
13. *Journal of Experimental Biology*, Vol. 30 (1953): 268.
14. Matthews, *Journal of Experimental Biology*, Vol. 28, *op. cit.*
15. H. L. Yeagley, *Journal of Applied Physiology*, Vol. 18 (1947): 1035; Vol. 22 (1951): 746.
16. Vol. 28, *op. cit.*
17. G. Ising, *Arkiv Mat. Astron. Fysik*, Vol. 32A, No. 18 (1946): 1.
18. Matthews, Vol. 28, *op. cit.*; Griffin, *op. cit.*
19. W. J. Beecher, *Science Monthly*, Vol. 75 (1952): 19.
20. G. Kramer, and U. v. St. Paul, *Z. Tierpsychol*, Vol. 7 (1950): 620.
21. H. L. Yeagley, *op. cit.*
22. G. V. T. Matthews, Vols. 28 and 30, *op. cit.*
23. Vol. 30.
24. *Journal of Parapsychology*, Vol. 17 (1953): 34.
25. *Journal of Parapsychology*, Vol. 15 (1951): 81.
26. *Ibid.*, p. 85.
27. *Ibid.*, p. 86.
28. *Ibid.*, p. 113.
29. *Reach of the Mind*, p. 62.
30. *Ibid.*, p. 151.
31. *Ibid.*, p. 152.
32. P. Laslett, Editor (Oxford: Blackwell, 1950).
33. *Ibid.*, p. 64.
34. *Ibid.*, p. 25.
35. L. A. Jeffress, Editor (New York: Wiley, 1951).
36. R. W. Sperry, *American Scientist*, Vol. 40 (1952): 291.
37. *Science Monthly*, Vol. 44 (1939): 99.
38. *Reach of the Mind*, pp. 81-82.
39. *Ibid.*, p. 220.

40. E. W. Sinnott (Chapel Hill: University of North Carolina Press, 1950), pp. 49-50.
41. *Ibid.*, p. 55.
42. M. Minnaert, *Pub. Astron. Soc. Pacific,* Vol. 63 (1951): 272.
43. Vol. 16: 225.
44. L. Warner, *Journal of Parapsychology,* Vol. 16 (1952): 284.
45. Vol. 16: 225.

MIND-BODY AND 'PSI'

Michael Scriven and J. G. Pratt

Discussion by Michael Scriven: The service I hope to perform here is to set out some of the issues and the location on the battlefield of some of the forces, introduce you to a new force about which parapsychologists have not been fully informed despite the extensive discussion of it in journals, explain the relevance of the engagement to the problem of evidence and to certain general claims about the significance of parapsychological findings, and suggest my own conclusions.

On the major issue of the relation of the mind to the body and in particular to the brain, there are—as you know—two main schools of thought, the monists and the dualists. The monists, who believe there is only one fundamental substance or type of entity involved, may decide that it is mental (the idealists), physical (the physicalists—sometimes the term "materialist" is used synonymously with physical), or of some third kind (the "neutral" monists). In any case, it appears that they have no problem of explaining how the mind and brain affect each other; since there is only one thing involved, there cannot be a problem about any causal relation, which would involve two things. Their problem is to explain why there *seems* to be a distinction between mind and body, and a correlation or causal connection between them.

The dualists accept the existence of two fundamentally different kinds of entity, and are then faced with the problem of deciding how they are related. The parallelists maintain there is a constant correlation or synchronicity between mental and physical events, but not a causal connection between them, although within each separate sequence of events there may be causal connection; the epiphenomenalists believe that all mental events are caused by physical ones, though not vice versa, and that, unlike physical events, no mental events cause other mental events; and the interactionists (as I shall interpret their position, which is sometimes ambiguous) believe that both mental and physical phenomena can cause phenomena of the same and of the other kind. I assume that "mechanism" means much the same as physicalism and materialism in contemporary philosophical parlance, but I shall try to avoid the term.

In our own field, we find Smythies as a monist, sub-species physicalist (he thinks sense-data are "end products of the causal chain of perception" and in the brain), with most of the rest being dualists; Zorab and Grey Walter being epiphenomenalists; Pratt, Rhine, Broad, and Burt being—probably—interactionists. I am pleased to say that everyone seems to agree on

This selection is reprinted from *The Journal of Parapsychology*, Vol. 25 (1961), 313-18, 14-16, 23-27. Used by permission of the editor.

two rather important propositions. (1) that there is an external world, which rules out idealism, and (2) that some mental states are caused by some physical ones, e.g., headaches by excessive drinking, which rules out parallelism.

At this stage the disagreements start. In order to keep our feet on the ground I shall take four putative phenomena, two normal and two paranormal, and examine their implications for the mind-body problem, rather than talking at the theoretical level.

As the first phenomenon, consider the existence of a correlation between mental and physical states such that every variation in the former is accompanied by a variation in the latter (though not necessarily vice versa). This is a fundamental premise for physicalism and epiphenomenalism and is not usually denied by interactionists, hence its *truth* does not decide the dispute. But if it were *false,* only interactionism could still hold. So a great deal hangs on its truth in this sense. *Is* it true? We shall return to that question in a moment. I shall also comment on the exercise of the will to command the body, which R. H. Thouless and Cyril Burt take to be the everyday case of PK, and which the epiphenomenalists and physicalists take to be an illusion; on telepathy, which Rhine and Pratt take to disprove physicalism; and on survival which is thought by Broad and Zorab to disprove both physicalism and epiphenomenalism. Let us turn to the first putative phenomenon.

Is there a separate brain-state for every mental state? We have a quite negligible amount of direct evidence for this Hypothesis of Neurophysiological Determinism, as it is sometimes called, but we certainly have no evidence to the contrary, and there is a reasonable though not overwhelming presumption in its favor stemming from the immense, though not unrestricted, success of determinism in general. It could apparently be disproved only if we could perform the physically virtually impossible experiment of observing the brain state to remain unchanged while the subject's thoughts changed. This is physically virtually impossible because the brain is never static and it is not only sustaining but also functional circuits that are in constant flux; moreover, the brain stem is almost inaccessible from complete observation, being masked by the outer layers.

Nevertheless, it appears conceivable that we might decide to abandon the Hypothesis of Neurophysiological Determinism (HND). Suppose, for example, that examination of the brain processes of individuals who come to a decision after meditation displays a condition during the meditation absolutely indistinguishable from the process during any other reflections, problem-solving, etc., terminating in a burst of activity in the centers appropriate for implementing the decision. In that case, interactionism would be in and the rest out. (I may add that it is in fact rather hard to reconcile interactionism with the HND, though interactionists rarely see this.)

Now, unless this unlikely and wholly nonparapsychological discovery is substantiated, the usual arguments in our journals will not suffice to defeat physicalism. Telepathy, for example, may be *thought* of as the influence of mind on mind, but then being in love is often thought of as a communion of souls and neither phenomenon has the least logical force against a carefully thought out position by those who are skeptical about minds or souls. For if physicalism is true, then telepathy is simply an example of a hitherto unknown inter-brain reaction which could be regarded as analogous to the discovery of magnetism. Of course, telepathy might be a useful accessory in an assault on the Hypothesis of Neurophysiological Determinism: a super telepath might be able to provide an independent check on whether a given subject *was* actually thinking when his electroencephalogram remained constant. But *only* through disproving that hypothesis could physicalism—materialism be disproved.

The same discouraging remarks must be made about the exercise of the will. If this is a case of mind affecting matter (the brain) and if interactionism is true, then it is or it could be a model for the PK effect, but until those premises are established (by disproof of HND) it can be perfectly well accounted for by the physicalists and the epiphenomenalists. It is most undesirable for parapsychologists as scientists to commit themselves to a theory of extrasensory perception which requires the falsehood of the basic tenet of neurophysiological psychology, when all our phenomena can perfectly well be handled within a framework which is consistent with it. We should not fight at the new frontiers of the brain unless we have to.

Now surely there is *one* parapsychological phenomenon which has the most direct bearing on the mind-body problem. Broad, Thouless, and Ian Stevenson have recently argued that the IPA phenomenon, or survival, demonstrates the independence of the mind from the body. Broad indeed puts it by saying that this is the absolutely crucial and only parapsychological phenomenon which counts against monism and hence materialism. To this I would say, first, that it is then quite essential we apply to the evidence here the same "back-to-bedrock" attitude I have recommended with respect to the ESP work, noticing particularly how very long it is since we had good evidence and viewing the cross-correspondences as long overdue for critical reassessment. Secondly, I would say that we must not imagine we can show water vapor is fundamentally different from water by showing that it continues to exist when we remove the saucepan of water from which it originated. The mind may be a kind of field or emanation or related form of the brain which is eventually and rarely capable of independent temporary existence. This would not prove materialism to be false or dualism true in the supposed sense. I would myself think this kind of hypothesis inherently *more* likely than a radical two-substance dualism, partly because we have many analogs for it in nature and it would permit of explanation without the introduction of special correlation laws.

I am thus suggesting that we have often been too quick to think in a stereotyped way about the interpretation of parapsychological phenomena; carefully evaluated, they count less in favor of dualism than has been usually supposed among parapsychologists, if indeed they count in that direction at all. I view this as fortunate since I think we may expect an advance of the frontiers of the brain, of materialism if you will, which could well be of the greatest service to us and should not be thought of as a threat to ESP in the way in which the advance of electromagnetic technology, exemplified by the snooperscope, was a threat to the physical mediums. There is no need to suppose that the identification of an ESP organ, or of an ESP mechanism perhaps analogous to known fields, would constitute either absorption or evaporation of our field. To discover that ESP is just as brain-dependent as abstract thought is not to discover it does not exist. Surely that point must be clear and we must not arouse opposition among neurophysiologists by behaving as if we were fundamentalists facing the development of evolutionary biologists. So far from being threatened by the subject, it can—and already has—afforded us new ideas and tools of great value. I think we have only a limited chance of survival as a science if we commit ourselves on what I see as purely dogmatic grounds to the denial of materialism. This would be the more tragic since I believe there are perfectly good logical grounds for rejecting monistic materialism. Moreover they apply to and overpower a much more sophisticated form of materialism than is usually discussed in parapsychological circles, a version which has replaced behaviorism as the philosophically "in" physicalist thesis. I add two cautions in case this sounds more exciting than it is: the weaknesses in this new version (known as the Identity Theory) are neither very novel nor in any way related to parapsychology. The plain facts of our own experience, logically analyzed, demonstrate the irreducibility of sensations to brain states. The development of the Identity Theory recently has been largely in the hands of Feigl and Smart and I shall not attempt to do more than bring it to your attention. Feigl's article "The Mental and the Physical" in *Minnesota Studies in the Philosophy of Science* (Volume II, ed. H. Feigl et al.) provides the most comprehensive exposition and a stupendous bibliography.

Dualism is true, but two questions remain. The obvious one: Which version of dualism? And an important but subtle one: How can science ever explain the fact dualism apparently must take as fundamental; viz., the existence of an enormous number of basic correlations of certain sensations, e.g., sharp shooting pain, with certain brain states? Cyril Burt sees this problem but answers it by saying these correlations would be inexplicable—just some more of the basic postulated correlations in science. But I can think of only one or two such, compared with the *embarras des richesses* psychophysical dualism yields. This is contrary to the spirit of scientific economy and yet apparently inescapable. There is just one ray of hope here. The correlations are not between two independently identifiable properties, a fact recognized in the old "Perhaps when you see green, you see what I see when I see red" puzzle. I believe this ray of hope actually sheds enough light to get us out of the dualistic darkness and into the (dualistic) light. Similarly, I think we can demonstrate the truth of interactionism as an answer to the first question—which kind of dualism should we adopt. But I only *think* this: I have not yet found or constructed such a proof.

• • •

What does "physical" mean? There are many entities in modern physics which lack the characteristics of everyday physical objects such as chairs and tables. An electromagnetic field is physical in that it is an entity of physics but it is not physical in the sense of being visible or tangible to normal senses. Obviously psi is nonphysical in the latter sense, but this would not make an interesting claim. At the moment, it is nonphysical in the first sense. But even that is not a very interesting claim, since the same was true of electromagnetic fields not so long ago. Physics is always expanding its frontiers. Now the interesting claim would be that there is some *impossibility* about the idea of a physics encompassing psi. But I see no possible way of justifying that claim any more than the claim that science could never explain the origin of life on earth.

It seems to me that a good parapsychological experiment is *by definition* one which shows there is something new under the sun, i.e., creates the necessity for *expanding* physics (and probably psychology). But it is just as misleading to assert it demonstrates the existence of something nonphysical, as it would have been for Helmholtz or Michelson or Einstein to say this of their discoveries which demonstrated the inadequacies of the physics of their day.

More remains to be done before we can assert definitely that the varied resources of contemporary physics cannot cope with psi. Even the simpler inverse-square-law forces have not been absolutely ruled out, and modern field theories have included discussions of causally reversed processes, perhaps the most awkward psi phenomenon. It need not weaken our enthusiasm for parapsychology to realize that the opposition to it is largely based on an absurdly parochial idea of the limitations of physics. We should be progressive physicalists, not reactionary anti-physicalists!

The idea of physical causation operating across a vacuum was just as repugnant to the conservatives of earlier physics as ESP is to some of our contemporaries, but the experimenters who showed that a magnet could affect iron filings in a vacuum did not claim to have discovered a nonphysical phenomenon. Yet probably a majority of parapsychologists today would make that claim about ESP. Why? I believe the real explanation is the fact that a *person* is involved in ESP, and that we are always more willing to accept the idea that *we* transcend the limitations of things. Remarkable though we are, however, we are remarkable *objects*—physical objects with some capacity for locomotion, communication, and reproduction. But it might be said that we are absolutely unique in our possession of a mind, and psi is a specifically mental, and in that sense nonphysical, phenomenon.

The mind-body problem cannot be resolved in this space, but a possible treatment of it can be stated and may be of some interest. 1. We are not unique in possessing a mind. Animals have them, and I see no impossibility in the supposition that we shall create robots or living things who also have them. 2. Mental events are not analyzable behavioristically, nor are they (though they appear to be correlated with) brain events. 3. They are sometimes caused by brain events. 4. They can sometimes correctly be said to cause other mental events and also actions, but not brain events. 5. To say that a twinge of pain (mental event) led one to go to a doctor (action) is not to deny that another entirely adequate causal explanation referring only to the brain can be told (whereas it can not be said that an adequate mental causation explanation can be given of cases where direct electrical stimulation of the brain produces mental events). 6. Any system capable of behaving like humans with respect to (i) stimulus discrimination and (ii) symbolic manipulation, has a mind.

This account is (a) dualistic, (b) materialistic, in a certain sense, (c) epiphenomenalistic, (d) interactionistic, in a certain sense, (e) novel, as far as I know. It has the following consequences:

A. ESP and PK have no relevance to it; they simply become extra powers of the mind-brain unit. But if the correlation between mental events and physical events broke down or failed to appear with respect to certain mental events, psi might become an important datum for the new mind-body problem. I am thus suggesting that the oft-quoted "absence of an ESP organ in the brain" will be eliminated either by discovery or creation, i.e., by the correct insistence that if the owner of the brain has psi faculties, and can't do without a brain, then the brain *is* the ESP organ—though I naturally expect some slightly better localization than that. Since new fields and forces may be involved, it is not significant that no organ of the usual kind has been discovered.

B. Free will is a matter of causation of a certain kind, not an absence of causation. Morality is a system of rules for behavior and attitudes with a complex but potentially rational basis. Psi is again irrelevant.

C. Post-mortem survival is made extremely implausible but not logically impossible; and here telepathy might provide the departed spirits with a providentially disembodied means of communication. Survival would simply prove the basic correlations nonuniversal; and the mind-body problem would take a new form and new solutions. (But other psi phenomena do not make survival likely.)

In summary, psi phenomena are psychological phenomena and hence—in certain aspects—physical phenomena, that appear to be of a categorically different kind from the usual phenomena of perception and causation. The difference lies in the impossibility of giving a causal account of the kind enshrined in classical nineteenth-century physics (as clearly demonstrated by Professor Broad), and has no relevance whatsoever to the mind-body relationship as I conceive it, nor to the freedom of the will and morality.

Discussion by J. G. Pratt: Psi phenomena include those, and only those, effects that appear not to represent physical principles, and I would agree that this, more than any other distinctive feature, defines the field.

This statement does not, as far as I can see, conflict with Prof. Broad's definition that "for a phenomenon to count as an instance of psi it is necessary and sufficient that it should conflict with one or more of several 'basic limiting principles.'" His limiting principles are themselves formulations of physical laws generally assumed to apply to the behavior of living organisms.

Still another way of defining parapsychology, which some workers seem to prefer, is simply to list the phenomena with which the research is concerned. This kind of definition is unsatisfactory, since it merely leaves unstated the principle that leads to the grouping of certain phenomena and the exclusion of others.

Of course we do not know all about the physical world at present. In this sense we cannot give a complete and final meaning to the word *physicality*. But to recognize that physics has its own frontier of knowledge is not to say that psi must be assumed to be a part of the unexplored physical world.

Since this discussion turns largely upon the meaning of words, it is essential to be explicit regarding the definition of some key concepts. *Physics* is the branch of science which deals with conditions and changes within the material universe that are capable of being described in terms of time-space-mass-energy relationships. *Physics is not synonymous with science.* If one starts with the assumption that it is, as it seems to me Dr. Scriven does, of course there is no possibility of making any basic distinction between physicality and psi. But such an assumption begs the question. If there ultimately should prove to be some range of natural (parapsychical) phenomena that are irreducibly beyond the scope of physics, this state of affairs would not of itself be a contradiction of the concepts of that area of knowledge. It is simply a question of whether parapsychology represents an extension of physics or an extension of science beyond the borders of physics, as that branch can properly be defined.

Parapsychology, as a branch of science, needs to be defined in relation to other branches of science. The only way such a definition can be stated with any precision is in terms of present-day scientific concepts. Psi and physics are irreconcilable in terms of what we know today, and present knowledge is the only knowledge we have at our disposal in trying to relate them.

To say that psi phenomena are those personal events that are unexplainable by physical principles is not to say that no way will ever be found to reconcile the two. Indeed, inasmuch as the facts of physics and parapsychology are both parts of the same universe, it is certain that they *are related* even though we do not understand how. Future advances of scientific knowledge will, we trust, reveal the nature of this "unity." But from our present position, it is just as reasonable to suppose that the reconciliation will be achieved by extending the concept of the nonphysical as by a broadening of the concept of the physical.

No one, I think, would claim that psi is the science of nonphysical aspects of nature in any sense except that of our present knowledge. We can safely leave to the future the revision of existing concepts or the formulation of new ones to keep us in step with new scientific facts. But we need to know what parapsychology is *at this time* in relation to present-day scientific thought.

Psychology, the science of the behavior of living organisms, obviously includes parapsychology, and the latter is only one of many aspects of the former, the parent field, which border upon and overlap with physics. The precise degree of overlapping with physics for each special function investigated by psychologists is not known at present. Many psychological phenomena can be described rationally in terms of physical concepts, even if only on a theoretical basis. Psi phenomena are precisely those psychological events which defy description in terms of any physical theory now available. The difficulties of explaining the findings of parapsychology in physical terms have only become greater as the research has advanced. The failure of the physicists to claim psi phenomena during eighty years of scientific study of these effects surely justifies a serious doubt whether the psi processes *are* physical. If this inference be wrong, let the physicists welcome psi as a part of their own area and show how it fits into their existing body of knowledge!

The mind-body problem has remained an open question in spite of centuries of philosophical debate about the great issue involved. The question of the bearing of mental and physical processes upon the nature of the universe could not be settled because of the ambiguity of the data of observation and experience which gave rise to the mind-body problem. Different views of the nature of reality, especially of man as a part of existence, have therefore advanced or receded in accordance with the cultural and scientific climate forming the background of philosophical thought. The philosophy of materialism has in our period gained the ascendency in Western scientific thinking. This position of influence is not based upon direct evidence in favor of physical monism; it is, rather, a result of the advance of physics, the science of the material world, the success achieved in extending physical principles into the areas of biology, medicine, and even psychology, and the understandable preference for an explanation of all observable phenomena that is as simple as possible.

Psi phenomena are the first experimentally demonstrated effects in man that cannot be theoretically reconciled with the current purely material (physical) operations. These effects thus provide direct evidence for operations in living organisms which involve something more than can be ascribed to the functions of the physical organism. Physics, for example, offers no help toward understanding how a person can have a noninferential accurate experience of a complicated event before it occurs. If we hold to our concept of a *physical* organism (as I most certainly do), psi thus makes it necessary to recognize the occurrence of something in addition to the physical (as we know it or can conceive it)—a kind of basic duality.

Freedom of the will does not imply an absence of causation; I agree with Dr. Scriven that it is a question of the kind of causation. By freedom of the will, I take it we mean an ability of the individual to make choices that are in some degree independent of the physical order. If all action, including behavior, were reducible to purely physical effects, free will in this sense could not exist. But if there is an order of mental causation which is to some degree independent of the physical order, then the concept of choice becomes meaningful at least as a logical possiblity. Psi effects are events which establish the existence of this second order of causation. (Again, we need to remember that we are at the beginning of our scientific knowledge, not at the end.)

Ethics, as Dr. Scriven indicates, is a system of rules for behavior, but in which sense may an individual's conduct conform to the rules? If his morality only represented behavior over which he had no control, there would be no basis for assigning personal responsibility for keeping or breaking the rules. As far as society is concerned, the rules might serve a purpose as a sort of program for the regulation of human automata. But is there any aspect of human nature which indicates that an individual may be truly capable of making ethical decisions? Here psi *is* relevant.

Psi as a nonphysical aspect of man's nature points to the possibility of some sort of survival of personality after death. Such survival would be impossible for a purely materialistic "personality" that could be proposed in terms of the physics which we know today or of any advances in physical knowledge of which we can conceive. Within the limits of present knowledge, therefore, any surviving aspect of personality would not be physical.

• • •

Psi is by general agreement not explainable in terms of present-day physics. This fact alone is sufficient to indicate the *possiblity* that it *may be* nonphysical. Certainly, in terms of present knowledge, it is demonstrably beyond the scope of natural operations that can be expected to occur on a purely physical basis.

If there *is* a true and fundamental distinction between psi and those operations in the world of matter which form the domain of physics, this is easily the most important scientific generalization about psi phenomena which we can make. The degree to which psi has challenged explanation in terms of known physical laws suggests that the distinction may be a basic one. To hesitate to recognize it at this time because we do not yet know all there is to know about the material world is to risk obscuring what may be the essential characteristic of these mysterious findings. Today, physics and parapsychology are the two branches of science that stand most strikingly opposed to each other. When, where, and under what terms may they become reconciled? Our job as parapsychologists is to help to answer this question.

MINDS AND MYSTIFICATION

A. G. N. Flew

The first recorded investigation of possible "psychic" capacities was carried out under the instruction of King Croesus of Lydia in the middle of the sixth century B.C. Herodotus tells us that the king, wishing to test the powers of various oracles, sent embassies to them, each with instructions to ask its particular oracle, on a prearranged day, "What is King Croesus, the son of Alyattes, now doing?" The answers were to be written down and brought back to him. On the day appointed, the king, we are told, "devised a thing impossible to guess: he cut in pieces a tortoise and a lamb, and himself boiled them together in a cauldron of brass." When the embassies returned it was discovered that the oracle of Delphi, and that alone, had given the right answer, recognizably correct although couched in its customary cryptic hexameters.

The earlier investigations of the Society for Psychical Research often had the dramatic qualities of this first royal research project. Members dealt mainly with such phenomena, or alleged phenomena, as spirit communications, materialisms in the séance room, hauntings by ghosts, and the spritely pranks of poltergeists. Today, though the society still tries to follow up any specious reports of such occurrences, the main emphasis has shifted towards humdrum laboratory work. Its president, Dr. S. G. Soal, has commented slyly on this change: "Mr. Noel Coward," he says, "can at any time whistle up a poltergeist from the vasty deep; in real life one may whistle but he seldom comes. And infra-red rays appear to have frightened away all the materialising mediums. So what is the poor investigator to do? The lack of more exciting material condemns him to card-guessing, dice-throwing, and suchlike tame pursuits." But although less exciting than work on the so-called "spontaneous phenomena," these tests can be made under properly controlled laboratory conditions: and they can be repeated often enough to allow the use of statistical methods and of the calculus of probability. It is therefore primarily in this way that things like telepathy and clairvoyance are now studied.

The terms "telepathy" and "clairvoyance" are tending to drop out: both because the progress of the research has made it doubtful whether it is even possible—much less useful—to maintain the old distinction between mind to mind as opposed to mind to thing intuition which they were intended to mark; and because they carry theoretical implications which, in the present state of our ignorance, are unwanted and unjustified. Investigators now are inclined to use theoretically neutral words, defined in terms of the experiments themselves. So

This article is reprinted from *The Listener*, Vol. 46, No. 1178 (1951), 501-02, 515. Used by permission of the editor and A.G.N. Flew.

when I later go on to describe the sort of experiment being done I shall also simultaneously be explaining the main technical terms. But, briefly, the whole group of phenomena are called the psi-phenomena (the Greek letter Ψ); the capacity to guess better than by chance selection is called ESP capacity; the alleged capacity to influence the movements of things without the use of means or mechanism is called PK capacity. "ESP" and "PK" started life as abbreviations for "extra-sensory perception" and "psychokinesis" (that is, movement by the mind): but they have since tended to lose all theoretical implications, becoming mere labels for the things which happen in the experiments. Increasingly—and significant of the change which I have pointed out—the new American word "parapsychology" is replacing the older "psychical research": it marks a transformation of the subject; and at the same time expresses the researchers' hope that their study, like that of hypnotism before it, will some day be accepted into the academically respectable society of official psychology.

Card-Guessing Tests

But though parapsychologists have abandoned dramatics for the pedestrian round of laboratory routine, most of them still seem to compensate themselves with the conviction that their work has profound metaphysical significance. In these talks I shall suggest that, whatever may be the truth about these phenomena, this at least is a mistake: a mistake which derives partly from misunderstanding the logic of the terms in which they are popularly described; and partly from applying, often unconsciously, explanatory models which are in vital respects certainly inappropriate. It is a most unfortunate mistake, because it helps to generate around the whole subject an aura of philosophical sensationalism. This gives many cautious and hardheaded people an excuse for dismissing parapsychology out of hand, as the private precinct of cranks and charlatans.

I am sure they are quite wrong to do this. But it is easy to sympathize with their attitude. Take, for example, two widely circulated books, *New Frontiers of the Mind* and *The Reach of the Mind*, by Professor J. B. Rhine, of Duke University, North Carolina. Both are full of mystifying talk about "the mind." "The thread of continuity," he writes, "is the bold attempt to trace as much as we can see of the outer bounds of the human mind in the universe." Accounts of research are spiced with references to the mind, its powers, frontiers, and manifestations, to its unknown, delicate, and subtle capacities. The work is in sum supposed to show that "the mind does interact with matter, not only in the thought-brain relation, but also in some sort of contact with external objects in the ESP and PK experiments.... Accordingly a distinct difference between mind and matter, a relative dualism, has been demonstrated by the psi-experiments; and whether we like it or not the evidence is now overwhelming." Or so Rhine thinks.

Now just what is this experimental evidence which so overwhelmingly proves these metaphysical conclusions? The ESP experiments are mainly card-guessing experiments. The sort of thing which the experimenter does is this. He takes a pack of so-called Zener cards, a special pack consisting of twenty-five cards in five suits of five identical cards. The pack is shuffled. The subject has to guess at least one complete pack, a series of twenty-five cards, before he is told which and how many guesses were right and how many were wrong. Usually there is someone—either the experimenter or a third person—acting as what is called an agent. His function is to turn up and look at each target card in turn while the subject guesses. (But sometimes there is no agent: and then no one at all knows the answers until the scores are checked.) In the best, though certainly not in all, experiments the possibility of cheating by using, consciously or unconsciously, sensory clues or clues seems to have been eliminated. Yet in spite of all precautions many subjects have, in test after test, guessed right not merely the average of five times out of twenty-five, which is what would have been expected from chance selection, but significantly more often than this, six, seven, or eight times out of twenty-five; and this on average over large numbers of tests.

The upshot seems to be that, even after discounting all the work—and this certainly includes most early tests at Duke—in which the precautions to exclude conscious and unconscious cheating were inadequate, the proportion of right answers, of hits, in genuine guesses has been too high, with too many subjects in too large an aggregate of guesses, to be dismissed on the grounds that a certain proportion of guesses are bound to be right, and that a certain number of high scores are bound to be made "by the law of averages." The results, that is, seem to be "statistically significant." So it is said that these results reveal the presence of a new factor "beyond mere chance," a capacity for what is called extra-sensory perception (ESP). This is very unexpected; and very baffling.

But there is worse to come. For the rate of scoring does not seem to vary either with the distance of the object guessed nor yet with the time when the guess is made; scores equally good seem to be made when the guesser and the agent with the target cards are a hundred yards, a mile, or 100 miles apart as are achieved when they are in adjacent rooms or even in the same room: scores statistically just as significant have been accumulated when the card to be guessed had been turned up before the guess was made, when it was turned up simultaneously with the guess, and when it was only to be turned up and looked at after the guess had been made. And this is very unexpected indeed.

At one time these phenomena seemed to be confined to the American continent. But Dr. Soal, of London University, in his work on Mrs. Stewart and Mr. Shackleton, has impressively confirmed in our own less exuberant intellectual climate many of the findings of Professor Rhine and his colleagues in North Carolina. Dr. Soal got very significant scores from Mrs. Stewart while the agent was turning up and looking at the target cards in another house 150 yards away. This surely eliminates decisively the possibility of cheating, whether intentional or unconscious, by using using sensory clues. (Hyper-acute hearing by the subject of sub-vocal whispering by the agent, or shrewd spotting by the subject of minute marks on the backs of the cards cannot explain away results achieved when subject and agent were in different houses. But those who wish to assess the quality of the best experiments should consult the publications of the Society for Psychical Research; above all Dr. Soal's reports on his own work.)

No Metaphysical Conclusions

In addition to the records of card-guessing tests and other similar experiments done under laboratory conditions, there is a great mass of evidence pointing to the spontaneous occurrence of parallel phenomena. It consists of innumerable well-authenticated tales—preserved in the archives of the society and elsewhere—of people having hunches about, or seeing visions of, occurrences which were taking place out of the range of their senses, or which had not yet taken place at all; and which they could not have learned about by ordinary means, or forecast by rational inference from information which was available to them. Taken by itself, this material is of little value as evidence. For it is almost impossible—owing to the notorious difficulties of proving a negative—ever to know that the person who had the hunch or vision really could not have inferred that, whatever it was, was occurring or would occur. And it is always possible for the skeptically inclined—and I must confess to being of them—to say that the fact that the premonition turned out right was "just a coincidence"; if a lot of people have hunches and visions—and they do—some of them must turn out to be right "by the law of averages"; and, after all, people just do not report the hunches which turned out to be wrong. It was to meet these very reasonable objections that the laborious, dull, and repetitive card-guessing tests were devised: in simple laboratory experiments it is far easier to exclude all possibility of normal knowledge and inference; by repeating again and again the same procedures we can remove the objection that the correct guesses are got "by mere chance." But now that this has been done we can allow weight to the records of the spontaneous phenomena—which originally suggested that the laboratory work might be worth undertaking, and may now suggest further useful lines of research.

Perhaps passing mention should also be made of "the dice work." This is supposed to show that some people can influence the fall of dice by just "willing"; and thus to reveal a capacity for what is called psychokinesis (PK). Personally I should be more impressed if more, and more varied, work had been done; and if it had been better confirmed. But fortunately, my arguments would apply even if we had to accept the PK effect as genuine.

I am not so much trying to decide what the facts are as to find what theoretical implications follow from the facts, if facts they be; though I hope I have said enough to suggest that the claims of the parapsychologists deserve attention. But allowing that the psi-phenomena, the ESP (and even the PK) effects occur, surely this has not the slightest tendency to prove Professor Rhine's dualist metaphysical conclusions? When they are described, as we have described them, austerely, with no picturesque talk about minds, it is hard to see how anyone could think they did. No one has found, or even claimed to have found, elusive objects called minds interacting with familiar things like cards and dice. All that has been found is that some people can guess cards right far more often than they have any business to do (and some perhaps can even influence dice by just "willing"). These are remarkable discoveries: but they prove no metaphysical conclusions.

The source of the trouble is, I think, this "mind"-terminology in which Professor Rhine insists on describing and interpreting his results. He misconstrues its logic. What I mean is this. When, sententiously, we talk of the triumph of mind over matter, such impressive expressions can always be replaced, with a loss of pomposity but a gain in precision, by workaday statements about the things people can do. Mind-matter idioms suggest that we are in the presence of some metaphysical dichotomy. Mind-body idioms suggest that people consist of a sort of Webb partnership—a corporeal Sidney mated to an incorporeal Beatrice. But picturesque idioms must not be taken seriously. To do so is to misunderstand their logic.

This is what Professor Rhine, and others, seem to have done. Taking the word mind to refer to some object, some sort of not-brain, he assumes that minds and brains can significantly be said to interact; and tries to interpret his results in terms of this supposed interaction—which, not surprisingly, is found to be mysterious. In his own words, "Science cannot explain what the human mind really is and how it works with the brain." This is to make a mystery out of a muddle. "Mind" is not that sort of word at all. He complains that the student (I quote again) "finds ... in modern psychology ... very little on the mind as a distinct reality. Instead he studies "behavior" and its relations to brain fields and pathways." But this does not convict psychologists of shirking the study of the mind: studying certain human capacities, feelings, and performances is—is what is meant by—studying the mind. Mind talk is an alternative description of the same phenomena: it does not help to explain those phenomena; nor does it record the occurrence of further phenomena. Rhine starts a chapter on "The Reach of the Mind in Space" by remarking, "Experiences suggesting that the mind can transcend space are plentiful." He continues, "The spontaneous awareness of distant events, of which no knowledge could be acquired through recognized channels, is reported fairly frequently"; and then describes ESP work in which the subjects—the guessers—scored significantly when widely separated from the target cards.

But these phenomena are not evidence for further ghost phenomena taking place, as it were, offstage. They are part of what is meant by this talk of the reach of the mind in space. Confused by his own mystifications, Rhine apologizes because his "simple, monotonous procedure seems an almost childish way to investigate the possibility of the human mind's possessing powers not recognized by scientists or by the majority of laymen." But how else could guessing capacity be investigated than by studying how well people guess?

Psychologists tend to avoid "mind" idioms precisely because these do generate such mystifications and muddles. Professor Rhine is certainly not the first nor yet the only person to become entangled in this terminology. We need to get rid of it altogether. It tends to conceal from the layman what is actually being done; to confuse the researcher about what needs to be done; and to generate around the whole subject an atmosphere of philosophical sensationalism. Suspicion of work done in such an atmosphere delays the acceptance of even the best established results. And so it handicaps the investigation of these very remarkable, and rather disturbing, psi-phenomena.

MATTER, MIND AND PRECOGNITION

A. Campbell Garnett and G. I. Mavrodes

A. Campbell Garnett: The two great philosophical objections to precognition are: (1) that it requires a radical reconstruction of our whole common-sense and scientific conception of the causal order of the universe; (2) that it undermines the concepts of human freedom and responsibility in any sense of those terms which assumes that human understanding, foresight, voluntary decision, and effort can change the course of events from what it would have been if these processes had been otherwise or ineffective. The purpose of this paper is to present the essential features of a theory of the nature, relation, and operation of matter and mind which shows how precognition may occur without involving either of these objectionable features.

The first part of this theory adopts a view favored by many physicists and advocated by Heisenberg:

> The physicists today try to find a fundamental law of motion for matter from which all elementary particles and their properties can be derived mathematically. This fundamental equation of motion may refer either to waves of a known type, to proton or meson waves, or to waves of an essentially different character which have nothing to do with any of the known waves or elementary particles. In the first case it would mean that all other elementary particles can be reduced in some way to a few sorts of "fundamental" elementary particles; actually theoretical physics has during the past two decades mostly followed this line of research. In the second case all different elementary particles could be reduced to some universal substance which we may call energy or matter, but none of the different particles could be preferred to the others as being more fundamental. The latter view corresponds to the doctrine of Anaximander, and I am convinced that in modern physics this view is the correct one.[1]

It should be noted that it is the search for a connecting link between the different known entities and operations of the physical world that leads to this postulate. The discreteness of the quanta from each other and of their properties of wave function and particle function call for an explanation, not in terms of the functioning of some known entity, but of some unknown, of which all the known entities and operations may be functions. Heisenberg speaks of this unknown as a "substance which we may call energy or matter," but these terms are so much loaded with further connotations that their use here is inadvisable. The argument simply points to the need of postulating a *medium of connection* between known entities that are otherwise discrete and separate and apparently irreducible one to the other. All that is necessary is that this otherwise unknown something should be such that the known events can be functions of it and the known entities have their existence in it. We had better refer to it, then, by the one function we are primarily attributing to it and call it simply the "medium of connection," or, for short, M, a letter which stands for "medium" and is conveniently neutral as between matter and mind.

When we turn from consideration of matter to that of mind we find two other features of the situation which seem to require postulation of an otherwise unknown factor. These are, first, in the connection of mental and physical events. The events which physics describes are so unlike those which we experience as the appearance and disappearance of sense *qualia* and images, and as expectations, intentions, and so forth, that the notion that further research in physics, chemistry, and physiology could reduce the one to the other, or show how the former produce the latter, or how the latter can directly influence the course of the former, is nonsensical. For any suggestion as to the nature of such a connection we must go beyond the methods of the sciences to some philosophical postulate of a medium of connection which is not reducible to any one of the events or entities.

A similar need arises, in the second place, when we consider the problem of the origin of the individual mind, or of mental process in general. There is no real problem with regard to the continuity of all the processes of *one* individual mind, for the mind is not to be identified with consciousness. It can much better be conceived as a more or less well integrated system of interest processes only a small part of which is ever conscious, consciousness being only one of its functions. Such a mind appears as a cumulative organic process, growing from its earliest beginnings, decaying in old age, and ending in death. But since none of the events or entities that enter into its structure and process can be interpreted as reducible to any combination of physical events, or reducible to such an event, the question of its beginning in a world of such an alien kind presents a problem which is beyond the methods of either the physical sciences or psychology. So here again we are called upon for a philosophical interpretation, postulating some medium of connection between physical existence and the beginnings of the mental. The problem is the same whether we regard each individual mind as having its own separate beginning at some point in the growth of its own individual organism or, alternatively, regard it as an outgrowth of a stream of subconscious and conscious mental life going back through the parent organisms to the beginning of life on earth.

Faced with this demand for postulation of a medium of connection at these three points, the logical principle of parsimony requires that we postulate only one entity for all three functions unless there is some important reason to the contrary. There appears, however, to be none. M, which we have postulated as the ultimate medium of connection between all the discrete entities and events of physics, could well be both the source of all mental process and the medium and connection between mental and physical processes. This would appear to constitute difficulties if we had allowed M to be called "energy" or "matter," for the latter term very definitely has elements in its connotation which are incompatible with the second and third functions we are attributing to M, and the former also does so when it is so closely associated with the physical. The term "substance" also has disadvantages, for there is here no proposal that mental and physical entities and events should be considered as having a merely adjectival status as attributes of an underlying substance, as with Spinoza. M is here conceived as the *source* of the distinctive process or processes of life and mind, and if Hoyle's "continuous creation" theory of the physical universe is adopted it can be regarded as the source of the energy involved in the newly emerging hydrogen atoms. But, as the medium of connection between the mental and the physical and between otherwise discrete physical events, it is simply a condition of the operation of these events which determines that, if and when certain events of the one kind occur, then certain events of another kind shall also occur or shall occur in a different way than they would otherwise have done. Between two physical events, or between two mental events, there may be causal connections quite independent of M, and both types of events may have a spontaneity of their own quite independent of M. On these questions the postulate is thus far entirely open.

Having thus laid the groundwork in a theory of the nature and relation of the mental and the physical, we can now turn to the problem of precognition.

Precognition, as the term is today understood in parapsychology, implies that the response of the subject is influenced by something in such a way that it predicts the occurrence of some future mental or physical event which could not be inferred by any humanly possible knowledge of present facts and scientific laws. Since the response predicts a future event that is causally dependent on present events of the ordinary kind, it is reasonable to assume that these ordinary events have some effect upon the mysterious source of the influence which determines the precognitive response but the source of this mysterious influence cannot itself be any event of the kind now taken into consideration in the framing of scientific laws. It cannot be either mental or physical as we know such events and entities. If we had no other reason to suppose the existence of any such unique neutral entity, then the acceptance of precognition would require either the completely unsupported postulation of it or the acceptance of much more unwelcome philosophical consequences of the kind to which we have earlier referred. However, we are not in the position where it is the evidence of precognition alone which impels us to acceptance of such a postulate. As we have seen, this consequence also seems to follow from a consideration of the problem of the medium of connection among otherwise apparently discrete physical events and entities and the problem of the relation of the mental and physical.

The question, then, should be asked concerning this medium of connection which we have called M: Can M reasonably be conceived to have the further properties which would enable it to function as the source of the influence to which psi processes are apparently responsive in precognition? Such a condition in M would have to be causally dependent on the ordinary present existing world in such a way that it would contain a pattern corresponding to future events of that world as far ahead as precognition is found to function. The psi process in cognition could then be understood as responsive to this present existing pattern. But is such a pattern reasonably conceivable?

The answer here is in the affirmative. Such a pattern would be supplied if the present lines of force of existing physical events could be understood as producing in M an instantaneous projection of their future course that is in accord with natural laws of the continuity and relation of ordinary physical events, such projection reaching as far ahead as is required to explain demonstrated cases of precognition. Such a pattern in M would not need to be a pattern of spatially related events and, being instantaneous and simultaneous, its parts would not be temporally distinguished. Both spatial and temporal relations, and also the masses and energy units related, would have to be represented in M by a distinctive set of symbols and it is to this symbolic representation of the course of future events that we would have to assume the psi process as responding. Such a pattern might not only be limited in time, representing only a few months or years of the future. It might also be limited in space, representing only the interrelated set of events of a single planet and incorporating into its structure a representation of only the statistical expectation of energy received into the planet's system from outside. If so, the representation would not be completely accurate in detail and psi might be to that extent misled. For example, a change in solar weather might effect a change in earth's weather which would not have been foreshadowed in the pattern in M which had been instantaneously created by the projective effect of the lines of force in the weather of the previous day. Any precognition, on that day, of the next day's weather would then be to that extent mistaken.

Thus far we have suggested only the projection in M of the lines of force of physical events. But if it is the case that there is interaction between brain changes and mental processes, then a complication is introduced. In order for these mentally produced changes also to be reflected in the pattern in M it would need to be the case that this pattern not only reflects an instantaneous projection of all the present lines of force, and reflects these as they will be influenced by each other in their future course in accord with natural laws, but that it reflects them as they will be affected by the future mental activity of human beings and animals so far as that is a carrying-out of the present set habits and purposes of their minds working in accord with the natural laws of such minds. There is no greater difficulty in conceiving the laws of mental operation as affecting the instantaneous projections of lines of force in M than there is in conceiving these projections as framed in accord with the physical laws of the relation of natural events; for M, we must remember, is postulated as the medium of connection of the mental and physical and the ultimate source of psychical processes, and perhaps of physical events also.

If human and animal minds work always in accord with their own natural laws, then (apart from the element of uncertainty due to possible spatial limitations) the pattern thus produced in M would give an accurate foreshadowing of the course of human and animal behavior as well as of merely physical events. On the other hand, if human decisions, whether made with or without ordinary foresight, do not always conform to rigid psychological or psycho-physical laws, then a further element of uncertainty is introduced into the pattern to which psi is assumed to respond, and the precognitive response may be further mistaken on this account. Where such changes are introduced by human agency into the course of natural events, and the lines of force are thus changed, we can assume an instantaneous corresponding change in the projected pattern in M, and it would be to this changed pattern that further precognitive processes would respond. But the free decision of human beings, if it is in reality non-predetermined, must be recognized as introducing a further element of uncertainty into precognitive responses, as it does with the normal process of inference.

This theory of the functioning of the neutral medium M thus enables us to conceive of the operation of precognition without any radical change in the notion of the ordinary causal relation of physical events and without denying the possibility that human foresight, decision, and effort can change the course of behavior in such a way that it can sometimes be said of a person that he could have acted differently and so must accept final responsibility for his action. It thus removes the two great philosophical objections which have deterred so many persons, sophisticated and unsophisticated, from accepting precognition as genuine. It does this at the cost of adopting two unverifiable postulates. The first of these is that of the existence of M as a neutral medium of connection between physical and mental processes and between the otherwise apparently discrete physical processes known to science. But this postulate, though unverifiable, has the logical advantage of serving to explain a large number of puzzling facts, and it has the psychological advantage of having been frequently propounded and widely adopted prior to and apart from any consideration of precognition. The second postulate has the logical weakness of being propounded solely to provide a way of fitting an acceptance of precognition into the ordinary and well established framework of our knowledge of the world. It does not, however, require any modification of that framework. It merely adds, speculatively, the concept of an extra and otherwise unknown effect and accompaniment of known physical and mental processes. And, if precognition must be admitted to be a fact, it provides a way of recognizing the fact without disturbing the basic presuppositions of our science and our society, as other theories seem to require.

This essay does not presume that precognition is established as a fact, nor is the writer entirely convinced. But recent experimental work at the Duke laboratory has been so well guarded against alternative hypotheses that the accumulation of evidence is making skepticism more difficult. The present writer must confess that a perusal of it has turned his thinking from efforts to show that the facts can be accounted for in other ways to an effort to accommodate the evidence at face value into the system of our well established knowledge and normal assumptions. The present paper is the result.

Comment

G. I. Mavrodes: Precognition has usually seemed to be the most theoretically disturbing of the psi capacities. The others seem to point to unusual ways of obtaining information or of influencing the world, and they may require a revision of our ideas about the nature of the mind and of its relation to other aspects of the world. Precognition, however, seems to have these consequences plus others which are even more radical. For it threatens to subvert the commonsense view of the linearity of time and the belief that events cannot temporally precede their causes. And these notions seem to be more fundamental and more deeply rooted than any theory of the nature of the mind or of psychological interaction.

Professor A. Campbell Garnett has set forth briefly a theory of precognition which would eliminate these more radical consequences and would thus render it no more disturbing than are other psi phenomena. In doing this, Garnett makes a valuable contribution to the theoretical discussion of psi phenomena, but he may also have partly misconstrued the nature of his own proposal. That proposal consists of two postulates which are logically quite independent. Garnett says that both postulates are unverifiable. But this seems to be a mistake, for one of them, as I will later show, is subject to experimental test. Garnett also believes that they both possess explanatory power relative to the occurrence of precognition. But I think that this is also mistaken; only one of them possesses such power. I turn to this last point first.

I

Garnett suggests that we postulate the existence of a "medium of connection" (M), whose nature is unknown, but which would serve to explain a number of phenomena whose common feature is that they all involve the interaction of diverse entities. For example, Garnett suggests that the primary physical particles (otherwise apparently independent of each other), along with their wave aspects, would all be "functions" of M, which Garnett also describes as a "source" of energy and matter. But M would also be the source of mental processes and events and would thus form the ground of the causal relations which hold between these mental events and the physical world.

M would then serve to explain three major classes of phenomena which otherwise might seem inexplicable. These are the relation of the primary particles to each other and their mutual interaction, the causal relations between mind and matter, and the origin of individual minds or mind in general in the "alien" world of matter. Garnett thus attempts to provide a monistic explanation of the relations of apparently diverse entities by postulating that the diversity has its source in a single neutral ground. He then incorporates the postulated M into his explanation of the particular phenomena of precognition.

Before considering that particular explanation, however, I want to suggest that the introduction of a postulated entity of unknown nature to explain the interaction of better-known entities is not a useful expedient and represents no real gain in intelligibility. For example, Garnett seems to suggest that mental events are so unlike physical events that any direct influence of one upon the other would be unintelligible. For the same reason the notion that mind could have its source in matter is likewise thought to be inconceivable.

Now, I am not convinced that these things are unintelligible, especially since the fact that one thing influences another or even arose out of another does not require that one of them should be *reducible* to the other. But the more important point is that if such relations are unintelligible, then the postulation of M will not serve to remedy the situation. For M must be different from both mind and matter. (If it were identical with one of them, then its relation to the other would simply be the original problem.) But then if a causal interaction between entities of different kinds is intelligible, the causal interaction between both mind and matter on the one hand and M on the other must also be unintelligible. No gain in explanatory power is achieved by simply attributing to M whatever properties will enable it to interact with both mind and matter. For we could achieve the very same result by simply attributing to mind and matter whatever properties will enable them to interact directly. That mind and matter can interact may be mysterious, but it is not more mysterious than that they could both interact with an unknown third entity which was neither mental nor physical.

In the same way, the notion that mind could arise out of something as unlike it as matter may be mysterious. But if so, there must be just as much mystery in the notion that two such different things as mind and matter could both arise out of a single substratum. (If there is thought to be an intolerable mystery here, we might decide that mind is just as basic and original a component of the universe as matter instead of being an intruder in an alien world.)

This type of monistic account, then, does nothing to explain diversity or interaction or to render them understandable, since it merely relocates these features in a new place where all the old problems (if indeed they are problems) arise again. Consequently, we may as well accept the experienced fact that there is psychophysical interaction, and consider it as evidence that mental and physical events or entities have whatever properties are necessary to make such interaction possible. I conclude, therefore, that Garnett's first postulate is lacking in explanatory power.

II

Garnett's second postulate is much different. It is an empirically testable hypothesis about the *modus operandi* of precognition. In effect, it says that precognition operates on the basis of an extrapolation from the present state of the world to a future state. On this view precognition would be rather similar to an astronomer's prediction of the future position of a planet, though in the case of precognition no conscious inference would be involved.

Garnett suggests that M contains a model of the present state of the world plus a model of its causal laws. This combination generates in M *at the present time* a model of the course of the world for some time into the future. The precognitive subject is somehow in contact with this *present* model of the future world and translates it into his prediction of some future event. Thus, precognition involves no distortion of commonsense temporal or causal orders, for it does not involve any direct apprehension of a future event nor any causal influence of a future event in the present. It is based rather upon the apprehension of a present model or representation of the future, and this model is in turn based wholly upon the present state of the world and its causal laws.

Thus an analogy which comes closer than the astronomer analogy which I mentioned above is that of a computer whose program includes a representation of the laws of celestial mechanics and into which are fed data (in a symbolic form) on the present position, velocity, etc., of a satellite. The computer then extrapolates the future orbit more rapidly than does the satellite itself, and the symbolic representation of that extrapolation which is produced by the computer is translated by the human operation into a prediction of the satellite's future position.

As before, the introduction of M here seems to be gratuitous. The properties and capacities here being attributed to the unknown M might as well be attributed to the mind of the precognitive subject. They are, of course, surprising, but they are no more surprising in one place than in the other, and we may as well avoid the problem of how the subject gets in touch with M. Consequently, I will make no more reference to M.

Apart from this, however, the extrapolation hypothesis is interesting, and its verification would be a very significant advance in this field.[2] And it is empirically testable if a significant proportion of precognitive *failures* are due to failures somewhere in the extrapolation process. For failures of this type can be selectively multiplied by suitable experimental techniques. For example, Garnett suggests that the extrapolation may sometimes fail because the model does not contain an accurate representation of some relevant factor, or because some events are affected by non-deterministic features of the world. To be more specific, if a deck of cards is to be shuffled through a certain number of cycles by a machine an extrapolation to its final order requires data on the present order of the cards, the present state of the machine, other impinging forces, and the relevant causal laws. But such an extrapolation may sometimes fail if the data on the present state of the machine are sometimes inaccurate. If that is so, then such extrapolation failures will increase, on the average, as the required data on the state of the machine increase. Therefore, precognition experiments which involve the shuffling of the deck in two machines, one after the other, should show a lower rate of scoring than those in which the deck is shuffled an equal number of cycles in a single machine. For errors involving the present state of the machine will be more frequent, on the average, when two machines are involved.

On the other hand, the extrapolation may sometimes fail because a "computational" error is made even with accurate data. (This is equivalent to saying that the natural laws are not perfectly mirrored in the model.) Such errors, if they occur at all, will on the average be more frequent in long extrapolations than in short ones. Thus, precognition experiments in which the cards are shuffled though ten cycles would show a lower scoring rate than those involving only five cycles. And similar differential experiments could be devised to test for other sources of extrapolation error, e.g., free will.

I have described the required sorts of experiments in a very simple manner. That should not, of course, suggest that the actual carrying out of such experiments will be easy or that their evaluation is a simple matter. Suitable measures must be taken to eliminate differences due to interest lag, time differences, etc. And, even so, problems may remain. For example, it is unlikely, even if the extrapolation hypothesis is true, that extrapolation failures account for all precognitive failure. The extrapolation might, for instance, be perfectly correct and it might precisely model the future state of the world, and still the translation of that model into the conscious form of a prediction might be a potent source of error. "Translation" errors of this sort will occur equally in the sorts of differential experiments which I described above. If they are far more common than the others, so that they account for the vast majority of precognitive failures, then they will tend to swamp and mask the differential effects of extrapolation errors in such experiments. Consequently, sophisticated statistical techniques may be required to detect the differential effects. And even with such techniques the failure to find such effects should probably be construed as less significant in falsifying the hypothesis than a success in finding them would be in verifying it. Nevertheless the attempt may be worth making.

Reply

A. Campbell Garnett: Mavrodes first raises a basic issue when he says, "The introduction of a postulated entity of unknown nature to explain the interaction of better known entities is not a useful expedient and represents no real gain in intelligibility." The issue raised is that of the sense in which a metaphysical hypothesis can be said to "explain" anything. It certainly does not explain, as science does, by showing particular cases to be examples of general laws. This is no place for an essay on the nature and function of metaphysics, but briefly I would claim that there is an important philosophical task, which may be called "metaphysics," which consists in the analysis and definition of all the categories which we need to describe what we find. The test of the adequacy of such a descriptive metaphysic is that when what we find is taken to be fully described in terms of these categories, then none of the relations we find shall be rendered unintelligible. Cartesian dualism, for example, is a bad metaphysic because, if matter and mind are taken to be fully described, the former as extension, the latter in terms of the contents of private experience, then the interrelationship we find between them is rendered unintelligible. Cartesian dualism has then to be supplemented by occasionalism or pre-established harmony. But these developments suffer from the other metaphysical vices of too great complexity and lack of support from good analogy.

Now let us consider whether the sort of neutral monism involved in the concept of M presented in my paper, though certainly not serving as a scientific explanation, serves a useful function as part of a metaphysical description of minds and bodies. Suppose we start with *empirical* descriptions. We might say that a mind, as we actually find it, is an interrelated set of occurrences made up of such processes as sensations, images thoughts, efforts, likings, dislikings, intentions, and anticipations; a physical thing or piece of matter we might say is, as actually found, a center of resistance occupying some space, capable of movement, and associated in our experience with color expanses, sounds, touch data and other sensations whereby we can detect its presence without actually experiencing it as a center of resistance. Suppose now we make the metaphysical proposition that these empirical descriptions are analytically complete—that a mind and a physical thing are this, as described, *and nothing more*—we shall now find that our empirical characteristics, probably adequate for most purposes of empirical reference and scientific explanation, are inadequate as metaphysical descriptions. For if a mind and a body had just these characteristics *and nothing more* (if this were the whole being of a mind and a body) then the actual relations we find between them would be as incomprehensible as they were for Descartes. Each mind would be left as a solipsistic world to itself and the physical world would be sharply separated from the mental worlds.

To avoid this impasse we must suppose that our own minds and the world of physical things each involve *something more* than what is contained in these empirical descriptions of what is found in the discretely given processes. To suppose this does not *explain* the connections in the sense of a scientific explanation, but it enriches the concepts of mental process and physical process in such a way that it is no longer either self-contradictory or miraculous to think of each mind and each thing as a unity manifesting a multiplicity of processes, and also to think of all minds and all physical things as parts of one interconnected unity, one world. Since the function of this "something more" is simply to constitute a connection between the processes, mental and physical, which present themselves discretely in our experience, I have called it M, the medium of connection. The neutral term makes for clarity. To call it either "matter" or "mind" leads to confusion. These terms should be kept for the organized sets of *processes,* empirically given, which constitute particular minds and physical things, and which can be thought of as processes or activities of the one connecting medium.

M is metaphysically required because the different types of physical process and the still more different sets of mental processes of each private consciousness, if thought of as *nothing but* such processes as given, are too discrete to be thought of as interacting parts of one world. M, of course, is also different from the processes, and Professor Mavrodes raises the question as to how, if it also is different, it can function any better to make interaction intelligible, but the reply here is that M differs from its processes as that which undergoes a process differs from the processes it undergoes, not as one process differs from another. Two processes, as given in our experience, may be so different as to have nothing in common but the fact of change, in which case, if they are nothing more than what they appear as given, their interaction becomes inconceivable. But there is no reason why two such processes should not be processes of, activities of, or changes in, one and the same entity. And if so, the entity may be such that a process of one kind within it may be always (or never) followed or accompanied or preceded by a process of a certain other sort. If so, this entity would function as the medium of connection between such processes.

Our theory postulates that M is such an entity. In this way, and in this way only, it is an explanatory metaphysical principle.

It should be noted, then, that M is not, as Professor Mavrodes suggests, a sort of third entity, distinct from both matter and mind, but having properties which produce them and interconnect them. I am not proposing a triple substance theory to replace dualism, but rather a neutral substance theory which suggests that all the distinct kinds of process we can find, however unlike they may be, are processes (events, changes, or activities) of and within the one common medium which thus interconnects them. Professor Mavrodes himself recognizes that to admit the possibility of interaction of mental and physical events we must recognize that they are something more than what they appear as we immediately find them, and he proposes that we attribute to mental and physical events "whatever properties are necessary to make such interaction possible" (p. 174). But this is, surely, only a vaguer statement of what I have proposed. For these further "properties" which are required to make interconnection possible must constitute a "medium" of connection, and the principle of Occam's razor requires that we conceive this medium as an entity as simple as possible, therefore common to all the different kinds of discrete process, mental and physical. We should avoid complicating the postulate in the way suggested by use of the word "properties," as though we need to attribute to mental processes one set of further properties and to physical processes another set of properties and postulate that these additional sets of properties are such as to make interaction possible. Thus M, as the medium of connection common to all kinds of process, physical and mental, seems to be the simplest category we can postulate to make adequate a descriptive metaphysics which clearly recognizes both the distinctions and the interconnections of mental and physical processes. Mavrodes' suggestion of further unknown "properties" of the mental and physical suffers from the metaphysical defect of being unduly complicated.

Turning to the part of my thesis concerned with precognition, Professor Mavrodes misrepresents my conception of M by saying that "M contains a model of the present state of the world plus a model of its causal laws." This would make M an entity separate from both the physical world and human minds, merely reflecting a model of them. On my view M *contains the present state of the world,* physical and mental, with its causal laws, not merely a model. To explain precognition I then further postulate that M contains a model, determined by this present state of the world within it, which extrapolates the lines of force of a limited region within the present state of the world for some time ahead, and thus foreshadows the future states of this region for this period as they will be if those lines of force are not interfered with by human volition or unusual forces from outside the region. We then postulate that the precognitive subject is subconsciously responsive to this model or foreshadowing of things probably to come.

If we now take up Mavrodes' analogy of the computer, then the computer is that part of M which is sensitive to the radiations of the satellite and extrapolates them into a symbolic model of its future course; and the precognitive subject, which is also a part or feature of M, subconsciously reads and interprets this symbolic model. Mavrodes, however, questions the explanatory value of our hypothetical model in M. "The properties and capacities here being attributed to the unknown M," he says, "might as well be attributed to the mind of the precognitive subject." But this would require that we attribute to this subject all the resources that we attribute to M. It would have to be subconsciously responsive to all the lines of force in a wide region of space and capable of extrapolating them in accord with causal laws and the set voluntary tendencies of other minds whose activity might be relevant. If a mind is nothing more than the set of processes we are empirically aware of, then, in the light of our knowledge of their natural history, this is incredible. On the other hand, if a mind is a special development of certain kinds of process (intentional activity and sensitivity) within a continuum, M, which also includes the physical world, and if that continuum also contains a projection of the course in which events are moving, then it is not incredible that such a mind could be subconsciously responsive to such a projected pattern. And in such a theory of mind there is nothing incompatible with our knowledge of its natural history.

My final comment on Mavrodes' critique is concerned with his interesting suggestion for testing my "extrapolation" hypothesis. He points out that it would receive some degree of confirmation if it were found that interference with the method of determining the target after the guesses are made increased the number of errors. If it did not, this would indicate that the guesses are independent of any sort of projection by means of causal laws from conditions of the experiment obtaining at the time the guesses are made. If it did, this might indicate that some such projection or extrapolation is involved. This is an interesting possibility. If a significant correlation were found between increase in the number of failures of a fairly consistent scorer and changes in the conditions whereby the target is determined (made after the guesses are complete), this would indicate that correct guesses were not achieved by some sort of direct envisioning of a future state of affairs but by extrapolation from the conditions of the experiment. However, it would not serve to indicate the method of this extrapolation, nor would a lack of correlation decisively indicate that no extrapolation was involved, for even a change in the target, voluntarily made by the experimenter after the guesses were in, would not preclude the possibility that conditions obtaining at the time of the guesses still determined the form that volition of the experimenter would take, and so would be reflected in the projection in M. We can never know when and to what extent, if at all, a volition is "free" from antecedent conditions. A negative result of the proposed experiment would therefore be indecisive, and a positive result would be of very limited significance. Also, it would require the use of a subject capable of a consistent success that has rarely, if ever, been obtained as yet. Nevertheless, given such a subject, it would be worth trying.

NOTES

1. Werner Heisenberg, *Physics and Philosophy* (New York: Harper and Brothers, 1958), pp. 61-62.

2. In what follows I am not offering any opinion as to the likelihood of the extrapolation hypothesis' being true.

FIFTH SYMPOSIUM

PERSONAL IDENTITY: OPENING NOTE
Peter A. French

PERSONAL IDENTITY AND BODY EXCHANGE
John Locke

PERSONAL IDENTITY
Charles Daniels

MEMORIES, BODIES AND PERSONS
D. E. Cooper

"I can't explain myself because I am not myself you see"

PERSONAL IDENTITY: OPENING NOTE

Peter A. French

What has the study of the philosophical problem of personal identity to do with psychical research? In order to answer that question it will first be necessary to clarify the problem. A major distinction must immediately be drawn: the philosophical problem is not begotten with the question "What kind of person is he?" but is generated by the question "What particular person is he?" Hence the problem of personal identity is primarily that of clarifying the grounds we have for deciding whether someone is the same person today as we once knew. Philosophers dealing with personal identity are attempting to account in some way for reidentification, to provide a justification for our certainty that this person standing before us is the same person we once knew, despite the passing of many years. Obviously people change over a period of time. Hair recedes, waistlines expand, visions dim, etc. Almost nothing about us appears the same as we once were. Some philosophers, following David Hume,[1] argue that sameness and change are not compatible notions; that unless one stipulates that some essential element of the person remains unchanged while all else is changing, it cannot be said that he is the same person as he was only a few minutes earlier. Hume's search for such a stable element, however, proved futile and he felt constrained to conclude that personal identity (the unity of a self) is a product of our imagination.

Most philosophers who attempted to deal with the problem of personal identity, however, have denied (or at least have not assumed) that sameness and change are always antithetical. They have sought to establish criteria of identification. Generally speaking, there have been two basic and competing views on what constitutes the primary criterion of personal identity: continuity of a body through time (bodily identity) or a set of memories (memory identity). Many philosophers such as John Locke have argued that these two criteria are fundamentally different in that different things are identified in the application of each.[2] But in practice it would seem that we apply either bodily or memory criteria to suit the circumstances and without excluding one or the other as a criterion. Nevertheless, it does seem appropriate to ask which of the two criteria is more fundamental, which is necessary, and if either is in itself sufficient to establish identity. The most often used device by philosophers defending one or the other criterion is that of inventing puzzle cases. Puzzle cases are tales in which there appears to be a clear-cut conflict between the two criteria. The assumption is, of course, that the resolution of the conflict in a particular case indicates which of the two criteria is primary. An example of such a puzzle case is the following from John Locke:

> Should the soul of a prince, carrying with it the consciousness of the prince's past life, enter and inform the body of a cobbler, as soon as deserted by his own soul, every one sees he would be the same person with the prince, accountable only for the prince's actions: but who would say it was the same *man*? The body too goes to the making the man and would, I guess, to everybody determine the man in this case, wherein the soul, with all its princely thoughts about it, would not make another man; but he would be the same cobbler to every one besides himself.[3]

Locke would have us decide between the two criteria in favor of memories.

Reports of mediumistic communication raise questions as to whether the ostensibly communicating spirit is actually the same person who once lived on earth. Consider the following account of a seance with the famous medium Mrs. Leonard:

> On Monday the first part of the time was taken up by what one might call a medley of descriptions, all more or less recognisable, of different people, together with a number of messages, some of which were intelligible and some not. Then Feda (as I am told the control is called) gave a very correct description of my husband's personal appearance, and from then on he alone seemed to speak (through her of course) and a most extraordinary conversation followed. Evidently he was trying by every means in his power to prove to me his identity and to show me it really was himself, and as time went on I was forced to believe this was indeed so.

All he said, or rather Feda for him, was clear and lucid. Incidents of the past, known only to him and me were spoken of, belongings trivial in themselves but possessing for him a particular personal interest of which I was aware, were minutely and correctly described, and I was asked if I still had them. Also I was asked repeatedly if I believed it was himself speaking, and assured that death was really not death at all, that life continued not so very unlike this life and that he did not feel changed at all. Feda kept on saying: "Do you believe, he *does* want you to know it is really himself." I said I could not be sure but I thought it must be true. All this was very interesting to me, and very strange, more strange because it all seemed so natural.[4]

The files of the societies for the study of psychic phenomena are replete with accounts of people who believed themselves to have been visited by spirits of the dead, for example:

> 80, Mayes-Road, Wood Green,
> February 1st, 1897

Madam,
Mother has this morning brought your letter to Emma over to me, as I could better write what happened on July 16th, 1895, as it was me that saw Mr. Edward with another gentleman in the garden (as I thought). I remember it all so well that I have been able to write it just as it happened.

> Yours respectfully,
> E. Nichols

P.S. I have signed the other paper with my name as it was then.

On Tuesday, July 16th, 1895, between the hours of one and two o'clock, I was doing some work in our bedroom and, looking out of the window, saw (as I thought) Mr. Edward Benecke with another young gentleman walking in the garden, and I went at once to mother and told her Mr. Edward had come home, and she said something must have prevented him from starting, as we knew he was going to Switzerland for his holiday, for I was positive it was him I saw. When nurse came in on the Thursday, mother asked her if Mr. Edward had come home, and she said "no" and then we only said "I thought I saw him," and we thought no more about it until the sad news reached us.

> Ellen Carter

In answer to some questions from Mrs. Benecke, Mrs. Nichols writes further:

> 80, Mayes-Road, Wood Green,
> February 4th, 1897

Madam,
I am glad to be able to answer the questions you have asked me. I

did see another young man with Mr. Edward (as I thought it was) and the look was not momentary, for I was so surprised to see him that I watched him until he turned round the path; he was coming, as he sometimes did after luncheon, from the stable yard, along the path and turned towards the house. He was smiling and talking to his friend, and I particularly noticed his hair, which was wavy as it always was; he had nothing on his head. It was all that that made me feel so sure it was him, and I felt that I could not have been mistaken, knowing him so well. I cannot tell you anything (about) what the other young gentleman was like, as he was walking the other side; also I hardly noticed him at all, being so surprised to see Mr. Edward. Mother was doubtful when I told her about it and said I must be mistaken; but I said I was sure I was not, and I was positive I had seen him, and I felt sure he had come home until nurse came in and said he had not been home, and then I thought how strange it was, and even then I could not think I was so mistaken, and often have I thought about it and feel even now that it was him I saw. Mother did say perhaps some accident had happened to his friend that he was to travel with and so was prevented from going; that was the only remark that was made about an accident.

If there is any other question I can answer, I shall be only too glad to do it for you.

E. Nichols

Mrs. Benecke gives the following particulars:

Teddy was in the habit of walking regularly in the garden, from 10 minutes past 12 till one o'clock, and again directly after luncheon, varying, according to the time this meal took us, from 1:30 or 1:45 till 2:30. He was so regular that I could tell the time by his footfall on the stairs. He never, except in the very coldest weather—to please me—wore a hat or cap in the garden. The laundress often watched him walking up and down the garden paths, noticing the wind playing with his wavy hair. She even, at times, would get up on a stool to watch him, especially when Margaret was with him. She says they looked so bright and happy together. She has left us owing to her health, and her daughter married quite lately.

Teddy was devoted to his "dear mountains," they were a "second home" to him; but all his letters prove that his thoughts were very much with us on the climbs. He wrote to me in 1892 that when bivouacking out even in his Bietschhorn, "it felt strange to be so far away, so high up, and as I wrapped myself in my rug, I thought of you all, sitting round the lamp, etc." In 1895 he wrote, after his successful crossing the Wetterlucke, (a climb he was quite delighted with) "at 8:30,—just as you were coming down to breakfast, I was thinking—we were through." The last climb he wrote about to both Margaret and myself he said: "The last half-hour was not pleasant: it was the only time during the climb that I was *not* sorry you (Margaret) were not with us." With a heart so full of thought and love of us at home, even when intensely interested and occupied in his dearest pursuit, it seems natural that when called to leave us once more, he should have turned towards us and sent his loving thoughts home. That they took his shape and were seen once more on his familiar path seems very wonderful and of course inexplicable, but to me seems a fact. I believe that he was taken when his form appeared here. It makes it somewhat more difficult to conjecture where it happened, as he intended to be back by 4 and this time—between 1 and 2—gives therefore only 3 hours from Ried.

I wrote to our former laundress with respect to her having seen Teddy on July 16th, 1895. Our old nurse told me that it was the younger daughter, Emma, who had seen him. I could not, at the time Mrs. Carter left our service, November, 1895, trust myself to speak to her about it; therefore, I was rather uncertain as to what really had been said, and when I received the first letter, I wrote for a few more particulars.

It was through this letter that I heard, for the first time, that Ellen Carter saw two forms, which seems all the more remarkable to me. I therefore wondered if she could remember the face of the friend. I had understood she had seen him "about one o'clock" and had thought it was in his morning walk, but Ellen is positive that it was later. His coming out of the stable yard is quite likely; he often fetched the dog. I asked her if it was a "momentary passing view" she had, as in the first letter she writes almost as if she had merely looked out and then gone to her mother.

When I heard this talked about, I remembered the word "accident" and asked her if it was mentioned. Her answer in (the second) letter refers to this question.

In answer to our further enquiries, Mrs. Benecke wrote:

Norfolk Lodge, Barnet
February 15th, 1897

I will do my best to answer your questions and to do it clearly and systematically.

Ellen Carter lived with her mother and sister in a cottage in our garden. I have tried to give you an idea of the cottage by (a sketch not reproduced). I took this sketch from our dining-room window, past which the broad path leads, which I called A. Along this path my son went daily and often have I watched his light swinging steps till he had gone through the little gate I called B. This leads into our kitchen garden. I had understood that when Ellen saw him on July 16, 1895, he was coming back from his first walk through the gate B and had turned towards our house down the path A. You will easily understand that during the first months, I could not ask questions about the events of that day,—nor, in fact, can I now. But I was told of Ellen having seen my son almost directly after my return, and Mr. Benecke heard of it at once. I will return to this directly. Ellen was in her mother's house tidying their bedroom (which has the window I have marked I), when, looking up, she saw my son. She tells

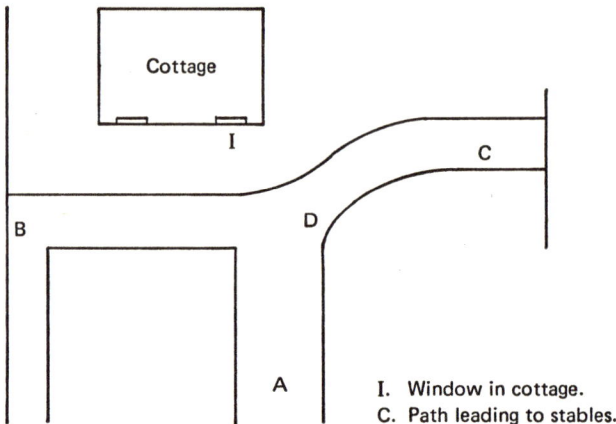

I. Window in cottage.
C. Path leading to stables.

about that herself and that he "was coming out of the stable yard." That would not be quite his usual direction, because he mostly jumped out of the window after luncheon, but still it did happen that he would fetch the dog, or put him away, in the yard. The door leading into the yard is behind bushes and he would, according to Ellen's account, have come from there and out where the path D comes out towards out house. You will, I hope, understand from this about the distance from the cottage to the path, and that it would be quite easy for Ellen, who seems to have quite good sight, to have seen him distinctly and for a minute at least.

Mrs. Carter cannot write, so it would only be what Ellen wrote for her which we should get by asking for her version. Our old nurse, who can write, is very confused about what and when she first heard of it, and therefore she can write down nothing. I have asked her several times about it all, but she varies each time in her statements, except that she remembers Mrs. Carter asking her if "Mr. Teddy had come home," and then her saying "Oh, I told Nellie she was mistaken, when she thought she saw him." She could not have spoken like that if the conversation had taken place after we heard the terrible news. Mr. Benecke remembers that the gardeners told him, after the news, that Ellen had said she had seen Mr. Teddy, and the general impression has certainly been that she had said so, and therefore had believed it, that she had seen him in the garden, on that day. (She is convinced) that it was "Mr. Teddy, no one else" she saw, for she said that she knew his pretty wavy hair too well to make a mistake, and she quite sulked when it was proved to her that she was mistaken.

We heard the terrible news on Saturday morning, July 20th, and I started five minutes later to catch the train and go over to Switzerland. Of course the servants heard of it at once, and Nellie then is said to have been very much startled when she heard it. There has never been any doubt in our minds here that she had all along said she had seen him on the Tuesday.

There have been printed notices of my dear boy's loss in many papers. We have no means of fixing the hour of it. All we know of his plans for

> July 16th was that he started with Mr. Cohen at 3 a.m. from Ried, and was seen at 3:30 at Blatten, and that he had arranged with the guides of Ried to meet him there at 4 p.m. o'clock on the Tuesday, 16th, to settle details for a tour on the 17th. My son was very accurate and always planned his tours exactly before starting. The guides told me that he knew every inch of ground in the neighborhood. He was working for Mr. Coolidge and there was but one ridge of rock not yet explored in the district assigned to him. I feel certain that the two friends started for that ridge "Feenkundl" and that there they are now resting. This conviction has gradually become clear to me, but since I have understood the whole question, the weather has made all search impossible....

> Mrs. Benecke also sent us the accompanying ground plan (not drawn to scale) lettered as in her sketch, showing the position of the percipient in relation to the place where the apparition was seen.

What criterion is to be applied in deciding whether it makes sense to say such phantasms are the persons they are claimed to be?

Another phenomenon which has drawn the attention of psychical researchers and in which questions of personal identity are central is that of multiple personality. Psychical researchers have argued that such famous cases as the Beauchamp and "Three Faces of Eve" cases are prima facie evidence that more than one person can inhabit a single body.[5] The phenomenon of multiple personality has also been used to account for the relationship between a trance medium and her/his control (the purported spirit which serves as a go-between from the spirits of the dead to the medium). Note the following account of "Feda," Mrs. Leonard's control:

> Feda has not a high opinion of Mrs. Leonard, ... she ... never conveys any impression that she likes her. She frequently indeed expresses open scorn of Mrs. Leonard's opinions, likes or dislikes, and speaks of her as of a not very satisfactory and distinctly inferior instrument, who must be protected and humoured merely because such as she is, there is none better to hand.[6]

Attempts to understand these phenomena hinge on the conception of personal identity adopted. It could be argued that the philosophical problem of personal identity underlies an explanation of most of the spontaneous and mediumistic cases of the psychical world. The question of personal identity is also central to any attempt to understand the purported inhabiting of persons by devils, demons and evil spirits and the phenomenon of exorcism as practiced by certain religious sects.

NOTES

1. Hume wrote: "A change in any considerable part of a body destroys its

identity; but it is remarkable, that where the change is produced gradually and insensibly, we are less apt to ascribe to it the same effect. The reason can plainly be no other, than that the mind, in following the successive changes of the body, feels an easy passage from the surveying of its condition in one moment, to the viewing of it in another, and in no particular time perceives any interruption in its actions. From which continued perception, it ascribes a continued existence and identity to the object." (From *A Treatise of Human Nature* (1739) Section 6, Pt. IV, Bk. I)

2. Locke maintained: He that annexes the name man to a complex idea, made up of sense and spontaneous motion, joined to a body of such shape, has thereby one essence of the species man; and he that, upon further examination, adds rationality, has another essence of the species he calls man: by which means the same individual will be a true man to the one which is not so to the other. I think there is scarce any one will allow this upright figure, so well known, to be the essential difference of the species man; and yet how far men determine of the sorts of animals rather by their shape than descent, is very visible; since it has been more than once debated, whether several human foetuses should be preserved or received to baptism or no, only because of the difference of their outward configuration from the ordinary make of children, without knowing whether they were not as capable of reason as infants cast in another mould: some whereof, though of an approved shape, are never capable of as much appearance of reason all their lives as is to be found in an ape, or an elephant, and never give any signs of being acted by a rational soul. Whereby it is evident, that the outward figure, which only was found wanting, and not the faculty of reason, which nobody could know would be wanting in its due season, was made essential to the human species. (From *Essay Concerning Human Understanding* (1960) Book III, Ch. VI)

3. *An Essay Concerning Human Understanding*...Bk. II, 1690.

4. From a letter written to Lady Troubridge on December 29, 1917, and reported in "An Examination of Book-tests obtained in Sittings with Mrs. Leonard," by Mrs. Henry Sidgwich, *Proceedings of the Society for Psychical Research*, 1921, Vol. 31, pp. 253-260.

5. Locke wrote: Could we suppose two distinct incommunicable consciousnesses acting the same body, the one constantly by day, the other by night; and, on the other side, the same consciousness, acting by intervals, two distinct bodies, as much as one man is the same in two distinct clothings? Nor is it at all material to say, that this same, and this distinct consciousness, in the cases above mentioned, is owing to the same and distinct immaterial substances, bringing it with them to those bodies; which, whether true or no, alters not the case: since it is evident the personal identity would equally be determined by the consciousness, whether that consciousness were annexed to some individual immaterial substance or no. For, granting that the thinking substance in man must be necessarily supposed immaterial, it is evident that an immaterial thinking thing may sometimes part with its past consciousness, and be restored to it again: as appears in the forgetfulness men often have of their past actions; and the mind many times recovers the memory of a past consciousness, which it had lost for twenty years together. Make these intervals of memory and forgetfulness to take their turns regularly by day and night, and you have two persons with the same immaterial spirit, as much as in the former instance two persons with the same body. So that self is not determined by identity or diversity of substance, which it cannot be sure of, but only by identity of consciousness . . . (From *Essay Concerning Human Understanding* (1690) Book II, Chapter XXVII)

6. "The *Modus Operandi* in So-called Mediumistic Trance" by Lady Troubridge, *P.S.P.R.*

PERSONAL IDENTITY AND BODY EXCHANGE

John Locke

The identity of the same man consists in nothing but a participation of the same continued life, by constantly fleeting particles of matter, in succession vitally united to the same organized body. He that shall place the identity of man in any thing else, but, like that of other animals, in one fitly organized body, taken in any one instant, and from thence continued under one organization of life in several successively fleeting particles of matter united to it, will find it hard to make an embryo, one of years, mad and sober, the same man, by any supposition, that will not make it possible for Seth, Ismael, Socrates, Pilate, St. Austin, and Caesar Borgia, to be the same man. For if the identity of soul alone makes the same man, and there be nothing in the nature of matter why the same individual spirit may not be united to different bodies, it will be possible that those men living in distant ages, and of different tempers, may have been the same man: which way of speaking must be, from a very strange use of the word man, applied to an idea, out of which body and shape are excluded. And that way of speaking would agree yet worse with the notions of those philosophers who allow of transmigration, and are of opinion that the souls of men may, for their miscarriages, be detruded into the bodies of beasts, as fit habitations, with organs suited to the satisfaction of their brutal inclinations. But yet, I think, nobody, could he be sure that the soul of Heliogabalus were in one of his hogs, would yet say that hog were a man or Heliogabalus.

7. Identity suited to the idea. It is not therefore unity of substance that comprehends all sorts of identity, or will determine it in every case: but to conceive and judge of it aright, we must consider what idea the word it is applied to stands for; it being one thing to be the same substance, another the same man, and a third the same person, if person, man, and substance are three names standing for three different ideas; for such as is the idea belonging to that name, such must be the identity: which, if it had been a little more carefully attended to, would possibly have prevented a great deal of that confusion, which often occurs about this matter, with no small seeming difficulties, especially concerning personal identity, which therefore we shall in the next place a little consider.

8. Same man. An animal is a living organized body; and consequently the

---

This selection is extracted from "Of Identity and Diversity," Book II of *An Essay Concerning Human Understanding,* London, 1690.

same animal. as we have observed, is the same continued life communicated to different particles of matter, as they happen successively to be united to that organized living body. And whatever is talked of other definitions, ingenuous observation puts it past doubt, that the idea in our minds, of which the sound man in our mouths is the sign, is nothing else but of an animal of such a certain form: since I think I may be confident, that whoever should see a creature of his own shape and make, though it had no more reason all its life than a cat or a parrot. would call him still a man; or whoever should hear a cat or a parrot discourse, reason and philosophize, would call or think it nothing but a cat or a parrot; and say, the one was a dull irrational man, and the other a very intelligent rational parrot. A relation we have in an author of great note is sufficient to countenance the supposition of a rational parrot. His words are:

> I had a mind to know from Prince Maurice's own mouth the account of a common, but much credited story, that I heard so often from many others, of an old parrot he had in Brasil during his government there, that spoke, and asked, and answered common questions like a reasonable creature: so that those of his train there generally concluded it to be witchery or possession; and one of his chaplains, who lived long afterwards in Holland, would never from that time endure a parrot, but said, they all had a devil in them. I had heard many particulars of this story, and assevered by people hard to be discredited, which made me ask Prince Maurice what there was of it. He said, with his usual plainness and dryness in talk, there was something true, but a great deal false of what had been reported. I desired to know of him what there was of the first? He told me short and coldly, that he had heard of such an old parrot when he had been at Brasil; and though he believed nothing of it, and it was a good way off, yet he had so much curiosity as to send for it: that it was a very great and a very old one, and when it came first into the room where the prince was, with a great many Dutchmen about him, it said presently, What a company of white men are here! They asked what it thought that man was? pointing to the prince. It answered, "Some general or other;" when they brought it close to him, he asked it, "D'ou venez vous? It answered, "De Marinnan." The prince, "A qui estes vous?" The parrot, "A un Portugais." Prince, "Que fais tu la?" Parrot, "Je gardez les poulles." The prince laughed and said, "Vous gardez les poulles?" The parrot answered, "Oui moi, et je scai bien faire,"* and made the chuck four or five times that people used to make to chickens when they call them. I set down the words of this worthy dialogue in French, just as Prince Maurice said them to me. I asked him in what language the parrot spoke, and he said, in Brasilian; I asked whether he understood Brasilian; he said, no, but he had taken care to have two interpreters by him the one a Dutchman that spoke Brasilian, and the other a Brasilian that spoke Dutch; that he

---

* "Whence come ye?" It answered, "From Marinnan." The prince, "To whom do you belong?" The parrot, "To a Portugese." Prince, "What do you there?" Parrot, "I look after the chickens." The prince laughed, and said, "You look after the chickens?" The parrot answered, " Yes, I, and I know well enough how to do it."

asked them separately and privately, and both of them agreed in telling him just the same thing that the parrot had said. I could not but tell this odd story, because it is so much out of the way, and from the first hand, and what may pass for a good one; for I dare say this prince at least believed himself in all he told me, having ever passed for a very honest and pious man: I leave it to naturalists to reason, and to other men to believe, as they please upon it; however, it is not, perhaps, amiss to relieve or enliven a busy scene sometimes with such digressions, whether to the purpose or no.

I have taken care that the reader should have the story at large in the author's own words, because he seems to me not to have thought it incredible; for it cannot be imagined that so able a man as he, who had sufficiency enough to warrant all the testimonies he gives of himself, should take so much pains in a place where it had nothing to do. to pin so close not only on a man whom he mentions as his friend, but on a prince in whom he acknowledges very great honesty and piety, a story which if he himself thought incredible, he could not but also think ridiculous. The prince, it is plain, who vouches this story, and our author, who relates it from him, both of them call this talker a parrot; and I ask any one else, who thinks such a story fit to be told, whether if this parrot, and all of its kind, had always talked, as we have a prince's word for it this one did, whether, I say they would not have passed for a race of rational animals: but yet whether for all that they would have been allowed to be men, and not parrots? For I presume it is not the idea of a thinking or rational being alone that makes the idea of a man in most people's sense, but of a body, so and so shaped, joined to it: and if that be the idea of a man, the same successive body not shifted all at once, must, as well as the same immaterial spirit, go to the making of the same man.

9. Personal identity. This being premised, to find wherein personal identity consists, we must consider what person stands for; which, I think, is a thinking intelligent being, that has reason and reflection, and can consider itself as itself, the same thinking thing in different times and places; which it does only by that consciousness which is inseparable from thinking, and as it seems to me essential to it: it being impossible for any one to perceive, without perceiving that he does perceive. When we see, hear, smell, taste, feel, meditate, or will any thing we know that we do so. Thus it is always as to our present sensations and perceptions: and by this every one is to himself that which he calls self; it not being considered in this case whether the same self be continued in the same or diverse substances. For since consciousness always accompanies thinking, and it is that which makes every one to be what he calls self, and thereby distinguishes himself from all other thinking things; in this alone consists personal identity, *i.e.* the sameness of a rational being: and as far as this consciousness can be extended backwards to any past action or thought, so far reaches the identity of that person: it is the same self now it was then; and it is by the same self with this present one that now reflects on it, that that action was done.

10. Consciousness makes personal identity. But it is farther inquired, whether it be the same identical substance? This few would think they had reason to doubt of, if these perceptions, with their consciousness, always remained present in the mind, whereby the same thinking thing would be always consciously present, and, as would be thought, evidently the same to itself. But that which seems to make the difficulty is this, that this consciousness being interrupted always by forgetfulness, there being no moment of our lives wherein we have the whole train of all our past actions before our eyes in one view, but even the best memories losing the sight of one part whilst they are viewing another;—and we sometimes, and that the greatest part of our lives, not reflecting on our past selves, being intent on our present thoughts, and in sound sleep having no thoughts at all, or at least none with that consciousness which remarks our waking thoughts;—I say, in all these cases, our consciousness being interrupted, and we losing the sight of our past selves, doubts are raised whether we are the same thinking thing, *i.e.* the same substance or no. Which, however reasonable or unreasonable, concerns not personal identity at all: the question being, what makes the same person, and not whether it be the same identical substance, which always thinks in the same person; which in this case matters not at all: different substances, by the same consciousness (where they do partake in it), being united into one person, as well as different bodies by the same life are united into one animal, whose identity is preserved, in that change of substances, by the unity of one continued life. For it being the same consciousness that makes a man be himself to himself, personal identity depends on that only, whether it be annexed solely to one individual substance, or can be continued in a succession of several substances. For as far as any intelligent being can repeat the idea of any past action with the same consciousness it had of it at first, and with the same consciousness it has of any present action, so far it is the same personal self. For it is by the consciousness it has of its present thoughts and actions, that it is self to itself now, and so will be the same self, as far as the same consciousness can extend to actions past or to come; and would be by distance of time or change of substance, no more two persons, than a man be two men by wearing other clothes today than he did yesterday, with a long or a short sleep between: the same consciousness uniting those distant actions into the same person, whatever substances contributed to their production.

11. Personal identity in change of substances. That this is so, we have some kind of evidence in our very bodies, all whose particles, whilst vitally united to this same thinking conscious self, so that we feel when they are touched, and are affected by, and conscious of good or harm that happens to them, are a part of ourselves; *i.e.* of our thinking conscious self. Thus the limbs of his body are to every one a part of himself: he sympathizes and is concerned for them. Cut off a hand, and thereby separate it from that consciousness he had of its heat, cold, and other affections, and it is then no longer a part of that which is himself, any more than the remotest part of matter. Thus we see the substance, whereof personal self consisted at one time, may be varied at another, without the change of personal identity; there being no question about the same person, though the limbs, which but now were a part of it, be cut off.

12. Whether in the change of thinking substances. But the question is, "Whether if the same substance which thinks be changed, it can be the same person; or, remaining the same, it can be different persons?" And to this I answer, first, This can be no question at all to those who place thought in a purely material animal constitution, void of an immaterial substance. For whether their supposition be true or no, it is plain they conceive personal identity preserved in something else than identity of substance; as animal identity is preserved in identity of life, and not of substance. And therefore those who place thinking in an immaterial substance only, before they can come to deal with these men, must show why personal identity cannot be preserved in the change of immaterial substances, or variety of particular immaterial substances, as well as animal identity is preserved in the change of material substances, or variety of particular bodies: unless they will say, it is one immaterial spirit that makes the same life in brutes, as it is one immaterial spirit that makes the same person in men; which the Cartesians at least will not admit, for fear of making brutes thinking things too.

13. But next, as to the first part of the question, "Whether if the same thinking substance (supposing immaterial substances only to think) be changed, it can be the same person?" I answer, that cannot be resolved, but by those who know what kind of substances they are that do think, and whether the consciousness of past actions can be transferred from one thinking substance to another. I grant, were the same consciousness the same individual action, it could not: but it being a present representation of a past action, why it may not be possible, that that may be represented to the mind to have been, which really never was, will remain to be shown. And therefore how far the consciousness of past actions is annexed to any individual agent, so that another cannot possibly have it, will be hard for us to determine, till we know what kind of action it is that cannot be done without a reflex act of perception accompanying it, and how performed by thinking substances, who cannot think without being conscious of it. But that which we call the same consciousness, not being the same individual act, why one intellectual substance may not have represented to it, as done by itself, what it never did, and was perhaps done by some other agent; why, I say, such a representation may not possibly be without reality of matter of fact, as well as several representations in dreams are, which yet whilst dreaming we take for true, will be difficult to conclude from the nature of things. And that it never is so, will by us, till we have clearer views of the nature of thinking substances, be best resolved into the goodness of God, who, as far as the happiness or misery of any of his sensible creatures is concerned in it, will not by a fatal error of theirs transfer from one to another that consciousness which draws reward or punishment with it. How far this may be an argument against those who would place thinking in a system of fleeting animal spirits, I leave to be considered. But yet, to return to the question before us, it must be allowed, that if the same consciousness (which, as has been shown, is quite a different thing from the same numerical figure or motion in body) can be transferred from one thinking substance to another, it will be possible that two thinking substances may make but one person. For the same consciousness being preserved, whether in the same or different substances, the personal identity is preserved.

14. As to the second part of the question, "Whether the same immaterial substance remaining, there may be two distinct persons?" which question seems to me to be built on this, whether the same immaterial being, being conscious of the action of its past duration, may be wholly stripped of all the consciousness of its past existence, and lose it beyond the power of ever retrieving again; and so as it were beginning a new account from a new period, have a consciousness that cannot reach beyond this new state. All those who hold pre-existence are evidently of this mind, since they allow the soul to have no remaining consciousness of what it did in that pre-existent state, either wholly separate from body, or informing any other body; and if they should not, it is plain, experience would be against them. So that personal identity reaching no farther than consciousness reaches, a pre-existent spirit not having continued so many ages in a state of silence, must needs make different persons. Suppose a Christian Platonist or Pythagorean should, upon God's having ended all his works of creation the seventh day, think his soul hath existed ever since; and would imagine it has revolved in several human bodies, as I once met with one, who was persuaded his had been the soul of Socrates (how reasonably I will not dispute; this I know, that in the post he filled, which was no inconsiderable one, he passed for a very rational man, and the press has shown that he wanted not parts or learning); would any one say, that he being not conscious of any of Socrates's actions or thoughts, could be the same person with Socrates? Let any one reflect upon himself, and conclude that he has in himself an immaterial spirit, which is that which thinks in him, and in the constant change of his body keeps him the same; and is that which he calls himself: let him also suppose it to be the same soul that was in Nestor or Thersites, at the siege of Troy (for souls being, as far as we know any thing of them in their nature, indifferent to any parcel of matter, the supposition has no apparent absurdity in it) which it may have been, as well as it is now the soul of any other man: but he now having no consciousness of any of the actions either of Nestor or Thersites, does or can he conceive himself the same person with either of them? Can he be concerned in either of their actions? attribute them to himself, or think them his own more than the actions of any other men that ever existed? So that this consciousness not reaching to any of the actions of either of those men, he is no more one self with either of them, than if the soul or immaterial spirit that now informs him had been created, and began to exist, when it began to inform his present body; though it were ever so true, that the same spirit that informed Nestor's or Thersites's body, were numerically the same that now informs his. For this would no more make him the same person with Nestor, than if some of the particles of matter that were once a part of Nestor were now a part of this man; the same immaterial substance, without the same consciousness, no more making the same person by being united to any body, than the same particle of matter, without consciousness united to any body, makes the same person. But let him once find himself conscious of any of the actions of Nestor, he then finds himself the same person with Nestor.

15. And thus we may be able, without any difficulty, to conceive the same person at the resurrection, though in a body not exactly in make or parts the same which he had here, the same consciousness going along with the soul that inhabits it. But yet the soul alone, in the change of bodies, would scarce to any one, but to him that makes the soul the man, be enough to make the same man. For should the soul of a prince, carrying with it the consciousness of the prince's past life, enter and inform the body of a cobbler, as soon as deserted by his own soul, every one sees he would be the same person with the prince, accountable only for the prince's actions: but who would say it was the same man? The body too goes to the making the man, and would, I guess, to every body determine the man in this case; wherein the soul, with all its princely thoughts about it, would not make another man: but he would be the same cobbler to every one besides himself. I know that, in the ordinary way of speaking, the same person, and the same man, stand for one and the same thing. And indeed every one will always have a liberty to speak as he pleases, and to apply what articulate sounds to what ideas he thinks fit, and change them as often as he pleases. But yet when we will inquire what makes the same spirit, man, or person, we must fix the ideas of spirit, man, or person in our minds; and having resolved with ourselves what we mean by them, it will not be hard to determine in either of them, or the like, when it is the same, and when not.

16. Consciousness makes the same person. But though the same immaterial substance or soul does not alone, wherever it be, and in whatsoever state, make the same man; yet it is plain consciousness, as far as ever it can be extended, should it be to ages past, unites existences and actions, very remote in time, into the same person, as well as it does the existences and actions of the immediately preceding moment: so that whatever has the consciousness of present and past actions, is the same person to whom they both belong. Had I the same consciousness that I saw the ark and Noah's flood, as that I saw an overflowing of the Thames last winter, or as that I write now; I could no more doubt that I who write this now, that saw the Thames overflowed last winter, and that viewed the flood at the general deluge, was the same self, place that self in what substance you please, than that I who write this am the same myself now whilst I write (whether I consist of all the same substance, material or immaterial, or no) that I was yesterday. For as to the point of being the same self, it matters not whether this present self be made up of the same or other substances; I being as much concerned, and as justly accountable for any action that was done a thousand years since, appropriated to me now by this self-consciousness, as I am for what I did the last moment.

17. Self depends on consciousness. Self is that conscious thinking thing (whatever substance made up of, whether spiritual or material, simple or compounded, it matters not) which is sensible or conscious of pleasure or pain, capable of happiness, or misery, and so is concerned for itself, as far as that consciousness extends. Thus every one finds, that whilst comprehended under that consciousness, the little finger is as much a part of himself, as what is most so. Upon separation of this little finger, should this consciousness go along with the little finger, and leave the rest of the body, it is evident the little finger would be the person, the same person; and self then would have nothing to do with the rest of the body. As in this case it is the consciousness that goes along with the substance, when one part is separate from another, which makes the same person, and constitutes this inseparable self; so it is in reference to substances remote in time. That with which the consciousness of this present thinking thing can join itself, makes the same person, and is one self with it, and with nothing else; and so attributes to itself, and owns all the actions of that thing as its own, as far as that consciousness reaches, and no farther; as every one who reflects will perceive.

18. Objects of reward and punishment. In this personal identity is founded all the right and justice of reward and punishment; happiness and misery being that for which every one is concerned for himself, and not mattering what becomes of any substance not joined to, or affected with that consciousness. For as it is evident in the instance I gave but now, if the consciousness went along with the little finger when it was cut off, that would be the same self which was concerned for the whole body yesterday, as making part of itself, whose actions then it cannot but admit as its own now. Though if the same body should still live, and immediately, from the separation of the little finger, have its own peculiar consciousness, whereof the little finger knew nothing; it would not at all be concerned for it, as a part of itself, or could own any of its actions, or have any of them imputed to him.

19. This may show us wherein personal identity consists; not in the identity of substance, but, as I have said, in the identity of consciousness; wherein, if Socrates and the present mayor of Queenborough agree, they are the same person: if the same Socrates waking and sleeping do not partake of the same consciousness, Socrates waking and sleeping is not the same person. And to punish Socrates waking for what sleeping Socrates thought, and waking Socrates was never conscious of, would be no more of right, than to punish one twin for what his brother twin did, whereof he knew nothing, because their outsides were so like that they could not be distinguished; for such twins have been seen.

20. But yet possibly it will still be objected, suppose I wholly lose the memory of some parts of my life beyond a possibility of retrieving them, so that perhaps I shall never be conscious of them again; yet am I not the same person that did those actions, had those thoughts that I once was conscious of, though I have now forgot them? To which I answer, that we must here take notice what the word I is applied to; which, in this case, is the man only. And the same man being presumed to be the same person, I is easily here supposed to stand also for the same person. But if it be possible for the same man to have distinct incommunicable consciousness at different times, it is past doubt the same man would at different times make different persons; which we see is the sense of mankind in the solemnest declaration of their opinions; human laws not punishing the mad man for the sober man's actions, nor the sober man for what the mad man did, thereby making them two persons: which is somewhat explained by our way of speaking in English, when we say such a one is not himself, or is beside himself; in which phrases it is insinuated as if those who now, or at least first used them, thought that self was changed, the self-same person was no longer in that man.

21. Difference between identity of man and person. But yet it is hard to conceive that Socrates, the same individual man, should be two persons. To help us a little in this, we must consider what is meant by Socrates, or the same individual man.

First it must be either the same individual, immaterial, thinking substance; in short, the same numerical soul, and nothing else.

Secondly, or the same animal, without any regard to an immaterial soul.

Thirdly, or the same immaterial spirit united to the same animal.

Now take which of these suppositions you please, it is impossible to make personal identity to consist in any thing but consciousness, or reach any farther than that does.

For by the first of them, it must be allowed possible that a man born of different women, and in distant times, may be the same man. A way of speaking, which whoever admits, must allow it possible for the same man to be two distinct persons as any two that have lived in different ages, without the knowledge of one another's thoughts.

By the second and third, Socrates in this life, and after it, cannot be the same man any way but by the same consciousness; and so making human identity to consist in the same thing wherein we place personal identity, there will be no difficulty to allow the same man to be the same person. But then they who place human identity in consciousness only, and not in something else, must consider how they will make the infant Socrates the same man with Socrates after the resurrection. But whatsoever to some men makes a man, and consequently the same individual man, wherein perhaps few are agreed, personal identity can by us be placed in nothing but consciousness (which is that alone which makes what we call self) without involving us in great absurdities.

22. But is not a man drunk and sober the same person,—why else is he punished for the fact he commits when drunk, though he be never afterwards conscious of it? Just as much the same person as a man that walks, and does other things in his sleep, is the same person, and is answerable for any mischief he shall do in it. Human laws punish both, with a justice suitable to their way of knowledge; because in these cases they cannot distinguish certainly what is real, what counterfeit: and so the ignorance in drunkenness or sleep is not admitted

as a plea. For though punishment be annexed to personality, and personality to consciousness, and the drunkard perhaps be not conscious of what he did; yet human judicatures justly punish him, because the fact is proved against him, but want of consciousness cannot be proved for him. But in the great day, wherein the secrets of all hearts shall be laid open, it may be reasonable to think, no one shall be made to answer for what he knows nothing of, but shall receive his doom, his conscience accusing or excusing him.

23. Consciousness alone makes self. Nothing but consciousness can unite remote existences into the same person; the identity of substance will not do it. For whatever substance there is, however framed, without consciousness there is no person; and a carcass may be a person, as well as any sort of substance be so without consciousness.

Could we suppose two distinct incommunicable consciousness acting the same body, the one constantly by day, the other by night; and, on the other side, the same consciousness acting by intervals two distinct bodies: I ask, in the first case, whether the day and the night man would not be two as distinct persons as Socrates and Plato? And whether, in the second case, there would not be one person in two distinct bodies, as much as one man is the same in two distinct clothings? Nor is it at all material to say that this same and this distinct consciousness, in the cases above-mentioned, is owing to the same and distinct immaterial substances, bringing it with them to those bodies; which, whether true or no, alters not the case; since it is evident the personal identity would equally be determined by the consciousness, whether that consciousness were annexed to some individual immaterial substance or no. For granting that the thinking substance in man must be necessarily supposed immaterial, it is evident that immaterial thinking thing may sometimes part with its past consciousness, and be restored to it again, as appears in the forgetfulness men often have of their past actions: and the mind many times recovers the memory of a past consciousness, which it had lost for twenty years together. Make these intervals of memory and forgetfulness to take their turns regularly by day and night, and you have two persons with the same immaterial spirit, as much as in the former instance two persons with the same body. So that self is not determined by identity or diversity of substance, which it cannot be sure of, but only by identity of consciousness.

24. Indeed it may conceive the substance, whereof it is now made up, to have existed formerly, united in the same conscious being: but consciousness removed, that substance is no more itself, or makes no more a part of it, than any other substance; as is evident in the instance we have already given of a limb cut off, of whose heat, or cold, or other affections, having no longer any consciousness, it is no more of a man's self than any other matter of the universe. In like manner it will be in reference to any immaterial substance, which is void of that consciousness whereby I am myself to myself: if there be any part of its existence which I cannot upon recollection join with that present consciousness, whereby I am now myself, it is in that part of its existence no more myself than any other immaterial being. For whatsoever any substance has thought or done, which I cannot recollect, and by my consciousness make my own thought and action, it will no more belong to me, whether a part of me thought or did it, than if it had been thought or done by any other immaterial being any where existing.

25. I agree, the more probable opinion is, that this consciousness is annexed to, and the affection of, one individual immaterial substance.

But let men, according to their diverse hypotheses, resolve of that as they please, this every intelligent being, sensible of happiness or misery, must grant, that there is something that is himself that he is concerned for, and would have happy; that this self has existed in a continued duration more than one instant, and therefore it is possible may exist, as it has done, months and years to come, without any certain bounds to be set to its duration; and may be the same self, by the same consciousness continued on for the future. And thus, by this consciousness, he finds himself to be the same self which did such or such an action some years since, by which he comes to be happy or miserable now. In all which account of self, the same numerical substance is not considered as making the same self; but the same continued consciousness, in which several substances may have been united, and again separated from it; which, whilst they continued in a vital union with that wherein this consciousness then resided, made a part of that same self. Thus any part of our bodies, vitally united to that which is conscious in us, makes a part of ourselves: but upon separation from the vital union, by which that consciousness is communicated, that which a moment since was part of ourselves is now no more so than a part of another man's self is a part of me; and it is not impossible but in a little time may become a real part of another person. And so we have the same numerical substance become a part of two different persons, and the same person preserved under the change of various substances. Could we suppose any spirit wholly stripped of all its memory or consciousness of past actions, as we find our minds always are of a great part of ours, and sometimes of them all, the union or separation of such a spiritual substance would make no variation of personal identity, any more than that of any particle of matter does. Any substance vitally united to the present thinking being is a part of that very same self which now is: any thing united to it by a consciousness of former actions makes also a part of the same self, which is the same both then and now.

PERSONAL IDENTITY

Charles Daniels

Suppose that someone says to you, "Let me think about it for a moment," "I'll clear off the dishes," "I gave it some thought while you two were discussing the course options, and. . .," or "Well, I've cleared off the dishes, let's watch TV." When you verify by observation that the person now talking to you has done or will do something in the very recent past or near future, one observes his body; and the body one observes is a spatio-temporally continuous entity. The problem of personal identity is that of whether or not bodily continuity is a *necessary* condition of personal survival.

The issue is complicated by a further factor: one does not normally make such observations about oneself. We do not live surrounded by mirrors; and even if we did, we would still not verify that we observed our bodies by observing ourselves observing our bodies. As Sydney Shoemaker has pointed out,[1] we do not use criteria of spatio-temporal continuity in the verification of the personal components of our own perceptual and memory claims.

Yet it has recently been forcibly argued that bodily continuity *is* a necessary condition of personal survival.[2] My aim in this paper will be to provide a summary and critical evaluation of the arguments *pro* and *con*. Let me straightaway disclose my view on all this. I find that the arguments put forward to support the thesis that bodily continuity is a necessary condition of personal survival simply do not prove this conclusion; and here I side with the many people on earth who, in believing that reincarnation is actual, are committed to its possibility. If bodily continuity were a necessary condition of personal survival, these people would be taking a necessary falsehood for a contingent truth. I do part company with the believers in reincarnation, however, for while I believe that reincarnation is possible, I am doubtful that it ever in fact occurs.

A case, whose source is unknown to me but which has circulated widely among philosophers by word of mouth, will serve to illustrate the in's and out's of these matters admirably.

Science marches on. A machine is built that will, when a person enters it, record the type and position of each molecule in his body and then disintegrate him. The process takes only a few seconds and ends with a pile of atomic debris lying on the floor of the recording chamber. The tape which contains the information about the molecular structure of the individual's body can then be fed back into the machine; and after the requisite raw materials are added, the

---

An earlier version of this selection appeared in the *American Philosophical Quarterly*, Vol. 6, No. 3 (July, 1969), 226-232. Professor Daniels has substantially expanded and revised his essay for this anthology. Used by permission of Charles B. Daniels and Nicholas Resher, editor of the *American Philosophical Quarterly*.

machine will fabricate a person who not only looks and talks exactly like the one who entered the machine in the first place, but also believes that he is that person. No one who emerges from the machine complains of any suffering that he has undergone. Many of these machines are built.

People become accustomed to "travel" *via* these machines. They walk in, are taped and disintegrated, the information on the tape is beamed to their destinations where other machines await, and there they are reconstructed.

"Operations" are performed that never were possible before: a technician makes a few emendations in the tape before feeding it back into the machine for the reconstruction. Broken bones are mended, and happier "memories" are furnished for those who simply cannot cope with their real ones.

Here an objection might be raised. Since it is possible to duplicate tapes or for a machine to record its information on two tapes, such duplicate tapes can be fed into separate machines and there will emerge two people who both claim to be the same person.

Now in one way it is possible for the same person to be in two places simultaneously: for example, someone might be both inside and outside his house if he were, say, standing astride the doorway. But one person cannot, it seems, simultaneously be situated in two places that are not connected by some path between them, both of which have him situated in them. This is what is normally meant by saying that a person cannot be in two different places at the same time.

If the two individuals that emerge from the two machines are the one person they claim to be, then one person *can* be in two places at the same time. But one person can't. So they both can't be the person they believe themselves to be. But to say that one of them is and the other is not the person who entered the machine in the first place is arbitrary in a case like this, at least more arbitrary than saying that neither of them is. So that is the best thing to say: neither of them is. And since it is always possible to make two people from a tape, these considerations will obtain even when in fact only one happens to be made. It would be very strange, indeed, if your being who you think you are depended upon the fact that someone has not secreted a duplicate of the tape you were made from and has not made use of it in some far corner of the earth.

But what this objection fails to note is that the two people who emerge from the machines do not claim that they *are now* the same person, i.e., each other. They can see very well that they are not. What each claims, on reflection, is that he *was* the fellow that entered the machine, say, an hour before.[3] So both *can agree* (i) that they are now different people and (ii) that they were once one and the same person. One can imagine them getting very chummy reminiscing about the things that happened when they were the same person.

Other uses of the machine can now be envisaged. Two women fall madly in love with me to the point of desperation. I walk into the machine. A tape is made in duplicate. The two tapes are fed into two machines and both of my admirers and "I" live happily ever after. But all is not sweetness and light. Criminals can now duplicate themselves a hundredfold after committing the most heinous of crimes. Are the courts to condemn them all—especially the few that turn into saints during the prolonged pretrial period? Probably not, because while it is true that they *were* the person that committed the crime, it is not true that they *are* the person that committed it. They can remember that they *were* the one that did it, but not that they *are* the one that did it. Fortunately, however, the poor woman that was their wife is not their wife now.

There is another objection to consider, however. A horrible rumor has begun to circulate about the entrepreneurs who control these machines. The machines have only *some* of the capacities we have been told they have. They can record the type and position of each molecule in a person's body, and they can, given raw materials and a suitable tape, fabricate people, but they cannot perform the disintegration operation.

What really happens, once the tape is made, is that a trap door opens in the bottom of the recording chamber, and the poor unsuspecting soul inside falls down into the basement, where he is seized by a band of sadists, bound, tortured until nearly dead, and at last thrown half alive into a vat of acid in which he dies and is quickly decomposed leaving no trace—and all the while on the floor above the accomplices of these fiends are manufacturing a duplicate. One can hear them now: "How's it going down there? Boris is almost ready to pull the duplicate" will come the shout from above, and from below, "Oh, we've all had our fun. He's in the bath now."

So the duplicate is merely a duplicate, like a photocopy, and not the original. And why do we say that the duplicate and the original are different people? Because a person ceases to exist when his body does—by dissolving in acid, *or* by being disintegrated by a machine—even though, like any of the items of mass production, there may be any number of people with bodies just like his. Since lack of bodily continuity between the person entering the machine and the person emerging from it seems to entail that the person before and the person after are different people, we might conclude then that a logically necessary condition of personal survival over time is bodily continuity over time. At least this is how the argument goes.

And that the person before and the person after are in fact different people is in a case like this the correct answer, I think, but another consideration seems to suggest that our judgment to this effect is not based upon seeing an *entailment,* i.e., bodily continuity over time is not a *logically* necessary condition of personal survival over time. Cases of reincarnation, if such things are logically possible, are precisely cases in which there is personal survival over time in the absence of bodily continuity.

Suppose my best and oldest friend awakes one morning thoroughly convinced that he is Henry Morgan, the pirate. I know little of Morgan, but from what I do know I judge that my friend has taken on the personality and character traits of Morgan. This may, of course, simply be due to an unconscious desire on his part to preserve his deluded conviction that he is Morgan; to keep in character he must behave like him. In any event, people can have the same character and personality traits, mannerisms, likes and dislikes, and still be different people, so having Morgan's character and personality traits certainly isn't sufficient to make my friend be Morgan.

But there are other more disquieting elements. He seems to know vastly more about the intimate details of Morgan's sordid life than the John Dokes I have known from childhood could possibly be in a position to know. As boys we played at pirates, but I know for a fact that he took no more than the passing interest I did in the lives of the pirate notables. He insisted, moreover, in making a trip to the Caribbean "to convince all you skeptics"; and near Ocho Rios, after having oriented himself to the now altered lanscape, he pointed to a spot where we dug up a fabulous treasure and the bones of the men he claimed he had murdered so as to preserve the secret of its location.

If we decide that Dokes is a reincarnation of Morgan (or that Morgan's soul has informed Dokes' body, or something of the sort), we do so having judged that the claims Dokes makes that he *remembers* being Morgan, burying the treasure, killing the crew, etc., *are true*; it is a real case of remembering, and this judgment forms the basis of our judgment that Dokes is Morgan. However, our basis for judging that Dokes *remembers* being Morgan, burying the treasure, killing the crew, etc., is that we know or have good reason to believe that *Morgan* buried the treasure, killed the crew, and whatever else Dokes claims *he* did, and that Dokes has some, to say the least, very extraordinary *insight* into Morgan's life and deeds.

But now another objection must be raised. We might account for Dokes' strange insight in another way than by saying that it is a case of remembering. Dokes might simply have clairvoyant knowledge of what Morgan did, felt, thought, etc., and be mistaken when, believing it to be true, he says he *remembers* being Morgan, burying the treasure, killing the crew, etc. One can think one is remembering events which one is, say, merely imagining, and one can think one is merely fantasizing events that one is really remembering. So, too, it seems possible that one may have clairvoyant knowledge of something one *only thinks* one remembers.

Suppose I claim to have a wonderful clairvoyant power to know things. When asked to give examples of things I know this way, I say,"I know that I had bacon and eggs for breakfast this morning, and that my good friends, the Smiths, came to visit my flat last night and we had a good time together." This isn't clairvoyance at all. I was present when these things happened and am remembering them. You know this by knowing that the body I now have was in a position this morning for me to be seated at the breakfast table and to know that I was, etc.

It seems, then, that bodily continuity plays an important role in distinguishing what is to count as a case of clairvoyance from what is to count as a case of remembering. This is undoubtedly true. It might be argued further, though, that when bodily continuity is absent as it is in cases of reincarnation or "change of bodies," the distinction between the two collapses. Remembering is one thing when it is distinct from clairvoyance; it is quite something else when it is not.

If this line of reasoning is accepted it is suggestive of further argument. First, that if "remembering" doing something in a former life entails that one did it, the concept of *person* we are dealing with differs significantly from our normal one. For example, no present court would adjudge Dokes guilty of the murders of the crew members even if it accepted that he "remembered" (in our novel sense) committing them and, hence, was the "person" (in a novel sense) that committed them, nor, I imagine, would it judge that he was not married to Dokes' wife, if it accepted that prior to his awakening as that "person" he was not that "person"—although this change might serve as grounds for divorce. And although we might find much objectionable in his present character, even viewing him with suspicion as a potential criminal because of these traits we would not, I think, regard him with the same moral disapproval as we would if he had committed murders in his present life and remained unrepentant.

Secondly, there seems to be no reason to hold that the implications of "remembering" (which is not distinct from clairvoyance) will resemble those of our normal remembering (which is distinct from clairvoyance). In particular, the fact that remembering that one has done so-and-so entails that one has done it, when the presence of bodily continuity preserves the distinction between remembering and clairvoyance, provides no clear reason for holding that the entailment obtains when the absence of bodily continuity collapses the distinction. So the fact that Dokes "remembers" burying the treasure and killing the crew is no longer a reason for saying that he did do it. It may still be a reason for saying that someone did it, for remembering-clairvoyance still has some element of knowledge in it.

Yet to all of this a believer in the possibility of reincarnation will simply and, I think, correctly reply that *there is* a distinction between remembering and clairvoyance despite the fact that in such cases bodily continuity is absent:[4] if Dokes remembers killing the crew and if Morgan singlehandedly killed the crew, then Dokes is Morgan; if Dokes merely has clairvoyant knowledge that Morgan killed the crew, he isn't (and perhaps cannot be) Morgan. The fact that we do not seem to be able to figure out a way of coming to know which is in fact the case does not *imply* that it is impossible for one and only one of them to be Morgan.

Yet the question does remain of how we—including those of us who seem to ourselves to remember former lives—can tell in such cases who is really remembering and who isn't. If in normal cases bodily continuity is treated merely as an inductive ground for saying yea or nay to the question of who is really remembering and who isn't, there must be an independent way of telling which is which if we are to establish empirically that it is a good inductive ground, or so it seems. It might be, of course, that we just see that X is remembering and that Y isn't. But if this is our answer, shouldn't we simply forget about remembering that one is so-and-so, a sufficient condition of identity, and just say that we see that X is so-and-so and that Y is not? If the answer takes either of these forms, though, we can still perhaps be jollied out of it.

Suppose that I am an anthropologist who has been living with a tribe long enough to have sufficient command of their language to carry on a fairly decent conversation in it. One day the chief and I are sitting outside his dwelling watching the men of the tribe practice archery. One of them is particularly inept with the bow and arrow, invariably missing the target completely. I remark to the chief, "He's certainly not much of an archer," and to my surprise the chief answers, "Oh, he *is* in the next village." I ask, "Do you mean that he becomes a good archer when he goes to the next village?", and the chief replies, "No, I mean that he is *now* a good archer in the next village. I ask, "Do you mean that he is in the next village now, besides being here too?", and the chief answers, "Yes, and what's more he is sitting over there too, but that's not him over there," pointing in the first instance to a woman nursing a child and in the second to a girl in her teens. It seems clear to me at this point, if the old boy isn't pulling my leg, that these people have a different concept of a person than we do.

I then ask the chief how he knows that the man in question is in the next village and he replies, "I see that he is. I'm there too." I ask him how one tells which of these figures I see are the same person and which aren't and he says, "Well, it's just one of those things, like sameness of color, that one sees, or one doesn't. A few of us are 'person-blind' and simply can't do it. There have been cases where a foreigner who has spent time living with us and learning our ways has finally gotten the knack of it. You may be suspicious, but if you take the trouble to stick it out here, you will find that you have good reason to believe that we can see these things, just as blind people have good reason to believe that those of us who claim to have the power of seeing colors actually do see them. Blind people know that there is overwhelming agreement about what the colors of things are. They know that this agreement cannot be traced to authority; you don't need traffic policemen standing out on every corner shouting, 'Now the light is red. You must stop.' They know, moreover, what organ would have to be fixed if they were to come to have this power. It is the same with you. You will find that we agree about what things are the same person and what are not. Our agreement doesn't come from authority. And your eyes may well need fixing. But then, again, perhaps just practice will do."

Now the person who believes in the possibility of reincarnation might not be convinced that his concept of remembering or of person differs from the normal simply because he realizes that this tribe has a different concept of person from the normal. But the chief's kind of argument does have a sufficiently strong cajolery force to make it hard for him to say that he simply sees the difference between remembering and clairvoyance or between the same and different people and that the rest of us are blind in these respects. And there is the further difficulty that our world is full of instances of the same color, just as the tribesmen's world is full of instances of the same "person" in their sense. Cases of the Dokes type of insight simply don't occur, so questions of whether one would be driven to take the "simply seeing" line if they did become difficult to answer in the absence of further information.

This is an important point and it can be illustrated by the difference between the machine case and the case of reincarnation or "change of bodies." When we read the details of the machine case, we find they fit easily into a whole set of background beliefs we have about how things actually work in the universe. The people emerging from the machines have the characters, personalities, and beliefs they do *because* character, personality, and belief is determined by the position and type of certain molecules in one's body—at least that is what we believe about these matters. And when we realize that the people who emerge from the machines are not the ones who first entered, we are *still* able to give this explanation of why they act, talk, and believe as they do. We do not *have* to fall back upon such outlandish things as clairvoyance or queer rememberings to explain the phenomena (not that a thing cannot be explained by both the concept of molecules at work and by the concept of remembering). But if we didn't have the background beliefs we do have, the machine case might be on a par with the reincarnation case. Except for the inclusion of a lot of unnecessary trappings.

Why do the people act, talk, and believe as they do? Because they have a certain kind of molecules at work in certain parts of their bodies. Why does Dokes act, talk, and believe as he does? Same reason. Why are these molecules there and structured in just that way in the bodies of the people who emerge from the machines? Because someone by means of the machines put them there and arranged them that way. Why are the molecules there and arranged in just that way in Dokes' body? We just don't know, not that we can't know. Perhaps Morgan's spirit entered and informed his body, causing a molecular rearrangement. Perhaps a combination of clairvoyant power and mental instability made him that way. Perhaps the type and arrangement of molecules in one's body has nothing to do with how one acts, talks, and believes. Imagine a case of the machine type or the John Dokes type happening in an *Oz*-like world of tin men and straw men in which molecules had nothing to do with what its inhabitants did or thought. What would be the right thing to say here?

I think the difficulties in deciding what would be the right thing to say arise from two factors: (a) a suppressed demand for physical possibility and (b) a lack of relevant information. Another case may help.

Sydney Shoemaker offers the following counterexample to the thesis that bodily continuity is a necessary condition of personal survival:

> ... suppose that medical science has developed a technique whereby a surgeon can completely remove a person's brain from his head, examine or operate on it, and then put it back in his skull (regrafting the nerves, blood vessels, and so forth) without causing death or permanent injury; we are to imagine that this technique of "brain extraction" has come to be widely practiced in the treatment of brain tumors and other disorders of the brain. One day, to begin our story, a surgeon discovers that an assistant has made a horrible mistake. Two men, a Mr. Brown and a Mr. Robinson, had been operated on for brain tumors, and brain extractions had been performed on both of them. At the end of the operation, however, the assistant inadvertently put Brown's brain in Robinson's head, and Robinson's brain in Brown's head. One of these men immediately dies, but the other, the one with Robinson's body and Brown's brain, eventually regains consciousness. Let us call the latter "Brownson." Upon regaining consciousness Brownson exhibits great shock and surprise at the

appearance of his body. Then, upon seeing Brown's body, he exclaims incredulously, "That's me lying there!" Pointing to himself he says, "This isn't my body; the one over there is!" When asked his name he automatically replies, "Brown." He recognizes Brown's wife and family (whom Robinson had never met), and is able to describe in detail events in Brown's life, always describing them as events in his own life. Of Robinson's past life he evidences no knowledge at all. Over a period of time he is observed to display all the personality traits, mannerisms, interests, likes and dislikes, and so on that had previously characterized Brown, and to act and talk in ways completely alien to the old Robinson.[5]

Shoemaker himself has doubts about what is the right thing to say here. I will limit myself to commenting on the case as it is presented above.

It seems to me, right off, that Brownson is Brown. One is inclined to say this because he has Brown's brain and behaves as the story says. Brain continuity is not, however, a logically necessary condition of personal survival.

Shoemaker goes on to argue:

> ... if upon regaining consciousness Brownson were to act and talk just as Robinson had always done in the past, surely no one would say that this man, who looks, acts, and talks just like Robinson, and has what has always been Robinson's body, must really be Brown rather than Robinson because he has Brown's brain. Here we would conclude simply that there is not the close causal relationship we had supposed there to be between the state of a man's brain and his psychological features, i.e., his personality and his ability to report events in his past history. If we did not think there to be such a causal relationship we should not think that having the same brain has anything more to do with being the same person than, say, having the same liver.[6]

If Brownson were to awake acting and talking like Robinson, I myself do not think we would immediately conclude that brains do not have the intimate relationship we think they have to psychological features. There is simply too much other evidence that they do, e.g. the effects of frontal lobotomies and brain tumors, etc. Rather, I think it would take an incredible amount of evidence to persuade us to the view that the assistant had really made such a mistake.

But if there were such evidence, perhaps several movie crews taking films of the whole thing, I think that then Brownson's case would become an anomaly, and many other alternative explanations would have to be explored before we would resign ourselves to saying that as regards an explanation of human consciousness brains play about the same role as livers and that these other "effects" (of frontal lobotomies, brain tumors, etc.) are sheer coincidence.

Suppose, for instance, that Brown has had a history of clairvoyant interludes and also has shown signs of mental instability. Immediately before his operation he had heard that someone named Robinson was undergoing a similar operation. Perhaps he is now fulfilling a wish to be someone else and has picked on Robinson. This is farfetched, but it seems no more farfetched than the supposition that Brownson wakes up believing that he is and acting like Robinson, given that he has Brown's brain. Equally farfetched would be the case in which Brown awakened thinking and acting like Robinson after receiving a transfusion of Robinson's blood.

What all of this shows is, I think, that we have a natural tendency, when presented with made-up cases like these, to fill in the missing details in such a manner as to make the imagined world, the one we have in mind, as much like the actual world with respect to unspecified detail and physical possibility as we can, given the limitations of the statement of the case and our beliefs as to what the actual world is like and what is physically possible. If, for instance, we harbor a belief, however fuzzy or confused, that there is an identity in fact between mind and brain, we will take it for granted that there is this identity in the world we are asked to imagine in a case like Shoemaker's and say that Brownson is Brown. Robinson's brain now lies encased in the inessential part of Brown's body—inessential in the way fingernails, hair, fingers, livers, etc., are inessential to his body, while the essential part of Brown's body, which is in fact his brain, lies encased in the inessential parts of Robinson's body. (Suppose that brains could be manufactured by a machine so that they exactly resembled our own brains and suppose also that they could be transplanted in our skulls in an operation like the now successful kidney or heart transplants. But remember the possibility that sadistic fiends might be in control!)

Or if we want to use the word "body" in Brown's, perhaps more normal, way, we will say that despite the fact that one's bodily continuity is not essential to one's survival, *spatio-temporal continuity of something*, whatever one cares to call it, may still be; and this something in the imagined world and our own is in fact the brain. And because we believe this we say that Brownson is Brown.

But suppose further details are given: suppose that the fact that there has been a mistaken switch in brains is proved and that Brownson's opposite number, call him Rown, doesn't die, but awakens *also* thinking, talking, and acting like Brown—we don't know what to say because we don't know who is who. And we don't know who is who, because now, it seems, we don't know enough relevant details.

But the tendency to make the presented world as much like what we believe the real world to be, within the framework of detail actually given to us, still operates; and this determines what kinds of further details we feel ought to count as relevant. Given a belief in the identity of mind and brain, the case becomes mysterious, because we want to reconcile this belief with the story told. Then when further details are given that make it clear that brain-mind identity does not hold in the hypothetical world, other beliefs about the real world still retain their hold over us: we believe that in fact a person could not be such a lucky guesser that he would with no knowledge whatsoever about the life of another guess all the details of that other's life with the facility and accuracy that the other could remember them, that he would not have this detailed clairvoyant knowledge, he could not be so mistaken about his own identity, that he could not be so mistaken about whether he was guessing blindly, being clairvoyant, or remembering, that he could not react in just the same way as the other to people and situations, that in all probabilty there are no cases anyway of clairvoyance or of reincarnation or of one soul, mind, or what have you, informing different bodies at different times, etc. Any of these beliefs might be false; none of them are, in my opinion, logically necessary truths.

At this point I am handicapped by the fact that I have no sufficiently detailed analysis of knowledge or rational belief to offer, so what I say in the following will have no other basis than my own intuitions. I ask the reader to test mine against his. Let us operate under the assumption, though, that the worlds presented in these cases differ from the actual world, represented partially by the truth of the set of beliefs stated above, only as much as the details stated in the description of the case and taken in a generous spirit require.

In the original brain-transfer case, we should, I think, barring sheer stupidity, *know* that Brownson was Brown.

In the case of Dokes-Morgan, I think we might have fairly good reason to suspend judgment, to wait and see what turned up. In fact, if no other such cases occurred, generations in the fairly remote future would probably have good grounds to doubt existing accounts that said that the case of John Dokes ever really occurred, unless, of course, investigations into the connections between mind and brain take a very surprising turn. Even then, the stories might be viewed with great suspicion—like the "explanation" that the "immaculate conception" was really a case of parthenogenesis.

But if such cases were to begin to occur with some regularity, provided, of course, only one good candidate appeared each time, we would have good reason to believe—and we might perhaps even come to know—that Dokes was Morgan. The mind-brain identity thesis would have to be scrapped, but minds could still be thought of as having an exceptional intimate causal relationship to brains during those periods when the minds were in fact incarnate. Also, to be sure, we would start believing that cases did occur of minds informing different bodies at different times. Our reasons for believing Dokes to be Morgan would, I imagine, be that we knew that in all normal cases the likelihood that memory was the source that provided a vast store of true information about the past doings and thoughts of someone is far and away greater than the likelihood that it came *via* clairvoyance or sheer uninformed lucky guessing. Also, we regard it as wildly unlikely that a man could be mistaken on so grand a scale about whether he was remembering, being clairvoyant, or just guessing blindly. And we could still say that there were no cases of real clairvoyance. *And*, to be sure, there are all those other cases; Dokes-Morgan is not unique. Of course, the problem of determining the relationship between the mind and the brain would become far more difficult and puzzling for the scientists, perhaps requiring a new physical theory.

Similarly in one isolated case of competing candidates, whether it is a case where no spatio-temporal continuity is apparently present or one like the case where both Brownson and Rown act like and believe themselves to be Brown, judgment is best suspended.

In most circumstances that come to mind, we would, I think, want to hold it to be true that in the absence of physical continuity at most one of the competing candidates is who he claims to be, i.e., that in the absence of such spatio-temporal continuity two competing candidates cannot have been one person in the past. The qualification as to spatio-temporal continuity is required in view of another kind of case: if children were born fully able to reason and to talk, and each firmly believed it had done and thought the things its mother had done and thought, we might want to say that the mother and child had once been the same person.

Indeed, it cannot only be made to seem plausible that two such individuals *were* the same person, but also that they *are* the same person, i.e., that a person can be in two different places at the same time. The following case I owe to a recent article by Derek Parfit:[7]

Suppose that the bulk of the information a person has is stored in duplicate in the two hemispheres of his brain and that in the event that one hemisphere is destroyed the other will take over the work of the whole and continue to regulate bodily and mental functions. Suppose further that it is found that certain individuals are capable of voluntarily dividing their minds, i.e., pursuing two trains of thought concurrently without a unifying consciousness overseeing the effort. One of these gifted individuals could, for instance, when faced with a problem, decide that there were two quite different lines of approach to a possible solution. He might then, to save time, divide his mind for a period of time, in order to pursue both to see whether one of them might prove fruitful. Sometimes upon reunification he would find that neither worked; other times he would have his solution in hand.

Neurophysiologists then determine that a mind division is in fact a division of labor between the two hemispheres of the brain. After a period of training, anyone who happens to have both hemispheres intact turns out to be able to divide his mind at will. But those individuals who lack two functioning hemispheres are simply incapable of doing so. Finally, it is found that subjects are able to divide (and unify) their minds even when the neural connections between the two hemispheres are severed. Indeed, they are capable of doing so when the two hemispheres are transplanted into bodies that lack brains. Of course, in the case of such transplants there are at first grave difficulties in adjusting to and controlling two spatially separate bodies. But the difficulties are not in principle greater than those involved in controlling two spatially separate arms or legs. Thus it seems quite possible that one mind could inhabit two different bodies simultaneously.

But barring considerations like these, when it becomes the regular thing for good, and on the face of it equally good, competing candidates to appear, our whole stock of basic beliefs are, considering the intent of the case, called into question. Whether or not there are cases of minds informing different bodies or brains, there are cases rampant of clairvoyance, incredibly lucky guessing, being mistaken on the grand scale about the bases of one's beliefs, persons being in two different places simultaneously, or something else.

As to the "something else," perhaps there is an ingenious and powerful god or

Martian causing these things to happen, making some minds inform different brains at different times, causing others to believe that they are yet other minds and filling them with information—perhaps by causing changes in brains. And given time, the god or Martian might even be wise, eloquent, and patient enough to be able to explain to us how he goes about doing it. Faced with such going's on, we are somewhat in the position of a Bushman in a physics lab.

But this sort of explanation of what is going on is not meant to be available. On the one hand, our background beliefs and sophistication about the actual world don't help; and on the other, we are not meant to be allowed to develop a new set to take their place. So by the very nature of the case, if we are to know which are "change of body" cases and which are not, we seem to be reduced simply to seeing that so-and-so is actually remembering and that so-and-so is being clairvoyant or guessing blindly. It is worth noting, however, that in some possible world people could have full-blown and sophisticated sets of background beliefs about these matters, about why they happen and what mechanisms are at work, rather than having to view them from the eyes of someone, very much unlike us, who never explains but merely identifies.

But from his eyes spatio-temporal continuity is now not an aid for making the distinction, and if criteria are demanded, like those we could perhaps name for a thing's being a unicorn, we fail to come up with them. It is a mistake, though, at this point to become mesmerized by the case of colors and to turn it into a paradigm for all cases in which we simply see that so-and-so is the case without being able to name interesting criteria, inductive or otherwise, for its being the case.

I believe that seeing that something is changing or moving is also of this sort. Wittgenstein suggests other cases. What are the criteria for a thing's having a gentle look, a benign look, a stern look? Talented artists can capture these features, on canvas or on stage, but we and they are at a loss to name criteria for them (unless, of course, gentleness and the like are treated as their own criteria).

What makes a thing a gentle look seems far more complicated than what makes it, say, red. Parts of an entirely red surface can be removed and the remainder will still be red. Parts of a face that has a gentle look cannot so easily be removed so as to leave the gentle look intact. If a person has trouble making these distinctions in practice, his problem seems to be much less one of the organs of sight than one of sensibility, the cure less amenable to drugs or operations than to practice, training, experience, and perhaps even a change in character and interests.

We are dealing, of course, not with a sharp distinction here: wine tasters and color experts by their vast training and experience develop extraordinary sensitivity, as do actors, sculptors, and social workers. Art connoisseurs often spot extremely good forgeries on sight, without knowing precisely what it is about the work that gives it away. Furthermore, the ability to make subtle distinctions like these is not always a gift of the practiced or talented few. All English speakers that are not deaf or hard of hearing can distinguish the sounds of the words "bed" and "bad," "bitch" and "beach." Few Spaniards can.

My suggestion is that the distinction between remembering, being clairvoyant, and lucky guessing might be viewed this way too, and what makes a thing a case of one rather than another is perhaps even more complicated than its having a gentle, benign, or stern look. We are handicapped, too, by the fact that there simply are no cases in the actual world of clairvoyance and such wildly lucky guessing, even though there are plenty of cases of remembering. We lack the opportunity to practice. It is as if there were only one flavor of tea in the world, and we were asked to imagine a world in which there were others.

In summary, then, I think that the believer in the possibility of reincarnation or bodily transfer is right on logical grounds in insisting that there is a distinction between remembering on the one hand and clairvoyance or uninformed lucky guessing on the other even if bodily continuity is absent. I fail to see why there would cease to be a distinction, even if it were true that it was logically impossible for us *to know* which was a case of one, which a case of the other—much less if it were merely impossible in practice. But I have also suggested that it *would* be possible for us to know which was which and even to explain the hows and whys of the phenomena. I have also suggested that we do distinguish many things of high complexity, unlike shades of color, without being able to say, except trivially, what distinguishes them and that the present distinctions might be of this kind.

But in judging whether we are still talking about the same thing by the word "person" in describing a world where competing candidates occurred frequently, other details would be relevant:

Does change of sex ever occur when one mind informs different bodies? Is there an institution of homosexual marriage? Does one have to obtain a divorce from someone who has changed bodies? Is one guilty of crimes committed when one had another body? Is one's eye-witness testimony accepted in court after a change of bodies? Can one's named heirs inherit when one dies? Do minds survive in space invisibly when they are not incarnate? Do the scientists of the world attempt to test for the presence of disembodied minds in space?

Here, I would imagine that the answers to these questions could be filled in with ingenuity in such a way as to make it fairly plausible that we are still using the word "person" in the regular way and that change of bodies might occur in the absence of any form of spatio-temporal continuity.

NOTES

1. Much of the material in this essay is taken directly from my article, "Personal Identity," *American Philosophical Quarterly*, Vol. 6, No. 3, July, 1969, pp. 226-232.

2. Sydney Shoemaker, *Self-Knowledge and Self-Identity*, Ithaca: Cornell University Press, 1963.

3. Many of the points that are discussed here can be found stated or at least hinted at in two articles by B. A. O. Williams: "Personal Identity and Individuation," *Proceedings of the Aristotelian Society*, Vol. LVII, 1956-57, pp. 229-52; "Bodily Continuity and Personal Identity: a Reply," *Analysis*, Vol. 21, No. 2, 1960, pp. 43-48.

4. The problem of formalizing such claims is extremely difficult. Yet one thing an analysis must not do is to turn them into necessarily false claims. The possibility that a person might be split into two people such that each resultant can see that he is now

not the other and yet can remember having been the original seems so plausible that that in itself seems to provide a good reason for rejecting any analysis that does make them necessarily false.

Normally identity is thought to be a two-term relation. Here, however, it seems to be taken as a three-term relation: A is identical to B at time t. The following rules characterize the two-term identity relation in natural deduction systems:

$$\begin{array}{ll} | x = x & (= \text{in}) \end{array} \qquad \begin{array}{l} \phi(x) \\ x = y \\ \cdot \\ \cdot \\ \cdot \\ \phi(y) \quad (= \text{out}) \end{array}$$

One is tempted to characterize the three-term identity relation by the following rules:

$$\begin{array}{ll} | I(t,x,x) & (I \text{ in}) \end{array} \qquad \begin{array}{l} \phi(t,x) \\ I(t,x,y) \\ \cdot \\ \cdot \\ \cdot \\ \phi(t,y) \quad (I \text{ out}) \end{array}$$

Using these rules, however, it can be proved that if x is identical to y at one time, x is identical to y at any other time:

1. $I(t,x,y)$ hyp.
2. $I(t',x,x)$ I in
3. $I(t',x,x) \& I(t,x,y)$ 1,2, & in
4. $I(t',x,y) \& I(t,x,y)$ 1,3,I out
5. $I(t',x,y)$ 4,& out

It is clear that to obtain the kind of three-term identity relation called for, further restrictions will have to be put on at least one of the two I rules above. What these restrictions are is not clear.

5. It is perhaps worth pointing out here that the believer in the possibility of reincarnation, in making this reply, in no way commits himself to a standard or to a non-standard view of identity. In the standard view, the identity relation is reflexive, symmetrical, and transitive. The principle of the Identity of Indiscernibles is a second-order *theorem*. Spatiotemporal continuity has absolutely nothing to do with it. On the other hand, if some non-standard view of identity is adopted (see, for instance, the preceding footnote), it is still not obvious that spatiotemporal continuity must, or even will, enter in.

6. Sydney Shoemaker, *Ibid.*, pp. 23-24.

7. *Ibid.*, p. 24.

8. Derek Parfit, "Personal Identity," *Philosophical Review*, Vol. LXXX, No. 1, January, 1971.

MEMORIES, BODIES AND PERSONS

D. E. Cooper

Traditionally, philosophical writings on personal identity have taken the form of attempts to discover the dominant criterion for deciding when a person at one time is identical with a person at some other time. Among the candidates for the role of dominant criterion have been bodily continuity (or continuity of some appropriate part of the body) and memory (or the ability, in principle, to remember). In the normal case, where a person P is identical with a person P' at some earlier time, it is true that P and P' share a continuous body, that P can remember experiences of P', and that many other relationships (e.g. similarity of character) hold between P and P'. Consequently, the debate as to which of the normal criteria is the dominant one has usually taken the form of imagining strange cases in which one or more of the normal criteria are lacking, and attempting to say, in such cases, who is identical with who. The scene was set, at least for modern times, by Locke's prince/pauper example, in which, according to Locke, the ability to remember experiences of a person having a different body guarantees, nevertheless, that one is that person—and hence that the memory criterion is dominant over the bodily identity one.

Attempts, like Locke's, to draw conclusions about personal identity from what we would say about such strange cases have usually failed to convince all philosophers of what the dominant criterion is. Many, for example, would not share Locke's intuitions on the prince/pauper example as to who is who. In recent years, indeed, doubt has been cast upon the propriety of asking the question, "What is the dominant criterion of personal identity?" It has been argued that we can only settle questions about who is who in normal situations where all, or most, of the normal criteria jointly apply. The concept of a person, it has been said, is a "cluster" concept, one for whose application there is a cluster of criteria no one of which dominates over the rest. So, in a case like that of the prince/pauper there is literally no answer to the question, "Who is who?" Instead we must, in a more or less arbitrary manner, make a decision as to what to say. We could select memory, say, as the dominant criterion, but the important point is that it would be a selection, not a correct (or incorrect) answer.

Not the least reason for this somewhat defeatist outlook has been the inconclusiveness of reflections upon what we should say about the strange cases. If people's intuitions as to what should be said differ so strongly, is this not good evidence for supposing that there is no right or wrong thing to say, and hence no dominant criterion to be found?

This selection is reprinted from *Philosophy*, Vol. 49, No. 189 (1974), 225 ff. Used by permission of the editor and D.E. Cooper.

Acceptance of this defeatist outlook has been too hasty. For recently it has been made relatively clear *why* it is that intuitions differ on how strange cases are to be described. And once one can see why intuitions differ one is at once in a better position to assess the value and weight of the various intuitions.

Suppose we have the case where the memory criterion comes into conflict with the bodily continuity criterion; a person, say, appears to remember vividly the experiences of a person occupying a different body. How do we describe what has happened? Has a person changed bodies or not? The problem here—and Professor Bernard Williams has recently put his finger on it[1]—is that our answers will tend to depend upon which perspective we view such a case from. In particular, there is an asymmetry between what we feel like saying from the perspective of persons prior to a putative case of body-changing, and what we feel like saying from the perspective of persons after such a putative case. To point this out is not to answer the question, "What is the dominant criterion of personal identity?" but the difficulty is highlighted. For we can now ask if each perspective is equally privileged, and if what we say from the two perspectives can be given equal weight. In fact I shall argue that the perspective which tempts us to say that changes of body do occur is less privileged, so that less weight should be given to the intuition that persons can change bodies, and therefore that we should regard bodily continuity as the dominant criterion.

I shall make my point by analyzing an imaginary experiment, and the perspectives from which it may be viewed. But first, I want to add a few words on what I have called the defeatist view. Philosophers who take the view that there is no dominant criterion of personal identity stress that we often do not know what to say about strange cases. This is very often so. But it does not follow that our inability to be clear is due to the fact that the concept of personal identity does not stretch to cover such cases. Instead it may be because we are completely in the dark as to what events have taken place, because no intelligible scientific story can be told about the sequence of events. Suppose a man wakes up one morning and relates vividly experiences which only Guy Fawkes could have had. If this is all we know, then we are in a desperate position, since we have no idea how it is that the man can display this talent. It is little use, even, suggesting that the man is Guy Fawkes, for we have no idea how Guy Fawkes, having lain dormant for centuries (where? how?), can suddenly have injected himself into this body. But suppose, instead, that we can tell a quite intelligible story of brain transplantation to explain how it is that a person in one body can recall the past of a person in another body. Then we are in a much better position to decide on questions of personal identity. The same is true in the case of the identity of material objects. There is all the difference between the two following instances: first, where my statuette vanishes into thin air, and ten minutes later its place on my desk is taken by a round lump of matter that appears to materialize out of nowhere; second, where I see my statuette melted by a flame and then molded into a round lump. The question, "Is the round lump the same thing as my statuette?" is much easier to answer in the second case.[2] In general it is wrong to confuse difficulties in answering questions about identity which derive from the opacity of that concept, with those that derive from our not knowing what the empirical facts are in situations where these questions might arise. I feel that those who have opted for the defeatist view might be guilty of just this confusion. At any rate, the example I shall be analyzing is one that is scientifically intelligible, and one about which it is possible to make a rational decision on personal identity.

The experiment—ignoring for the moment the weighted perspectives from which it may be viewed—is this: a scientist takes two persons, A and B who occupy, respectively, body-A and body-B. He links the brains of the men together, and by an ingenious electrical process obliterates those neural patterns in the brain of body-A which were the physiological basis for A's memories, and artificially reproduces these patterns in the brain of body-B. An analogous transfer from the brain of body-B to the brain of body-A is performed. The net result of this experiment is that the person in body-A is able to relate many experiences which only the person who, prior to the experiment, occupied body-B could have had. Equally the person now in body-B is able to recount past experiences which only the occupier of body-A could have had.[3]

One might say that the person now in body-A can remember experiences which the person once in body-B had originally had. This would have the disadvantage of sounding like question-begging; at least it would if we accept the principle that a person can only remember having experienced things which *he* experienced. So we would be begging the question in favor of saying that the person now in body-A is, in fact, B. I do not know if the above principle is acceptable or not. I think there could be reasons for saying that beliefs about past experiences are memories even where the person remembering is not the person who originally had the experiences. But, in case the principle is acceptable, I shall take the time-honored expedient of placing "memory," and its cognates, inside quotes, so that when I speak of a person "remembering" an experience, it is not entailed that he is the same person as the original subject of the experience. (Equally, it does not entail that he is not the same.)

Let me now fill in some of the events preceding the experiment, so as to move towards looking at it from the perspective of the persons after the experiment has been performed. Before the experiment, the scientist announces to A and B that they are to be subjected to this complete "memory"-transfer. He also announces that, after the transfer, one of the bodies will have red-hot pins stuck into it, while the other will receive a delicious massage. Finally he asks A to decide which of the bodies is to receive which treatment. A decides that it shall be body-A that will receive the torture, and body-B the massage. Let us call this decision D. Meanwhile, B has witnessed A making decision D. The two persons are then subjected to the "memory"-transfer.

What will the persons say and think after they have come round from the experiment? The following would be entirely natural for the person now in body-A to say, immediately and unreflectingly, as the pins are stuck into his body: "How unjust! I, who now feel pain, am the one who had no choice as to which body would be tortured, for I merely witnessed the person, then in body-A, make decision D." (I shall refer to this as sentence Sa.) It would be quite natural for the person now in body-A to utter Sa, since he can "remember" having witnessed decision D. Equally, it will be perfectly natural for the person who, after the transfer, is in body-B to say: "Thank goodness! I am now receiving a delicious massage and no pain, so I made the right decision when I chose body-A to be the victim of torture." (I shall refer to this as sentence Sb.) It will be entirely natural for the person in body-B to say this, since he can "remember" having made decision D.

It is the fact that Sa and Sb, and sentences like them, would be quite natural for the persons to utter after the experiment that tempts us, and them, to speak of a change of bodies having taken place. For how can the person now in body-A use "I" to refer both to the person in body-A and the person who, prior to the experiment, was in body-B, unless the two persons are the same? I am not suggesting, of course, that he must be right to employ "I" to refer to both, or that the two persons are generally right to utter sentences like Sa and Sb. What I do claim, though, is that Sa and Sb, and the use of "I" to refer to occupants of different bodies, sound reasonable enough and natural enough. We might put it like this: I put "remember" in quotes when I said that the person now in body-A can "remember" B's experience of witnessing the making of decision D. But the person in body-A would feel no need to put "remember" in quotes. Nor would a writer of science-fiction telling such a story put "remember" in quotes; and I doubt if many of his readers would condemn him for any laxity. I am claiming that the onus is very much on those who deny that a change of bodies has occurred to show why, despite the naturalness of Sa and Sb, they are nevertheless incorrect. Or, what comes to the same thing, they must explain why "remember" must be put in such cautious quotes. So I shall assume that if we regard the experiment from the perspective of what the persons would naturally say and think after it, then we are intuitively tempted to speak of a change of bodies, to opt for the memory criterion as being the dominant one.

Now I want to look at the experiment from the perspective of what might be naturally said and felt before the transfer. This time the preamble to the experiment is somewhat different. The scientist says to A: "Red-hot pins are going to be stuck into "your" body (body-A) in a short time." A, naturally, is horrified. The scientist then adds: "But by the time 'you' feel the pain, 'you' will have no memories of 'your' life up until the present moment." This will scarcely comfort A; insult, in the form of amnesia, is being added to injury. The scientist then adds: "'You' will, however, be equipped with a complete set of false beliefs about 'your' past." This will, if anything, worsen A's fears; torture, amnesia, and total delusion! Finally the scientist adds: "Incidentally, these false beliefs do fit the past of another person, B, who is, moreover, going to be equipped with false beliefs which fit 'your' past." This will be no comfort to A; delusions are still delusions even if they are delusions of being someone who actually existed. And what is it to A if some other unfortunate, B, is to go through the same process?

It would seem, then, that nothing the scientist tells A about the psychological changes that are to be induced, can comfort A's fears as to what is going to happen to body-A in a short time, namely torture by pins. Since it is the future of his own body that is of most concern to A, then it appears that he identifies the future of his body with the future of body-A. He is not tempted at all to suppose that he is going to change bodies as a result of the psychological changes, for his fears remain fears for body-A whatever the scientist tells him. In order to avoid begging the question I placed "you" and "your" in quotes during the scientist's conversation. But the scientist would not feel the need to do this; nor would A find anything odd in the scientist employing "you" and "your" unquoted. That is, A would find it quite natural for the scientist to employ "you" to refer to the occupant of body-A while he is talking, and to the occupant of body-A after the experiment. In other words, A takes it that, after the experiment, the person in body-A will be himself, despite the psychological changes that are to be induced. It seems, then, that from the perspective of what would be naturally said and felt before the experiment, it is not at all tempting to suppose that a change of bodies will take place.

Here, then, is the asymmetry I mentioned between what we are tempted to say from different perspectives. We have taken one and the same experiment; regarded from the perspective of what would be said afterwards we are tempted to say a change of bodies has taken place, but regarded from the perspective of what would be said before the experiment, we feel no temptation to say that a change of bodies will take place.

We could resolve the problem if we could show that what is said and felt from one perspective is less privileged than what is said and felt from the other. And we could do this if we could show either (1) that Sa and Sb are things persons would naturally utter even where, definitely, no change of bodies has taken place, or (2) that the concern A feels for the future of body-A is something he would naturally feel even where, definitely, he will change bodies.

I shall concentrate on (1). There would be an obvious difficulty in trying to establish (2), namely that there are no cases in which it is obvious that a person changes bodies. Our experiment is as good a case of putative body-changing as one could get, but it is hardly obvious that persons really do change bodies. No similar problem arises in trying to establish (1) for there are, of course, innumerable cases in which it is definite that persons do not change bodies. I, for example, have definitely never changed bodies.

It was the naturalness of saying, and accepting, Sa and Sb that was given as the sole reason for saying that a change of bodies had taken place; so if (1) can be established, it follows that we have no reason for thinking that, since it turns out that Sa and Sb are the sorts of things it would be natural to say even where no change of bodies has occurred. If Sa and Sb would be said anyway, then their utterance can count as no reason for suggesting that a change of bodies has taken place. To this extent, the perspective of what is said and felt after the experiment is less privileged; so that we should take more seriously what is said and felt before it.

Can (1) be established? I think so. Suppose, as before, the scientist tells A and B that a complete "memory"-transfer is to take place, and that it is up to A to decide which body will be tortured, and which massaged. A, as before, makes decision D, which B witnesses. Then they are anaesthetized for the experiment. This time, however, the scientist plays a trick. Instead of transferring all of A's "memories" to the brain of body-B, he transfers just one. This is the "memory" of having made decision D in the light of his belief that there would be a complete "memory"-transfer. Equally only one "memory" is transferred from B to the brain of body-A. This is the "memory" of having witnessed A make decision D. In this situation, plainly, no one would even suggest that a change of bodies has occurred. The transfer of one of my "memories" to your body clearly does not involve my being transferred to that body. So A is still in Body-A, and B in body-B.

Now what would it be natural for A and B to say after the experiment, when the torture and the massage begin? The following would be entirely natural for the person in body-A, A himself, to say: "How unjust! I, who now feel pain, am the one who had no choice as to which body would be tortured, for I merely witnessed the person, then in body-A, make decision D." It would be quite natural for him to say this, since he can "remember" having witnessed decision D. Equally, it will be perfectly natural for the person now in body-B, B himself, to say: "Thank goodness! I am now receiving a delicious massage and no pain, so I made the right decision when I chose body-A to be the victim of torture." It will be entirely natural for him to say this, since he can "remember" having made decision D.

Now A has uttered Sa, and B has uttered Sb, just as after the real experiment the person in body-A uttered Sa, and the person in body-B uttered Sb. So it turns out that the persons in body-A and body-B would naturally utter Sa and Sb respectively both after the real experiment and after the trick one. Since, after the trick one, there has definitely been no change of bodies, then we cannot regard the naturalness of Sa and Sb as reason for saying that a change of bodies has occurred even after the real experiment.

It is no good saying that, after the real experiment, it is the *conjunction* of (a) a complete "memory"-transfer with (b) the naturalness of Sa and Sb, that is reason for thinking that a change of bodies has taken place, for, as far as I can see, the fact of the complete "memory"-transfer tempts us in no particular direction. If someone is told, merely, that certain neural patterns have been removed from one brain and reproduced in another, I doubt that he would feel intuitions one way or the other concerning a possible change of bodies. It is only when we mention what is said and felt as a result of the electrical operation that we are tempted towards the body-change hypothesis. But, so I am arguing, since this might just as well result from a much more modest operation, in which definitely no change of bodies takes place, we should not be so tempted.

A more threatening objection would be that, after the trick experiment, A and B could use some of their memories to make them very quickly aware that a trick has been played, and so remove the temptation for them to say things like Sa and Sb. Suppose A had been in Paris in 1960. Then, after the real experiment, it will be the person in body-B who has "memories" of being in Paris in 1960; whereas, after the trick experiment, it will be the person in body-A, A himself, who remembers being in Paris. However, it is unclear how A is meant to use this memory so as to realize that a trick has been played. For if he believes that there has been a complete "memory"-transfer, and that he is the person who witnessed, and did not make, decision D, then he will presumably believe that although he was in Paris, this was during his occupancy of body-B.

The objection would have to be strengthened by insisting that some of A's memories are body-specific, in the sense that they are of body-A, and no other, being, e.g. in Paris in 1960. If so, then A will quickly realize, because most of his memories fit only the past of the body he occupies and not body-B, that a trick has been played, that only one or a few "memories" have been switched.

I think this objection can be dealt with by circumscribing more exactly the nature of the experiment. But it is also worth mentioning that very few of our memories are body-specific in the sense that they could fit only the history of this, rather than that, body. For example, my memory of eating breakfast does not contain an image of a mouth which could fit only this mouth, the one I at the moment have. It is, of course, reasonable to say that I remember employing my mouth at breakfast; but this is because of the reasonable assumption that I have not changed mouths since then. I certainly do not use specific images of this, my present mouth, to infer that this is the very mouth I ate with at breakfast. Now once A makes the assumption that he no longer inhabits his old body, it is not clear that many memories would jibe with this assumption. While, for example, he may remember the Champs Elysées well enough, it is doubtful if he recalls that this foot, rather than that one was walking upon it. Which feet he thinks were walking along the Champs Elysées will depend upon which body he thinks he occupied then, rather than vice-versa.

Anyway, I believe one can handle the problem of memories which might at once fail to jibe with the natural tendency of A and B, after the trick experiment, to say things like Sa and Sb, by adding some complications into the experiment. There are various things we might do. We might, for example, make A and B identical twins; so that any of A's memories which contain specific memories of body-A could, nevertheless, quite happily fit the history of body-B—in the way in which my memory of the Mona Lisa fits the past of a good reproduction of that painting but does not fit the past of the Night Watch. A, for example, could not tell, just by looking at B, that B's body is not the one that figures in his memories. Or we might introduce into the experiment a fairly radical plastic surgery, one which makes both bodies unrecognizably different. In this case, too, A could not, just by looking at B's body, tell that this is not his old body, since he knows that, whichever his old body is, it is no longer at all as he remembers it. Or we might so arrange things after the trick experiment that neither A nor B is able to inspect his own body, so that neither is able to tell that his own body is the one that figures in his memories. To make matters more convincing, A could then be confronted with an animated, life-size waxwork copy of himself, which will fit his memories of his body, and which, since he can observe it at a distance from himself, he will conclude he no longer inhabits.

The experiment has now become pretty fantastic, but I think we are entitled to make it as fantastic as we like. For all that needs to be shown is that there are circumstances in which it would be just as natural to say things like Sa and Sb after the trick experiment as it was after the real experiment. It is not, incidentally, necessary for me to show that A and B would never, on reflection, come to reject Sa and Sb after the trick experiment. But then it is equally true that the persons after the real experiment might, on sufficient reflection, come to withdraw Sa and Sb. The person in body-A—A himself, I would argue—might reason as follows after the real experiment: "At first I was tempted to say things like Sa, since I seemed to remember having witnessed, rather than made, decision D. But since I know what happened, that neural patterns have been removed and others implanted into my brain, I no longer feel tempted to say this. I simply falsely believed that I witnessed decision D. In the future, whenever I am tempted to say "I remember experiencing . . .," I shall stop myself; for it was not me who had the experience, but B." If I am right, this is how A should reason with himself.

I conclude, then, that faced by the choice between the memory criterion and the bodily continuity criterion of personal identity, the latter is the wiser to opt for.[4] For the intuitions, in strange cases, which tempt us to hypothesize changes of bodies, emerge from the less privileged perspective.

NOTES

1. "The Self and the Future," *Philosophical Review* (April, 1970).

2. *Easier,* not easy. See D. Wiggins' discussion of such cases in his *Identity and Spatio-Temporal Continuity* (Oxford, 1967).

3. This experiment, and my accounts of the two perspectives from which it may be viewed, are very similar to those given by Williams (*op. cit.*).

4. I should stress that I am aware of, but have not tried to discuss, the very tricky problem of what *parts* of the body are relevant in devising a bodily continuity criterion.

SIXTH SYMPOSIUM

ESP, P. K. AND KNOWLEDGE: OPENING NOTE
Peter A. French

MIND OVER MIND AND MIND OVER MATTER
H H. Price

NORMAL COGNITION, CLAIRVOYANCE AND TELEPATHY
C. D. Broad

AN ANALYSIS OF FACTUAL KNOWLEDGE
Peter Unger

*"Somehow it seems to fill my head with ideas—
only I don't exactly know what they are"*

ESP, P. K. AND KNOWLEDGE: OPENING NOTE

Peter A. French

What is the nature of knowledge? What is it to know? Questions regarding the definition and scope of knowledge have played focal roles throughout the Western tradition of philosophy. Philosophers have argued that knowledge is justified, true belief. What does that mean? It would seem that one can only have knowledge of what is true. "He possessed false knowledge of X," if it has any sense at all, must mean something like "He held unsupportable beliefs about X." It would be an inappropriate use of language to say, "I know that the cat is on the mat, but 'The cat is on the mat' is false." It is only a common-sense truism that no one can know that which is not so. Of course, people often claim to know what is not so, but then they are mistaken or lying or confused, etc. No one, however, can sensibly admit that some statement is false and yet protest that he knows it to be the case. If I know that the cat is on the mat, no one else can know that the cat is not on the mat; which is to say that there is in common use a strong sense of "know" which is incompatible with making a mistake.

Knowledge seems to entail more than simply having true beliefs. Each of us has experienced any number of occasions when what we believed would happen did happen but about which we would not, even retrospectively, say that we had known all along that it was going to happen. Beliefs which just happen to be true, but which were supported only by the vaguest of reasons are not generally described as knowledge. If someone says, "I know that an earthquake will destroy Los Angeles in a matter of days," or, simply, "An earthquake will destroy Los Angeles in a matter of days," the appropriate retort is to say, "How do you know?" And not just any sort of answer will be acceptable. For example, should he respond that he saw the horrible destruction of Los Angeles in a dream or that the local fortune teller saw it in her crystal ball and told him so, we are likely to frown and utter, "But you don't really know. You're just guessing. You just believe it. It's your opinion." Although one's beliefs may be true, they must be justified by a demonstration that it is not accidently the case that they are true before we are prepared to count them knowledge. In other words, it must be possible for one to answer, "How did you come to know?" questions in at least one of a number of specifiable and conventional ways.

These obviously complicated issues are related to the field of psychical research because the subjects of ESP tests purport to know certain things. In fact, unless ESP experiences result in knowledge claims by the subjects, they are not special or even interesting; they are dismissable as sheer guesswork, lucky though they may sometimes be. If all that is claimed is that the subject of a telepathy experience is a better than average guesser concerning some specific things, then there would seem to be little reason to examine the purported phenomena in depth. Psychical researchers, however, do claim that "sensitives know" more than the rest of us or at least have ways of coming to know which we either do not have or which we do not usually exercise.

This symposium is concerned with a series of questions which may be grouped under the general heads of "Are ESP experiences genuine justifying grounds for knowledge claims? Can we understand what is purported to be going on during an ESP experience?" and "Does the notion that knowledge is justified, true belief really satisfy our concept of what it is to know?" We shall also explore various kinds of ostensible ESP experiences: telepathy, clairvoyance and psychokinesis, mainly in order to (a) understand what each is said to involve and (b) discuss the issue of whether they, or some of them, can appropriately be deemed perceptual experiences and as such supportive of knowledge claims.

Before beginning this symposium let us acquaint ourselves with one attempt to isolate and study a form of ESP. The following excerpted account is of the Pearce-Pratt distance tests of ESP which was originally published in the *Journal of Parapsychology*, Vol. 18 (1954), 165-77.

> *Procedure.* A single subject, H. E. P., was tested for his ability to identify ESP test cards manipulated by the experimental assistant, J. G. P., in another building, part of the time at a distance of 100 yards and part of the time at a distance of more than 250 yards from the location of the subject. The experiment was designed to test for the clairvoyant type of ESP; and J. G. P., accordingly, did not know the card order in the test.
>
> Aside from planning the experiment, J. B. R. participated only in the independent checking of results, except for Series D in which he

participated with J. G. P. as the witness to the operation of the test.

There were, in all, four subseries, A, B, C, and D, totaling 74 runs through the pack of 25 cards; and the series extended from August, 1933, into March, 1934. The testing days were not consecutive, though within a given subseries they were more or less so. They were selected, however, at the mutal convenience of H. E. P. and J. G. P. Subseries C was begun in October, 1933, and four runs were added to it in March, 1934, with Subseries D following thereafter. Specific dates may be found in Table 1. Subseries A was done with the 100 yards distance, Subseries B at 250 yards, and the other two subseries back at 100 yards. The 74 runs represent all the ESP tests made with H. E. P. during this experiment under the condition of working with the subject and target cards in different buildings. It was, in fact, the only distance test involving different buildings done at the Duke Laboratory at the time.

Series A was set up with an advance commitment on termination point. It was agreed that 300 trials were to be given H. E. P. The following Subseries B, was intended to be a duplication with only the additional distance involved, but the experimenters were interested in the big shift of scoring level from day to day which was shown at the longer distance. It was decided to allow H. E. P. to continue further so as to see what would happen. Subseries C was intended to be a repetition of Subseries A, consisting of 300 trials designed to discover whether the lower scoring rate of Subseries B at the longer distance was a result of the altered situation or whether H. E. P. had declined in scoring ability. Subseries D, as has been stated, was intended as introducing a check on J. G. P., and its length was agreed upon in advance (150 trials, or six runs).

In actual operation the experiment proceeded as follows, regardless of which subseries was involved: at the time agreed upon, H. E. P. visited J. G. P. in his research room on the top floor of what is now the Social Science Building on the main Duke campus. The two men synchronized their watches and set an exact time for starting the test, allowing enough time for H. E. P. to cross the quadrangle to the Duke Library where he occupied a cubicle in the stacks at the back of the building. From his window J. G. P. could see H. E. P. enter the Library.

J. G. P. then selected a pack of ESP cards from several packs always available in the room. He gave this pack of cards a number of dovetail shuffles and a final cut, keeping them face down throughout. He then placed the pack on the right-hand side of the table at which he was sitting. In the center of the table was a closed book on which it had been agreed with H. E. P. that the card for each trial would be placed. At the minute set for starting the test, J. G. P. lifted the top card from the inverted deck, placed it face down on the book, and allowed it to remain there for approximately a full minute. At the beginning of the next minute this card was picked up with the left hand and laid, still face down, on the left-hand side of the table, while with the right hand J. G. P. picked up the next card and put it on the book. At the end of the second minute, this card was placed on top of the one on the left and the next one was put on the book. In this way, at the rate of one card per minute, the entire pack of 25 cards went through the process of being isolated, one card at a time, on the book in the center of the table, where it was the target or stimulus object for that ESP trial.

In his cubicle in the Library, H. E. P. attempted to identify the target cards, minute by minute, and recorded his responses in pencil. At the end of the run, there was on most test days a rest period of five minutes before a second run followed in exactly the same way. H. E. P. made a duplicate of his call record, signed one copy and sealed it in an envelope for J. B. R. Over in his room J. G. P. recorded the card order for the two decks used in the test as soon as the second run was finished. This record too, was in duplicate, one copy of which was signed and sealed in an envelope for J. B. R. The two sealed records were delivered personally to J. B. R., most of the time before J. G. P and H. E. P. compared their records and scored the number of successes. On the few occasions when J. G. P. and H. E. P. met and compared their unsealed duplicates before both of them had delivered their sealed records to J. B. R., the data could not have been changed without collusion, as J. G. P. kept the results from the unsealed records and any discrepancy between them and J. B. R.'s results would have been noticed. In subseries D, J. B. R. was on hand to receive the duplicates as the two other men met immediately after each session for the checkup.

Thus, from day to day as the experiment proceeded, H. E. P. was kept informed, as he had been in all his earlier experiments, as to the rate of success achieved. The practice of expressing enthusiastic congratulations should be mentioned as a part of the procedure. If, as rarely happened, the scoring rate was low, favorable emphasis was placed on the overall performance, the general average maintained, and the high standing of the subject in the comparative scale of ESP subjects. Throughout the series the paramount objective of high-order performance was held before the subject with all the vigor and expectation that could be communicated.

General Evaluation: Since they were one series of tests carried out under essentially the same conditions, the four subseries (totaling 74 runs, or 1850 trials) may be pooled. Mean chance expectation is 20%, or 370 hits. The total number of successes actually scored for the series is 558, which is better than 30%. The theoretical standard deviation derived on a conservative basis is 17.57. This total of 558 hits is 188 above the theoretical expectation and it gives a critical ratio of 10.70. The probability that a critical ratio so large as this would occur on the basis of random sampling is less than 10^{-22}. In the determination of the critical ratio given above, allowance is made for the slight correction applicable when, as in this experiment, the balanced ESP deck is used; that is, when there are five of each symbol in each pack. The variance of scores obtained with the 5 x 5 ESP deck depends upon the frequency with which the subject calls the different symbols. The largest variance results when the subject always calls exactly five of each symbol, and the SD of 17.57 was obtained on this assumption (2). However, the subject rarely called five of each symbol in a run, and the exact SD would therefore be smaller than the one used here, which makes the estimate of statistical significance a conservative one.

TABLE: Pearce-Pratt Distance Series: General Results

Subseries	Dates		Runs	Dev.	SD	CR	P
	Start	End					
A	8/25/33	9/1/33	12	+59	7.07	8.35	$<10^{-14}$
B	9/2/33	9/30/33	44	+75	13.54	5.54	$<10^{-6}$
C	10/18/33	3/10/34	12	+28	7.07	3.96	.000075
D	3/12/34	3/13/34	6	+26	5.00	5.20	$<10^{-6}$
Total.	8/25/33	3/13/34	74	+188	17.57	10.70	$<10^{-22}$

MIND OVER MIND AND MIND OVER MATTER

H. H. Price

The questions I want to discuss are not questions of fact or evidence, but questions of theory, and highly speculative theory at that. I think such a discussion is needed. The theoretical side of psychical research has lagged far behind the evidential side. And that, I believe, is one of the main reasons why the evidence itself is still ignored by so many, and especially by so many highly educated people—not rejected but just disregarded. It is because these queer facts apparently "make no sense" and "don't fit in anywhere," that they tend to make no permanent impression on the mind, even if one has had firsthand experience of them. If we could devise some theoretical explanation or interpretation in terms of which the facts *did* make sense and did fit into some kind of comprehensive conceptual framework, it would be a great gain. Such an explanation is needed for its own sake; and it is also needed to get the evidence attended to and considered.

It is usual to divide the whole field of supernormal phenomena into two main groups, mental and physical. Telepathy, clairvoyance, precognition, and at least some apparitions would be called mental phenomena; so would automatic writing, because its cognitive aspect is more important than its physical aspect. The physical phenomena include poltergeists, materialization, spiritual healing, levitation of tables, human bodies and other physical objects. It would generally be said that the evidence for the mental phenomena is better than for the physical. But there is some evidence for the physical phenomena, too, and even some laboratory evidence (Dr. J. B. Rhine's experiments on influencing the fall of dice by means of will or thought). I think there is at any rate enough evidence for the physical phenomena to compel the theorist to sit up and take notice, lest he be caught napping some day.

Let us first consider the mental phenomena. I want to suggest that all of them, including apparitions, can be reduced to two basic ones—telepathy and clairvoyance. Precognition, I believe, is not a separate mental function, but rather a name for the fact that both telepathy and clairvoyance are in some degree independent of physical time. I am, however, going to assume that telepathy and clairvoyance are two distinct processes, though I know that some very distinguished authorities disagree with this. I shall say no more about clairvoyance here (except for a word or two by way of postscript at the end). So far as the mental phenomena are concerned, I shall confine myself to telepathy.

If we now turn to the physical phenomena, we find that the situation is

This selection is extracted from *Enquiry*, Vol. 2, No. 1 (July, 1949) and Vol. 2, No. 3 (September, 1949). Used by permission of H.H. Price.

simpler from the classificatory point of view even though more difficult from the evidential point of view. I think it will be safe to group all the physical phenomena under the term psychokinesis, or PK for short, which I borrow from Dr. Rhine. PK may be provisionally defined as the influence of thought upon matter, independently of the muscular mechanism of the body.

Telepathy and PK

I can now state the problem I want to discuss. On the face of it, telepathy and PK seem to be utterly different things. In the one, mind influences mind; in the other, mind influences matter. All they seem to have in common is that both are supernormal, i.e., things which *ought* not to happen if our ordinary scientific assumptions about the world are correct. I want to suggest that telepathy and PK are much more closely connected than this, and are, in the end, two different manifestations of the same thing. But to reach this agreeable conclusion, I am afraid you will have to accompany me on a long and difficult journey; and you may suffer considerable shocks on the way.

The first step is to remove a certain misconception which is, I think, the greatest of all obstacles to progress in psychical research: the assumption that the individual mind is a separate and indivisible unit—just the mind of Jones or Smith, and that is all about it. This assumption is really part of the intellectual heritage of Descartes. Descartes divided the created universe into two great divisions, matter and mind (his famous dualism); and he divided the individual human being into two parts, mind and body. He thought that the material half of the universe could be regarded as one single substance, whose essence was extension in space. But the mental half, he supposed, was arranged on quite a different plan. Within the mental half he thought there were hard and fast divisions. It consisted, according to him, of many *separate* minds, each of which was by itself a substance. Each of these minds was supposed to be a complete and separate unit, and none of them interacted directly with any other. Each of them did interact with matter, but only with a special piece of matter, its own brain. He supposed, also, that consciousness was the essence of mind, as extension in space was the essence of matter; and if we define mind in this way it follows, of course, that unconscious mind is an absurdity, like a square circle.

Descartes

The philosophy of Descartes has come to be part of the mental background of all of us in the West. It seems to us to be just common sense; and because it does, phenomena which contradict it are either not believed, or, if they are with difficulty believed, they have to be labeled supernormal or abnormal. They are regarded as things which violate common sense.

But I believe that if we are to make any progress in psychical research, or in psychopathology either, we must get rid of this seeming common sense. It is not common sense at all. It is just a philosophic theory, a very brilliant theory, and a very useful one (since without it modern science would probably not have got started) but a theory still. And in our time it has become a nuisance, for facts have turned up in psychical research, and in abnormal psychology, too, which cannot be squeezed into this particular theoretical framework. So we must try to construct a better one.

The first thing we must do, I believe, is to divide human nature into *three* parts instead of Descartes' two—into body, mind and spirit, instead of just body and mind. The word "spirit" is, of course, a most unsatisfactory one. I am using it here to mean the fundamental "I," the pure ego, the *Atman* of the Hindu philosophers. Whether this "I" is analyzable or unanalyzable I do not wish to inquire. And a mind, at this rate, is not something that one *is,* but something that one *has.* Perhaps we can say of the spirit that it is something permanent and indivisible, and that its essence is consciousness—or perhaps we cannot really say anything about it at all (not even whether it is one or many), because none of the familiar categories of our thought are applicable to it. The main point is that psychical research is not concerned with it. The discussion of the spirit or ego belongs rather to metaphysics or to the philosophy of mystical experience. What concerns us is the second member of the triad—mind, or what the Neoplatonist philosophers called "soul" or *psyche*. Mind, as distinct from spirit or ego, is the subject matter of psychical research and of all the psychological sciences. I shall henceforth use the word "mind" in this sense, for something distinct from the spirit, on the one side, and from body on the other. This terminology may not be very satisfactory; but let us use it for want of a better. Perhaps the greatest difficulty of the philosophy of psychical research is that at present we simply have not got a terminology for saying what we want to say.

Now I believe it is a fundamental error to suppose that a *mind* is an indivisible entity, or separate from other minds. It is not, I believe, true that its essence is consciousness. On the contrary, many and perhaps most of the processes which go on in it are subconscious or unconscious. Again, it is not necessarily true that the only piece of matter which a mind directly acts upon is its own brain, as Descartes said it was. This is a question of empirical fact.

It seems to me that the philosophical notion of a substance, a persistent and indivisible entity separate from all others, does not apply to minds at all. Such unity as a mind does have is precarious and unstable, and only a matter of degree. Its unity is tighter at some times and looser at others. There is a sense in which we are all mad—mentally disintegrated—when we are dreaming. I am trying to suggest that a mind is not an absolutely unitary being, as Descartes thought. The unity of a mind has two aspects, internal and external, and in respect of both it is a matter of degree, and not of all or none. The facts of abnormal psychology show that *internally* the unity of the mind is unstable and precarious, and that sometimes it splits into two or more parts, as in the phenomena of multiple personality. The facts of psychical research show that *externally* also the unity of the mind is a matter of degree. They show that one mind is not separated from another by any hard and fast line, and that two minds may overlap.

The Main Problem

It becomes clear, then, that if we are to make any sense of either abnormal or supernormal phenomena, the individual mind is not a suitable unit to work with.

If we are to make any progress we must change the unit. We must take as our unit not a mind, as Descartes did, but what I shall call an *idea*. (I shall not try to define the word "idea"; I shall assume that its meaning is sufficiently well understood.) The ultimate elements of the mental world, let us say, are ideas. We can then build up the various grades of psychical entity out of these new units, from not very purposive ghosts and Freudian complexes at the one end, to the complete and healthily integrated individual human mind at the other. I will add, however, that none of these mental entities, not even the healthily integrated waking human mind of the sane and normal Mr. Jones, is completely autonomous or completely coherent. All have ragged edges, and the internal unity of each is precarious and unstable. If all this seems to disintegrate human personality too much, remember that I am still distinguishing the mind from the spirit or "I."

After these preliminaries, we are now in a position to tackle our main problem: can we show that there is some link between the two main groups of supernormal phenomena, mental and physical, which appear at first sight to be entirely different and disconnected? If telepathy is the basic phenomenon on the mental, and PK on the physical side, our question comes to this: can we show that there is any kind of link between telepathy and PK? Let us begin by reconsidering PK.

Taking the idea, not the complete mind, as our unit, let us see what more might be said about the nature of an idea. Every idea, we may assume, originates in somebody's consciousness. Let us suppose, however, that once an idea has come into existence it has, so to speak, an independent life of its own. Let us suppose that it remains in existence for a short or long time (in some cases, perhaps, longer than the lifetime of the body) but presumably only for a finite time. Moreover, let us suppose that an idea, once it is in being, is no longer wholly under the control of the consciousness which gave it birth. Though it began its career in consciousness, it persists outside of consciousness ("in the unconscious" as we say). It may return into consciousness from time to time, or it may not. Moreover, we will also suppose that every idea is endowed with *causal efficacy;* and that it not only exists but also operates independently, apart from the consciousness in which it originated.

What kind of causal efficacy shall we attribute to it? Let us suppose that every idea has an inherent tendency to realize itself in a physical form, to make itself concrete, or to "materialize" itself. (I do not mean that every idea has a tendency to *create* a material embodiment *ex nihilo* for itself; but that it tends to realize itself by rearranging existing material particles in some way.) This tendency may, of course, be resisted by the inhibiting action of other ideas, which are also trying to realize or materialize themselves. Again, this tendency may be only partly fulfilled. Thus an idea may succeed in manifesting itself in an imaginative or pictorial form, as a mental image, but not in a physical form. This is, as it were, a half-way stage toward material self-realization, because a mental picture is at least something spatial, even though the space it is in is not the space of the physical world. The next stage is a visual or tactual hallucination, and then a quasi-public apparition, common to two or three observers. But every idea, I am suggesting, tries to go even further than this. It tries actually to embody itself in the physical world, to express itself in a fully material form.

The most familiar and obvious way in which ideas get embodied in the physical world is through the nervous systems and muscles of human beings and other animals. Much of the physical environment of civilized man, especially town-dwelling man, consists of ideas or thoughts which have materialized themselves in this way, such as houses, factories, streets buses, machines of all kinds. But I suggest that this commonplace and familiar way in which ideas materialize themselves is only a special case of something wider. That is what we *must* suppose if PK is a genuine fact. We must suppose that sometimes an idea succeeds in materializing itself in a physical object or event without making use of anybody's brain or muscles. We must treat the familiar operation of ideas by means of nerves and muscles as merely one manifestation among others of the inherent tendency ideas have to materialize themselves if they can.

Ideo-Motor Action

To put it in another way: I think we must generalize the notion of what psychologists call ideo-motor action. Any idea which occupies one's attention tends to fulfil itself by means of muscular action, unless it is inhibited by other ideas. If the bicyclist *thinks* of turning to the right he does find himself turning to the right. If the thought of running into the old lady crossing the street occupies his mind, the chances are that he will run into her. Or if a man walking across a plank thinks of falling into the water, the chances are that he will fall in. The so-called "nervous" person, who is always thinking of the things he wishes to avoid, is likely to do these very things, just *because* the thought of them occupies his attention. And what is called "good nerve" consists in keeping such thoughts out, and focusing one's attention upon the desired object instead. The examples I have given are *unwilled* actions. But will itself is only the conscious utilization of this same ideo-motor mechanism. What is called strength of will consists in concentrating attention upon the thing you want to do, and keeping other ideas out; and the idea then executes itself automatically through the muscular apparatus of the body. The function of will is to keep that thought before the mind and to keep other thoughts out.

If we now proceed to *generalize* this notion of ideo-motor action, we come back to where we were, to the hypothesis that every idea has an inherent tendency to manifest itself in physical form. PK is ideo-motor operation occurring apart from the nervous system and muscles, instead of by means of them. You will observe, with suitable horror, that this is just one of the fundamental assumptions of primitive magic. I cannot help it; perhaps primitive magic has a little grain of sense in it after all, along with a very great deal of nonsense and superstition. But you may also observe that a much more respectable activity—prayer—seems to be based on a similar assumption. I suspect that prayer does work sometimes, although we are by no means compelled to accept the theologians' theory of how it works.

I cannot forbear to add that if there is any truth in this hypothesis, thought is a very dangerous thing. It is said that hard words break no bones, but perhaps they sometimes may, if there are hard thoughts behind them. For it follows from what I have said that what anybody thinks has some tendency to come about in fact just because it is thought of; and it still has that tendency even when the thought is no longer in anybody's consciousness. If it does not, that is because there are other contrary thoughts which are opposed to it. Ideas are dangerous things because they have a tendency, however slight, to come true.

Now let us turn to telepathy. Please remember that we are still taking the individual idea rather than the individual mind as our fundamental unit. The phenomena of telepathy seem to me to show that there is a common unconscious, that at the unconscious level there is no sharp distinction between one mind and another. But we may have to distinguish, as Jung does, between the personal unconscious and a "deeper" impersonal unconscious. This, however, is only a difference of degree. We may explain it, following a hint of Carington's, in terms of degrees of probability. If a certain idea is more likely to emerge into my consciousness than into anyone else's, then it belongs to my personal consciousness. But if it is as likely to emerge into anyone's consciousness as into anyone else's, then it belongs to the impersonal or collective unconscious. Any idea is capable, in principle, of emerging into anyone's consciousness, and there is some small probability that it will. Before telepathy was discovered it was assumed that an idea, once it had come into existence, could *only* emerge thereafter in the consciousness of the person who originally formulated it—that ideas orginating in A's past experience could only emerge into A's consciousness thereafter. The discovery of telepathy shows this assumption is false.

It will now be useful to introduce the notion of the *threshold* of consciousness. If it is unfamiliar to any of my readers, I would point out that the word "subliminal" used by Myers and others is only the Latin for "beneath the threshold." The threshold is conceived as a kind of barrier or dividing line between conscious and unconscious. Not all the ideas which try to get into consciousness succeed in doing so. There is a kind of competition among them, and some have to stay out. This is partly because of what I called the narrowness of consciousness. The number of ideas of which anyone can be conscious at any one time appears to be limited. But that is not all. The ideas which get in easily are those which appeal to our dominant interests and purposes. The ones which are opposed to these interests and purposes tend to be kept out. Indeed ideas which are completely opposed to one's own ideas and purposes are permanently kept out of consciousness, repressed; though that of course does not prevent them from still existing and operating—quite the contrary.

Now I think we have to suppose that every idea has our inherent tendency to cross the threshold and emerge in a consciousness if it can. This is parallel to the tendency which every idea has to materialize itself. Indeed, as I hope to show later, it is another aspect of the same thing.

Telepathy

Let us now apply this notion of the threshold to the phenomenon of telepathy. Suppose I receive telepathic communication. Then an idea which was originally in someone else's consciousness (he need not, of course, be conscious of it now) has got into mine. To do this, it first had to cross my threshold and compete with all the other ideas there which were trying to do the same. Crossing the threshold is rather a difficult job, as I have tried to explain. It is difficult even for ideas which were originally my own. Even my own personal memories are liable to be permanently repressed if too distasteful; and then they can only emerge, if at all, in a distorted and symbolic form as dreams, for example. And every idea, even if it is my mind, has to compete with others to get in. The difficulty is only greater still if it is *not* my own. I think we can now see why telepathy is a relatively rare occurrence. It is because of the difficulty of crossing the threshold. If the threshold were not there, or if it were a weaker barrier than it is, we should be having telepathic experiences all the time. The right question to ask about telepathy is not "Why does it happen at all?" but "Why doesn't it happen more often?" And I believe this is the answer to it. According to my assumption, every idea has a tendency to emerge into consciousness if it can. And if telepathy is a genuine fact (as I am sure it is) every idea has a tendency to emerge into *any* consciousness, no matter whose. But wherever it tries to emerge, it always comes up against this barrier of the threshold, and only in rare cases does it succeed in getting through.

We must not, however, suppose that the threshold is a mere nuisance; on the contrary, it is a kind of protective mechanism, indispensable to the maintenance of our personalities. So the question, "Why doesn't telepathy happen all the time?" can also be answered in another way. If it did happen all the time, our personalities would be disrupted. We literally could not bear it. The unity of our mind—such as it is—would collapse under the strain. The integrity of each man's personality depends upon a relatively stable set of interests and purposes, or, if you like, upon a relatively stable set of dominant ideas. If other ideas were continually getting in which have nothing to do with these, or are even opposed to them, his whole conscious life would become completely incoherent. If the threshold were not there, we should all be mad; as indeed we all are to some degree in dreams, when the threshold is much weaker than it is in waking life. A certain narrowness and concentration seem to be a necessary condition of personal identity; and the function of the threshold is to preserve our personal identity. One of the ways in which it does so is to ensure that telepathy is not too frequent. If it were universal we should no longer be persons at all. There would be no such thing as an individual mind.

I must add, however, that telepathy may be rather less simple than it seems at first sight. The threshold may sometimes be crossed by guile when it cannot be crossed by force. An idea may be able to get across in symbolic and distorted form, when in a literal form it cannot. A little may get across and the rest be left out. It may blend itself with other ideas which are more acceptable and get in in that way, though in isolation it could not. Or it may get across in the form of a general emotional tone or coloring of our whole state of mind, a feeling of gloom or a elation pervading all our thoughts, even when it cannot get across in the form of a distinct "message." In one or other of these ways, many of our conscious thoughts may be partly telepathic in origin, though few are wholly so.

So far, my main conclusions are these. Taking as the basic unit the idea (rather than the complete mind), I have suggested that every idea may have two fundamental properties: (1) an inherent tendency to materialize itself in a physical form, which is the explanation of PK; (2) an inherent tendency to emerge into consciousness—into *any* consciousness, no matter whose, and not merely into the consciousness of the person who originally conceived it. In other words, every idea has an inherent tendency to cross *any* threshold. And that is the explanation of telepathy. The collective unconscious is like a vessel with many different lids on it, and all its contents are continually pressing against all the lids.

The Link Between

Let us now ask whether we can establish any link between telepathy and PK. We can see already that they have one important feature in common. Both are ways by which ideas operate. The two operations do, of course, seem very different. Crossing the threshold of consciousness, you may say, is one thing; causing a change in the physical world is quite another. But I believe they are not so different as they look.

First we should notice that there are intermediate cases between telepathy and PK. Telepathy need not be merely cognitive. A telepathically received idea may express itself in bodily behavior. Automatic writing is the most familiar example. I fancy that in some card-guessing experiments the process works in this way. Often the so-called percipient is not conscious of receiving any telepathic "message" at all; he just writes down a word or number, and it turns out to be the correct one. Sometimes automatic speech occurs, instead of automatic writing, and here again the subject may not know what he is saying; but here too the process is often telepathic, because the idea expressed by his words came from another mind. I should expect that sometimes the telepathically expressed idea might express itself in a symbolic action, a piece of action whereby the telepathic message is acted out, in dumb show; but the only instance I can quote is a very old one, the behavior of the Prophet Agabus, in the *Acts of the Apostles,* ch. 21. As you will remember, he bound St. Paul with Paul's own girdle, to signify that he was going to be a prisoner, which later he was. You will notice that whenever a telepathically received idea manifests itself in bodily movement there is a blend of telepathy and PK. It is PK, because an idea in the mind of A causes a change in a piece of matter other than his own brain; and at the same time it is telepathy, because that piece of matter is the body belonging to another mind B, and the change in that body is of an informative kind, a communication of something.

Something similar must happen in "absent" psychic healing, if this is a genuine fact. Here again an idea in the mind of another causes a change in the patient's body, without entering the patient's consciousness. This too is a kind of blend of PK and telepathy, or something intermediate between the two. It is nearer to PK than automatic writing and speech are, in so far as no message is conveyed. (Or might it be said that the absent healing is a message—a "lesson"—to the patient himself?) But it has also some kinship to telepathy because it is an interpersonal process; the piece of matter affected is the body of another mind.

So far I have been trying to say that there are intermediate phenomena between pure PK and pure telepathy. Of course it might still be true that for theoretical purposes we must draw a sharp distinction between them, even though in actual fact they are often combined. But I now want to go farther. I want to show that fundamentally they are two manifestations of the same thing.

What I want to say can be put in two different ways which I hope are not incompatible, but complementary. The first way of looking at it is this:

(1) It will be remembered that I attributed two tendencies to every idea: (a) a tendency to get itself embodied in matter, (b) a tendency to emerge into consciousness wherever it can find a threshold which it is able to cross. Now it could be argued that this second tendency is just a special case of the first. If an idea can get into someone's consciousness, it then has a much better chance of being realized in a physical form. It can then make use of the ordinary mechanism of ideo-motor action. Once the idea is in consciousness it will be executed automatically through the muscular mechanism of the body, unless there are other ideas to inhibit it. To speak picturesquely, if an idea *wants* to materialize itself (and we are supposing that all ideas do want it), then the best thing it can do will be to get itself into someone's consciousness if it can. If the consciousness of its original owner is barred to it for some reason, temporarily or permanently, it will get into another whose threshold is less difficult to cross; then we have a case of telepathy. But from the point of view of the idea itself (if I may put it so), this irruption into another mind would only be a means, a means towards getting itself materialized, which would be its ultimate and fundamental aim. Thus, according to this way of looking at it, telepathy is, as it were, an incomplete process, a half-way stage towards something else. And that something else is the materialization of ideas in the physical world. Of course, telepathy of the pure or classical kind—"thought transference," as it is sometimes called—belongs to the cognitive side of our nature. The recipient is *aware* of something, an image or dream or phantasm or hallucinatory voice. But as psychologists are always telling us, the cognitive side of our nature is incomplete by itself; cognition exists not for its own sake but for the sake of action, to enable us to make changes in our physical environment. If this is true, or in so far as it is, it must apply to telepathic cognition as well as to other sorts. The mere receiving of a telepathic message must likewise be something incomplete, and the process is only completed when the recipient *does* something about it.

Let us apply this to the most striking of all telepathic phenomena, the crisis apparition. If we consider the telepathic apparition from a teleogical point ot view, if we ask what its point or purpose is, it is obvious that the mere seeing of the apparition is not the end of the story. And the idea conveyed to the recipient is not just that something has happened (e.g., that A has had an accident or is dead), but also that something must be done about it, some practical readjustment made. The process is not complete unless or until the recipient acts appropriately upon the telepathic communication he has received.

This, then, is one way in which we might try to show that the two tendencies which I have attributed to ideas are reducible to the same one. According to this way of looking at it, their tendency to materialize themselves is the fundamental one, and their tendency to emerge into consciousness is derived from this. This amounts roughly to saying that PK is the fundamental supernormal phenomenon and telepathy is a partial and incomplete form of it, incomplete until the telepathically received idea is realized in action.

PK as a Partial Process

But perhaps we could also look at the matter the other way around, and treat PK as a partial and incomplete manifestation of the tendency which ideas have to get themselves into consciousness. We could treat it as an indirect and roundabout way of *getting across the threshold*. If an idea cannot get directly into consciousness, it may still manage to do it indirectly by embodying itself in the physical environment. The physical object or event in which it is embodied may then be perceived by someone; so the idea does get into consciousness in this roundabout way, by means of his sense organs. The threshold is more permeable to sense perceptions than to thoughts or images. According to this way of looking at it, all PK phenomena will have a symbolic or informative character; they will be messages or communications, in the same sort of way as automatic writing or automatic dumb show, and the whole point of them will be to get themselves noticed or understood by some observer. According to *this* view of the matter, it is PK, and not telepathy, which is the incomplete process, and it is only complete when the psychokinetic occurrence is perceived by someone. According to this way of looking at it, the idea embodies itself in matter in order to get itself into someone's consciousness; in the other way of looking at it, it is the other way round—the idea crosses the threshold of someone's consciousness in order to get itself embodied in matter.

So far, then, the problem of finding a unitary theory which will cover both telepathy and PK seems to have two different solutions. If we consider the two tendencies which every idea has, it would seem so far that either of these tendencies could be reduced to a special case of the other. According to the one solution, ideas tend to emerge in any consciousness they can get into, because they have a tendency to materialize themselves, and this is one of the easiest ways of doing it—by means of ordinary ideo-motor action. According to the other solution, they tend to materialize themselves because this is one of the easier ways of getting into someone's consciousness—by means of the mechanism of the sense organs. Either of these solutions is plausible, and either seems to cover the facts. This being so, it does look as if both these tendencies—both the tendency to break into consciousness and the tendency to materialization—must somehow be effects or derivatives of something more fundamental. What can this something be? I will now suggest an answer, but it is far from clear and I am not at all satisfied with it. Perhaps the fundamental tendency ideas have may be described as a tendency to *express* themselves. I shall not try to define the word "express," any more than I have tried to define the word "idea." I suspect the notion of expressing is one of the fundamental undefinables of all the psychological sciences, including psychical research and, indeed, sociology also. But I think we are all sufficiently familiar with the notion that works of art express something in the mind of the artist, and that a man's words or gestures or grimaces express his state of mind.

Embodiment in Matter

There are very many alternative ways in which an idea may express itself. It may express itself as a mental image by words, by gestures. These images, words or actions may belong not to the original owner of the idea, but to someone else; then we have telepathy. Another way it may express itself is by hallucination; and that, too, may be telepathic, for here again the hallucination is sometimes experienced not by the original owner of the idea but by someone else. Finally, an idea may express itself by embodying itself in the material world. That happens, perhaps, in works of art. It also happens in PK. Moreover, there is an approximation to it in dreams, for the dream image is a kind of half-way state towards complete embodiment. Thus the self-materializing tendency of ideas is one aspect of their fundamental tendency to express themselves by any means available.

But there is another point to be mentioned about this notion of "expressing." Expression, I think, is always expression *to someone,* to some consciousness; it is not completed till someone is aware of it. A statue which nobody, not even its maker, ever looked at, a poem which nobody read, would have failed in its purpose. Thus when we say that every idea has a tendency to express itself, we also say that it has a tendency to get itself into consciousness. This tendency to get itself into consciousness is really just an aspect of its tendency to express itself. If I am right, then, both telepathy and PK are manifestations of one fundamental property which all ideas have, their need or urge to express themselves by any means available. But we must, of course, remember that the collective unconscious contains a vast and perhaps innumerable multitude of different ideas, and normally the self-expressive tendency of one idea is resisted by the self-expressive tendencies of other ideas. So they are liable to cancel each other out. That is one reason why telepathy and PK are relatively rare occurrences, because of mutual inhibitions. It is also a reason why they may fail to occur if there are skeptical spectators. Indeed, the skeptics need not even be spectators. It will be enough if the general climate of opinion is skeptical. But this is itself just another manifestation of the self-expressive tendency of ideas. The negative idea, "Such things do not happen," expresses itself by preventing the phenomena from occurring, or at least by making it more difficult for them to occur. In any age of faith, when the general climate of opinion is credulous, instead of skeptical, it is presumably the other way around. It really is easier for "queer events" to happen just because everyone thinks that they do happen.

This brings me to the end of my attempt to suggest a unified theory which will cover both telepathy and PK phenomena, which seem at first sight to have nothing to do with one another. Both alike, I suggest, are manifestations of the inherent tendency, the urge or impulse which all ideas have, to express themselves by any means they can.

Conclusions

The theory is certainly a very queer one on the face of it, though perhaps no queerer than the phenomena to be explained. But, queer or not, I want to emphasize that it does all depend upon the two assumptions I stated earlier: (1) that human personality is to be divided into three parts, spirit, mind and body, and not just into two, as Descartes supposed; and (2)—an even more important assumption—that in the mental sphere the fundamental unit is not the individual mind but something more elementary, which I have called, for want of a better name, the idea; and that every idea has a causal efficacy.

I must add a final word on clairvoyance. It will be remembered that I deliberately left this out at the beginning. If I am right, telepathy and PK are two manifestations of the same thing. One single hypothesis, that of the self-expressive tendency of ideas, will account for both. But it will not account for clairvoyance as well. Clairvoyance is something radically different from either of them. It cannot be explained as a way in which ideas *operate*. On the contrary, it is a way in which ideas are *acquired*, and in that respect (though perhaps not in others) it is analogous to ordinary sense perception. In both telepathy and PK the ideas are already in existence. Clairvoyance is a way of getting new ones. All I can say about it at present is that I think it requires a great deal more investigation, both experimental and theoretical.

NOTES

1. In the Herbartian terminology, it tends to prevent them from "crossing the threshold" or at any rate to prevent the memories of them from doing so. What appears unintelligible, what seems to make no sense, tends to be repressed for that very reason; particularly in a highly educated mind, trained to value intellectual coherence and consistency.

NORMAL COGNITION, CLAIRVOYANCE AND TELEPATHY

C. D. Broad

The forms of supernormal cognition which have been alleged to occur may be roughly classified as follows. We may divide them first into supernormal cognitions of contemporary events or of the contemporary states of things or persons, and supernormal cognitions of past or future events or the past or future states of things or persons. Under the first heading would come clairvoyance and telepathy. Since clairvoyance, if it happened, would involve no complications about other *minds* than that of the cognizer or other *times* than that at which he has his cognition, I shall begin with it. I shall then consider telepathy.

Clairvoyance

Suppose that a person correctly guesses the number and suit of a card in a new pack which he has never touched, and which has been mechanically shuffled so that no one else has the information in his mind at the time. If this were to happen often under test conditions, there would be a *prima facie* case for postulating pure clairvoyance. It would then be reasonable to raise the following question: "Supposing that pure clairvoyance does occur, how far, if at all, is it analogous to ordinary sense perception?" This is the question which I am now going to discuss.

Normal Sense perception: Plainly we cannot hope to answer this question until we have stated clearly what happens in normal sense perception. I shall therefore begin by giving what seems to me to be, on the whole, the most reasonable account of this in view of all the known facts. We shall have to consider it in its psychological, its physiological, and its physical aspects. The subject is very complex and highly controversial, and I shall have to be rather dogmatic in order to be reasonably brief.

I think that the first point to be made is that there are several forms of *sense* perception which are, *prima facie,* fundamentally different in nature. Philosophers have too often confined themselves to a certain one of them, viz., visual perception, in discussing the subject. It is essential that we should not make this mistake if we are seeking for analogies between clairvoyance and normal sense perception. I begin, therefore, by dividing sense perception into "extrasomatic" and "intrasomatic." In the former the percipient seems to himself to be perceiving foreign bodies and events; in the latter he seems to

This selection is reprinted from *Proceedings of the Society for Psychical Research,* Vol. 43 (1936), 397ff. Used by permission of the editor.

himself to be perceiving the inside of his own body and processes going on in it. Now there are at least three important forms of extrasomatic sense perception, viz., hearing, sight, and touch, which seem, *prima facie,* to be unlike each other in certain fundamental respects.

Sight and hearing agree with each other and differ from touch in that they seem to reveal to us things and events which are located at various distances out from our bodies. But hearing differs from sight in the following important way. When I say that I hear a *bell* I should admit that this is an elliptical expression. Strictly speaking, I hear a *noise* of a rhythmic booming kind which seems to be emanating from a distant place and coming to me in a certain direction. I take it that this place contains a bell, and that a certain rhythmic process in it is causing it to make the noise. On this point there would be no difference in principle between the account which an unscientific percipient would give of the experience as it seems to him and the account which a scientist would give iof it from the standpoint of physics. But, when I say that I *see* a bell, I do not readily admit that I am using an elliptical expression, as I should admit that "I hear a bell" is short for "I hear a bell *tolling.*" I seem to myself to be directly and intuitively apprehending a remote colored area which I take to be part of the surface of an independent foreign body. I may learn from the scientists that the situation, in its physical aspect, is very much like that which exists when I hear the bell. I may learn that certain rhythmic processes are going on in the place where the bell is, that these cause a disturbance to be emitted in all directions from this center, and that this disturbance eventually travels to my body and produces a visual sensation. But, even if I accept this as proved, it remains a fact that the situation does not present itself to me in that way when I am having the experience. I continue to seem to myself to be directly apprehending the surface of a remote extended object and to be actively exploring it with my eyes. In this respect visual perception resembles tactual perception, except that the objects are perceived as remote from the percipient's body in the one case and in contact with it in the other.

We may sum up these likenesses and unlikenesses as follows. We may say that hearing is *projective* in its epistemological aspect, and is *emanative* in its physical aspect. We may say that sight is *ostensibly prehensive* and not projective in its epistemological aspect, but is *emanative* in its physical aspect. And we may say that touch is *ostensibly prehensive* in its epistemological aspect, and is *noncumulative* in its physical aspect.

Now the question at once arises whether sight and touch are really, as well as ostensibly, prehensive. We will now consider the two kinds of perception in turn. The mere fact that sight is physically emanative does not, as some people have thought, suffice to prove that it cannot be epistemologically prehensive. It is logically possible that the function of the light-waves which emanate from a distant object, strike the percipient's eye, and thus eventually affect his visual brain centers, should be purely that of evoking and directing a cognitive act and not in the least that of producing or modifying a cognizable object. In fact the disturbance in the percipient's brain, produced by the light waves, *might* simply cause his mind to apprehend directly the colored surface of the remote object from which the waves emanated. If so, visual perception would really be prehensive. But, although this is *logically* possible, I think it may quite safely be dismissed as inconsistent with the facts taken as a whole. The argument for this conclusion is cumulative. Each kind of fact which seems to conflict with the view that visual perception is prehensive can, perhaps, be squared with it if we choose to make a complicated and ingenious enough supplementary *ad hoc* hypothesis. But these various suplementary hypotheses are logically independent of each other; and, when one takes them all together, the prehensive view becomes as complex and artificial and incredible as the Ptolemaic system of astronomy had become just before it expired.

I shall content myself with mentioning one particularly obvious difficulty. Light travels with a finite velocity. It is therefore possible that, when the light which started from a distant star reaches my eye, the star should have moved away from its original position, changed its original color, or blown up completely. If sight were really prehensive the result of the light now striking my eye and affecting my brain would be that I now directly apprehend the surface of the star as it was when the light left it perhaps a thousand years ago. My act of direct acquaintance would thus have to bridge a temporal gap of a thousand years between the date of its own occurrence and the date of existence of its own immediate object. Yet the object which I see is most certainly perceived by me as simultaneous with my act of seeing it.

I conclude that visual perception, though ostensibly prehensive of external objects, is not *really* so. All the facts conspire to support the following conclusion. When I have a visual perception I seem to myself to be directly apprehending an area of a certain size and shape, colored in a certain way, and forming part of the surface of a certain material thing at a certain position outside my body. But the shape and size and position which I perceive it as having, and the color which I perceive as pervading it, are completely and finally determined, on the physical side, by certain processes which are going on at the time in a certain part of my brain. Provided that these processes are going on in this part of my brain, and that my mind is functioning normally, I shall have exactly this kind of visual experience no matter how the brain process may have been set up, and no matter whether there is or is not an external body such as I seem to myself to be directly apprehending. If the brain process has been set up by light which has traveled from an external source through a homogeneous medium to my eye, the visual perception will be as nearly veridical as it is possible for a visual perception to be. If it has been set up by light which has traveled from an external source but has undergone reflections or refractions before reaching my eye, the visual perception may be highly misleading in many respects, but it will not be utterly delusive. If it has been set up by events in my own body, as in dreams or delirium, or by such abnormal causes as the suggestion of a hypnotist, the visual perception will be utterly delusive. Thus, even in the most favorable case, where there is or has been an external source and where the visual perception gives the percipient correct information about its shape, position, and physical state, the connection between the act of perceiving and the external source is extremely remote. Even in this case the source and the processes going on in it are at most a *remote causal ancestor* of the visual perception and are never *the immediate object* of it. Thus there is always a certain element of delusiveness in even the most normal and veridical visual perception. For the percipient always seems to himself to be *directly apprehending* the surface of a remote object *as it now is*, whereas at best he is only cognizing *very indirectly* certain facts about an emitting source *as it formerly was*. Owing to the very great velocity of light the time error is practically unimportant except when the source is at an astronomical distance from the observer. But ostensible prehensiveness, like original sin, is a taint which equally and systematically infects all visual perceptions, good, bad, or indifferent.

One important consequence of this is the following. Consider the statement: "You and I are seeing the same part of the surface of the table." There is no reason to doubt that such statements often record facts, and that they do this quite efficiently for most of the practical purposes of daily life. Nevertheless there is a *suggestio falsi* about them. They suggest that there is a certain part of the surface of a certain external body which you and I are both directly apprehending. But the fact which they record, when they do record a fact, is much more complex and of a very different kind. It would be more accurately expressed by the statement: "This visual experience of mine and that visual experience of yours, though they are not prehensions of a common object, have a common causal ancestor in an emitting source outside our bodies."

We can now turn our attention to tactual perception. As I have said, this is ostensibly prehensive in its epistemological aspect, and is non-emanative in its physical aspect. In tactual perception we must distinguish three factors. (i) Awareness of various sensible qualities, such as hotness and coldness, roughness and smoothness, etc. This may be compared with awareness of auditory qualities in hearing and of colors in seeing. (ii) Awareness of shape and extent. This may be compared with the corresponding factor in visual perception. There is, I think, nothing like it in hearing. (iii) The experience of actively pulling and pushing foreign bodies which are in contact with one's own. I will call this *dynamic* experience. I know of nothing anlogous to it in any other form of perception.

It is this dynamical factor in tactual perception, and the systematic way in which variations in it are correlated with variations in the non-dynamic factors, which makes it difficult even for the most skeptical to doubt that tactual perception is really prehensive of external objects. We may admit at once that there is not here, as in the case of visual perception, a large coherent mass of facts which it is difficult or impossible to reconcile with the prehensive view. It might even be argued with some plausibility that, unless we *really are* directly acquainted with foreign bodies in the experience of active manipulation, we should never have *seemed to ourselves* to be directly acquainted with them in visual perception. But we must not let ourselves be rushed into accepting the prehensive view of tactual perception until we have noted one important fact which may bear in the opposite direction.

Tactual perception shares with sight and hearing a characteristic which we have not yet mentioned. It is *transmissive* in its physiological aspect, i.e., it depends on the existence and functioning of nerves which connect the periphery of the body to the brain and convey disturbances at a finite rate inwards and outwards. Now it is certain that the occurrence of a characteristic kind of disturbance in my brain is a *necessary* condition without which I shall not have a perception of myself as touching and interacting with a foreign body. The question is whether the occurrence of such a process in my brain is also the *sufficient* physical condition of my having such an experience. If it is sufficient I should have exactly the same tactual experience, provided that this process in my brain were to occur and that my mind were working properly, even if there were no foreign body in contact with my skin. If this were so, my tactual perceptions could not be prehensive. It is difficult to settle this question conclusively, because it is doubtful whether precisely that kind of brain state which occurs when I am actually manipulating and struggling with a foreign body ever does arise from purely internal causes. But the fact that I can dream that I am struggling with a foreign body, though I am in fact doing nothing of the kind, certainly suggests that even the experience of active tactual manipulation may not be really prehensive.

My own tentative view is that tactual perception is probably not prehensive of external objects, but that, in spite of this, it justifies us in being practically certain that there are foreign bodies and that they do interact with our own bodies. It seems to me just conceivable, though extremely unlikely, that I might have had the kinds of experience which I describe as "seeing" or "hearing" foreign bodies even if there had been no foreign bodies or if they had never emitted light waves or sound waves to my body. But I find it almost impossible to believe that I could *ever* have had the kind of experience which I describe as "pushing" or "pulling" or "struggling with" foreign bodies unless there had been foreign bodies and they had *quite often* interacted dynamically with my own body through contact. Granted that this has quite often happened, it is not hard to explain how occasionally, in dreams or delirium, I may have a close imitation of this experience although no foreign body is then interacting dynamically with mine.

There is one important point on which I want to insist before leaving the topic of extrasomatic perception. I have argued that, when we have the experience of hearing, seeing, or touching something, we are not in fact apprehending directly the foreign body, if such there be, which we say we are hearing, seeing or touching. Now at this stage there is a risk of making a serious mistake. It might be thought that, because hearing, seeing, and touching are indirect and mediate, in the sense of being non-prehensive, they must be indirect and mediate in the sense that they involve inference. This would be a profound mistake. Even in the case of hearing I do not *argue,* from the fact that I am hearing a booming recurrent noise and from certain general principles of physical causation, that there is probably a bell tolling in a certain place outside my body. The fact is that my auditory experiences have been closely correlated with certain of my visual and tactual experiences in the past, and this correlation has established a persistent system of traces and dispositions in my mind. When I now hear a booming recurrent noise a certain part of this dispositional system is excited, and the auditory sensation is at once invested with an aura of acquired meaning in terms of a remote visible and tangible source. It is still more obvious that there is no element of inference in the experience which I call "seeing this" or "touching that." I doubt whether we can account psychologically for the ostensible prehensiveness of visual and tactual perception by any process of acquirement of meaning through association in our early years. I think we must assume that visual and tactual experiences are taken by us, from the very first, as revelations of an external material world. No doubt all the later detailed development of this primitive vague conviction depends on the actual course of our experience and on the particular associations which are established in our early years.

So much for the purely psychological point. There is a logical point closely connected with it. Beliefs which were not reached by inference may be capable of being supported or refuted by inference. Now, in my opinion, something like the commonsense belief in a world of extended movable interacting bodies can be shown to be highly probable, on the basis of our auditory, visual, and tactual perceptions and their correlations, if and only if the following premise is granted. Our primitive uncritical conviction that our visual and tactual perceptions are manifestations of an external material world, and that distinctions and variations in them are signs of distinctions and variations in it, must be allowed to have an appreciable antecedent probability. There is no way of proving this indispensable premise. Some people may find it self-evident and count it as an axiom. I am content to take it as a postulate. We can call it the *Postulate of Perceptual Transcendence*.

Finally we must consider intrasomatic perception, i.e., the perception which each of us has of his own body, and of no other body, by means of organic sensations. Each of us is almost always aware of a general somatic background or field, which is vaguely extended and fairly homogeneous in quality throughout its extent. It is fairly constant in general character, though its specific tone varies from time to time. Such variations are recorded by expressions like: "I am feeling tired," "I am feeling well," "I am feeling sick," and so on. No doubt the general character changes very slowly as we get older, and it may undergo profound and fairly sudden modifications in illness or at certain periods of normal life such as puberty. Against this fairly homogeneous and constant background there happen from time to time outstanding localized feelings which are independent of one's volition, e.g., a sudden twinge of toothache, a prolonged and voluminous stomach ache, and so on.

We might compare the general somatic field to the visual field of which one would be aware if one lay on one's back and looked up at the sky when there is not much movement among the clouds. And we might compare the occasional localized outstanding toothaches, stomach aches, etc., to the visual sensa which we should sense if there were occasional flashes of lightning, dark masses of cloud, and so on, in the sky.

Lastly, we must notice that, whenever we deliberately act upon or react against a foreign body, there are characteristic localized changes in the somatic field, connected with the pressures, tensions, and movements of our muscles and joints.

The following points are of special importance for us to notice. (i) Intrasomatic perception, like all other normal perception, is transmissive in its physiological aspect. If I am to have the kind of experience which I record by saying "I am feeling a pain in my toe," it is not *sufficient* that there should be a process of a certain kind going on in my toe. It is *necessary* that a certain process should be going on in my brain. Moreover, we are told on good authority that persons who have had a limb amputated may yet have experiences of the kind which they would record by saying "I have a pain where my amputated limb used to be." It therefore looks as if the occurrence of a certain process in the brain were the final and *sufficient* physical condition of the occurrence of this kind of experience. If so, intrasomatic perception cannot be *really* prehensive of one's own body, however much it may seem to be so to the percipient. (ii) There is, however, no reason to doubt that the brain process, which is the final and sufficient physical condition of an intrasomatic perception, generally arises from and corresponds in structure with a certain process in a certain other part of the percipient's body, such as his stomach or a tooth or a toe. Thus, although intrasomatic perception is probably not prehensive, there is no reason to doubt that it is generally veridical in outline if not in detail. (iii) One's awareness of one's somatic field as extended, and one's awareness of this or that outstanding bodily feeling as happening in this or that part of it, are, I think, psychologically quite primitive experiences. But the identification of this extended somatic field with the region occupied by one's body as a visible and tangible object, and the correlation of each part of the former with a certain part of the latter, are, I am sure, products of early experience and association.

Clairvoyance and Sense Perception: Let us now turn from normal perception and consider an alleged case of clairvoyance. It is essential to take something quite concrete and not to talk vaguely. I will suppose that a special pack of cards has been made on the following plan. Every card has for its face a white background on which are either squares or circles, but not both. Every card has black pips or red pips, but no card has a mixture of both. There are thus four suits, which we can call Red Squares, Black Squares, Red Circles, and Black Circles. Lastly, in each suit there are ten cards in sequence from ace to ten. The backs of all cards are uniformly brown. Let us suppose that the percipient correctly guesses that the sixth card from the top of a new and mechanically shuffled pack of this kind is the eight of red squares. And let us suppose that such guesses of his have so often been right that we cannot ascribe his success to chance. Could we suppose that anything analogous to normal sense perception is taking place?

To assert that a certain card is the eight of red squares is to assert three independent propositions, viz., that there are *eight* outstanding patches on the surface, that these are *square* in outline, and that they are *red* in color. Now all these propositions could be known by sight to a person who could look directly at the front of the card in white light. This implies that there are eight square patches on the card, which differ physically from the background in such a way that they selectively reflect the red-stimulating light waves while the background reflects equally light of all wave lengths in the ordinary spectrum. Let us try to suppose that the clairvoyant gets his information by some mode of perception analogous to sight or hearing.

We shall have to suppose that the percipient's body is being stimulated by some kind of emanation from the front of the sixth card in the pack, although the back of the card is towards him. We shall have to suppose that the five cards which are on top of the selected one are transparent to this emanation, though they are not transparent to light. We shall presumably have to suppose that the five cards which are on top of this one and the thirty-four which are beneath it are all equally emitting radiation of this kind. Thus the emanation from the selected card will reach the percipient's body mixed up with the emanations from all the other cards in the pack. Next we shall have to assume that, although the emanation is not light, yet there is a characteristic difference between the emanation from the pips and the emanation from the background, correlated with the difference between red-stimulating and white-stimulating light waves. Without this there is no hope of explaining how the clairvoyant can tell that there are pips and a background and judge the number of pips. Still less could we explain how he can tell the color of the pips on the selected card. When we look more carefully into the last mentioned assumption we find that it is equivalent to the following supposition. We are, in effect, supposing that the physical difference between the pips and the background, which makes the former selectively reflect red-stimulating light waves and the latter indifferently reflect a whole mixture of light waves, is correlated with another physical difference which is concerned with another and unknown kind of emanation. This is certainly not very plausible.

We have not yet attempted to deal with the clairvoyant's knowledge that the pips on the sixth card from the top are square in outline. No assumption that we have so far made will account for this. If the face of the card were being looked at directly in white light, the light reflected from its surface would travel in straight to the percipient's eye. There it would pass through the pupil and be focused by the lens on the retina. There it would excite different parts of a certain area in various ways. The area as a whole, and the distribution of the excitement over it, would be geometrically a projection of the surface from which the light came. From this excited area, through the optic nerve, a corresponding pattern of excitement would be transmitted to the brain. At this stage the percipient would directly apprehend an outstanding oblong patch in his visual field, with a white background and eight red squares scattered about it. This he would automatically and uncritically, but erroneously, take to be the surface of the card. In order to have any analogy with all this we should have to assume that the emanation travels in straight lines through the medium between the card and the percipient's body, and that there is in his body some organ for collecting it and focusing it on a sensitive surface. I need hardly say that we know of no part of our bodies which could plausibly be regarded as such an organ. Moreover, the fact that we have had to assume that ordinary matter is transparent to this emanation makes it difficult to see how a material organ could collect and focus it. It is like being asked to construct a camera, or a telescope, or a microscope when the only material provided is clear transparent glass.

I have now dealt with the physical and physiological assumptions which would be involved in supposing that clairvoyant cognition is analogous to sight or hearing. It remains to consider the psychological aspects of this supposition. In the first place, we should have to assume that the ultimate result of this emanation being received by the appropriate organs, and of the disturbance being transmitted to the appropriate part of the brain, is that the clairvoyant directly apprehends a total sense-field of a characteristic kind. This experience must be analogous to the normal man's apprehension of his visual or his auditory field. So far as I know, there is no introspective evidence for the occurrence of any such experience in persons who claim to be clairvoyant. We should therefore have to assume that this peculiar kind of sensory experience belongs to a part of their mind which they cannot interpret in normal waking life.

Next we must assume that this peculiar sense-field is differentiated, and differentiated in a very special way. There must be in it an outstanding sensum which in fact corresponds to the sixth card from the top of the pack, and there must be in this sensum eight outstanding differentiations which in fact correspond to the eight pips on the face of this card. Moreover, there must be a certain determinate sensible quality in these eight outstanding differentiations which in fact corresponds to the visible squareness of the pips as they would appear to sight. There must also be a certain other determinate sensible quality in these eight outstanding differentiations which in fact corresponds to the visible redness of the pips as they would appear to sight. Although emanations are coming in on top of each other from all the cards in the pack, and presumably from the table and the walls too, we must assume that the sensum specially connected with the emanation from any particular card is distinct enough to be discriminated from the rest of the sense-field by the percipient if he pays enough attention. We must also assume that such a sensum has enough discriminable detail to display those features in the card which would appear to sight as a certain number of pips of a certain shape and a certain color.

It must be admitted that this involves a very heavy draft on the bank of possibility. I think that the nearest known analogy is provided by hearing. The waves from a number of simultaneously sounding sources, such as the instruments in an orchestra, do come in on top of each other. Yet it is possible with practice and attention to discriminate the noise which in fact comes from one instrument from the noise which in fact comes from another. It is also possible to distinguish overtones, if one has an acute ear, in the noise which comes from a certain instrument. This analogy, though it is not to be despised, does not carry us very far. The noise which in fact comes from a certain instrument has no auditory quality which is invariably correlated with the *shape* or the *color* which that instrument manifests to sight. The analogy would be a little closer if, when we looked at the various instruments, they appeared to be visibly vibrating at various rates and with various amplitudes. Then there really would be a systematic correlation between the *auditory* qualities of the *noise* which comes from a certain instrument and certain *visible* characteristics in the appearance which that instrument would present to *sight*.

We are not yet at the end of the psychological assumptions which we should have to make. It is not enough that there should be in the clairvoyant's peculiar sense-field a certain discriminable sensum which *in fact* corresponds to the sixth card from the top of the pack. If he is to answer our question: "What is the sixth card from the top?" he must *know* or have reason to *believe*, with regard to a certain discriminable sensum in his field, that *it* corresponds to the sixth card from the top. Again, it is not enough that this sensum should have eight differentiations which *in fact* correspond to the eight differentiated areas on the card which appear to sight as eight red squares. If he is to answer our question, he must *know* or have reason to *believe* that the eight differentiations in this sensum correspond to eight differentiated areas on the card which would appear to sight as eight red squares. He must therefore know or have reason to believe, with regard to a certain sensible quality of these differentiations in this sensum, that it corresponds to visible squareness. And he must know or have reason to believe, with regard to a certain other sensible quality of these differentiations, that it corresponds to visible redness. Unless the clairvoyant knew these facts he would be in much the same position as a man born blind who had acquired plenty of tactual experience and was then suddenly enabled to see. In the visual field of such a man there would be outstanding colored patches which are *in fact* visual appearances of various things from which he has already received tactual sensations. And the visible shape of these visual sensa would *in fact* correspond to the tangible shape of the corresponding tactual sensa. But the newly cured blind man would not *know* these facts or have any reason to suspect them. So, if we were to ask him a question about an object which he has touched in the past and is no longer touching but is seeing for the first time, his visual experience would not help him in the least to answer it. It is not until his experiences of sight and touch have become correlated and associated, so that a certain kind of visual appearance has come to *represent for him* a certain kind of tactual appearance, that his newly acquired power of visual perception will enable him to answer our questions about external objects.

How could the clairvoyant acquire such knowledge or belief as we have had to assign to him? The extremely intimate association between sight and touch, which is established in infancy in all normal people, seems to provide the only helpful analogy. Here we must substitute for it an intimate association between sight and the peculiar kind of sense-experience which we have assumed the clairvoyant to possess. We shall have to suppose that all or most things which are visible also emit the peculiar emanation which gives rise to this peculiar kind of sense-experience when it reaches the clairvoyant's body. And we must suppose that every variation in the light reflected from bodies is correlated with a corresponding variation in this emanation. On this assumption, the clairvoyant will from infancy have been apprehending two coexisting and intimately correlated sense-fields, viz., the normal visual field and the peculiar sense-field connected with the emanation. This may be compared with the case of the plain man who apprehends from infancy a visual and a tactual field which are intimately correlated with each other. The difference is that the normal man is constantly aware of apprehending both the visual and the tactual field, while the clairvoyant in ordinary waking life is not aware of apprehending the peculiar sense-field connected with the emanation. In consequence of this constant and detailed correlation between the contents of the visual sense-field and those of the peculiar sense-field, in the clairvoyant's case, an intimate association will be established in his mind between the two, just as an intimate association is established in the case of the normal man between his visual and his tactual sense-fields.

When a normal man in the dark has a tactual sensation of a certain familiar kind, which has become associated through frequent past experience in the light with a certain kind of visual appearance, he is able to describe in visual terms the object which he is at present only touching and not seeing. Similarly, when the clairvoyant has a familar sensation of his own peculiar kind, which has become associated through frequent past experience with a certain kind of visual appearance, he will be able to describe in visual terms the object which is evoking this sensation by its emanation but is at present hidden from his view.

It seems at first sight most implausible to postulate in the clairvoyant's mind a whole special group of sensations of which he is totally unaware, and then to postulate that they are intimately correlated with his ordinary visual sensations and eventually become associated with the latter. Yet it must, I think, be confessed that a very similar postulate is unblushingly made by the most orthodox psychologists in trying to explain normal visual perception of distance and solidity. We are told a great deal by these scientists in this connection about sensations of accommodation and sensations of convergence. We are told that these become so intimately associated with purely visual sensations that the minutest variation in the one represents to the percipient a corresponding variation in the other. But the fact remains that most of us at most times are quite unaware of these constantly occurring and continually varying sensations of accommodation and convergence. If we focus our eyes for a long time on a very small and very near object, we may begin to notice sensations of accommodation. If we indulge in elaborate and deliberate squinting, we may notice sensations of convergence. But it is only in these exceptional circumstances that such sensations are noticed or noticeable by the person who, presumably, is in fact never free from them. So orthodox psychologists are not in a position to cast stones at the postulates which would have to be made about the clairvoyant's special sense-field.

I have now enumerated and explained the various assumptions, physical, physiological, and psychological, which would have to be made if clairvoyance is to be regarded as a peculiar kind of sense perception, emissive in its physical aspect, like sight or hearing. It must be confessed that they make a formidable list. But it is better to set them out fully and to face them squarely than to talk vaguely of analogies to wireless and television and "the marvels of modern science." Many people will be inclined, when faced with this list of necessary assumptions, to conclude that the attempt to make clairvoyance analogous to sight or hearing must be dropped.

Now, unless clairvoyance is analogous to a physically emissive form of sense perception, like sight or hearing, it can hardly be analogous to *any* form of normal sense perception. If we tried to compare it with touch, we should have to suppose that the clairvoyant's body is provided with invisible and intangible organs, supplied with sensitive spots on their surface and with conducting nerves. We should have to suppose that he can thrust these out and poke them between two cards which are, and remain throughout the experiment, visibly in continuous contact with each other. And we should have to suppose that the square areas on the card which differ from the background by selectively reflecting red-stimulating light waves also differ from the background by giving a special kind of stimulus to the sensitive spots on this quasi-tactile organ. It seems hardly worthwhile to linger over these fantastic suppositions, or to consider what others might be needed in addition to them.

Perhaps some psychical researchers will welcome these conclusions. They will remind us that they have always insisted that clairvoyance cannot be analogous to any form of sense perception, and they will feel that I have only been underlining the obvious. I cannot share their satisfaction. Have those who believe that clairvoyance occurs, and deny that it is analogous to any form of sense perception, any positive notion of its psychological nature or its *modus operandi*? If they have, it is most desirable that they should expound it. If they have not, they are just postulating what Locke would have called "a something, I know not what." Since their postulate will then have no discernible analogy or connection with anything that is already known and admitted to be a fact, it will be impossible to assign a degree of antecedent probability or improbability to it. In that case we shall be unable to come to any rationally justified degree of belief or disbelief when they produce their empirical evidence, however impressive it may be.

Clairvoyance as Non-sensuous Prehension of Physical Objects: The only intelligible positive interpretation which I can put on this view of clairvoyance is the following. Those who deny that clairvoyance is analogous to any form of sense perception might suppose that the clairvoyant *really does* directly apprehend remote physical objects, as the ordinary man *seems to himself to do* in sight and touch. This supposition is, I think, *prima facie* intelligible. As I have said in discussing normal sense perception, each of us really does directly apprehend *something* when he is seeing, hearing, etc. In seeing, e.g., one is directly apprehending an extended continuous variegated colored field; though one uncritically mistakes it for something else, of a quite different nature, which one does not directly apprehend. So we can understand, in general outline at any rate, what we are being asked to suppose in the case of the clairvoyant.

But, as soon as we begin to consider the suggestion in detail, it becomes less and less intelligible. The card called the "eight of red squares" is a physical object which, when suitably illuminated, reflects light-waves. If these reach the eye of a normal human observer, they stimulate it in a characteristic way, and at a certain stage in the process a characteristic kind of disturbance is set up in his optic centers. If and only if all this should happen, the card will be represented in the observer's visual field by an outstanding white oblong sensum with eight outstanding square spots on it. There is not the faintest reason to believe that the card itself, which is the locus of a remote causal ancestor in this long and variegated chain of events, has literally and intrinsically any color whatever. That which corresponds in a physical object to the color which it is perceived as having is presumably some special configuration or some rhythmic motion of its minute constituents, which causes it to reflect certain kinds of light waves and to absorb others. If, then, the clairvoyant directly apprehends the card, as it intrinsically and independently is, he will *not* apprehend it as a thing with a white continuous surface on which there are eight square red spots; for it is almost certainly nothing of the kind. He might, perhaps, apprehend it as a swarm of very small colorless electric charges in very rapid rhythmic motion; for, according to the best information available at present to those of us who are not clairvoyants, this or something like this is what the card most probably is.

Now, if clairvoyants do *directly apprehend* physical objects as having those characteristics which scientists *laboriously infer* that they must have, they show no sign of being aware of their own knowledge. If they were, they could presumably put it, at least roughly and in outline, into words. They would then be invaluable helpers in all physical laboratories; for their information, artlessly expressed but "straight from the horse's mouth," would suffice to head scientists off from plausible but false theories and to suggest fruitful lines of experiment and speculation. We shall have to assume, then, that the clairvoyant's direct apprehension of physical objects, as they intrinsically are, occurs in a part of his mind which is cut off from his ordinary waking experience.

The clairvoyant describes the unseen card in terms of colors, visible shapes, etc., and not in terms of electric charges, waves, and rhythmic motions. We shall therefore have to explain how he translates his direct apprehension of the unseen card, as it intrinsically is, into the colors, visible shapes, etc., which it would appear to have if it were being seen by a normal human being in daylight. It will be remembered that there is a rather similar problem for those who regard clairvoyance as a peculiar form of sense perception. The suggestion which I made in that connection might, perhaps, be modified to deal with the present problem. We shall have to suppose that the clairvoyant has, from infancy, been continuously though unconsciously apprehending directly all those objects which he has also been cognizing indirectly through sight and touch. Then we can suppose that an association would be set up between, e.g., the conscious experience of seeing an object as red and the unconscious experience of directly apprehending it as having that intrinsic characteristic which makes it selectively reflect red-stimulating light waves. Suppose that, on some future occasion, such an object, though no longer visible, is still being directly but unconsciously apprehended by the clairvoyant. He will still apprehend it as having that intrinsic characteristic, whatever it may be, which has now become associated in his mind with the visual appearance of redness. Consequently the idea of it as a red-looking object will arise automatically in his mind, and he will announce that the unseen object is red.

I have now stated and tried to work out in some detail two alternative views of what clairvoyance would be if it took place. Neither of them is in the least attractive or plausible, but I know of no other alternative that is even intelligible. I hope that some of those who think that there is adequate evidence for clairvoyance will be inspired to suggest some other view of it which will be equally intelligible and much more plausible. Though I can offer no hint of a solution, I may possibly have given them some help by setting out elements of the problem in a clear and orderly way.

Telepathy

Telepathic Interaction: It is commonly assumed that one embodied mind can affect another only in an extremely roundabout way. It must first affect its own body; then this change in its own body must set up a series of physical changes which eventually affect another ensouled body; and, finally, this change in the other ensouled body must produce a change in the mind which animates it. Thus the process involves a psychophysiological transaction at one end, a physiologico-psychical transaction at the other end, and a purely physical causal series between the two. A further restriction is commonly imposed on this general scheme. It is usually assumed that the process set up within the one ensouled body must issue in some overt macroscopic change of it, such as emitting a sound, making a gesture, or assuming a new facial expression; and it is assumed that this must affect the other ensouled body by sight, hearing, touch, or some such form of normal sensory stimulus. The wider assumption may be summed up in the following general principle: "The only thing, other than itself, with which an embodied mind can directly interact is the brain and nervous system of the body which it animates." It this be granted, the rest follows.

We can now imagine various stages in which the commonsense assumption might be given up. (i) We might keep the general principle, but drop the further restriction which is commonly put on it. We might suppose that, in certain cases, the disturbance set up in A's brain by an event in his mind initiates a physical process of an emanative kind which travels out in all directions; that this may set up a disturbance in B's brain, if it reaches the latter; and that this disturbance in B's brain may affect his mind. On this view there need be no overt macroscopic change in A's body, such as emitting a noise, making a gesture, etc. And B's brain need not be stimulated through any of the ordinary sense organs by what is happening in A's body. Yet the general principle about interaction will remain intact.

(ii) The next stage would be to drop one half of the general principle and keep the other half. This would give two possible alternatives. (a) We might continue to assume that A's mind can directly affect only A's brain, and that B's mind can directly affect only B's brain. But we might now suppose that A's mind can, in some cases, be directly affected by disturbances in B's brain; and that B's mind can, in some cases, be directly affected by disturbances in A's brain. (b) We might continue to assume that A's mind can be directly affected only by A's brain, and that B's mind can be directly affected only by B's brain. But we might now suppose that A's mind can, in some cases, directly produce disturbances in B's brain; and that B's mind can, in some cases, directly produce disturbances in A's brain.

(iii) Lastly, we might drop the general principle altogether. We might suppose that, in certain cases, one embodied mind can affect or be affected by another embodied mind *directly*, without any physiological or physical mediation. I propose to call the first alternative the "Brain-wave Theory," and the third alternative the "Theory of Direct Intermental Transaction." Theories of the second kind might be called "Theories of Extended Psycho-physiological Interaction." I cannot pretend that this is a "snappy" title, but I think it is accurately descriptive.

If either of these three suppositions were ever realized in practice we should say that there had been a case of "Telepathic Interaction." If it were an instance of the Brain-wave Theory it would involve no supernormal interaction between mind and matter or between mind and mind. It would involve nothing but an unusual transaction between two brains and an intervening physical medium. If it were an instance of either form of the Theory of Extended Psycho-physiological Interaction it would involve supernormal interaction between mind and matter, but no direct interaction between mind and mind. The supernormality of the transaction would consist in the fact that an event in *one man's mind* directly affects or is directly affected by an event in *another man's brain*. If it were an instance of the Theory of Direct Intermental Transaction it would involve supernormal interaction between two embodied minds, but it would not necessarily involve any supernormal interaction between mind and matter.

If the Brain-wave Theory would fit the empirical facts, it would be preferable to the other two in respect of antecedent probability. But the general opinion of those who have studied the facts seems to be definitely adverse to this theory.

In favor of the Theory of Extended Psycho-physiological Interaction it may be said that we do know that each embodied mind directly affects and is directly affected by *at least one* brain and nervous system, though this kind of transaction has to be accepted as a completely mysterious brute fact. This one brain and nervous system is, of course, that of the one material system to which this mind stands in the peculiar relation of "animating." Now the theory under discussion is that this direct interaction between minds and brains, which is admitted to occur, is not necessarily or invariably restricted within these limits. Either the range within which direct interaction between a mind and a body is possible extends beyond the limits marked out by the relation of animation, or the relation of animation extends more widely than commonsense recognizes. The latter suggestion amounts to supposing that an embodied human mind may animate a material system which includes, in addition to one human body, parts of another human body which is animated by another human mind. This relation might be mutual as between two human individuals A and B. A's mind might animate a material system which includes, beside what we call "A's body," a part of what we call "B's body"; and B's mind might animate a material system which includes, beside what we call "B's body," a part of what we call "A's body." In some cases of multiple personality it looks as if there were two minds simultaneously animating either the whole of a common brain and nervous system, or, at any rate, animating two parts of it which overlap each other. This at least supplies empirical support for the general conclusion that the relation of animation between minds and bodies is not always one-to-one. If two minds can animate one body, it may not be unreasonable to contemplate the possibility that one mind may animate one body and a bit of another body.

These speculations are, I know, very wild; but I make no apology for them on that account. The admitted relation of animation between the mind and the body of a normal human individual, and the admitted interactions between the two, are so mysterious that we are left with a wide field for legitimate conjectures. The situation is very different from that which faced us when we were considering normal sense perception and alleged clairvoyance. We have a great deal of positive knowledge about normal sense perception, in its physical, its physiological, and its epistemological aspects; so the field for legitimate conjecture is there much narrower.

Passing finally to the Theory of Direct Intermental Transaction, we must, I think, assign to it the lowest antecedent probability of the three typical theories. So far as I am aware, it is supported by no known analogy with admitted facts. We should, therefore, hesitate to resort to it unless the evidence rules out all theories of the other two types.

Telepathic Cognition: We have so far considered the possible *causal relations* between two embodied minds; we must now turn our attention to what primarily concerns us in this paper, viz., the possible *cognitive relations* between them. It is important to be quite clear that these are different problems, for the word "telepathy" seems often to be carelessly used to cover both supernormal causal influence of one embodied mind on another and supernormal cognition of one embodied mind by another. We have given the name "telepathic interaction" to the former, and we will call the latter "telepathic cognition." Probably telepathic cognition would be impossible without telepathic interaction, but there is not the least reason why there should not be telepathic interaction without telepathic cognition. Cognizing or being cognized, on the one hand, and affecting causally or being affected causally, on the other, are utterly different relations. If either of them can be analyzed, which is doubtful, it is certain that neither of them forms any part of the analysis of the other. So there can be no *logical* impossibility in two terms being related by one of them and not by the other. And, if it be granted that two minds could influence each other telepathically at all, it is quite easy to imagine that two minds which remained completely ignorant of each other might yet be in fact influencing each other frequently and profoundly by telepathic interaction.

Having made this distinction clear, we can now turn our attention to the cognition by one mind of another mind and its experiences. I shall begin by stating and explaining two principles which are commonly, if tacitly, assumed to apply to embodied human minds and their normal cognitions. The first is that one and the same experience cannot be owned by more than one mind. I do not think that anyone would question this. It is true that we sometimes use expressions which, if literally interpreted, would imply that one and the same experience is owned by several minds. We might, e.g., say of two people who both believe that Francis wrote the *Letters of Junius* that they both have the same belief about the authorship of the *Junius* letters. But we all recognize at once that such statements are not to be taken literally. One belief that Francis wrote these letters occurs in A's mind and not in B's; another belief that Francis wrote these letters occurs in B's mind and not in A's. When we talk of *the same* belief occurring in two minds we mean that *two beliefs*, which stand in a common relation to *one and the same fact*, viz., the actual but unknown authorship of the *Junius* letters, are occurring, and that one belongs to one mind and the other belongs to the other mind. A similar interpretation would have to be put on any statement that seemed to conflict with our principle. We will call this the "Principle of Unique Ownership of Experiences."

We come now to the second principle. It may be stated as follows. Any particular existent which can be directly apprehended by an embodied mind can be directly apprehended *only by one* such mind. Let us consider what kinds of particular existents a given embodied mind M can directly apprehend. They are (i) M itself, perhaps; (ii) some, if not all, of M's experiences; (iii) certain mental images; (iv) somatic sensa connected with the processes in M's body; and (v) certain visual, tactual, auditory, and other kinds of extrasomatic sensa. Of course the plain man would have included in this list something which we have not included, viz., the surfaces of certain foreign bodies and of his own body, and certain kinds of events happening from time to time in such bodies. And he would not have mentioned certain items which we have included, viz., various kinds of sensa. The cause of both these differences is the same, viz., the fact that the plain man mistakes what he directly apprehends in sense perception for parts of physical objects and events in such objects. We have seen that he does not directly apprehend such particular existents, and so we have had to exclude them from our list. But we have also seen that he really is apprehending particular existents of *some* kind in sense perception, and so we have had to introduce them into our list under the technical name of "sensa."

Now let us go through the list, and we shall see that, if it is exhaustive, it proves our principle. (i) Everyone would agree that normally no embodied mind but M could directly apprehend M. (ii) Everyone would agree that normally no embodied mind but M could directly apprehend any of M's experiences. (iii) Everyone would agree that normally no embodied mind but M could directly apprehend any mental image that M can directly apprehend. (iv) Everyone would agree that normally no embodied mind but M could directly apprehend the aches and pains and pressure data and so on which arise in connection with processes in M's body. (v) As regards extrasomatic sensa a difference of opinion might arise, but it would certainly be due to verbal confusion. A person might say: "A noise is an extrasomatic sensum. Now we all know that M and N may both hear the same noise. So N can directly apprehend an extrasomatic sensum which is also being directly apprehended by M." There is nothing in this argument. When M and N are correctly said to be "hearing the same noise" *each* is directly apprehending a *different* auditory sensum. But these two auditory sensa are related in a certain characteristic way to each other, and they are manifestations of a common physical event at a remote common source. When the fact that normal sense perception is not *really* prehensive of external objects is clearly understood and firmly grasped, and when the various verbal confusions which have arisen from its being *ostensibly* prehensive have been removed, we see that there is not the least reason to believe that, in normal life, N can ever directly apprehend any sensum which M can directly apprehend, or vice versa.

Now I think that, with the explanations which I have just given, it will be admitted that the above list includes all the various kinds of particular existents which any embodied mind, under normal conditions, could directly apprehend. And we have now seen, with regard to each of these classes of particulars, that any member of it which *can* be directly apprehended by any one embodied mind M *cannot*, under normal conditions, be directly apprehended by any other embodied mind. And so we reach our second general principle: "Any particular existent which can be directly apprehended by an embodied mind can be directly apprehended *only by one* such mind." I will call this the "Principle of the Privacy of Prehensible Particulars."

Before going further I will make some remarks on these two principles. (i) The Unique Ownership of Experiences is in a much stronger position than the Privacy of Prehensible Particulars. Many people would say that it is self-evidently impossible that one and the same experience should literally be an experience of two minds, no matter whether the minds were embodied or disembodied, in a normal or an abnormal condition, or what not. Without committing myself to this view, I must admit that it is highly plausible. Now the Privacy of Prehensible Particulars, as a general principle, is not in the least self-evident. We reached it simply by a process of enumeration and inspection, and there is no apparent absurdity in supposing that there might be exception to it. As we have seen commonsense does unhesitatingly take for granted that, in normal visual perception, one and the same particular can be, and often is, directly apprehended by several embodied minds. We rejected this, not in the least because it seemed *intrinsically* absurd or impossible, but because it was impossible to reconcile it with the relevant empirical facts taken as a whole. The outcome of this comparision between the two principles is that an alleged exception to the Privacy of Prehensible Particulars has an appreciable antecedent probability, while an alleged exception to the Unique Ownership of Experiences has far less, if any at all.

(ii) Some people have held that images and sensa are themselves experiences. Many others, who have not gone so far as this, have taken a view which may be roughly expressed as follows. They have held that a mental image can exist only as a logically inseparable factor in someone's experience of imaging it, and that a sensum can exist only as a logically inseparable factor in someone's experience of sensing it. If either of these views were accepted, we could replace the Privacy of Prehensible Particulars by the following principle: "No embodied mind can directly apprehend anything but itself, its own experiences, and objects which are logically inseparable factors in its own experiences." This principle does not seem to me to have any better claim to be self-evident than the Privacy of Prehensible Particulars. And I am not convinced that either of these two views about sensa and images is true. So I prefer to keep the second principle in the form in which I originally stated it.

(iii) Some people have held that, whenever a mind *has* an experience, it *directly apprehends* that experience. Others have held that, whenever a mind *has had* an experience, it *could have directly apprehended* that experience if it had attended, though it may not in fact have done so. If we accept either of these views, and combine it with the Privacy of Prehensible Particulars, the Unique Ownership of Experiences follows as a logical consequence. For suppose, if possible, that two minds, M and N, both owned a certain experience E. According to the view under discussion M could or would directly apprehend E, since E is an experience of M's. Similarly, on the view under discussion, N could or would directly apprehend E, since E is also an experience of N's. Therefore E could be directly apprehended by two different minds, which is contrary to the Privacy of Prehensible Particulars. So the supposition that E could be owned by two minds must be rejected if the Privacy of Prehensible Particulars is to be retained and the view under discussion is to be accepted.

This result seems to me to be of logical interest rather than of practical importance. In the first place, the view that, whenever a mind has an experience, it directly apprehends that experience, seems to me obviously false. And the view that, whenever a mind has had an experience, it could have directly apprehended that experience if it had attended, seems to me quite uncertain. But, even if one or other of these doctrines were indubitable, it would still be a logical perversion to base the Unique Ownership of Experience on it and the Privacy of Prehensible Objects. For, as we have seen, the Unique Ownership of Experiences has some claim to be self-evident, while the Privacy of Prehensible Objects has no such claim. We should therefore be basing the stronger of two propositions on the weaker. I conclude then that the two principles are best regarded as independent propositions.

Telepathic Prehension: We have now stated, explained, and commented on the two principles which are assumed by commonsense to govern the region with which we are at present concerned. We can look upon telepathic cognition as involving a real or apparent breach of one or other of these principles. Any breach of the Privacy of Prehensible Objects would, *ipso facto*, be an instance of telepathic cognition. To be more precise, it would be an instance of what I will call "Telepathic Prehension." Under this heading would come the following five possible cases. (i) One mind directly apprehending another mind as a unit. (ii) One mind directly apprehending an experience which is occurring in another mind. (iii) One mind directly apprehending a mental image which is being imaged by another mind. (iv) One mind directly apprehending a somatic sensum which is being sensed by another mind and is the manifestation of a process going on in the body which that other mind animates. (v) One mind directly apprehending a visual, tactual, or auditory sensum which is being sensed by another mind in seeing, touching, or hearing an external object. Telepathic prehension of the first kind seems to be claimed for Mrs. Willett (see Lord Balfour's paper, *Proc. S.P.R.*, Part 140, pp. 90-94). There are plenty of cases which look, *prima facie*, as if they were instances of the four remaining kinds. Are they really so?

In considering this question the first point to notice is the following. A breach of the Unique Ownership of Experiences would not be *ipso facto* an instance of telepathic prehension, for in itself it would not be an instance of *cognition* at all. It would best be described as an instance of "Intermental Confluence." But, if intermental confluence were to take place, telepathic prehension would almost certainly follow as an immediate consequence of it. Suppose, e.g., that, through mental confluence, N's experience of sensing a certain sensum or of imaging a certain mental image were also an experience of M's. Then M would be sensing or imaging the very same sensum or image which N is sensing or imaging. Now sensing and imaging are instances of directly apprehending. So M would be directly apprehending a sensum which N is sensing or an image which N is imaging. And, of course, the converse would also be true. So, if there were intermental confluence of this kind between M and N, there would necessarily be telepathic prehension of sensa or images by *both* M and N. This particular example can at once be generalized. If any experience which is a direct apprehension of a particular were, through mental confluence, owned by both M and N, M would be directly apprehending something which N is directly apprehending, and conversely.

We have seen, however, that intermental confluence would be ruled out by many people as self-evidently impossible. So we may now put the following question. Supposing that we rule out intermental confluence, is there any need to assume that telepathic prehension occurs? It seems to me quite unnecessary to assume this in order to account for successful experimental results in which one person conveys supernormally to another figures which he sees or draws, images which he calls up and fixes, or bodily feelings which he is experiencing. All that we need to suppose here is a particular form of telepathic *interaction*. It is enough to suppose that the occurrence of a certain sensation or imagination or bodily feeling in M's mind causally determines in N's mind the occurrence of a sensation with a similar sensum, or of an imagination with a similar image, or of a bodily feeling with a similar quality and feeling-tone. In experiments it may be generally assumed that N knows that it is *M*, and no one else, who is trying to convey an impression to him. And it may generally be assumed that he knows roughly *at what time* M is going to try the experiment. Suppose that, at about the agreed time, N suddenly has a sensation or bodily feeling or becomes aware of an image. Suppose that there is no noticeable feature in N's surroundings at the time, or in his immediately previous train of thought, which would supply an obvious normal explanation for the occurrence of just this experience at just this moment. Then he will naturally suspect that the experience is caused by M, whom he knows to be experimenting at the time. So there is no need whatever to assume that N has any telepathic prehension of M or of M's experiences, however successful such experiments may be.

So far as I can see, it is quite possible that each of us may be often, or even continuously, influenced telepathically by other minds, and yet this fact might always have escaped notice. Suppose that an event in M's mind does in fact determine telepathically an event in N's mind. N will have no reason to regard this as an instance of telepathic interaction unless all the following conditions are fulfilled. (i) The effect on N must take the form of an experience which he can and does notice. Now the effect might equally well be a change in his mental dispositions, or be an experience which he does not or cannot notice.

(ii) This experience must be so discontinuous with his other contemporary and immediately past experiences and with his usual trains of association that he is surprised by it and is led to suspect that it is not caused normally. Now this condition would seldom be fulfilled. Very often I suddenly image an image, visual or auditory, which seems quite disconnected with my other contemporary and immediately past experiences and with my usual trains of association. But even I, who am professionally interested in such things, tend to dismiss it as just one more unexplained oddity in the workings of my mind. Most people are occupied for most of their lives in practical dealings with other people and things; so an experience of theirs would have to be very odd indeed before they would seriously raise the question whether it was or was not caused normally. Moreover, if an experience in N's mind be telepathically caused by an event in M's mind, the event in M's mind would never be the *complete* immediate cause of it. It would at most be one of the immediate necessary conditions. Another, and equally necessary, factor in the total immediate cause of this experience of N's would be the permanent dispositions, the acquired associations, and the contemporary or immediately past experiences of N himself. There is therefore no reason to believe that most telepathically caused experiences would be so outstanding and discontinuous as to attract the special attention of the experient.

(iii) Even if N notices this experience with surprise, and is led to wonder whether it may not be telepathically caused, he can get no further unless he can discover that, at about the same time, a certain other person was having an experience which was specially closely related to his own. Now this condition could not be fulfilled unless all the following conditions were also fulfilled. (a) M, the person who is in fact the telepathic agent in this transaction, would need to be known to N, the telepathic patient, or they would need to have common friends. Now it is obvious that M and N might be complete strangers. (b) The event in M's mind which telepathically determined this experience in N's mind would have to be an experience which M noticed and could describe to N or to their mutual friends. Now the event might not have been an experience at all; it might have been a change in the dispositional structure of M's mind. Or the event might have been an experience which M did not or could not notice. (c) There would have to be some specially intimate observable relation between M's experience and N's experience, which would make it reasonable to single out the former as a factor in the total cause of the latter. The only two relations that I can think of in this connection are likeness and the relation of fulfillment to intention. The first would hold if the two experiences were alike in quality or if they were prehensions of similar objects. The second would hold if M's experience were that of intending to produce in N an experience of a certain kind, and if N's contemporary experience were in fact of the kind intended. Plainly there is not the least reason to suppose that either of these very special relations would hold as a rule between the telepathic cause-factor and the experience which it cooperates in producing. An effect may be extremely unlike every one of the factors in its immediate total cause. And most telepathic interaction may be entirely unintentional.

The upshot of the above discussion is this. If telepathic interaction takes place at all, it may well be a very common occurrence. But it will be noticeable only when a large number of independent and rather special conditions are simultaneously fulfilled. And, when these conditions are fulfilled, so that it does become noticeable, the experience which is telepathically produced in N will be very liable to be mistaken for a telepathic prehension by N of that experience of M's which is its telepathic causal determinant. It is easy to find analogies in the physical sciences to the situation which I have just shown to be possible about telepathy. Consider, e.g., ordinary magnetic forces, and the history of our knowledge of them. Such forces occur whenever electric charges are moving or electric forces are varying, and they pervade all space at all times and are profoundly important factors in the physical world. Yet they would hardly have been discovered had it not been for the happy accidents that the earth contains a good deal of the one element, viz., iron, which is very strongly susceptible to magnetic forces; that it contains natural magnets, viz., lodestones; and that it is itself a natural magnet. For centuries magnetism seemed to be a freak of nature which occurred exclusively in connection with certain very special kinds of matter. Yet in fact it was all the time operating everywhere. And the very special characteristics which it displays in connection with iron and with permanent magnets, masked its real nature almost as much as they revealed it.

I have now said all that seems necessary in support of my contention that experiments in telepathy, however successful they may be, would prove only telepathic *interaction*, of one or other of the three kinds which we distinguished as theoretically possible. They would not force us to abandon the Privacy of Prehensible Particulars and to postulate telepathic prehension. It remains to consider two other kinds of ostensibly telepathic phenomena, for which there is ample evidence, some of which is of excellent quality. The first is spontaneous telepathy, such as is reported in *Phantasms of the Living*. The second is the supernormal knowledge which mediums often display with regard to facts known to the sitter or to some other living person.

A good many cases of spontaneous telepathy can be regarded as similar in principle to the cases of experimental telepathy which we have already considered. Suppose that M, sitting in his dining room in a mood of intense depression, eventually takes poison, suffers great bodily pain, and dies. Suppose that there arise in N's mind, through telepathic interaction, visual sensations or visual imaginings very much like those which M is experiencing through normal visual perception of his surroundings. If N is familiar with M's dining room, his telepathically induced visual experiences will naturally make him think of that room and of M. Suppose next that there arises in N's mind, through telepathic interaction, a feeling of intense depression very much like that which M is experiencing because of illness, financial trouble, or some other normal cause. It will be natural for N to connect together these two simultaneous abnormal experiences, and to suspect that there is something seriously wrong with M. Suppose finally that there arises in N's mind, through telepathic interaction, a sensation of intense bodily pain very much like that which M is experiencing in consequence of the action of the poison on his body. It will be natural for N to assume that M must be very ill and perhaps dying. If N should be asleep or in a dreamy state when the telepathic interaction takes place, it is extremely likely that the data supplied, and the normal associations which they excite, will be supplemented by a great deal of imagery. The whole thing may then be worked up into a vivid dream or waking hallucination, with the gaps filled in and the inconsistencies smoothed out correctly or incorrectly. No kind of telepathic prehension needs to be postulated here. Nothing need be assumed except the special kind of telepathic interaction, which we postulated to explain the experimental results, together with the normal workings of pre-formed associations in N's mind.

Telepathic Discursive Cognition: It is doubtful whether all well-attested cases of spontaneous telepathy can be dealt with on these lines. And it is fairly certain that this cannot be a right explanation of the supernormal knowledge which mediums often display with regard to facts known only to the sitter or to some other living person. We may best approach the subject in the following way. There are at least two fundamentally different, though intimately connected, kinds of normal cognition, viz., prehensive and discursive. So far we have considered only the possibility of telepathic *prehension* and we have found no direct evidence for it. Now it looks as if the mediumistic cases, and some of the spontaneous telepathy cases, might involve telepathic *discursive* cognition. I will now explain these statements and consider whether there is reason to postulate such cognition.

The distinction between prehensive and discursive cognition is roughly identical with the familiar distinction between "directly apprehending" and "thinking about." It is illustrated, e.g., by the difference between actually hearing a set of noises which form a tune and knowing or believing that this tune consists of a series of noises of certain pitches and durations following each other in a certain order. We may, of course, have discursive cognition about a particular which we are also directly apprehending; and the ground of our discursive cognition about it may be what is manifested to us in our prehension of it. But we can have discursive cognition about objects which we are not at the time prehending, about objects which we never have prehended, and about objects which we never could prehend. We can also have an experience which would properly be described as "thinking of an x," e.g., a dragon, or "thinking of the y," e.g., the King of the Fairies, although there may be nothing answering to the description "an x" or the description "the y." But it would be impossible to have an experience which would properly be described as "directly apprehending an x" or "directly apprehending the y" unless there were something answering to the description "an x" or to the description "the y," respectively.

Discursive cognition consists in either *knowing a fact* or taking up one of a number of alternative *cognitive attitudes* towards a *proposition* which may be either true or false. Among these cognitive attitudes are included believing, disbelieving, opining, uncritically accepting, supposing, and probably many others. All such cognitive attitudes towards a proposition equally presuppose a more fundamental cognitive experience which may be called "entertaining" the proposition. One and the same person may entertain the same proposition on many different occasions, and he may take towards it the same or different cognitive attitudes on different occasions. At one time he may doubt it, at another he may believe it, and so on. Again, several people may entertain one and the same proposition on the same occasion, and they may take various cognitive attitudes towards it. Smith and Jones may both believe it, while Brown doubts it and Robinson disbelieves it. (In saying these things I do not mean to imply that there is a peculiar class of entities called "propositions." I think it most likely that all the statements which I have just been making could be restated without introducing the word "proposition" or any synonym for it. But the translations would be extremely complicated and verbose. The use of the word "proposition" enables me to express in a reasonably simple verbal form what everyone admits to be facts about discursive cognition. No further excuse is needed for continuing to use it.)

There is one other general fact of very great importance which we must mention before we can profitably consider telepathic discursive cognition. At any moment far the greater part of any man's "knowledge" or "beliefs" or "opinions" certainly does not take the form of *experiences* of knowing such and such facts or believing or opining such and such propositions. The truth about him is that he *would* have these experiences *if* he chose to direct his attention in a certain way, or *if* he were to be suitably stimulated. We may express this by saying that, at every moment of our lives, much the greater part of our knowledge, beliefs, and opinions consists of relatively permanent *dispositions* to know certain facts or to believe or opine certain propositions. It is always assumed that, to every such relatively permanent cognitive disposition, there must correspond some relatively permanent *actual existent*. This is generally supposed to be some actual modification of the structure of our minds or our brains, or to be some actual persistent unobservable process in our minds or our brains.

It is as well to recognize that we know nothing at all about the intrinsic nature of the actual existents which are supposed to correspond to our cognitive dispositions. We do not know whether they are persistent structural features or persistent unobservable processes. And we do not know whether they are modifications of our minds or our brains or of both or of neither. All that we know of them is that they are produced and modified by our actual experiences, and that they are important factors in producing and modifying our experiences. There is very good reason to believe that the actual existents which correspond to the various dispositions of various kinds of *matter* are special peculiarities in the spatial arrangement and the motion of the ultramicroscopic particles of which bodies are composed. But, unless we assume that the actual existents which correspond to *mental* dispositions are themselves purely material, we cannot suppose that they are spatial arrangements or modes of motion of ultramicroscopic particles. Now it is extremely difficult to form any positive conception of purely *mental* structures or of non-introspectible *mental* processes which could plausibly be supposed to correspond to our mental dispositions. So we are between the horns of the following dilemma. If we put the correlates of all mental dispositions into the brain, we get a theory which is familiar and intelligible in outline but incredible when we come to consider detail. If, on the other hand, we postulate mental structures and non-introspectible mental processes as the actual correlates of our mental dispositions, we have no clear idea of what we are postulating and we run the risk of paying ourselves with words.

We are now in readiness to consider telepathic discursive cognition. Suppose that M knows the fact F or entertains the proposition P. The only normal way in which M's knowledge of F or his entertaining of P can cause another mind N to think of this fact or to entertain this proposition is the following. M must express the fact or the proposition by uttering or writing a sentence which expresses it in accordance with some conventional system of symbolization. N must hear or see or in some other way perceive with his senses either this spoken or written sentence itself or some reproduction of it, e.g., on a gramophone record or in a book. Of course profound physical transformations may take place during the process which intervenes between M's utterance and the occurrence of the reproduction of it which N perceives; but a fundamental identity of structure must be preserved throughout, though it may be realized in very different media at different stages. This is well illustrated by telephonic or wireless transmission of speech. Next, the sentence which N eventually perceives must mean for him, in accordance with some system of conventional symbolization with which he is familiar, the same fact or proposition which M expressed by his original sentence. If N perceives M's sentence itself, it is essential that he should be familiar with the system of symbolic conventions which M uses. If N perceives only a reproduction of M's original sentence, this condition need not be fulfilled, but another will have to be substituted for it. M might express himself in French; and N, who knows no French, might still be caused to entertain the proposition which M was entertaining provided that N perceives a sentence which is an English translation of M's sentence. But, in that case, it is essential that there should have been a third person T, familiar with both M's and N's systems of conventional symbolization, who made a translation from one set of symbols to the other.

The following remarks are worth making at this stage. (i) M's knowledge of F or his entertainment of P may be an essential factor in causing N to think of F or to entertain P; and yet N may have no knowledge or thought of M or of M's cognitions. If N perceives and understands a sentence, and if he cares to reflect on the matter, he will indeed recognize that some mind or other must have entertained the proposition which this sentence means and must have expressed it in a sentence. And he will recognize that this event in another mind must be a causal ancestor of his own entertainment of this proposition. But N need not know or believe anything more definite about this other mind. (ii) Suppose that N perceives and understands a certain sentence, and also knows that it was uttered by M or is a reproduction of one of M's utterances. N will then know, or have very strong reason to believe, that the proposition which he has been led to entertain has also been *entertained* by M. But he may know nothing about M's *cognitive attitude* towards this proposition. If N has any beliefs on this subject, they may well be mistaken; as is abundantly proved by the occurrence of successful lies and political propaganda, which are taken by the duped hearer to express the *knowledge* or the *beliefs* of the lying speaker.

It is now easy to define the phrase "Telepathically Induced Discursive Cognition." Suppose that a certain mind N thinks of a fact F or entertains a proposition P at a certain moment. Suppose that N would not have done this unless a certain other contemporary mind M were knowing this fact or entertaining this proposition. Lastly, suppose that M's knowledge of F or his entertaining of P does not bring about N's thought of F or his entertainment of P by the normal process which we have just described. Either M never expresses the fact or the proposition in a sentence, or N never perceives the sentence or any reproduction of it, or N cannot understand the sentence or the reproduction of it which he perceives. If these conditions, positive and negative, were fulfilled, we should say that N was having telepathically induced discursive cognition of this fact or this proposition. And we should say that he was deriving this cognition telepathically from M's mind. Now it looks as if telepathically induced discursive cognition, in the sense just defined, were involved in some cases of spontaneous telepathy between normal people and in many cases of trance-mediumship. Can we say anything further about it?

(i) I suspect that some people have at the back of their minds a certain tacit assumption about the *modus operandi* of telepathically induced discursive cognition. It may be stated as follows. Suppose that N is cognizing a fact or a proposition, and that this cognition of N's is derived telepathically from M's mind. Then, it is assumed, N must be telepathically *prehending* M's *cognition of* this fact or proposition. And in so doing, it is further assumed, N will *ipso facto* be himself cognizing the fact or proposition which M is cognizing. To sum up the theory in a sentence: "N's telepathically induced cognition of *what M discursively cognizes* depends upon N's telepathic prehension of *M's experience of cognizing*."

I should very much hesitate to accept this theory. In the first place, we have so far found no reason to admit the occurrence of prehensive cognition by one mind of experiences belonging to another mind. Secondly, I would question the assumption that, if N directly apprehended M's experience of knowing the fact F or cognizing the proposition P, he would *ipso facto* be himself cognizing F or P. It is, no doubt, true that a person could not directly apprehend *his own* experience of knowing a fact F or cognizing a proposition P unless he were knowing F or cognizing P. For, unless he were knowing F or cognizing P, there would be nothing answering to the description "his experience of knowing F or cognizing P." And, unless there were an experience answering to this description, he could not directly apprehend such an experience. But this argument will not lead to the desired conclusion if we apply it to N's prehension of M's cognitive experiences. The only conclusion to which it leads in this case is quite trivial. The conclusion is merely that, if N directly apprehends M's experience of knowing F or cognizing P, then M must be knowing F or cognizing P. The desired conclusion is that N must be thinking of F or entertaining P. And this certainly does not follow.

Now, if the fallacy which I have just indicated is avoided, there seems to be no reason to accept the assumption under discussion. Why should not N directly apprehend an event, which is *in fact* M's experience of knowing F or cognizing P, without realizing that the event which he is apprehending answers to this description? And, if this is possible, why should N *ipso facto* think of F or entertain P?

It might be plausible to maintain that N could not directly apprehend an experience of M's without *ipso facto* being aware of its *psychological quality*, e.g., without apprehending it as an experience of knowing or as one of believing or as one of doubting, as the case might be. But it is not plausible to maintain that N could not directly apprehend an experience of M's without *ipso facto* being aware of its *epistemological object*, i.e., of the fact of which it is a knowing or of the proposition of which it is a believing or a doubting. Yet, when telepathy takes place from M to N, the result is usually that N cognizes a fact or a proposition which M is cognizing, but remains unaware of the psychological quality of M's cognitive experience. So there seems to be very little to be said in favor of the theory which we have been discussing.

Before we leave this theory there is one more remark to be made about it. If it were acceptable on other grounds, it could be applied to explain the apparently telepathic prehension by N of images which M is imaging or of sensa which M is sensing. The explanation would, of course, take the following form. N, it would be said, telepathically prehends M's experience of imaging the image I or sensing the sensum S. In doing this, it would be assumed, N *ipso facto* prehends the image I or the sensum S which is the object of M's experience. The general principle assumed is that, is prehending any experience which is itself a prehension of an object, one would be *ipso facto* prehending its object. I see no reason to accept this principle; and I have already tried to show that the results of experimental telepathy can be interpreted in quite a different way, which involves telepathic interaction but does not involve telepathic cognition.

(ii) I think that certain cases of telepathically induced discursive cognition could be explained on the same lines as the simple cases of experimental telepathy. Suppose that M knows the fact F or cognizes the proposition P. Although he does not utter or write a sentence which would express F or P in his own language, he may image a series of auditory or visual images corresponding to such a sentence. Certainly when I am thinking I often find myself doing this. Suppose now that a series of visual or auditory images, similar to these, were produced by telepathic interaction and imaged by another mind N. If N knew the language in which these image-sentences are composed, he would automatically entertain the proposition or think of the fact which they express in that language. He would thus have been telepathically induced to entertain the proposition which M is cognizing or to think of the fact which M is knowing.

It must be noticed that this theory presupposes that N knows the language in which M would express himself if he were to speak or to write. It therefore could not explain how an Englishman could telepathically induce in a Frenchman, who knew no English, a cognition of a fact which the Englishman knows or a proposition which he cognizes. I do not know whether there is good evidence of telepathically induced discursive cognition in such cases. It would be a very important subject for experimental investigation.

(iii) Even if the explanation just proposed should be true of some cases of telepathically induced discursive cognition, I do not think that it could possibly cover all or most of them. In most cases it seems certain that the person from whom the cognition was telepathically derived was not thinking at the time of the fact or proposition concerned. And, if he was not thinking of it, he was *a fortiori* not imaging a set of spoken or written words which would express it in his own language. When N derives telepathically from M a cognition of a fact which M knows or a proposition which M believes, it is not usually the case that M is actually having an experience of knowing the fact or believing the proposition. Usually M's knowledge or belief is at the time purely dispositional, as most of our knowledge and our beliefs are at every moment. It is possible, of course, to evade this contention by saying that M must have been "unconsciously" having an actual experience of knowing the fact or of believing the proposition at the time when the cognition is telepathically induced in N. This, however, would be a wholly gratuitous assumption, for which there is no independent evidence, and I shall ignore it.

The position, then, seems to be this. Suppose that N telepathically derives from M a cognition of a fact F, which M knows, or of a proposition P, which M believes. Then the operative factor on M's side will not as a rule be any actual cognitive experience which M is having at the time. The operative factor on M's side will usually be what we may call his "potentiality of knowing F" or his "potentiality of believing P." By M's "potentiality of knowing F" I mean that persistent modification of structure or process, whatever it may be, which ensures that, whenever M is suitably stimulated by a reminder, he will have an actual experience of knowing F. By M's "potentiality of believing P" I mean that persistent modification of structure or process, whatever it may be, which ensures that, whenever M is suitably stimulated by a reminder, he will have an actual experience of believing P. I have already said that we know nothing whatever about the intrinsic nature or location of these assumed persistent modifications. We know them only as relatively permanent *after-effects* of actual experiences, and as relatively permanent *cause-factors* in producing and modifying subsequent experiences. Let us call them "Experientially Initiated Potentialities of Experience."

Now the normal rule is this. Any such potentiality which is a cause-factor in producing or modifying M's *later experiences* has been acquired from M's *earlier experiences*. I wish to point out that this is merely an empirical rule based on normal experience. Since we know nothing about the intrinsic nature or location of experientially initiated potentialities of experience, we cannot possibly see any kind of necessity in this or any other rule about them. It is logically possible that a potentiality which is an after-effect of M's past experiences should be a cause-factor in producing or modifying, not only M's future experiences, but also those of N. Many cases of telepathically induced discursive cognition seem to suggest that this logical possibility is in fact something realized.

Let us begin by considering normal thinking. Here, as we have said, the only experientially initiated potentialities which affect a person's later experiences are those which were initiated by *his own* earlier experiences. In low-grade thinking, such as day-dreaming, it would seem that some one potentiality is activated by some very contingent experience of the thinker, and that this then activates another, and this in turn another, and so on, in an almost automatic way dependent on association by contiguity, similarity, etc. The result is a series of thoughts or images which have very little logical interconnection; though the thinker himself, if he reflected on them, or a psychologist, if he performed a psychoanalysis, might be able to conjecture why the experiences had followed each other in this particular order. If, on the other hand, the person is actively pursuing a directed train of thought on some definite problem, those potentialities which would give rise to experiences relevant to the problem will tend to be stimulated and those which would give rise to experiences irrelevant to the problem will tend to be kept quiet. Even here the potentiality which would give rise to an experience highly relevant at a certain stage in the process often fails to be activated at the appropriate moment. And potentialities which give rise to irrelevant or misleading experiences often do get activated. Even when a process of thinking, directed to solving a certain problem, is eventually successful, the thoughts which are the stages in this process seldom arise in their proper logical order. The right logical order usually comes as a result of retrospective reflection on the process by the thinker, followed by an act of rearrangement.

The point which I want to emphasize now is the following. When normal directed thinking is contrasted with normal low-grade thinking, it may fairly be called a "voluntary" process. And it may fairly be said that the thinker "deliberately selects," out of the mass of potentialities of experience which his past experiences have initiated, those which would give rise to relevant experiences if they were stimulated. But it is most important not to be deceived by such phrases. We must not imagine that the thinker *perceives* the various potentialities of experience, as a man might perceive a lot of ties and socks and shoes and pullovers in his bedroom, and then *deliberately activates a certain selection from them*, as a man might deliberately put on a certain tie, a certain pair of socks, a certain pair of shoes, and a certain pullover, in order to produce a certain color scheme. The following analogy may make the fallacy quite plain. When the process of constructing a machine with one's hands is contrasted with blinking or jerking one's knee, it may fairly be call a "voluntary" process. And it may fairly be said that the agent "deliberately selects," out of a mass of potentialities of movement derived from his past bodily action, those which would give rise to the relevant overt movements if stimulated. But he certainly does not *perceive* his own motor-nerves and muscles, select certain of the former, and decide to send such and such nervous impulses down the former in order to activate the latter in such a way as to make his fingers move as he wants them to do. He is perceiving and thinking of nothing but his hands and the materials with which he is working. He is desiring nothing but to make certain complicated movements with his hand against the resistance of the materials. This *automatically*, and in ways utterly unknown to him, sets up unfelt processes in unperceived nerves. And, in the main, these are in fact the appropriate processes in the appropriate nerves; since, in the main, the expected and desired overt movements result. To imagine that a thinker literally selects and *deliberately* activates those potentialities of experience which are relevant to the problem that he is trying to solve is like imagining that a manual worker *literally* contemplates his own brain and nervous system as if it were a complicated switchboard and *deliberately* presses such and such buttons. The thinker or the manual worker wills that a certain process of thought or bodily action shall take place; and automatically, in ways unknown to him, his volition initiates and sustains, among unobservable entities, unobservable processes which do in fact tend to bring about the desired process of thought or bodily action.

I have insisted upon this point about normal thinking because it has an important bearing upon telepathically induced thinking. It seems to me that there are two ways in which we are liable to make needless difficulties for ourselves in connection with this subject. (i) We tacitly assume that potentialities of experience initiated by M's experiences must be located in M's brain or in M's mind; and similarly, *mutatis mutandis*, for N and for each other individual. (ii) We tacitly assume that, when a certain set of coexistent potentialities of experience are activated in such an order as to give rise to a certain coherent train of thought in M's mind, M must have contemplated a whole mass of coexistent potentialities and must have deliberately selected and activated this particular subgroup. Then we are faced with telepathically induced discursive cognition. We thereupon raise such questions as these. How can N contemplate potentialities of experience which are located in M's brain or in M's mind? How can N select from these just that subgroup which is relevent to his own problem at the moment? How can N activate this subgroup located in M's mind or brain? And, if N does this, why are the corresponding experiences produced in N's mind and not in M's?

Now these difficulties are at least lightened by the two following considerations. (i) Even if the potentialities of experience which are initiated by M's experiences are located in M's mind or M's brain, there is not the least reason to suppose that N would have to contemplate them and deliberately activate a certain selection of them. For we have seen that this is certainly not the way in which the set of potentialities which are relevent to a normal train of thought occurs.

(ii) We have very little ground for assuming that the potentialities of experience which are initiated by M's experiences are located in M's mind or in M's brain. If I say that an *actual experience* is located in M's mind, I know what I mean. I mean that it is one of M's experiences, and I know perfectly well what it is for a certain experience to belong to, or occur in, a certain mind. But *experientially initiated potentialities of experience*, whatever they may be, are certainly not themselves experiences. When I say that a certain acquired potentiality of experience is located in M's *mind* this can only be an abbreviated way of saying that it was produced by a past experience of M's and that it is a cause-factor in producing or modifying later experiences of M's. If the statement means anything more than this, I have no idea what it means. If, on the other hand, I say that it is located in M's *brain* I must mean that it is a more or less persistent modification in the spatial arrangement or the movements of the ultramicrosopic particles in some part of M's brain. Now there are well-known empirical facts about the loss of a person's normal memories through injuries to his brain and his subsequent recovery of these memories which make it very difficult to accept this view of experientially initiated potentialities of experience. So the statement that potentialities of experience initiated by M's experiences are located in M's *mind* seems to be either metaphorical or meaningless; and the statement that they are located in his *brain,* if taken as the whole truth, seems to be difficult to reconcile with admitted facts about the effects of brain-injuries on normal experience.

We must therefore consider seriously the possibility that each person's experiences initiate more or less permanent modifications of structure or process in something which is neither his mind nor his brain. There is no reason to suppose that this substratum would be anything to which possessive adjectives, such as "mine" and "yours" and "his" could properly be applied, as they can be to minds and to animated bodies. The situation would be this. The modifications which are produced in this common substratum by M's experiences *normally* affect only the subsequent experiences of M; those which are produced in it by N's experiences *normally* affect only the subsequent experiences of N. But in certain cases this normal causal "self-confinement," as we might call it, breaks down. Modifications which have been produced in the substratum by certain of M's past experiences are activated by N's present experiences or interests, and they become cause-factors in producing or modifying N's later experiences.

As we know nothing about the intrinsic nature of experientially initiated potentialities of experience, we cannot say anything definite about the intrinsic nature of the common substratum of which we have assumed them to be modifications. As there is no reason whatever to think that such potentialities of experience are, or could be themselves experiences, there is no reason whatever to suppose that the substratum is a mind. On the other hand, it could hardly be any particular finite body. It does not seem impossible that it should be some kind of extended pervasive medium, capable of receiving and retaining modifications of local structure or internal motion. But I do not think that we have at present any adequate data for further speculations about its nature.

AN ANALYSIS OF FACTUAL KNOWLEDGE

Peter Unger

I intend to provide an analysis of human factual knowledge, in other words, an analysis of what it is for a man to know that something is the case. I try to capture the conception of human factual knowledge that ordinary knowledgeable humans do in fact employ in making commonsensical judgments about the presence or absence of such knowledge. My analysis will depart most radically from all previously offered analyses and will, I think, be all the better for this departure.

The Presence of Knowledge and the Absence of Accident

In a recent critical paper,[1] after arguing to refute the idea that knowledge of most contingent matters must be based on experience, I put forward the following as providing a logically necessary condition of when a man's belief is an instance of knowledge:

> (0) For any sentential value of p a man's belief that p is an instance of knowledge only if it is not an accident that the man's belief is true.

Speaking of a man's belief as being an instance of knowledge may be too unnatural; at any rate it is not a very ordinary sort of thing to do. And, in the end, we are not so interested in when a man's belief might be an instance of knowledge, as we are in when a man might know that something is so. Thus, motivated by a consideration of (0), I now assert as a unified and univocal analysis of human factual knowledge:

> (1) For any sentential value of p (at a time t) a man knows that p if and only if (at t) it is not at all accidental that the man is right about its being the case that p.

To speak most clearly and correctly, a reference to specific times should be an explicit part of any adequate analysis of human knowledge. At one time it may be at least somewhat accidental that a man is right about a certain matter, although at another time it is not at all accidental that he is right. Thus, a man may believe that there is a rosebush on his vast estate simply because a servant told him so and convinced him of that. The servant did not know of the existence of any rosebush and only convinced the man for amusement, thinking,

---

This selection is extracted from *The Journal of Philosophy*, Vol. 65, No. 6 (March, 1968), 157-70. Used by permission of *The Journal of Philosophy* and Peter Unger.

indeed, that he had got his employer to believe something false. However, unbeknownst to the servant there was a rosebush in a far corner of the estate. One day the man may ride into that corner of the estate. We may suppose that he sees the rosebush. Before he sees the bush, it is entirely accidental that the estate owner has been right about there being a rosebush on his estate; when he sees the bush, it first becomes the case that it is not at all accidental that he is right about the matter. This is when the man first knows that his estate is so blessed. Again, and in contrast, a man who holds no opinion on the matter may see a rosebush and so first come to know and to be right that it is in a certain place. While he still has some but no very strong memory of the matter, he may believe that the rosebush is there and may have this belief as a result of his remembering that it is there. While he has this belief, a friend who has no knowledge of the rosebush, who simply wants to convince the man that there is a rosebush in the aforementioned place, may tell the man in most convincing and memorable terms that he, the friend, saw the rosebush there. When he hears the friend's story the man holds his belief about the rosebush both because he has seen it and remembers that it is there, and also because of the friend's story; either then being sufficient to ensure his then holding that belief. At this time the man does know; for, because he originally saw the bush, it is then not at all accidental that he is right about the location of the bush. Still later, the man may still believe that the rosebush is in the proper location but only because his friend so convincingly told him so. His originally seeing the bush will then be not at all responsible for his holding the (correct) belief. At this point, the man no longer knows; for at the time in question it is false that it is not at all accidental that the man is right about the matter. Indeed, at this time it is very much an accident that he is right about its being the case that the rosebush is in the place in question, and thus it is clear that at the time in question the man does not know the location of the bush.

It is essential, then, that we think of a man as knowing something *at a certain time* and say that *at that time* it is not at all accidental that he is right. With this understanding firmly in mind, we need not always refer to times in our subsequent discussion, and, to make matters easier, we often will not do so.

Irrelevant Accidents

What we properly regard as an accident, or as accidental, does appear to depend upon our various interests, as well as upon other things. Thus, even in the most physically deterministic universe imaginable, automobile accidents may occur, and it may be largely accidental that one man, rather than another, is successful in his competitive business enterprise. To provide an analysis of when something is an accident, or something accidental, is more than I am (now) capable of doing. Nor can I show in any helpful detail how our notion of an accident, or of something's being accidental, may be used to express or reflect the various interests we might have. Thus, I will rely on a shared intuitive understanding of these notions.

In my analysis of human factual knowledge, a complete absence of the accidental is claimed, not regarding the occurrence or existence of the fact known nor regarding the existence or abilities of the man who knows, but only as regards a certain relation concerning the man and the fact. Thus, it may be accidental that *p* and a man may know that *p*, for it may nevertheless be that it is not at all accidental that the man is right about its being the case that *p*. In other words, a man may know about an auto accident: when the car accidentally crashes into the truck, a bystander who observes what is going on may well know that the car crashed into the truck and accidentally did so. He will know just in case it is not at all accidental that he is right about its being the case that the car crashed into the truck and accidentally did so. Nor do I claim that there must be nothing accidental in the way that a man comes to know that *p*. Thus, a man may overhear his employer say that he will be fired and he may do so quite by accident, not intending to be near his employer's office or to gain any information from his employer. Though it may be an accident that the man came to know that he will be fired, and it may be somewhat accidental that he knows this to be so, nevertheless, from the time that he hears and onward, it may well be not at all accidental that the man is right about its being the case that he will be fired. Thus, he may know, whether by accident or not.

Of all the things that a man knows, none is more certainly known by him than the fact of his own existence. Thus, it must be most obvious that a man who, at a certain time, exists or is alive only as a matter of some accident may, even at that time, know about various matters of fact; he may, for instance, most certainly know that he exists. Though it may be largely accidental that he exists or is alive, it may be not at all accidental that he is right about various matters of fact: (indeed, necessarily, should he sincerely hold that he then existed, it would be not at all accidental that he was right about that matter). These points can perhaps be made more clear by our considering the following simple story: suppose that a man is looking at a turtle and even seeing that the turtle is crawling on the ground. This man may know that the turtle is crawling on the ground (and will in that he sees that it is); for because he is using his eyes (and because of other things as well), it may be that at that time it is not at all accidental that the man is right about its being the case that the turtle is crawling on the ground. However, suppose further that just at this time or immediately before it, a heavy rock would have fallen on the man and would have killed him then and there, smashing him to smithereens, but for the occurrence of an accidental happening which prevents the rock from falling and allows him to remain alive. Say, all of three terrible people who were pushing the rock that was to fall were themselves, coincidentally and simultaneously, hit on the head by three independently falling bricks and were killed upon impact. Each of the bricks quite independently of the others, just happened to fall loose from an ancient wall of which they all were a part. Thus, quite by accident, all three of the terrible rock pushers were killed, and the turtle watcher's life was spared, perhaps only until some later time. On these suppositions, it is indeed quite an accident that the turtle watcher is alive at the time he sees the turtle crawling on the ground before him. Yet, at that time, it is not at all accidental that he is right about its being the case that there is a turtle on the ground. And at that time, as we have supposed, the turtle watcher knows that there is a turtle crawling there upon the ground. These are the judgments that common sense and good sense would make about our case. Thus, it may be not at all accidental that a man is right about a certain matter, even though it is very much an accident that he then exists or is alive. Once we are clear about this, we can more fully appreciate the ability of my analysis to explain the cogency of Cartesian examples. Though it be accidental that a certain man exist, yet necessarily if he thinks that he exists, it is not at all accidental that he is right about the matter. An unwanted and accidental child, pursued by hapless rock pushers all his life, may grow up to know more than any of his brothers or sisters. He may do so even on my analysis of human factual knowledge, whether he fancy himself a Cartesian skeptic or whether he be entirely unconcerned with such philosophical profundities.

Accidents and Phenomena of Chance

The condition of my analysis is stronger than the necessary condition most naturally suggested by my earlier statement (0) and explicitly given by the following:

(2) For any sentential value of p, a man knows that p if and only if it is not an accident that the man is right about its being the case that p.

That such strength is required, that the weaker condition of (2) is not sufficient, can be most readily seen by considering our thought about phenomena of chance. Such a consideration will show, I think, how only our stronger condition, and none such as that of (2), adequately reflects tensions that often exist in the application of the concept of knowledge.

Let us, then, suppose a standard and simple sort of example: a man knows that a deck of cards contains ninety-nine white cards, one black card, and no others. He also knows that the cards have just been well shuffled and fairly so. On the basis of this knowledge, he concludes, as is his custom, that it is likely that the top card is white. Thus he may come to believe that the top card is white, and we may suppose him to do so. Let us further suppose that the top card is white: we are supposing that the man's belief is correct, that he is right about its being the case that the top card is white. The only reason that he has this (correct) belief is that he has reasoned in a certain way on the basis of the knowledge that we have supposed him to have. Now once we have made all these suppositions, we have supposed, not only that the man is right, but also, and with equal clarity, that it is not an accident that he is right about the matter. But, in contrast, it is *not* entirely clear that it is not at all accidental that the man is right. But, equally, it is *not* clear that it is *false* that it is not at all accidental that he is. In other words, there is a tension in the application of our analytic condition to the probabilistic case presented. This same tension is also in evidence when we consider the application of our concept of factual knowledge. For in the simple case presented, it is *neither* clear that the man does know *nor* clear that he does not. The suppositions neither allow nor yield any decisive answer as to whether the man knows the color of the top card.

The magnitude of the numbers involved may help to further our willingness to say that the man knows, to apply our concept of knowledge. But sheer consideration of number will not remove the tension entirely. Thus, were there a billion white cards, and only one of another color, we are more ready to say that the man who bets that the top card is white knows full well that he will win (assuming of course that he will win). Still, we may also find ourselves saying that he cannot really know that he has won until the color of the card is actually revealed. Similarly, such an increase in the chances furthers our readiness to apply our analytic condition, to say that it is not at all accidental that the man is right (assuming of course that he is right). But again, and equally I think, our willingness here is not so complete as it might be. Perhaps it is not really true, after all, that it is not at all accidental that he is right, even when such large numbers are involved. Thus, a consideration of our thought about such simple probabilistic cases gives some further support to the claim that our analytic condition mirrors well our concept of factual knowledge.

We may gain yet further support, I think, by considering the way in which our thought about more highly structured cases compares with what we think about such unstructured cases of the most simple probabilistic kind. In contrast to the first case of the card deck, let us consider the following, more structured sort of case, where considerations of probability enter rather less directly: a man is performing a hundred problems in addition and checking his answers by an independent arithmetic method. These problems each involve his adding three different numbers, each between 10 and 100. There is nothing mysterious here: the man uses the normal paper-and-pencil methods for both adding and checking. He always expresses the numbers in the decimal system, in the familiar arabic notation. Suppose the man, like most other men, characteristically to make only one mistake unspotted, and eventually to add and check correctly in ninety-nine of the hundred cases. And suppose him in *each* case to think the answer correct (though we may allow that he may not think he has been correct in *all* cases). Then, with respect to each problem that he worked and checked correctly, our common-sense judgment would be that he knew what the answer was. Having worked the problem correctly, he would know, for example, that 134 is the sum of 32 and 49 and 53. And equally, the common-sense attitude still prevailing, there is no doubt but that we should say that it is not at all accidental that the man is right about the sum. Such tension as was present in the purely probabilistic case of the card deck, is now absent from our judgment—both as regards our concept of knowledge and as regards our analytic condition. Exactly why cases like that involving fallible addition should differ so markedly from cases of pure probability is a deep question that cries out for further analysis and greater understanding. But though our understanding of these matters is presently quite limited, we may recognize that there are between the two sorts of cases just considered, notable differences in our willingness to apply our concept of factual knowledge. Even here, where my analysis leads us to no very important increase in our understanding of the relevant matters, we may say that the analysis has received some notable support.[2]

Justification, Evidence, and Knowledge

My analysis of human factual knowledge differs markedly from those analyses in which an attempt is made to consider such knowledge as some sort of justified true belief. Indeed, according to my analysis a man may know something without his being in any way justified in believing that it is so. And my analysis does not require, as does that of A. J. Ayer,[3] that

> (3) For any sentential value of p, a man knows that p only if the man has the right to be sure that p.

It also disagrees with Roderick Chisholm's claim[4] that

> (4) For any sentential value of p, a man knows that p only if the man has adequate evidence that p.

Let us consider a straightforward example which upsets these claims most decisively, and shows that no sort of justification is ever a necessary condition for knowledge. Thus, we may better understand my analysis by seeing how it conflicts with this other, more traditional view.

The example, which I first adduced in my aforementioned essay against empiricism, concerns a certain gypsy, one who, we must conclude, knows things of which others are ignorant. Our gypsy has been brought up to accept the messages of a certain crystal ball that he inherited from his family. Owing to forces in nature which no one understands, the ball always gives a correct report on any matter on which it provides a message. And, because of certain loyalties and beliefs instilled by his upbringing, the gypsy never checks up on the ball in any way whatever. We shall, indeed, suppose the gypsy to believe, what he inferred from what he learned later in life, that the ball will almost never give a correct report. But though the gypsy has this (false) general belief, which we may suppose him to be justified in having, when it comes to any particular matter, he cannot help but believe the message of the ball. Moreover, these acquired beliefs he holds most insistently though he is unable to provide any reasonable defense of these beliefs when challenged and is even wholly unconcerned with whether he is reasonable or not in holding them. We may even suppose that, despite his unreasonable attitudes and the lack of adequate evidence for his beliefs, the gypsy is entirely confident about the truth of each report despite his knowledge of its source and his belief about the general unreliability of the source. Where the fact that p is reported by the ball, on these suppositions, the gypsy does not have adequate evidence that p, and especially so when we further suppose him to have a wealth of evidence for thinking it false that p. Does the gypsy then have the right to be sure that p? Plainly not, unless everyone has the right to be sure of anything that is true. Such are the effects of the gypsy's early upbringing and certain later happenings.

But it does appear that, in the present case, the effects are not wholly and simply unfortunate ones. Owing to the gypsy's early upbringing and the operation of the crystal ball, the gypsy does have knowledge of those matters on which the ball delivers a report. This fact may be made especially clear by supposing that the gypsy's parents knew, by observational check or by some other means, that the ball gave only correct reports. On this basis they raised their gypsy child to accept unquestioningly the reports of the ball, whether these be of a pictorial sort or whether expressed in some sort of unusual writing. Thus, this gypsy, though he is only unreasonable in believing that *p,* knows that *p,* where the report that *p* is a report of the ball that the gypsy accepts. Though our gypsy does not satisfy the conditions of (3) or (4), he does have factual knowledge. For it is, after all, not at all accidental that he is right about the relevant matters. Thus we can see how my analysis conflicts with the fundamental claims of leading contemporary analysts, and how only my analysis survives this conflict intact.

As my analysis dictates, we must give up the idea that factual knowledge is any sort of justified true belief, or anything of the like. But even so, we may obtain both a better understanding of and further support for the analysis by examining another idea, one that derives from the attempt to understand our knowledge in this traditional way. This derivative idea is that a belief that represents knowledge on someone's part cannot be based on grounds that are entirely false. This derivative idea comes from a consideration of the standard sort of argument to show that epistemically justified true belief is not logically *sufficient* for factual knowledge. According to this standard argument, a man justifiedly deduces from justified beliefs of his that are entirely false, a true conclusion which he accepts on the basis of the deduction. Thus, by believing the conclusion, the man has an epistemically justified belief which, though true, represents no knowledge on his part.[5] It may be thought, then, that this justified true belief fails to be knowledge simply because it is based on grounds that are false. We might then require of a belief that some of its grounds be true, if the belief represent knowledge.

But such a requirement would be too strong. There are various examples in terms of which this may be seen. I should most like to adduce the main example of my aforementioned essay. In this example, knowledgeable scientists successfully duplicate a person who the scientists know to have a lot of important factual knowledge. They do this in order that there be more people who have this knowledge. The duplicate knows various things, say, various facts of physics. And we can now better say why he does: he knows because it is not at all accidental that the duplicate is right about these physical matters. But the beliefs that represent this knowledge on the part of the duplicate, all have as grounds beliefs that are entirely false. The duplicate, just like a normal scientist, bases his beliefs about the physical world on beliefs about his own personal history and experience: about what he has seen and read, about the experiments he has performed and heard about, and so on. But the duplicate has not done any of these things. Thus, these constructed duplicates, which satisfy the condition of my analysis, show that a belief may represent knowledge though it be based on grounds that are themselves entirely false.

Why, then, is there a lack of knowledge on the part of the man whose justified true belief is, in a simple and straightforward way, deduced from and based on grounds that are entirely false? The answer is, I think, that given by my analysis. Generally, with such a man, it is entirely accidental that he is right about the matter in question, whereas, for him to know, it must be quite the opposite. It must be not at all accidental that he is right about the matter.

In connection with our simple answer, we may note that there are other ways of seeing that justified true belief need not ensure factual knowledge. With such ways, no false belief is attributed to the man in question, and thus his failure to know is most clearly unrelated to his having any false grounds. One such way, it is interesting to note, is suggested by the card-deck examples we examined in the previous section. There, we noted that, with a very high proportion of white cards to black, it is not easy to tell or decide whether the man knows the top card to be white. But where we have, say, eighty-five white cards and fifteen black ones, it is *clear* that the man who reasons to the belief that the top card is white does not know the card to be white. On the other hand, it is also clear that the man is epistemically justified in believing the card to be white. Thus, though this man has no relevant false beliefs and though he reasons in no faulty manner, his epistemically justified true belief fails to represent knowledge. Again, the result is explained by my analysis: this man does not know because it is false that it is not at all accidental that he is right. So it is of interest that, in yet another way, a consideration of purely probabilistic cases lends support to my analysis while rendering it still more implausible that factual knowledge be some sort of justified true belief or, for that matter, anything of the like.

The Imprecision of the Concept of Knowledge

No doubt, any attempted analysis of factual knowledge will fail to take account of every imaginable case and example as nicely as one might wish. But, then, our concept of knowledge is itself not so exact with every imaginable case as one might wish it to be. Primarily in connection with certain matters peculiar to his own account of factual knowledge, Bertrand Russell warns against our having unrealistic expectations:

> But in fact 'knowledge' is not a precise conception: ... A very precise definition, therefore, should not be sought, since any such definition must be more or less misleading (*op. cit.*, p. 134).

Thus, though various examples may be brought to refute a putatively adequate analysis, whether such examples show the analysis to be inadequate is not always a very easy matter to decide.

Having expressed these thoughts, I will now put forward what has occurred to me as the example most likely to incline someone to reject the analysis that I offer. As might be expected, the example apparently could be used to show that the condition of my analysis is too weak, to show, that is, that at a certain time it might be not at all accidental that a man is right about its being the case that p and, even so, at that time he may not know that p. But I think that when this example is judged with impartiality and care, it is seen not to present any problem for my analysis of human factual knowledge. Indeed, such careful scrutiny, if anything, reveals that, when most clearly understood, the apparently damaging example actually may lend support to my analysis.

The example that I offer involves what might be called the fulfillment of a man's expectation about the future being brought about as a result of the man's having that expectation. Such happenings can, of course, occur in various ways, but rather than attempt to consider the entire variety, let us turn directly to the most bizarre sort of example, which is apparently most troublesome. Let us think, then, of a man who has a dream, and dreams that a certain horse will win a certain race. The man that I imagine generally believes only some of the things that he dreams will happen, and those that he believes simply as a result of a dream, he mumbles audibly upon awakening. Upon awakening from his dream about the horse race, the man mumbled that Schimmelpenninck, one of the horses to run in the 1965 Kentucky Derby, would be the winner of that race. Now, whenever our man awakes, he is wakened by his friend, who sees to it that the man has time to do his morning exercises. The friend knows that whatever the man mumbles upon awakening is what he has just dreamed about the future and thus believes will happen. The friend thus knows each of the man's beliefs that come to him simply as a result of dreaming, and he knows of each of these that it is the product of a dream. Hence, in particular, the friend knows that the man believes that Schimmelpenninck will win the 1965 Kentucky Derby, and he knows that the man acquired this belief simply as a result of his having an appropriate dream about that horse race. The friend, that morning, immediately decides to ensure the truth (or correctness) of his friend's belief; he resolves that the dreamer's belief be true. Now, the friend is an eminent veterinarian with access to all racing stables, and so he drugs all of Schimmelpenninck's competitors, endeavoring to fulfill the resolution that he made. I suppose that in this way the friend ensures that Schimmelpenninck is the winner of the 1965 Kentucky Derby; among other things, I here assume that Schimmelpenninck does finish first and that the veterinarian's activities are not detected. We may even suppose that once the veterinarian had made up his mind, it was no longer a matter of any chance which horse would win the race. In short, we may even suppose that the veterinarian knows that Schimmelpenninck will win. It is not very important here whether we suppose that without the doctor's intervention the horse would not have won, or whether we suppose the opposite, that the horse would have won anyway. In either case, the veterinarian knows the winner of the race. But the dreamer has no knowledge of the winner, for he always believes that Schimmelpenninck will win simply because he has a dream, a dream relevantly unconnected with the race to be run, and he never does in any way gain any relevant information.

It is clear that, on our suppositions, the dreamer does not know at any time. Yet, it may appear that, after the veterinarian makes his resolve or after he drugs the horse's competitors, it is not at all accidental that the dreamer is right about its being the case that Schimmelpenninck is the winner. But such appearances, I fear, would be most deceptive. Were it truly the case that at the relevant times it is not at all accidental that the dreamer is right, then we should have to make much stronger suppositions about our case than those we have made. Indeed, we should then have to make just such suppositions as render the case one most plausibly described as one in which the dreamer does know. To see that all of this is so, let us ask some questions of the presented case, questions which make it most dubious to suppose that the case is one which is correctly described by saying that it is not at all accidental that the dreamer is right about the outcome of the race.

The essential accidentality will not be fully brought out by asking what we should say were the veterinarian to make his resolve, not after his learning of the dreamer's acquisition of belief, but in advance of such information. To see this clearly, we may suppose the contrasting situation, that the doctor does make his resolve in advance, even long before the dreamer has the appropriate dream, and that he resolves that should his friend ever dream that a certain horse would win a certain running of the Kentucky Derby, he, the veterinarian, would ensure that his friend's belief be true. For even with such a supposition, the circumstances of which are unknown to the dreamer, we may ask: first, why did the veterinarian make just that particular resolve, which is still a rather specific one, and not some other one, or, better, some very general resolve whose fulfillment would entail the fulfillment of many particular resolves he might well make? And second, would the doctor be able to ensure the truth of other sorts of dream-produced beliefs that his friend might have, beliefs about future fluctuations of the stock market, future moon-rocket launchings, earthquakes, elections, and eclipses? These questions do, I think, bring out the large amount of accidentality that remains concerning the relevant matter, even after we have supposed that the veterinarian made his resolve long in advance of the particular dream or in advance of information of it. But, in contrast to the case so far considered, we may make suppositions that are quite extreme, and so rule out rather clearly any accidentality about the dreamer's being right about the subject of his opinion: we will imagine that the earth and all the life upon it were originally created by an extremely powerful and knowledgeable being. This being's chief fascination was with ensuring that a man's beliefs be true in case he acquired those beliefs simply as a result of a dream. In line with his most important desires, the being so created everyone that no man would ever have a dream-produced belief that conflicted with that of any other man; thus the being ensured that it be possible that he ensure the truth of every man's dream-produced belief about the future, for he also saw to it that no man would come to have any inconsistent beliefs simply as the result of a dream. Further, as the being well knew, it was well within his power to ensure the truth of any such belief that would ever actually be held. And the being, acting reasonably with respect to his chief fascination, proceeded to do what he knew to be well within his power. Now, though some philosophers might think otherwise, it strikes me as rather clear that a fair employment of our shared conception of factual knowledge dictates that, in such a world as this, the being has ensured that a man's dreams are a source of knowledge for the man (just in case the man believes that what he dreams about the future is the way that things will be). We have, then, presented a rather clear case of knowledge of the future which is of the relevant kind, enabling us to give an answer to what appeared to be the gravest problem that would befall my analysis of human factual knowledge. Happily, this example is quite in accord with that analysis, for it is on such extreme suppositions as those we have just made that it is most clear that, at the relevant time, it is not at all accidental that the man is right about the subject of his opinion.

Complete satisfaction with our extreme case allows us better to understand cases that are not so extreme, and thus not so clear. For example, we can now better understand and appreciate the following sort of case, one that lies somewhere between the last two we have considered: we suppose that a powerful and knowledgeable man makes a longstanding resolve that all of his dreaming friend's appropriate beliefs about the outcomes of all sporting events would be correct, and that the man succeeds in fulfilling this resolve, just as he knew that he would. About such a situation, we should not be so very disinclined to judge that the powerful man ensured that his friend's dreams were a source of knowledge for that man (just when he believes that what he dreams about the future is the way that things will be). Just so, about such a situation, we should be equally and not so very disinclined to judge that the powerful man ensured that at the relevant times it was not at all accidental that the dreamer was right about the subjects of his dream-produced beliefs.

Our putative counterexample, about the dreamer and his friend the veterinarian, has been shown to present problems that are only apparent. Indeed, by pursuing further these merely apparent difficulties, we have encountered relevantly similar cases that lend support to my analysis of human factual knowledge. Now, in all such cases of knowledge, as we suppose that the knower is wholly unaware both of the agent who makes it happen that he knows and of any happenings that help explain his knowledge, we may say that he does not know why he knows various things about the future, or at least that he knows almost nothing about why he knows. But still, should the man in such an example believe that he knows, this belief having as its source the same process of dreaming as does the belief that is supposed to represent knowledge on the part of the man, then, so far as I can see, there is no good reason for denying that the man knows *that* he knows, though he may lack completely knowledge of why he knows. Of course, we do know why the man knows; we know that a powerful agent makes it happen that at the relevant time it is not at all accidental that the man is right.

Apparent problems now appear to be resolved entirely, this resolution affording further support for my analysis of human factual knowledge.

NOTES

1. "Experience and Factual Knowledge," *The Journal of Philosophy*, Vol. 64, No. 5 (March 16, 1967): 152-73.
2. I have been much influenced on these matters and others that I have been writing about, by discussions with Robert Nozik and Michael Anthony Slote.
3. *The Problem of Knowledge* (London: Macmillan, 1956), ch. 1, "Philosophy and Knowledge," pp. 31-35, esp. p. 35.

4. *Perceiving: A Philosophical Study* (Ithaca, N. Y.: Cornell, 1957), ch. 1, "Epistemic Terms," esp. p. 16.

5. This standard argument is most influentially stated by Edmund L. Gettier in his "Is Justified True Belief Knowledge?" *Analysis,* Vol. 23, No. 6, n.s. 96 (June, 1963): 121-23. And it is earlier suggested by Bertrand Russell in *The Problems of Philosophy* (New York: Oxford, 1912), ch. 13, "Knowledge, Error, and Probable Opinion," esp. pp. 131 ff.

SEVENTH SYMPOSIUM

MEDIUMSHIP AND SURVIVAL AFTER DEATH: OPENING NOTE
   Peter A. French

SURVIVAL AND THE IDEA OF "ANOTHER WORLD" AND
MEDIUMSHIP AND HUMAN SURVIVAL
   H. H. Price

WHY I DO NOT BELIEVE IN SURVIVAL
   E. R. Dodds

CAN A MAN IMAGINE HIMSELF WITNESSING HIS OWN FUNERAL?
   Peter A. French

MYSTICISM AND THE PARADOX OF SURVIVAL
   J. J. Clarke

*"And she tried to fancy
what the flame of a candle looks like
after the candle is blown out"*

MEDIUMSHIP AND SURVIVAL AFTER DEATH:
OPENING NOTE

Peter A. French

In some of the earlier symposiums, especially II, IV and V, issues closely allied with the topic of this symposium were raised. Herein, however, we are specifically interested in a doctrine, a belief, that is essential to the standard (psychical researcher's) view of what is involved in non-fraudulent mediumistic communications. It is the hypothesis that men can and do survive the deaths of their earthly bodies. In some forms the survival hypothesis also involves the belief that disembodied existence is possible, that survival can occur in the absence of a post-mortem physical body or a body of any kind.

There are a number of philosophical problems interwoven with the concept of survival. The most central problem concerns the intelligibility of the notion itself. A large faction of the philosophical community is unprepared even to entertain the examination of the evidence of mediumistic communication because, as they argue, we have no clear idea at all of what survival after death might mean. We do, they admit, know what "survival" means, as, for example when written in a report of a naval disaster (we read of the dead and the survivors, and those are exclusive categories). But when "survival" is used in conjunction with death—"survival after death"—we have no clear notion of what is meant. Some philosophers, in fact, argue that the very idea of survival after death is inconsistent, that any attempt to explain the survival hypothesis is bound to be unintelligible despite an appearance of making sense.

One method philosophers have utilized in the examination of the intelligibility of the survival hypothesis has been to attempt to imagine what would have to be the case for a person to witness his own funeral. John Wisdom wrote:

> I know indeed what it would be like to watch my own funeral—the men in tall silk hats, the flowers and the face beneath the glass-topped coffin.[1]

But is this as simple as Wisdom suggests? Does it not require some account of disembodied or phantasmal existence, and does it not raise serious questions regarding whose funeral is actually being observed?

Even if the logical possibility of survival is allowed, major questions remain regarding the nature of such survival and the other world in which surviving persons exist. Due to the very strong influence of dualism (see Symposium IV) most of our conceptions of post-mortem existence are related to a quasi-spatial account of otherworldliness. In Symposim II we have seen the difficulties occasioned by such conceptions. Alternative views, however, have been offered which avoid the difficulties of dualism and the problems with multi-spatial myths. For example, afterlife might be conceived of in terms of a mystical model, the achievement of a oneness and harmony with the universe. A major drawback of the mystical account of survival is that it can explain ostensible mediumistic communications from departed persons only by denying that these phenomena occur in the advertised way.

It is a fact that there have been reported in the last 75 years or more an astounding number of cases of mediumistic phenomena, and only a relatively few can be written off as intentionally fraudulent. Trance mediums and automatic writers have given information to their sitters which those mediums and automatists could not have obtained by the ordinary ways of coming to know. Furthermore, these messages purport to originate from persons known to be dead. We seem to be bound to explain such phenomena in either one of two ways. Either the mediums receive their information telepathically from living persons or they actually do communicate with the dead and hence mediumistic communication would be *prima facie* a proof of survival after death. J. B. Rhine has written:

> We need, first of all, to learn everything we can about the more significant kinds of things that supposed incorporeal personalities or spirits are seriously reputed to do. The case must eventually rest on whether or not differences can be established between this range of phenomena and those of which the living are capable. Accordingly, a roundup of all the claims of spirit agency must necessarily precede any conception of an adequate test of the survival hypothesis.[2]

Those who explain mediumistic communication in terms of telepathy argue that nothing "communicated" at a seance is not already known by some living persons. Against such a view the phenomenon of cross correspondence has provided some truly dramatic counter-evidence. A cross correspondence is best described as a series of fragmentary sentences or even phrases generally given in automatic writing sessions, which in themselves seem to have no real significance, but when they are fitted together a message from the dead emerges. One of the most famous of such cases, one involving the American medium Mrs. Piper and the Englishwoman Mrs. A. W. Verrall and her daughter Helen Verrall, would seem at least to suggest that survival after death is not to be dismissed without serious investigation. But whether or not it constitutes a crucial test of the survival hypothesis is far from resolved. J. G. Piddington's account of the case, which is generally referred to as the "Hope, Star and Browning" case is as follows:

> Immediately following the extract from the sitting (with Mrs. Piper) of February 11, 1907 ... came these words:
> (Myers communicating) Did she (i.e. Mrs. Verrall) receive the word? Evangelical.
> *J.G.P.:* Evangelical?
> Yes.
> *J.G.P.:* I don't know, but I will enquire.
> I referred also to Browning again. (I had chosen on Dec. 18, 1906 some words from Browning's *Flight of the Duchess* for transmission to Mrs. Verrall by Myers, and he had claimed, though wrongly, to have succeeded in getting them written. It is to this that I think "again" refers—J.G.P.)
> *J.G.P.:* Do you remember what your exact reference to Browning was?
> I referred to Hope and Browning.
> Yes. (assent to reading as above.)
> I also said Star.
> (Miss Newton enters to announce the arrival of the sitter, Mr. Macalister.)
>
> . . .
>
> *J.G.P.:* Yes; I'm sorry, but we can, I hope, have a good talk the time after next.
> Meanwhile look out for Hope, Star and Browning.
>
> . . .
>
> I (J. G. P.) will now quote the scripts of Mrs. Verrall which I take to correspond with the words "Hope, Star and Browning":
>
> ### Script of January 23, 1907
> *Justice holds the scales.*
> That gives the words but an anagram would be better.
> Tell him that—rats star tars and so on. Try this.
> It has been tried before RTATS rearrange these five letters or again t e a r s
> $\qquad\qquad\qquad\qquad\qquad\qquad\qquad\qquad\qquad\qquad\qquad\qquad\qquad$ s t a r e
>
> s e a m
> s a m e

and so on
Skeat takes Kate's Keats stake steak.
But the letters you should give tonight are not so many—only three: a s t

Script of Jan. 28, 1907

Aster (star)
tépas (wonder or sign)
The world's wonder
And all a wonder and a wild desire—
The very wings of her
A WINGED DESIRE
ὑπόπτερος ἔρως (winged love)
Then there is Blake
and mocked my loss of liberty.
But it is all the same thing—the winged desire
ἔρως ποθεινός (passion) the hope that leaves
the earth for the sky—Abt Vogler for earth
too hard that found itself or lost itself—in the sky.
That is what I want
On the earth the broken sounds
                        threads
In the sky the perfect arc
The C major of this life
But your recollection is at fault

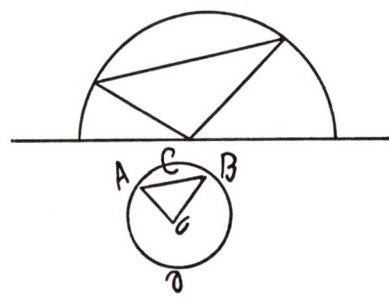

ADB is the part that unseen completes the arc.

    Mrs. Verrall had handed this script to me on Jan. 29, and pencilled on the envelope was this note:—
    "Jan. 29,/07. Is enclosed attempt at Bird? 'winged,' ὑπόπτερος, and 'Abt Vogler' (Vogel) suggest it. The later part is all quotations from R. B.'s *Abt Vogler* and earlier from the *Ring and the Book*. 'Oh, Lyric Love' etc."
    Mrs. Verrall might have added that "bird" was also suggested by the line which in the original precedes "And all a wonder and a wild desire", namely,
    "O lyric Love, half angel and half bird" . . .

Now as to the correspondence with the words "Hope, Star and Browning":—

Hope is found in the words "the hope that leaves the earth for the sky".

These words are a misquotation of

"The passion that left the ground to lose itself in the sky".

"Hope" has been substituted for "passion"; and it seems to me that by means of this very misquotation or substitution emphasis is thrown on the word "hope." ... Mrs. Verrall knew of the misquotation. She wrote to me on Feb. 15, 1907:—"I knew perfectly when I read the script that it should have been 'passion' which left the ground for the sky—and I was annoyed at the blunder." The ἔρως ποθεινός, which came straight out of a passage that I had been translating in the course of my work, represents 'passion.' And I wondered why the silly thing said 'Hope.'"

Browning pervades the whole script, and is besides definitely mentioned in Mrs. Verrall's pencilled note. (Some of these comments which Mrs. Verrall appends to her scripts bear, I fancy, much the same relation to the subject-matter of her scripts, as do the utterances of Mrs. Piper during the later part of the waking-stage to her trance-script. [J. G. P.])

Star is given prominently at the head of the script of Jan. 28 in the form Aster, the Greek for star ...

When, by reason of the coincidences involved, my mind began to concentrate itself on these two pieces of script and the words "Hope, Star and Browning" given in the Piper trance, a vague impression came over me that the string of words, "rats arts star," had somehow and somewhere come under my eyes before. At first I thought this must be mere fancy, and, when, after a little, I seemed to remember having seen them written on a piece of paper in Dr. Hodgson's handwriting when I went through his private papers in the early summer of 1906, at Boston, I was inclined to accuse myself of suffering from a delusion of memory. Still the memory—real or fancied—persisted, and to satisfy myself I wrote to Dr. Hodgson's executors in Boston, Mr. George Dorr and Mr. Henry James, Jr., and asked them to search among the odds and ends which, with other matter such as letters, I had handed over to them, for a scrap of paper with the words "rats art star" upon it. On August 23, 1907 Mr. James sent me the sheet of paper containing a rough draft of anagrams in the handwriting of Dr. Hodgson. . . .

But the coincidence does not end here.

We naturally were all considerably elated by the "Hope, Star and Browning" correspondence (though the full significance of the incident was not apparent till months later), and by way of encouragement Mrs. Verrall, on Feb. 15, gave her daughter a general description of the incident, being, however, careful to substitute imaginary words for the original ones. For "Star" "Planet Mars" was substituted, for "Hope" "Virtue," and for "Browning" "Keats." The script of Jan. 23 was not mentioned, and a general description only of the script of Jan. 28 was given. One correct detail only was Miss Verrall told, and that was that a *five* letter anagram had constituted a part of the success on Jan. 28.

Before, however, Miss Verrall had been told anything at all, she had on Feb. 3, written the following script:—

> Vulliamy not to be confused with the other.
> Williams more precious than rubies what was
> the name of the younger child Cecil Atl Mundellier
> (scribbles)

> quam ob rem in Sicillis proficiscitur (wherefore in Sicily he
>   sets out.)

> a green jerkin and hose and doublet where the
> song birds pipe their tune in the early morning
> therapeutikos ek exotikon (a healer from aliens)

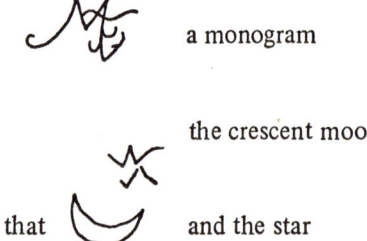

a monogram

the crescent moon

remember that   and the star

> like a thunder riven oak the grim remains
> stand on the level desolation of the plains
> a record of all ages of the span
> which nature gives to the weak labour of a man.

 bird.

After she had been told about the coincidence between her mother's script and that of Mrs. Piper, Miss Verrall wrote the following on Feb. 17, at which time she was away from home and at a distance from Mrs. Verrall:—

> androsace (?) Carthusian candelabrum

> many together

 that was the sign she will understand

when she sees it
No arts avail
diapason διαπασωγ ρυθμος (rhythm through all)
the heavenly harmony ως εφη οπλαγωγ (as Plato says)
the mystic three (?)

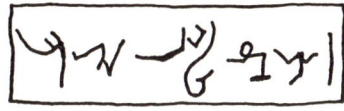

and a star above it all
rats everywhere in Hamelin town
now do you understand   Henry (?)[3]

William Roll, in his article "The Contribution of Studies of 'Mediumship' to Research on Survival After Death,"[4] has proposed possible ways of testing the spiritual theory of incorporeal personal agency (I. P. A.). His concluding remarks of that report are worth bearing in mind as we explore the problem of survival and its relationship to mediumistic communication. Roll writes:

> In the analysis of completed research as well as in planning further tests on the theory of mediumship the investigator's first thoughts are likely to be on methods to bypass the familiar types of ESP. When the opportunity for actual experimentation materializes his prime concern is again likely to be the inhibition of non-IPA ESP. But he has to be equally attentive to the possibility that the abilities of his subject can be smothered under an excessive load of experimental requirements. It is mainly for this reason that Rhine and Pratt recommend exploratory trials in ESP and PK before bringing in added resources for advanced testing. In survival research also we need the two-stage approach. The subject should not at once be faced with the many demands associated with the best types of IPA evidence. The emphasis should first be put on stimulating his psi abilities and only later on directing them towards the areas of most conclusive evidence.
>
> In both stages of his IPA research the experimenter will be at some advantage over the old workers, and such progress as he can hope to make will largely be due to the utilization of research resources and results from the scientific work of the last four decades. If he does not take advantage of this, or fails to read its implications, I fear that his work is only likely to be a faint echo of the efforts that were spent by a skilled and scholarly group of investigators. We need not only a sharpening of our means of

detection as proposed by Dr. Pratt, but also an added appreciation of what it is that parapsychologists have discovered about psi processes with their scientific tools.

We can now say what type of finding will indicate an incorporeal personal agent. It would consist in records which have motivational and personality factors foreign to the subject but typical of the deceased personality in question, as well as intellectual or cognitive characteristics that are not part of the furnishings of the subject's mind but were possessed by the supposed communicator. This type of material should be obtained in experiments in which there is no close linkage with living persons who have the personality traits or the technical knowledge shown in the record.

At the second stage of our research we should want to direct the subject and the supposed incorporeal agents more than has been done towards the desired kinds of responses. As part of our program we might apply Carington's method for comparative testing of the discarnate entities and the subjects they appear to communicate through to a larger sample than was at his disposal and perhaps utilize some of the other tools psychologists have made available. By adapting such tests for our purpose perhaps we will obtain a finer mesh for sifting out and discovering those conative or cognitive elements in the subject's personality which produce what we may call "the survival pose."

In addition to trying to find evidence of "another world" we should also try to tackle the problem by seeking among the living for survivable aspects of the personality. By utilizing both post- and ante-mortem procedures, and developing and refining them as the work progresses, there is, I believe, some hope for an answer to the survival problem.

NOTES

1. *Other Minds* (Berkeley, California: University of California Press, 1968), p. 39.
2. "The Question of Spirit Survival, *Journal of the American Society for Psychical Research* (1949): 51.
3. J. G. Piddington, "A Series of Concordant Automatisms," *Proceedings of the Society for Psychical Research,* Vol. 22 (1908): 59-77.
4. *Journal of Parapsychology,* Vol. 24 (1960): 275-76.

SURVIVAL AND THE IDEA OF "ANOTHER WORLD" AND MEDIUMSHIP AND HUMAN SURVIVAL

H. H. Price

This year is the seventieth anniversary of the foundation of the Society for Psychical Research. From the very beginning, the problem of survival has been one of the main interests of the Society; and that is my excuse, if any excuse is needed, for discussing some aspects of the problem this evening. I shall not, however, talk about the evidence for survival. In this lecture I am concerned only with the conception of survival; with the *meaning* of the Survival Hypothesis, and not with its truth or falsity. When we consider the Survival Hypothesis, whether we believe it or disbelieve it, what is it that we have in mind? Can we form any idea, even a rough and provisional one, of what a disembodied human life might be like? Supposing we cannot, it will follow that what is called the Survival Hypothesis is a mere set of words and not a hypothesis at all. The evidence adduced in favor of it might still be evidence for something, and perhaps for something important, but we should no longer have the right to claim that it is evidence for survival. There cannot be evidence for something which is completely unintelligible to us.

Now let us consider the situation in which we find ourselves after seventy years of psychical research. A very great deal of work has been done on the problem of survival, and much of the best work by members of our Society. Yet there are the widest differences of opinion about the results. A number of intelligent persons would maintain that we now have a very large mass of evidence in favor of survival; that some of it is of very good quality indeed, and cannot be explained away unless we suppose that the supernormal cognitive powers of some embodied human minds are vastly more extensive and more accurate than we can easily believe them to be; in short, that on the evidence available the Survival Hypothesis is more probable than not. Some people—and not all of them are silly or credulous—would even maintain that the Survival Hypothesis is proved, or as near to being so as any empirical hypothesis can be. On the other hand, there are also many intelligent persons who entirely reject these conclusions. Some of them, no doubt, have not taken the trouble to examine the evidence. But others of them have; they may even have given years of study to it. They would agree that the evidence is evidence of *something*, and very likely of something important. But, they would say, it cannot be evidence of survival; there *must* be some alternative explanation of it, however difficult it may be to find out. Why do they take this line? I think it is because they find the very conception of survival unintelligible. The very idea of a "discarnate

This selection is reprinted from the *Proceedings of the Society for Psychical Research*, Vol. 50 (January, 1953), 1-25. Used by permission of the editor and H. H. Price.

human personality" seems to them a muddled or absurd one; indeed not an idea at all, but just a phrase—an emotionally exciting one, no doubt—to which no clear meaning can be given.

Moreover, we cannot just ignore the people who have not examined the evidence. Some of our most intelligent and most highly educated contemporaries are among them. These men are well aware, by this time, that the evidence does exist, even if their predecessors fifty years ago were not. If you asked them why they do not trouble to examine it in detail, they would be able to offer reasons for their attitude. And one of their reasons, and not the least weighty in their eyes, is the contention I mentioned just now, that the very idea of survival is a muddled or absurd one. To borrow an example from Whately Carington, we know pretty well what we mean by asking whether Jones has survived a shipwreck. We are asking whether he continues to live after the shipwreck has occurred. Similarly it makes sense to ask whether he survived a railway accident, or the bombing of London. But if we substitute "his own death" for "a shipwreck," and ask whether he has survived it, our question (it will be urged) becomes unintelligible. Indeed, it *looks* self-contradictory, as if we were asking whether Jones is still alive at a time when he is no longer alive—whether Jones is both alive and not alive at the same time. We may try to escape from this logical absurdity by using phrases like "discarnate existence," "alive, but disembodied." But such phrases, it will be said, have no clear meaning. No amount of facts, however well established, can have the slightest tendency to support a meaningless hypothesis, or to answer an unintelligible question. It would therefore be a waste of time to examine such facts in detail. There are other and more important things to do.

If I am right so far, questions about the meaning of the word "survival" or of the phrase "life after death" are not quite so arid and academic as they may appear. Anyone who wants to maintain that there is empirical evidence for survival ought to consider these questions, whether he thinks the evidence strong or weak. Indeed, anyone who thinks there is a *problem* of survival at all should ask himself what his conception of survival is.

Now why should it be thought that the very idea of life after death is unintelligible? Surely it is easy enough to conceive (whether or not it is true) that experiences might occur after Jones's death which are linked with experiences which he had before his death, in such a way that his personal identity is preserved? But, it will be said, the idea of after-death *experiences* is just the difficulty. What kind of experiences could they conceivably be? In a disembodied state, the supply of sensory stimuli is perforce cut off, because the supposed experient has no sense organs and no nervous system. There can therefore be no sense perception. One has no means of being aware of material objects any longer; and if one has not, it is hard to see how one could have any emotions or wishes either. For all the emotions and wishes we have in this present life are concerned directly or indirectly with material objects, including of course our own organisms and other organisms, especially other human ones. In short, one could only be said to have experiences at all, if one is aware of some sort of a *world*. In this way, the idea of survival is bound up with the idea of "another world" or a "next world." Anyone who maintains that the idea of survival is after all intelligible must also be claiming that we can form some conception, however rough and provisional, of what "the next world" or "the other world" might be like. The skeptics I have in mind would say that we can form no such conception at all; and this, I think, is one of the main reasons why they hold that the conception of survival itself is unintelligible. I wish to suggest, on the contrary, that we *can* form some conception, in outline at any rate, of what a "next world" or "another world" might be like, and consequently of the kind of experiences which disembodied minds, if indeed there are such, might be supposed to have.

The next world, I think, might be conceived as a kind of dreamworld. When we are asleep, sensory stimuli are cut off, or at any rate are prevented from having their normal effects upon our brain centers. But we still manage to have experiences. It is true that sense perception no longer occurs, but something sufficiently like it does. In sleep, our image-producing powers, which are more or less inhibited in waking life by a continuous bombardment of sensory stimuli, are released from this inhibition. And then we are provided with a multitude of objects of awareness, about which we employ our thoughts and towards which we have desires and emotions. These objects which we are aware of behave in a way which seems very queer to us when we wake up. The laws of their behavior are not the laws of physics. But however queer their behavior is, it does not at all disconcert us at the time and our personal identity is not broken.

In other words, my suggestion is that the next world, if there is one, might be a world of mental images. Nor need such a world be so "thin and insubstantial" as you might think. Paradoxical as it may sound, there is nothing imaginary about a mental image. It is an actual entity, as real as anything can be. The seeming paradox arises from the ambiguity of the verb "to imagine." It does sometimes mean "to have mental images." But more usually it means "to entertain propositions without believing them"; and very often they are false propositions, and moreover we *dis*believe them in the act of entertaining them. This is what happens, for example, when we read Shakespeare's play *The Tempest,* and that is why we say that Prospero and Ariel are "imaginary characters." Mental images are not in this sense imaginary at all. We do actually experience them, and they are no more imaginary then sensations. To avoid the paradox, though at the cost of some pedantry, it would be well to distinguish between *imagining* and *imaging,* and to have two different adjectives "imaginary" and "imagy." In this terminology, it is imaging, and not imagining, that I wish to talk about; and the next world, as I am trying to conceive of it, is an *imagy* world, but not on that account an imaginary one.

Indeed, to those who experienced it an image world would be just as "real" as this present world is; perhaps so like it, that they would have considerable difficulty in realizing that they were dead. We are, of course, sometimes told in mediumistic communications that quite a lot of people do find it difficult to realize that they are dead; and this is just what we should expect if the next world is an image world. Lord Russell and other philosophers have maintained that a material object in this present physical world is nothing more nor less than a complicated system of *appearances*. So far as I can see, there might be a set of visual images related to each other perspectivally, with front views and side views and back views all fitting neatly together in the way that ordinary visual appearances do now. Such a group of images might contain tactual images too. Similarly it might contain auditory images and smell images. Such a family of interrelated images would make a pretty good object. It would be quite a satisfactory substitute for the material objects which we perceive in this present life. And a whole world composed of such families of mental images would make a perfectly good world.

It is possible, however, and indeed likely, that some of those images would be what Francis Galton called *generic* images. An image representing a dog or a tree need not necessarily be an exact replica of some individual dog or tree one has perceived. It might rather be a representation of a *typical* dog or tree. Our memories are more specific on some subjects than on others. How specific they are depends probably on the degree of interest we had in the individual objects or events at the time when we perceived them. An event which moved us deeply is likely to be remembered specifically and in detail; and so is an individual object to which we were much attached (for example, the home of our childhood). But with other objects which interested us less and were less attended to, we retain only a "general impression" of a whole class of objects collectively. Left to our own resources, as we should be in the other world, with nothing but our memories to depend on, we should probably be able to form only generic images of such objects. In this respect, an image world would not be an exact replica of this one, not even of those parts of this one which we have actually perceived. To some extent it would be, so to speak, a generalized picture, rather than a detailed reproduction.

Let us now put our question in another way, and ask what kind of experience a disembodied human mind might be supposed to have. We can then answer that it might be an experience in which *imaging* replaces sense perception: "replaces" it, in the sense that imaging would perform much the same function as sense perception performs now, by providing us with objects about which we could have thoughts, emotions and wishes. There is no reason why we should not be "as much alive," or at any rate *feel* as much alive, in an image world as we do now in this present material world, which we perceive by means of our sense-organs and nervous systems. And so the use of the world "survival" ("life after death") would be perfectly justifiable.

It will be objected, perhaps, that one cannot be said to be alive unless one has a body. But what is meant here by "alive"? It is surely conceivable (whether or not it is true) that *experiences* should occur which are not causally connected with a physical organism. If they did, should we or should we not say that "life" was occurring. I do not think it matters much whether we answer yes or no. It is purely a question of definition. If you define "life" in terms of certain very complicated physico-chemical processes, as some people would, then of course life after death is by definition impossible, because there is no longer anything to be alive. In that case, the problem of survival (*life* after bodily death) is misnamed. Instead, it ought to be called the problem of after-death *experiences*.

And this is in fact the problem with which all investigators of the subject have been concerned. After all, what people want to know, when they ask whether we survive death, is simply whether experiences occur after death, or what likelihood, if any, there is that they do; and whether such experiences, if they do occur, are linked with each other and with *ante mortem* ones in such a way that personal identity is preserved. It is not physico-chemical processes which interest us, when we ask such questions. But there is another sense of the words "life" and "alive" which may be called the psychological sense; and in this sense "being alive" just *means* "having experiences of certain sorts." In this psychological sense of the word "life," it is perfectly intelligible to ask whether there is life after death, even though life in the physiological sense does *ex hypothesi* come to an end when someone dies. Or, if you like, the question is whether one could *feel* alive after bodily death, even though (by hypothesis) one would not *be* alive at the time. It will be just enough to satisfy most of us if the *feeling* of being alive continues after death. It will not make a halfpennyworth of difference that one will not then *be* alive in the physiological or biochemical sense of the word.

It may be said, however, that "feeling alive" (life in the psychological sense) cannot just be equated with having experiences in general. Feeling alive, surely, consists in having experiences of a special sort, namely *organic sensations*—bodily feelings of various sorts. In our present experience, these bodily feelings are not as a rule separately attended to unless they are unusually intense or unusually painful. They are a kind of undifferentiated mass in the background of consciousness. All the same, it would be said, they constitute our feeling of being alive; and if they were absent (as surely they must be when the body is dead) the feeling of being alive could not be there.

I am not at all sure that this argument is as strong as it looks. I think we should still feel alive—or alive enough—provided we experienced emotions and wishes, even if no organic sensations accompanied these experiences, as they do now. But in case I am wrong here, I would suggest that *images* of organic sensations could perfectly well provide what is needed. We can quite well image to ourselves what it feels like to be in a warm bath, even when we are not actually in one; and a person who has been crippled can image what it felt like to climb a mountain. Moreover, I would ask whether we do not feel alive when we are dreaming. It seems to me that we obviously do—or at any rate quite alive enough to go on with.

This is not all. In an image world, a dreamlike world such as I am trying to describe, there is no reason at all why there should not be *visual* images resembling the body which one had in this present world. In this present life (for all who are not blind) visual percepts of one's own body form as it were the constant center of one's perceptual world. It is perfectly possible that visual images of one's own body might perform the same function in the next. They might form the continuing center or nucleus of one's image world, remaining more or less constant while other images altered. If this were so, we should have an additional reason for expecting that recently dead people would find it difficult to realize that they were dead, that is, disembodied. To all appearances they *would* have bodies just as they had before, and pretty much the same ones.

But, of course, they might discover in time that these image bodies were subject to rather peculiar causal laws. For example, it might be found that in an image world our wishes tend ipso facto to fulfill themselves in a way they do not now. A wish to go to Oxford might be immediately followed by the occurrence of a vivid and detailed set of Oxford-like images; even though, at the moment before, one's images had resembled Piccadilly Circus or the palace of the Dalai Lama in Tibet. In that case, one would realize that "going somewhere"—transferring one's body from one place to another—was a rather different process from what it had been in the physical world. Reflecting on such experiences, one might come to the conclusion that one's body was not after all the same as the physical body one had before death. One might conclude perhaps that it must be a "spiritual" or "psychical" body, closely resembling the old body in appearance, but possessed of rather different causal properties. It has been said, of course, that phrases like "spiritual body" or "psychical body" are utterly unintelligible, and that no conceivable empirical meaning could be given to such expressions. But I would rather suggest that they might be a way (rather a misleading way perhaps) of referring to a set of body-like images. If our supposed dead empiricist continued his investigations, he might discover that his whole world—not only his own body, but everything else he was aware of—had different causal properties from the physical world, even though everything in it had shape, size, color, and other qualities which material objects have now. And so eventually, by the exercise of ordinary inductive good sense, he could draw the conclusion that he was in "the next world" or "the other world" and no longer in this one. If, however, he were a very dogmatic philosopher, who distrusted inductive good sense and preferred a priori reasoning, I do not know what condition he would be in. Probably he would never discover that he was dead at all. Being persuaded, on a priori grounds, that life after death was impossible, he might insist on thinking that he must still be in this world, and refuse to pay any attention to the new and strange causal laws which more empirical thinkers would notice.

I think, then, that there is no difficulty in conceiving that the experience of feeling alive could occur in the absence of a physical organism; or, if you prefer to put it so, a disembodied personality could *be* alive in the psychological sense, even though by definition it would not be alive in the physiological or biochemical sense.

Moreover, I do not see why disembodiment need involve the destruction of personal identity. It is, of course, sometimes supposed that personal identity depends on the continuance of a background of organic sensation—the "mass of bodily feeling" mentioned before. (This may be called the somato-centric analysis of personal identity.) We must notice, however, that this background of organic sensation is not literally the same from one period of time to another. The very most that can happen is that the organic sensations which form the background of my experience now should be *exactly similar* to those which were the background of my experience a minute ago. And as a matter of fact, the present ones need not *all* be exactly similar to the previous ones. I might have a twinge of toothache now which I did not have then. I may even have an overall feeling of lassitude now which I did not have a minute ago, so that the whole mass of bodily feeling, and not merely part of it, is rather different; and this would not interrupt my personal identity at all. The most that is required is only that the majority (not all) of my organic sensations should be closely (not exactly) similar to those I previously had. And even this is only needed if the two occasions are close together in my private time series; the organic sensations I have now might well be very unlike those I used to have when I was one year old. I say "in my private time series." For when I wake up after eight hours of dreamless sleep my personal identity is not broken, though in the physical or public time series there has been a long interval between the last organic sensations I experienced before falling asleep, and the first ones I experience when I wake up. But if similarity, and not literal sameness, is all that is required of this "continuing organic background," it seems to me that the continuity of it could be perfectly well preserved if there were organic *images* after death very like the organic *sensations* which occurred before death.

As a matter of fact, this whole "somato-centric" analysis of personal identity appears to me highly disputable. I should have thought that Locke was much nearer the truth when he said that personal identity depends on memory. But I have tried to show that even if the "somato-centric" theory of personal identity is right, there is no reason why personal identity need be broken by bodily death, provided there are images after death which sufficiently resemble the organic sensations one had before; and this is very like what happens when one falls asleep and begins dreaming.

There is, however, another argument against the conceivability of a disembodied person, to which some present-day linguistic philosophers would attach great weight. It is neatly expressed by Mr. A. G. N. Flew when he says, "People are what you meet."[1] By "a person" we are supposed to mean a human organism which behaves in certain ways, and especially one which speaks and can be spoken to. And when we say, "This is the same person whom I saw yesterday," we are supposed to mean just that it is the same human organism which I saw yesterday, and also that it behaves in a recognizably similar way.

"People are what you meet." With all respect to Mr. Flew, I would suggest that he does not in this sense "meet" *himself*. He might indeed have had one of those curious out-of-body experiences which are occasionally mentioned in our records, and he might have seen his body from outside (if he has, I heartily congratulate him); but I do not think we should call this "meeting." And surely the important question is, what constitutes my personal identity *for myself*. It certainly does not consist in the fact that other people can "meet" me. It might be that I was for myself the same person as before, even at a time when it was quite impossible for others to meet me. No one can "meet" me when I am dreaming. They can, of course, come and look at my body lying in bed; but this is not "meeting," because no sort of social relations are possible between them and me. Yet, although temporarily "unmeetable," during my dreams I am still, for myself, the same person that I was. And if I went on dreaming *in perpetuum*, and could never be "met" again, this need not prevent me from continuing to be, for myself, the same person.

As a matter of fact, however, we can quite easily conceive that "meeting" of a kind might still be possible between discarnate experients. And therefore, even if we do make it part of the definition of "a person," that he is capable of being met by others, it will still make sense to speak of "discarnate persons," provided we allow that telepathy is possible between them. It is true that a special sort of telepathy would be needed; the sort which in life produces *telepathic apparitions*. It would not be sufficient that A's thoughts or emotions should be telepathically affected by B's. If such telepathy were sufficiently prolonged and continuous, and especially if it were reciprocal, it would indeed have some of the characteristics of social intercourse; but I do not think we should call it "meeting," at any rate in Mr. Flew's sense of the word. It would be necessary, in addition, that A should be aware of something which could be called "B's body," or should have an experience not too unlike the experience of *seeing* another person in this life. This additional condition would be satisfied if A experienced a telepathic apparition of B. It would be necessary, further, that the telepathic apparition by means of which B "announces himself" (if one may put it so) should be recognizably similar on different occasions. And if it were a case of meeting some person *again* whom one had previously known in this world, the telepathic apparition would have to be recognizably similar to the physical body which that person had when he was still alive.

There is no reason why an image world should not contain a number of images which are telepathic apparitions, and if it did, one could quite intelligibly speak of "meeting other persons" in such a world. All the experiences I have when I meet another person in this present life could still occur, with only this difference, that percepts would be replaced by images. It would also be possible for another person to "meet" me in the same manner, if I, as a telepathic agent could cause him to experience a suitable telepathic apparition, sufficiently resembling the body I used to have when he formerly "met" me in this life.

I now turn to another problem which may have troubled some of you. If there be a next world, *where* is it? Surely it must be somewhere. But there does not seem to be any room for it. We can hardly suppose that it is up in the sky (i.e., outside the earth's atmosphere) or under the surface of the earth, as Homer and Vergil seemed to think. Such suggestions may have contented our ancestors, and the Ptolemaic astronomy may have made them acceptable, for some ages, even to the learned; but they will hardly content us. Surely the next world, if it exists, must be somewhere; and yet, it seems, there is nowhere for it to be.

The answer to this difficulty is easy if we conceive of the next world in the way I have suggested, as a dreamlike world of mental images. Mental images, including dream images, are in a space of their own. They do not have spatial properties. Visual images, for instance, have extension and shape, and they have spatial relations to one another. But they have no spatial relation to objects in the physical world. If I dream of a tiger, my tiger image has extension and shape. The dark stripes have a spatial relation to the yellow parts, and to each other; the nose has a spatial relation to the tail. Again, the tiger image as a whole may have spatial relations to another image in my dream, for example to an image resembling a palm tree. But suppose we have to ask how far it is from the foot of my bed, whether it is three inches long, or longer or shorter; is it not obvious that these questions are absurd ones? We cannot answer them, not because we lack the necessary information or find it impracticable to make the necessary measurements, but because the questions themselves have no meaning. In the space of the physical world these images are nowhere at all. But in relation to other images of mine, each of them is somewhere. Each of them is extended, and its parts are in spatial relations to one another. There is no a priori reason why all extended entities must be in physical space.

If we now apply these considerations to the next world, as I am conceiving of it, we see that the question "where is it?" simply does not arise. An image world would have a space of its own. We could not find it anywhere in the space of the physical world, but this would not in the least prevent it from being a spatial world all the same. If you like, it would be its own "where."

It follows that when we speak of "passing" from this world to the next, this passage is not to be thought of as any sort of movement in space. It should rather be thought of as a change of consciousness, analogous to the change which occurs when we "pass" from waking experience to dreaming. It would be a change from the perceptual type of consciousness to another type of consciousness in which perception ceases and imaging replaces it, but unlike the change from waking consciousness to dreaming in being irreversible. I suppose that nearly everyone nowadays who talks of "passing" from this world to the other does think of the transition in this way, as some kind of irreversible change of consciousness, and not as a literal spatial transition in which one goes from one place to another place.

So much for the question "where is the next world?" if there be one. I have tried to show that if the next world is conceived of as a world of mental images, the question simply does not arise. I now turn to another difficulty. It may be felt that an image world is somehow a deception and a sham, not a *real* world at all. I have said that it would be a kind of dreamworld. Now when one has a dream in this life, surely the things one is aware of in the dream are not *real* things. No doubt the dreamer really does have various mental images. These images do actually occur. But this is not all that happens. As a result of having these images, the dreamer believes, or takes for granted, that various material objects exist and various physical events occur; and these beliefs are mistaken. For example, he believes that there is a wall in front of him and that by a mere effort of will he succeeds in flying over the top of it. But the wall did not really exist, and he did not really fly over the top of it. He was in a state of delusion. Because of the images which he really did have, there *seemed* to him to be various objects and events which did not really exist at all. Similarly, you may argue, it may *seem* to discarnate minds (if indeed there are such) that there is a world in which they live, and a world not unlike this one. If they have mental images of the appropriate sort, it may even *seem* to them that they have bodies not unlike the ones they had in this life. But surely they will be mistaken. It is all very well to say, with the poet, that "dreams are real while they last"—that dream objects are only called "unreal" when one wakes up, and normal sense perceptions begin to occur with which the dream experiences can be contrasted.

And it is all very well to conclude from this that if one did *not* wake up, if the change from sense perception to imaging were irreversible, one would not call one's dream objects unreal, because there would then be nothing with which to contrast them. But would they not still *be* unreal for all that? Surely discarnate minds, according to my account of them, would be in a state of permanent delusion; whereas a dreamer in this life (fortunately for him) is only in a temporary one. And the fact that a delusion goes on for a long time, even forever and ever, does not make it any less delusive. Delusions do not turn themselves into realities just by going on and on. Nor are they turned into realities by the fact that their victim is deprived of the power of detecting their delusiveness.

Now, of course, if it were true that the next life (supposing there is one) is a condition of permanent delusion, we should just have to put up with it. We might not like it: we might think that a state of permanent delusion is a bad state to be in. But our likes and dislikes are irrelevant to the question. I would suggest, however, that this argument about the "delusiveness" or "unreality" of an image world is based on confusion.

One may doubt whether there is any clear meaning in using the words "real" and "unreal" *tout court,* in this perfectly general and unspecified way. One may properly say, "this is real silver, and that is not," "this is a real pearl and that is not," or again "this is a real pool of water, and that is only a mirage." The point here is that something X is mistakenly believed to be something else Y, because it does resemble Y in some respects. It makes perfectly good sense, then, to say that X is not really Y. This piece of plated brass is not real silver, true enough. It only looks like silver. But for all that, it cannot be called "unreal" in the unqualified sense, in the sense of not existing at all. Even the mirage is something, though it is not the pool of water you took it to be. It is a perfectly good set of visual appearances, though it is not related to other appearances in the way you thought it was; for example, it does not have the relations to tactual appearances, or to visual appearances from other places, which you expected it to have. You may properly say that the mirage is not a real pool of water, or even that it is not a real physical object, and that anyone who thinks it is must be in a state of delusion. But there is no clear meaning in saying that it is just "unreal" *tout court,* without any further specification or explanation. In short, when the word "unreal" is applied to something, one means that it is different from something else, with which it might be mistakenly identified; what that something else is may not be explicitly stated, but it can be gathered from the context.

What, then, could people mean by saying that a next world such as I have described would be "unreal"? If they are saying anything intelligible, they must mean that it is different from something else, something else which it does resemble in some respects, and might therefore be confused with. And what is that something else? It is the present physical world in which we now live. An image world, then, is only "unreal" in the sense that it is not really physical, though it might be mistakenly thought to be physical by some of those who experience it. But this only amounts to saying that the world I am describing would be an *other* world, other than this present physical world, which is just what it ought to be; other than this present physical world, and yet sufficiently like it to be possibly confused with it, because images do resemble percepts. And what would this otherness consist in? First, in the fact that it is in a *space* which is other than physical space; secondly, and still more important, in the fact that the *causal laws* of an image world would be different from the laws of physics. And this is also our ground for saying that the events we experience in dreams are "unreal," that is, not really physical, though mistakenly believed by the dreamer to be so. They do in some ways closely resemble physical events, and that is why the mistake is possible. But the causal laws of their occurrence are quite different, as we recognize when we wake up; and just occasionally we recognize it even while we are still asleep.

Now let us consider the argument that the inhabitants of the other world, as I have described it, would be in a state of delusion. I admit that some of them might be. That would be the condition of the people described in the mediumistic communications already referred to—the people who "do not realize that they are dead." Because their images are so like the normal percepts they were accustomed to in this life, they believe mistakenly that they are still living in the physical world. But, as I have already tried to explain, their state of delusion need not be permanent and irremediable. By attending to the relations between one image and another, and applying the ordinary inductive methods by which we ourselves have discovered the causal laws of this present world in which *we* live, they too could discover in time what the causal laws of *their* world are. These laws, we may suppose, would be more like the laws of Freudian psychology than the laws of physics. And once the discovery was made, they would be cured of their delusion. They would find out, perhaps with surprise, that the world they were experiencing was *other* than the physical world which they experienced before, even though like it in some respects.

Let us now try to explore the conception of a world of mental images a little more fully. Would it not be a *"subjective"* world? And surely there would be many *different* next worlds, not just one; and each of them would be private. Indeed, would there not be as many next worlds as there are discarnate minds, and each of them wholly private to the mind which experiences it? In short, it may seem that each of us, when dead, would have his own dreamworld, and there would be no common or public next world at all.

"Subjective," perhaps, is a rather slippery word. Certainly, an image world would have to be subjective in the sense of being mind-dependent, dependent for its existence upon mental processes of one sort or another; images, after all, are mental entities. But I do not think that such a world need be completely private, if telepathy occurs in the next life. I have already mentioned the part which telepathic apparitions might play in it in connection with Mr. Flew's contention that "people are what you meet." But there is more to be said. It is reasonable to suppose that in a disembodied state telepathy would occur more frequently than it does now. It seems likely that in this present life our telepathic powers are constantly being inhibited by our need to adjust ourselves to our physical environment. It even seems likely that many telepathic "impressions" which we receive at the unconscious level are shut out from consciousness by a kind of biologically motivated censorship. Once the pressure of biological needs is removed, we might expect that telepathy would occur continually, and manifest itself in consciousness by modifying and adding to the images which one experiences. (Even in this life, after all, some dreams are telepathic.)

If this is right, an image world such as I am describing would not be the product of one single mind only, nor would it be purely private. It would be the joint product of a group of telepathically interacting minds and public to all of them. Nevertheless, one would not expect it to have unrestricted publicity. It is likely that there would still be *many* next worlds, a different one for each group of like-minded personalities. I admit I am not quite sure what might be meant by "like-minded" and "unlike-minded" in this connection. Perhaps we could say that two personalities are like-minded if their memories or their characters are sufficiently similar. It might be that Nero and Marcus Aurelius do not have a world in common, but Socrates and Marcus Aurelius do.

So far, we have a picture of many "semi-public" next worlds, if one may put it so; each of them composed of mental images, and yet not wholly private for all that, but public to a limited group of telepathically interacting minds. Or, if you like, after death everyone does have his own dream, but there is still some overlap between one person's dream and another's, because of telepathy.

NOTES

1. *University,* Vol. II, No. 2, 38, in a symposium on "Death" with Professor D. M. Mackinnon. Mr. Flew obviously uses "people" as the plural of "person"; but if we are to be linguistic, I am inclined to think that the nuances of "people" are not quite the same as those of "person." When we used the word "person," in the singular or the plural, the notion of consciousness is more prominently before our minds than it is when we use the word "people."

WHY I DO NOT BELIEVE IN SURVIVAL

E. R. Dodds

Before approaching the evidence from psychical research I ask myself what are the antecedent probabilities for, or against, survival. In its favor I find two distinct types of argument advanced. The first asserts under varying forms that our mind has a quality in common with the ultimate stuff of reality, or with the creator of reality, and that the possession of this quality assures its continuance: in theological language, it asserts man's immortality as a consequence from his divinity. On this argument two reflections occur to me. In the first place, it rests on a proposition about reality (or about its creator) which may be true, but which I do not certainly know to be true. I do not know of what ultimate stuff the universe is constituted, nor how it came into being; and certainly I find nothing in my experience which assures me that my continued existence is indispensable to it. But secondly, if this type of argument proves anything at all, it appears to me to prove too much. . . .

If we accept the metaphysical argument as a valid proof of survival, we must accept it also as a valid proof of pre-existence. This is, for me, unfortunate. For the doctrine of pre-existence is open to several objections which I do not know how to meet. Until these have been resolved for me, I feel constrained to reject the theory of pre-existence. . . . My next question is: Are there any positive antecedent grounds for *rejecting* the belief in survival? If this question means, "Can survival be shown on antecedent grounds to be impossible?", the answer is, I think, that it cannot, save on the materialist presuppositions which, as I said at the outset, I do not feel constrained to accept although they may be correct. But secondly: Are there any valid grounds for considering survival *improbable*? There are two considerations each of which seems to me to raise a presumption, fairly strong though falling short of proof, not indeed against all forms of the survivalist hypothesis, but against the particular form of it which is required to account for the supernormal phenomena. The first of these considerations is historical, and is in part an argument from silence. Now arguments from silence are notoriously dangerous; and in this case the absence of evidence for survival does not constitute evidence *against* it, since for all we know the conditions of existence after death may be such as to exclude the possibility of affirmative evidence being obtained. This is a perfectly satisfactory answer from the point of view of the orthodox Christian, who believes the dead to be segregated in Heaven, Hell or Purgatory; it is also satisfactory from the point of view of the man who says, "I believe that the dead survive, but I know nothing of their

This selection is reprinted from the *Proceedings of the Society for Psychical Research*, Vol. 42 (1932). Used by permission of the editor.

powers or their modes of existence, or their location in space." It is less satisfactory from the point of view of the spiritualist. For if the spiritualist interpretation of the supernormal phenomena is correct, we know a good deal about the dead. All spiritualists believe that the dead have both the will and the means to communicate with the living, either by controlling the hand or vocal organs of a medium or by influencing her mind telepathically. Most of them believe also that the dead can make their existence known by speaking to us directly, without the intervention of a human organism; by appearing in visible form; by the production of supernormal lights; by the supernormal movement of objects; and in various other ways. Now if the dead are really endowed with powers so varied and so remarkable; and if it is true, as they themselves tell us, that they are much occupied with the problem of comforting and assisting their surviving relatives; on these assumptions is it not surprising that they have refrained for so long from exercising their powers and making their existence known? During the two and a half millenia of which we have fairly full written records—say from 650 B.C. to A.D. 1850—they have failed so far as I know to produce satisfactory experimental evidence of their identity. Why? During certain portions of this period they might have endangered their surviving friends by attempting to communicate with them; but there were several centuries during which action on their part would have been perfectly safe. Nor was there any lack of the necessary machinery or the necessary interest on the side of the living; the evidence collected in Oesterreich's book on possession shows that the mediumistic trance is a fairly constant phenomenon in all ages and among all peoples; and curiosity about the state of the dead has left its mark on the literature alike of Greece and Rome, of the Middle Ages, and of the Renaissance. But there is something more singular still. The two groups of pre-nineteenth-century mediums about whom we have most information, those of the late Greco-Roman period and the witches of the sixteenth and seventeenth centuries, while performing a number of the feats performed by modern mediums, perversely attributed them in the one case to the agency of nonhuman gods or demons, in the other to the agency of the devil. Once again, why? A satisfactory answer may one day be forthcoming; but until it is, I cannot but feel some doubt about the correctness of the spiritualist interpretation of the contemporary phenomena....

What interpretation of psychical research am I to adopt? In the first place, where a normal explanation appears possible I shall certainly accept it. I am, however, satisfied that neither chance nor cheating, nor any combination of the two, will suffice to account for the *whole* of the mental phenomena of mediumship. (About the physical phenomena I am less certain; but these do not in any case come much in question here, since the great majority of them do not afford even *prima facie* evidence of survival.) As regards the mental phenomena, my choice is practically confined to three views: (a) that which attributes them to the exercise by the living of supernormal faculties, viz. telepathy, or a combination of telepathy and clairvoyance; (b) that which attributes them to the agency of nonhuman spirits; (c) that which attributes them to the agency of the surviving dead. I will call these respectively the telepathic, the demonist and the spiritualist hypothesis.

Now if my initial presuppositions are accepted, and my subsequent reasoning is valid, these three hypotheses vary widely in their antecedent probability. The telepathic hypothesis invokes no agency for whose existence there is not strong independent evidence: the independent evidence for regarding telepathy as a *vera causa* seems to me almost conclusive, and that for clairvoyance very substantial. The demonist hypothesis has the status of a bare, unmotived possibility: I know of no valid evidence against, but the only evidence in its favor is drawn from prescientific sources to which I can attach little weight. The spiritualist hypothesis seems to me, for reasons I have given, to start under the heaviest handicap of the three; not only is there no valid argument in its favor, but there is definite antecedent presumption against it, although this does not amount to disproof. This being so, an elementary canon of scientific method requires me to give the preference to the telepathic theory, *provided that it adequately covers the phenomena to be explained*. But does it cover them adequately? This is the crucial point of the whole inquiry, and to this I must now address myself.

I have made a list—doubtless not exhaustive—of nine objections which have been advanced against the telepathic hypothesis. I shall now proceed to consider them.

(1) It is objected that the telepathic hypothesis does not account for the fact that communications invariably *claim* to come from the surviving dead.

About this there are two things to be said. In the first place, the claim in question is by no means invariably made. Prior to the rise of the spiritualist movement in the nineteenth century the spirits of the dead were far from enjoying, if we can credit our documents, any monopoly of the control of mediums: the professed source of the communication was at least as often a nonhuman demon or familiar, while in many cases no agency is alleged other than that of the "seeress" or "wise woman" herself. And even today the asserted monopoly is not without exceptions. Dr. Osty, for example, has obtained numerous veridical communications both about the living and about the dead, comparable in range and accuracy with those of the best spirit mediums, from a subject, Mme Morel, who has no "controls" and no "communicators" and does not regard the dead as the source of her supernormal knowledge. It can hardly be doubted that were this lady imbued with the current spiritualist convictions her communications would emerge from the subconscious as orthodox "spirit messages."

For, in the second place, if we know anything about the working of the subconscious mind, we know (a) that it is addicted to dramatization, and (b) that its dramas are usually if not always wish-fulfillments; both points are abundantly demonstrated by the study of dreams. Remembering further that the great majority of recent mediumships have been developed in a spiritualistic environment, and that the great majority of sitters come to mediums not out of scientific curiosity but out of hunger for communion with the dead, I can find nothing in the facts here which I should not expect to find on the telepathic hypothesis.

(2) Dr. Prince argued in 1921 that the wholesale ascription to mediums of telepathic powers was unjustified, since the experimental evidence suggested that

only a very small minority of human beings possessed these powers in any recognizable degree, and there was no independent evidence that any medium possessed them.

The force of this argument has since been greatly weakened by the publication of a number of incidents which seem to have their origin in telepathy from sitter to medium. Perhaps the most striking of these is the John Ferguson case, published by Mr. Soal in *Proc., XXXV*. The communicator, "John Ferguson," was eventually shown to be a fictitious personality; but before this happened Mr. Soal (the sitter) had privately invented a number of hypotheses about "John Ferguson's" life and circumstances, which hypotheses were at subsequent sittings communicated to him as facts. This fictitious communicator also made a number of veridical references, the source of which could hardly have been any other than Mr. Soal's mind. Mr. Soal has himself mentioned the possibility that the medium (Mrs. Blanche Cooper) may have been assisted in her "mind-reading" by unconscious whispering on the sitter's part. The suggestion lacks proof and requires a deal of stretching to make it cover the facts; yet if the case stood alone it might be not unreasonable to discount it on the ground of this suspicion. In fact, however, it by no means stands alone. Dr. Osty has described numerous instances where different mediums have reproduced beliefs or hypotheses which were present in the minds of various sitters, but were subsequently proved to be erroneous. It is not easy to suppose that all these sitters (including Osty himself) gave themselves away by unconscious whispering or other means. . . .

(3) It is objected that if the telepathic hypothesis is to cover the facts we must credit mediums with the power of drawing on the contents of the minds of living persons quite unknown to them, who are not present at a sitting, and to whom their attention has not been in any normal way directed. Such an assumption, it is urged, goes far beyond any telepathic feats of which we have independent evidence; and if the phenomenon occurs only in spiritualistic conditions we must assume that spiritualistic conditions are requisite for its productions.

This objection is more formidable than the last; and it has been brought into special prominence by the striking successes achieved by Mrs. Leonard in "proxy" sittings. But, like the last, it loses a good deal of its force when we consider some of the incidents published by Dr. Osty. These seem to show (a) that correct information outside the normal knowledge of all present at the sitting, concerning private details of the life of absent persons, may be given by sensitives who do not profess to be assisted by "spirits"; (b) that incorrect information may be given which corresponds to the belief of a third party who is unknown to the sensitive. . . . Third-party telepathy, if it cannot be regarded as an established phenomenon, has considerably more than the status of a bare hypothesis. The independent evidence in its support is not very abundant, but it is not negligible. Its paucity need surprise no one who remembers (a) that in everyday life instances of long-distance telepathy from complete strangers, if they occur, are very unlikely to be recognized; (b) that in this country at any rate a "sitting" practically always means an attempt to obtain communications not from the absent living but from the dead. The remedy for the latter circumstances lies in our own hands.

(4) It is objected that the vivid presentation in trance of a personality normally unknown to the medium is not adequately explained save on the spiritualist hypothesis. . . .

To this contention there are two possible rejoinders. In the first place, skeptics may doubt, and have in fact doubted, whether in the circumstances of a sitting such "vivid presentation of a personality" ever has substantial value as evidence of identity. They point out that when the tones of the trance speech are recognized by the sitter as those of a familiar voice, or when certain mannerisms of *façons de parler* are felt by him to be characteristic of a certain person, it is very rarely possible to check the objectivity of the recognition, as can usually be done when a name, a date or an event is in question. The door is commonly left wide open to the insidious temptations of the will-to-believe—temptations whose potency in this context can be fully realized only by those who have either been sitters themselves or made an impartial study of the annotated records of sittings.

But secondly, whether evidence of this type has much or little value, there is some reason to think that certain mediums can on occasion "reproduce" the personalities of the unknown living with as much success as those of the unknown dead. . . .

(5) A further objection to the telepathic hypothesis is that it appears to involve an otherwise unexampled *selective* action of the medium's mind, in supernormally deriving from other human minds precisely those remembered facts which are required for the building up of a particular trance personality. . . .

But I do not think that the available evidence in the least requires me to picture the subconscious mind of the medium hunting through the subconscious mind of the assumed agent, as through a lumberroom, until its finds precisely the bit of information which it needs in order give verisimilitude to its impersonation of some deceased friend of the agent. I am equally free to imagine that when *rapport* is established between the medium's subconscious mind and that of the assumed agent, the nature of the material transmitted is determined by the relative emotive force of the agent's various complexes, or by the fact that the material belongs to an associative complex, some elements of which are already in the medium's mind, or by any other cause that you like to suggest. Selection does undoubtedly operate at some stage before the material is presented in a trance; but I see nothing to prevent its operating *after* the material has become part of the furniture of the medium's subconscious mind. I am free to imagine, in the first place, that the particular complex of feelings and images which underlies a particular trance personality attracts to itself only such elements of the newly acquired material as have some associative relevance to its existing content; and secondly, that the "control" who sits in the gateway of trance—Feda or Topsy, Phinuit or Rector—operates on occasion, like the Freudian "censor," to prevent the emergence of irrelevant or disturbing matter which might interrupt the illusion and break the continuity of the medium's dream. These are no more than guesses, although they derive a certain amount of support from the known mechanism of the normal dream. I claim no more for them than that they cover the observed facts as well as any other hypothesis, and better in one important respect than the hypothesis of possession. The degree of relevance and continuity to be observed in most trance communications is, to say the least, extremely limited. In Mr. Saltmarsh's words, "One of the most striking features of communications received through trance mediums is their disjointedness." This is what I should expect from the sort of psychological machinery I have suggested; it is not what I should expect if the communicators are what they say they are.

(6) A further objection to the telepathic hypothesis is that it fails to account for certain cases of "object reading" (popularly called "psychometry"). The cases in question are those where a relic is submitted to an entranced medium, its ownership and history being *unknown both to her and to the sitter*, and she nevertheless furnishes correct details about its present or former owner.

They are, it seems to me, puzzling occurrences on any hypothesis. The notion that the relic in some unimaginable way carries a permanent record of its own history, which the medium is able to read, is definitely put out of court by the fact that much of the information supernormally obtained in such cases refers to scenes in which the relic played no part whatever. It apparently functions not as a record but as a signpost pointing to some mind, living or dead, whence the information is then supernormally derived. How is this function exercised? On the telepathic theory, the source of the information will be a living mind, usually and perhaps always that of the contributor of the relic; but I do not know how the presence of a watch or a purse creates a rapport between the medium's mind and that of the contributor. Equally, on the spiritualist view, I do not know how the presence of a material object causes the particular spirit which once owned that object to present itself to two strangers at a particular time and place. We seem reduced here to a choice between two explanations—an unlikely coincidence, or "third-party" telepathy mediated by a material object.

(7) It is further objected that the amount and quality of the veridical information given varies not with changes of sitter but with changes of communicator—which is the contrary of what we should expect on the telepathic hypothesis.

The evidence on this point is not so abundant as one could wish, since most sitters always evoke the same communicator, and most communicators always manifest themselves in response to the appeal of the same sitter or group of closely associated sitters.... It is, however, a fact that some communicators, such as Mrs. Piper's "George Pelham," have been successful with a number of different sitters, while others have consistently failed with a variety of sitters. This is perhaps most easily explained on the spiritualist hypothesis. But other explanations are not impossible: e.g., that the dream figure called "George Pelham" emerged from a deeper stratum of Mrs. Piper's subconscious mind than the dream figure called "Stainton Moses," and was therefore more accessible to impressions telepathically received. And there is on the other side a fact which tells, so far as it goes, in favor of the telepathic hypothesis, namely that while some *sitters* consistently fail, others receive veridical information from a number of different communicators. My general conclusion is that little weight can be attached to objection 7. . . .

(8) It is further objected that the telepathic hypothesis does not satisfactorily account for cross-correspondences, in so far as these exhibit evidence of conscious design.

This objection leads me on to the most thorny and difficult ground in the whole field of psychical research—ground which I could not possibly attempt to traverse in detail at the end of a paper even if I felt myself adequately equipped for the task. All that I can do is to state the general impression which the evidence produces upon me, without demanding that others should acquiesce in my conclusion—or rather, in my absence of conclusions. For there are to my mind two points in which the evidence of cross-correspondences is inconclusive. In the first place, I cannot quite convince myself that in demonstrating pattern or coherence Mr. Piddington and other investigators have conclusively demonstrated design. The patterns are there, and I do not suggest that their occurrence is in all or even in most cases due to chance. But suppose we posit that an undesigned telepathic infiltration from time to time takes place between the subconscious minds of certain automatists. What chiefly then remains to be explained is (a) why the same idea frequently emerges in two automatists' scripts not in identical but in complementary forms; (b) why the emergence of a common idea is occasionally accompanied in the script by some such note as "seek elsewhere for this." I cannot feel that either of these peculiarities affords really clear evidence of design. . . .

(9) It remains to say a word about an objection which though demonstrably invalid is more frequent than any other on the lips of the uncritical. The spiritualist hypothesis, people say, is "so simple," the telepathic "so complicated."

If this means merely that the spiritualist explanation is more easily grasped by the unthinking, the statement is true, but irrelevant. We do not prefer Newton's picture of the physical world to Einstein's because it is more easily apprehended. If it is meant, on the other hand, that the spiritualist hypothesis is in the scientific sense simpler, the statement is relevant, but false. To a scientist, I take it, the simplest hypothesis is that which makes no assumption unsupported by independent evidence; the next simplest is that which makes the fewest and narrowest unsupported assumptions. Now the telepathic hypothesis assumes that mediums possess a supernormal faculty for whose reality there is substantial independent evidence; and it assumes further that they possess it in a degree for which there is a *slight* amount of independent evidence. The spiritualist hypothesis assumes:

(1) that many, if not all, human personalities survive bodily death;
(2) that they retain an accurate memory of many details in their past lives;
(3) that they have a detailed awareness of many physical events which have occurred among the living since their death;

(4) that they have in some cases access to the unspoken thoughts of the living;
(5) that they can at times communicate with the living, either by direct use of the organism of a medium or by telepathically influencing the medium's subconscious mind;
(6) that the unspoken wish of a living mind is in some cases sufficient to initiate this relationship between a particular deceased person and a particular medium.

These are I think the minimum assumptions which will cover the phenomena I have been considering. If the hypothesis is used as most of its advocates use it, to explain also book tests, newspaper tests, and the whole range of physical phenomena, a large number of additional assumptions are involved. Thus, far from being simple, the spiritualist hypothesis is hydraheaded. It is in fact not one hypothesis at all, but a series of hypotheses, of such a character that no later member of the series is a necessary, or so far as our knowledge goes, a probable consequence of an earlier member. If the dead survive, there is no positive probability that they will remember details of their past lives; if they survive and remember the past, there is no positive probability that they will be aware of terrestrial events after their death; and so forth. Whatever advantages the spiritualist view possesses, simplicity in the scientific sense is not one of them.

I have now considered all the objections known to me which seem to me to have a *prima facie* claim to consideration. To sum up my conclusions, objections 1, 5, 7, and 9 appear to me to have little or no cogency; indeed, all of them are capable of being turned against their advocates. Objections 2, 3, and 4 are to a considerable extent invalidated by evidence obtained under conditions which appear to exclude spirit agency. Objection 8 I am obliged to write off as inconclusive, for the reasons I have briefly mentioned. Finally, objection 6 calls attention to a set of phenomena which I cannot satisfactorily explain to myself on any theory.

Until, then, some stronger objection emerges, I must grant that the telepathic hypothesis covers the evidence as well on the whole as any other; and since it is the minimum hypothesis which does so, it commands my provisional acceptance. Until this conclusion is upset, I must regard survival as unproved; and I have stated my reasons for thinking that survival of the kind postulated by spiritualists, though not impossible, is antecedently improbable. It is in this sense that I do not believe in survival.

I must add that the two current forms of the spiritualist hypothesis—the theory of telepathy from the dead and the theory of possession—seem to me to differ widely in their evidential status. Against the former no conclusive objection has been drawn, or is likely to be drawn, from the trance phenomena, for the excellent reason that we know nothing at all about the conditions which might govern this kind of telepathy. Against direct possession there is evidence which I find insuperable....

There are other considerations, of a sufficiently obvious kind, which *tend* to discredit all forms of the spiritualist hypothesis, but tell most definitely against the theory of possession. It is, I think, fair to say that the "spirits" have so far failed to convey to us any distinctive impression of their present mode of life, their occupations, or their state of mind; and that they have never explained this failure. How comes it that these countless Columbuses, returning to us (if but for an hour) from the supreme voyage of discovery, described the life beyond the tomb in terms that are equally applicable to life in Putney, or alternatively, are borrowed from cheap theosophical literature? Can the vivid literary talent of a Verrall or the philosophic insight of a Myers do no more than this? And why, in general, do the "spirits" of intellectually gifted persons produce no evidence that they retain their gifts in the other world? No single valuable contribution to art or science has been made, so far as I know, by an artist or scientist liberated from the material body.... If there is an afterlife, it would appear on the evidence so far available to be a life which kills all interest in intellectual pursuits, as living men understand them. This may be indeed the case; yet I cannot but think it surprising, as well as extremely unfortunate from an evidential point of view.

CAN A MAN IMAGINE HIMSELF WITNESSING HIS OWN FUNERAL?

Peter A. French

> I can easily imagine, e.g., witnessing the funeral of my own body and continuing to exist without a body, for nothing is easier than to describe a world which differs from our ordinary world only in the complete absence of all data which I would call parts of my own body.
> —M. Schlick[1]

The purpose of this investigation is to raise what Butler in chapter one of the *Analogy of Religion* calls "strange difficulties" concerning the sense and imaginability of the question, "Can a man imagine himself witnessing his own funeral?"; i.e.; to examine Schlick's claim that the question is meaningful because the possibility under discussion is both conceivable and imaginable. In this regard two questions are crucial. The first deals with the notion of disembodied existence, while the second involves a clarification of the sense of "imagine" being used in this context. Question 1: "Is the notion of disembodied existence self-contradictory?" (If not, then we may take it to be, at least in this somewhat limited sense, meaningful, though not necessarily what Schlick maintains when he adds to the above the comment: "Immortality ... is an empirical hypothesis because it possesses logical verifiability. It could be verified by following the prescription, 'Wait until you die.' "[2]) Question 2: "What sense of 'imagine' must be involved in Schlick's claim?"

"Men (all men) survive (will survive) death." Some philosophers have claimed that this statement is self-contradictory. In effect they argue that the use of the words "death" and "survival" and their cognates is such that when in conjunction, as in referring to the "dead" and the "survivors" of an airplane crash, they are both exclusive and exhaustive terms. All those on the plane *logically* must either have died (been among the dead) or survived (were survivors). Furthermore, no one *logically* could have both died (been among the dead) and survived (been a survivor). To have died is one thing, to survive, another, but to be both dead and a survivor is not only peculiar but logically contradictory.

There is something both initially appealing and yet naggingly inconsequential in these philosophical arguments, however. After all there is claimed for that "logically unique expectation,"[3] i.e., that we shall have experiences after death, much more than that "man survives death" is not self-contradictory. Far from being a move intended to justify that "expectation," I take it to be a logical

---

This essay is reprinted from *The International Journal for the Philosophy of Religion* Vol. 5, No. 4 (1975). Used by permission of the editor.

derivative of other considerations. Schlick makes this point in two ways. In the first place he argues that that which is not only conceivable but imaginable cannot be self-contradictory (I shall deal with this under Question 2), and, secondly, he assumes that a description of "disembodied existence" can be given such that that notion not only is not self-contradictory but that it would render the hypothesis empirical and thereby verifiable if you only "wait until you die." If the latter is the case, then "men survive death" would be a logically noncontradictory assertion, i.e., in some sense meaningful.

The issue at hand, then, is to examine the intelligibility of (noncontradictory nature of) the concept of disembodied existence and this would seem necessarily to involve an examination of the use of person words. Schlick's claim again is that nothing is "easier than to describe" a disembodied world. The centrality of the notion of disembodied existence to the affirmative answer to the question, "Can a man imagine himself witnessing his own funeral?" cannot be overstressed. As long as the funeral in question is his, that it is not he imagining what his funeral might be like, an account of person words and their relationship (or nonrelationship) to bodies is essential. Briefly, if "his" entails "his body" or some bodily reference when we say "his funeral," then the sense of "himself" as a witness to the occasion is certainly peculiar, if not self-contradictory. On the other hand, and this is the perplexity which Schlick does not appear to recognize, if "his" does not involve some bodily reference—put differently, if "his" is understood at least upon certain occasions as calling for or even suggesting no bodily reference—then the sense of "himself" as a witness to the event is not odd, but the description of the event as "his funeral" seems to be only an arbitrary if not extremely peculiar locution. We must specify in what way we are to take the phrase "his funeral."

In fairness to Schlick, he talks only of imagining the "funeral of my body," but I think that this does not substantially alter the problem. "My body" as used here would seem to imply that person words are not dependent upon reference to bodily identification, i.e., that Schlick's notion of "I" is obviously related to something over and above bodily reference. "My" then is intended in the normal possessive sense: "my car, my book, and my body." The "my" of "my funeral," however, seems not quite to fit into this usage, and perhaps that is why Schlick chooses the rather uncommon expression, "the funeral of my body" for "my funeral."

Let us examine this point more closely. "My" as a possessive pronoun is generally associated with objects over which I have certain rights and privileges. I can do things with them: drive my car, lend you my book; perhaps even in some communities, sell my body, or will parts of it for research. My funeral is not mine in that sense. But, it should be readily seen, neither is "my cold" or "my state of confusion."

Those philosophers who argue for the self-contradictory nature of the hypothesis of disembodied existence rely almost exclusively upon a certain account of the use (and meaning) of pronouns and proper names. In effect they attempt to demonstrate that if "I" and "my" are used such that they are without reference to some body or other, they are unintelligible or meaningless.

The same is to be expected of proper names such as the surname "Jones." "Jones," it might be maintained, always stands for or refers to Jones's body (or a part of Jones's body).

Can we distinguish between the notion that "I" or "Jones" *refers to* my or Jones's body and "I" or "Jones" *stands for* my or Jones's body?[4] If "I" or "Jones" stands for "my body" or "Jones's body," it should be possible to substitute "my body" or "Jones's body" for all occurrences of "I" or "Jones" in ordinary discourse. (Perhaps we should alter the phrase "my body" to read "my body or a part of my body" and "Jones's body" to read "Jones's body or a part of Jones's body" to cover all of the alternatives.)

In the case of "I," consider the following sentences: "I saw the light, I remember my childhood days on the farm, I feel pain." Then replace "I" with "my body." The substituted "my body" (or a part of my body [my brain]) clearly does not result in a sentence with the same meaning as the original.[5] Few philosophers would deny that there are a number of uses of "I" or "Jones" in which the substitution of "my body" or "Jones's body" does not alter the meaning, for example, "I am six feet tall" or "Jones is six feet tall." In these cases the statement made entails (1) that "my body" is substitutable for "I" and (2) that a disparity between statements made about "I" or "Jones" and "my body" or "Jones's body" would be self-contradictory. In the case of (1), saying "I am six feet tall" is saying "My body is six feet tall," while (2) makes it clear that I cannot be five feet tall while my body is six feet tall. "I am six feet tall" is entailed by "My body is six feet tall." Clearly in a number of cases, then, "I" stands for "my body" and in others "I" does not stand or cannot stand for "my body." Yet there is a nagging problem about the phrase "my body." Can I understand the use of that phrase without making reference to "myself"; that is, can "my body" be translated into any phrase or set of expressions which are physical in every sense?

Suppose we define "my body" as "the body standing in a certain relation to *me*."[6] Imagine also that before us we have a model of my present body. "Does 'my body' mean 'the body of which this is a model'?" At first glance this seems attractive, but it assumes that it would be inconceivable that I might exist with a different body at a future moment. "The body of which this is a model" stands in a certain relation to me; i.e., it is mine in a so far unspecifiable way, but if at some future time I should have another body, then "the body of which this is a model" would stand in no relation to me at all. In short, if body transfer, reincarnation, etc., are possible, then "the body of which this is a model (in the case given) is *my* body" is a synthetic proposition and not, as it might first appear, an analytic one.

There are certain uses of "I" such that it cannot be replaced by "my body" without loss or change of meaning (call that case I^1), and there are other cases of the use of "I" in which it is proper to substitute "my body" for "I" (call that case I^2). My contention is that I^2 always involves reference to I^1, though I^1 does not necessarily refer to I^2. The analysis of sentences containing I^2 references will in part always consist of sentences containing the first-person pronoun as used in I^1. Briefly, the relationship between me and my body is a contingent one.

The individuation of this body as mine is an empirical matter.

Consider the other alternative, i.e., that though "I" does not stand for my body, "I" always refers to my body. By "refers to" is meant a weaker claim than that I can replace all occurrences of "I" with "my body" or "a part of my body." Instead, every statement in which "I" appears entails some proposition about my body. Our concern with this way of stating the referential relationship is that if it holds then the notion of disembodied existence is self-contradictory.

"I saw the light" (taken in a non-metaphoric way) would (if the above were the case) translate into "I saw the light and that entails certain propositions about my eyes, optic nerves, brain, etc." Furthermore, if "I" always refers to my body, then any proposition containing "I" would entail *a fortiori* that at the time I had a body.[7]

Although it might be possible to demonstrate that all propositions of what I have called case I^1 are causally dependent for their meaning on the existence of my body at a specifiable time—i.e., "I began to feel pain at 8:50 last night" could not be true unless I had a body at 8:50 last night—it may be possible to show that they are not logically dependent upon the existence of my body. But because my concern lies with problems of demonstrating the non-self-contradictory nature of the notion of disembodied existence, I will dismiss as irrelevant claims that the uses of "I" in case I^1 are causally dependent upon the existence of my body, simply on grounds that a causal implication is not a logical implication, and self-contradiction is a logical problem. That is, the causal implication that might in fact hold between statements which include "I" used in case I^1 has no bearing on the logical noncontradictory nature of the notion that "I can imagine myself existing without a body." The first-person pronoun does not (logically) stand for or refer to "my body."

Consider the statement, "I began to feel pain at 8:50 last night." (Perhaps this is the report of a woman in labor.) Must it entail the proposition, "I had a body at 8:50 last night?" Let us make a few observations before tackling this question. Certainly "I had a body at 8:50 last night" entails "A body existed at 8:50 last night" (the converse does not hold). The proposition, "I began to feel pain at 8:50 last night," would entail "A body (some body or other) existed at 8:50 last night" if it can be shown that "I began to feel pain at 8:50 last night" entails "I had a body at 8:50 last night." But does this entailment hold?

"I began to feel pain at 8:50 last night but I have never had a body" is a curious statement. What can we say about it? In the first place, it does not contradict "I began to feel pain at 8:50 last night and there has never existed a body." The proper name case, however, does appear to create a self-contradiction if substituted for "I" above; e.g., "French began to feel pain at 8:50 last night, and French has never had a body" and "French began to feel pain at 8:50 last night and there has never existed a body." Some philosophers argue that this self-contradiction only seems to arise because we want to distinguish between the "I" and the "French" case (because the latter is a third-person identification) in so far as we say "French began to feel the pain at 8:50 last night" entails "A body has existed at some time or other." On the other hand, "I began to feel the pain at 8:50 last night" does not entail "A body has existed at some time or other." I, however, think we can show that there is here, in fact, a self-contradiction.

When I say, "I began to feel pain at 8:50 last night," and you say, "French began to feel pain at 8:50 last night," you seem to be repeating the same thing I said. We both, it would seem, must be saying the same thing, and it would seem that what is entailed or not entailed by the one statement ought to be entailed or not by the other. If I say, "I began to feel pain at 8:50 last night," and you say, "French did not begin to feel pain at 8:50 last night," our statements appear to be contradictory. It could be argued: (1) if "French didn't begin to feel pain at 8:50 last night" does contradict "I began to feel pain at 8:50 last night," then "I began to feel pain . . ." entails "French began to feel pain . . ." (If $\bar{q}$ contradicts p it follows that p entails q); and the reverse, (2) if "I did not begin to feel pain at . . ." contradicts "French began to feel pain at . . ." then "French began to feel pain at . . ." entails "I began to feel pain at . . ." (If $\bar{p}$ contradicts q, it follows that q entails p).

The result of these logical entailments, however, poses a further problem. Three statements: (A) "I began to feel pain at 8:50 last night" does not entail "A body has existed at some time or other," (B) "French began to feel pain at 8:50 last night" entails "A body has existed at some time or other," and (C) "I began to feel pain at 8:50 last night" is logically equivalent to "French began to feel pain at 8:50 last night," all appear to be true, but their conjunction is a self-contradiction. We have, then, the major issue in this investigation of disembodied existence: is it the case that the conjunction (A) (B) (C) is a logical contradiction? What we have said regarding "I" neither always standing for nor always referring to my body would support the position that (A) cannot be denied. This leaves two possibilities for resolving the dilemma: (1) deny (B), then (A) and (C) could be maintained without contradiction; or (2) deny (C), and then (A) and (B) can be maintained.

Let us consider (C) first. "I began to feel pain at 8:50 last night" would seem to be equivalent to "French began to feel pain at 8:50 last night." But will this stand up to further analysis? The two statements are equivalent only if "I began to feel pain at 8:50 last night" entails "I am French." However, I am inclined to say that the statement "I began to feel pain at 8:50 last night and I am not French" is not a self-contradiction, i.e., that the needed entailment does not hold.

This issue turns on the question of whether "I am French" is an analytic statement. If "I am French" is not analytic, then any claims made about "French" should never logically be taken as claims made about me, and furthermore, what is true of "French" cannot automatically be translated as true of me, even if I were to agree that such and such were true of "French," i.e., that "French" were dead and I were witnessing his funeral.

The claim that "I am French" is synthetic is in obvious need of support. An interesting example might be constructed as follows: I have committed a serious crime and am "hiding out" at your apartment. The police enter the room and ask me, "Are you French?" I respond, "I'm not French . . . what has he done?" There is no doubt that I am lying, but what I have said does not appear to be self-contradictory. What makes my statement a lie is that I am "French." But in what sense am I "French" such that the denial, "I am not French," is a lie but not a self-contradiction? Perhaps I am "French" only in so far as I am identified as the person who has this body at this time or is seen and recognized by others to be the person having this body and called "French."

If lying about one's name is not to state a self-contradiction, we need to clarify what lying in this case might be. When I say to the policeman, "I am not French," it would seem that only one of two cases is true. Either I am in fact not "French," in which case the statement is true, or I am, in fact, "French," but wish to conceal that fact, and the statement is a lie. Perhaps we ought to question whether the use of "French" in "I am French" and in "French began to feel pain at 8:50 last night" is the same.

In "I am French," "French" might serve as the answer to the question, "Who are you?" "I am the one called 'French,' My name is 'French,' They call me 'French,' Call for 'French' and I'll come," etc. "Who are you?" "I am French, I am not Jones." Now, it seems to me that it is possible to conceive of circumstances in which "I am French" can be denied without self-contradiction. But not, I'm afraid, the policeman case. Such cases are very difficult to describe, but in order to show that "I am French" is a synthetic judgment, we shall have to wrestle with at least one of them.

Suppose that I were to awaken some future morning claiming to be Brendan Behan. I claim to remember events in Behan's life as events in my life. I have his characteristics of speech, his propensity for consuming alcoholic beverages, etc. I behave like him. When a friend calls on the telephone asking to speak to "French," I declare that no one with that name lives here. Have I contradicted myself? I am inclined to say that I have not. But was I not then lying?

What criteria could I offer to support my contention of being Brendan Behan? After all, it is quite conceivable that any number of people could have the character and personality traits of a Brendan Behan. How crucial are my memory claims relative to Behan's life? This point is not new. Certainly we should be inclined to accept that I am the same person as Behan if I factually and genuinely do remember episodes of Behan's life as my own. If memory claims are to count toward my contention, then the real issue is whether my "Behan-memories" could be real memories or cases of clairvoyance. Under normal conditions one can distinguish cases of remembering from cases of clairvoyance because the absence of bodily continuity signals clairvoyance. But my Behan-"reincarnation" case seems to blur the normal distinctions. (I take it that this is true for reincarnation cases in general.) We can see this by considering how I might be treated before the law. For example, even if the British authorities were to accept the fact that I genuinely remember committing Behan's IRA bombing excursions, they are not likely to find me guilty of treason and imprison me. They might, however, be reluctant to give me a visa to visit Northern Ireland. Or would they invoke an old injunction restricting Behan's travel? I think not. My remembering that I committed the bombings then is not reason for saying I did them in the case of reincarnation, though it would certainly count in a normal case of remembering.

What must I conclude about my "reincarnation" as Brendan Behan? I am afraid here I have given away the case. I spoke of "my" reincarnation. Strictly speaking, I am not sure that I can make sense of (or describe) a true case of reincarnation, but I am certain that I would be baffled as to the use of "I" and "my," etc., in attempting the description. I said, "Suppose I awoke as Behan." I take it that this would be the normal way of describing such a state of affairs. But when I say "I" here, to whom do I refer? What we must know is whether or not we are still talking about the same thing when we use person language in these puzzle cases, as in the cases of reporting the pain at 8:50 last night.

I may now be Brendan Behan but I have no claims to Behan's estate, wife, manuscripts, nor does the court treat me as Behan in any outstanding cases against him. Whether I have any claims to French's estate, wife, etc., I suspect might also come under legal scrutiny, though I suppose bodily continuity (recognition by others) might count toward my being rewarded them. What the reincarnation (or Behan-spirit-informing-my-body) case suggests is that proper names are not person words in the same sense as "I," "my," etc., are. I am not necessarily "French" in the sense that I am necessarily myself. "I am French" is contingent upon a number of things, most of which are related to the meeting of my body with others.[8]

The use of "French" in "French began to feel pain at 8:50 last night" is clearly of the type, "Which one is he?" "That one is French." "French" serves to delineate one of a number of people. "Who began to feel pain?" "He did," (pointing to a body) "that's French." I shall call this "Flew's sense of person words." The person "French" is something we can (though perhaps I cannot) meet. To put it in Flew's terms: "People are what you meet. Person words refer to men and women like you and me and the other fellow. They are taught by pointing at people. Indeed how else could they or should they be taught?"[9]

Flew cautions that this is not to say, however, that people or person words are merely substitutes for body words. "Person words do not mean either bodies or souls nor yet any combination of the two."[10]

Imagine the following conversation at a cocktail party:

> "Who are you?"
> "Me."
> "Well, of course, I know that, but I mean, what's your name?"
> "French."
> "Why, French (shaking hands), I've been dying to meet you."

A meeting has taken place. It is not like the meeting of crashing trains or automobiles. Human meeting is a social relation. "To say 'people are what you meet' amounts to saying that persons are entities with which one may have social relations: or rather, not 'with which' but 'with whom.'"[11] This, Flew would agree, means that persons are not just bodies, but he calls a person "a certain sort of corporeal object." If a social relationship, however, is essential in meeting, persons cannot be merely corporeal objects. In the idea of "meeting" we find entailed that consciousness is ascribable to both meeters by each other.

Yet, unless the two speakers above are corporeal entities, there can be no meeting at all. I take it then that being embodied is a necessary condition for carrying on social relations (I doubt that we would call telepathic communication "meeting"). I suspect that even the dualist would agree that part of what it is to be capable of meeting is to be able to perform certain expressive functions with one's body.

My point is that one need not disagree with Flew's person theory. I suggest that what he says, however, applies to the use of person words like "French" and perhaps also "he," "she," and "you." When we meet, you meet "French" and I meet "you." French's body is intimately involved in this affair. If this were as far as our analysis of person words were to go, then we must agree with Flew also that no one, not even French, can imagine French witnessing French's funeral. If the funeral is indeed French's, then French is no more; no one can meet him, and he cannot witness (a kind of social relation) the graveside activities.

I have maintained, however, that "I am French" is a synthetic judgment, that, to use Kantian language, the relationship is not thought through identity. "I" is not met, and, as we have shown, "I began to feel pain at 8:50" does not entail "I had a body at any time at all." What can be said of person words in Flew's sense cannot be said of "I" and "me." Although, as a matter of fact, I do ascribe "personal predicates"[12] to myself only after I have learned to ascribe them to others, that is insufficient reason for the claim that I logically must do so. For the use of "I" to apply to something it is not necessary that there have existed at some time or other a body to which one could have pointed and truly said, "This is I." Denying that (C) holds (i.e., " 'I began to feel pain at 8:50 last night' is logically equivalent to 'French began to feel pain at 8:50 last night' is false") resolves the difficulties of apparent self-contradiction, for certainly (A) and (B) are not contradictory.

A reluctance to take this route and instead to attempt to show (B) to be false might be traceable to the difficulty in finding anything wrong with the arguments that appear to show that "I began to feel pain at 8:50 last night" (p) and "French began to feel pain at 8:50 last night" (q) are equivalents. Again, the argument was that if $\bar{q}$ contradicts p then p entails q and that if $\bar{p}$ contradicts q then q entails p. I think, however, that this argument unwarrantedly assumed that "I am French" is analytic. If I can say "I am not French" without self-contradiction, then I fail to see how the denial of a statement about French necessarily contradicts the same statement made about me. In fact, of course, this may be so, but it is not logically so. Put differently, I think one might with little difficulty imagine circumstances in which the following would all be true: "I am French"; "I began to feel pain at 8:50 last night"; "French felt no pain at 8:50 last night."

Concerning Question 1 our analysis has shown that the notion of disembodied existence is not self-contradictory. We have shown that statements containing "I" need not entail statements about my body or a part of my body. We have also shown that "the body of which this is a model is mine" is synthetic and that "I am French" is also synthetic. "This is French," in fact, necessarily involves reference to some body (bodies) or other, while "This is I" need not. What can we then say regarding whether a man can imagine himself witnessing his own funeral? I think that here our analysis has not produced enough for unqualified affirmation of the possibility. Certainly "I am witnessing X's funeral" is no more of a problem than "I am watching X swim," as long as X is not identical to "I." However, when "I" is identical to X, I think our analysis gives us no reason to suppose that "I am witnessing my funeral" is anything but extremely (and logically) odd. "French's funeral" or "the funeral of my body" ("the body of which this is a model") would appear to be witnessable by me; that is, would be logically witnessable by me, though in fact the sense of witnessing here, as Flew rightly points out, cannot, I would think, be significantly linked to "I." "Witnessing" surely is a spatial notion, and the idea of disembodied existence, as we have shown, is not self-contradictory precisely because it does not entail that a physical body has ever existed in space. Whether one could make sense of "being there in spirit," it seems to me, does not substantially affect the issue.

Concluding Question 1 then, we can appreciate Schlick's choice of words, "funeral of my body," as necessitated by this formulation of the non-self-contradictory notion of disembodied existence.

Concerning Question 2, what sense of "imagine" is involved in Schlick's claim? I cannot hope to know certainly what Schlick had in mind, but I think we can distinguish at least three senses of "imagine," two of which would make the question, "Can a man imagine himself witnessing his own funeral (the funeral of his body)?" clearly inconceivable.

The ordinary uses of "imagine" would seem to involve cases in which mental imagery is called for, but this is not always the case.[14] "Imagine what would happen if the stock market fell one hundred points in one day." No mental picture is required for you to reply, "That will certainly throw us into a depression." Perhaps an accompanying picture of bankers and stockholders leaping from ten-story windows crosses your mind, but it need not. The imperative sense of "imagine" is interchangeable with the notion of "suppose," as in "Suppose what would happen if . . ." or even "Think of the outcome if . . ."

There is another use of "imagine" which does call for a mental picture or mental imaging. "I'm imagining the way it will look with the trees and grass all round." Here I am apparently entertaining a mental picture. A third sense of "imagine" would be as in the case where I say, "I imagined she would arrive before this time." Here "I imagined" seems only to be something like saying, "I thought that . . . but I was wrong."

Let us call the first sense of imagining (suppose), from Annis Flew, the "propositional entertainment" sense, the second sense "the imaging sense" and the third "the thinking (usually mistakenly)" sense. We can eliminate the third sense from consideration, for Schlick obviously did not mean "I imagined myself witnessing the funeral of my body . . . but it didn't work out that way."

This leaves us with the "propositional entertainment" sense of "imagine" and the "imaging sense." Schlick's use of "imagine" seems to be the "image sense."

His claim is that immortality is an empirical hypothesis and that one can describe a picture of "witnessing the funeral of my body." The problem is that a picture of the type called for, the straightforward production of the image of what it would be like to be at my own ("French's") funeral, cannot serve as an argument "that a doubtfully significant suggested description of itself does indeed make sense."[15] What Schlick needs to describe is an image of (picture of) me witnessing my own funeral. In view of what I have previously said about "I" and "French," I fail to see how such a picture of "I witnessing French's funeral" might be described short of identifying me in another body (one of the mourners, I would hope). The individuation problems which that would occasion, however, would diminish, I think, the significance of "witnessing the funeral of my body" about to the level of watching the barber cut my hair and then sweep up his shop.

Might we instead treat the "imagine" of our problem in the "propositional entertainment" sense? "Can a man imagine himself witnessing his own funeral?" then would be similar to "Can a man imagine what would happen if the stock market fell 100 points?" "Suppose," but suppose *what*. "Suppose that you were dead and ...." What are the limits on what can be supposed? I am inclined to say that anything short of a logical contradiction can be entertained in this way. Supposing the state of affairs after one's death is certainly not logically self-contradictory; a good deal of literature uses such a motif. But again the oddity of our particular question strikes. "Suppose that you were witnessing the funeral of your body." Although I don't deny this is odd, I cannot see where the command is self-contradictory or calls for the entertainment of a self-contradiction (given the answer to Question 1). Furthermore, I think that such a command would be intelligible to the ordinary man. I suspect he would respond, "Yes, I would find out then what they really do think of me."

To conclude, the examination of "imagine" suggests that only if it is understood as "suppose" can we make sense of the question, "Can a man imagine himself witnessing his own funeral?" But if taken in that sense I fail to see how the possibility of my doing so serves to prove that immortality is an empirical hypothesis. Any number of propositions which are not self-contradictory may be supposed and their possible consequences can be legitimately and often fruitfully discussed, but that does not make them empirical hypotheses.

NOTES

1. M. Schlick, "Meaning and Verification," *Philosophical Review*, Vol. XLV, No. 4 (1936): 356.
2. *Ibid.*, pp. 356-57.
3. See John Wisdom, "Gods," *Proceedings of the Aristotelian Society*, 1944-45.
4. Casimir Lewy, "Is the Notion of Disembodied Existence Self-Contradictory?" *Proceedings of the Aristotelian Society*, 1942-43. Lewy maintains that such a distinc-

tion is essential to understanding the proper use of these pronouns and proper names, that when properly understood they support the idea that disembodied existence is not self-contradictory.

5. The sentence "I saw the light" can be taken in more than one way. In the first case (call it the straightforward sense), "I saw the light" might be a part of the response of a motorist to the questions of a highway patrolman relative to the latter's contention that the motorist was not attentive to certain traffic conditions. The motorist's response in total might have been: "I saw the light and it was amber, not red." In the second case, "I saw the light" has a metaphorical sense, perhaps relative to certain religious matters (conversion). Heard in a church: "Why are you here?" "I saw the light." As used here the expression is not in reference to a physical light, let alone to a body or part of a body performing the act of seeing it. In fact, "seeing" as used here is not at all a normal perceptual word; though "I saw the light" is certainly a meaningful expression in the context of conversion.

6. *Ibid.*, p. 62. As Lewy does.

7. *Ibid.*, p. 64. "It would be claimed that the proposition 'I saw a flash of light at t' *logically entails* that I had a body at t, that the proposition 'I felt pain at t' *logically entails* that I had a body at t, and so on."

8. See A. G. N. Flew, "Can a Man Witness His Own Funeral?" *Hibbert Journal* (1956): 242-52, and *A New Approach to Psychical Research* (London: O. A. Watts & Co., Ltd., 1953), particularly ch. VII and Flew's comments on Price's paper, *Brain and Mind,* J. R. Smythies, editor (London:Routledge and Kegan Paul, 1965), pp. 24-28.

9. Flew, "Can a Man Witness His Own Funeral?" p. 249

10. *Ibid.*, p. 250. His example of the differences between things we might say about the living and the dead, however, I think are not as clear-cut as he would like. Notice that upon merely hearing "We brought him down from Z'mutt Ridge" and "We brought his body down from Z'mutt Ridge" one cannot tell whether the statements are or are not equivalent. Even if one were to accept Flew's claim that one can meet "him," but one can only bump into, trip over, etc., the body, is one forewarned as to what he is likely to see when he examines what was brought down from Z'mutt Ridge: person or corpse?

11. H. H. Price, "Reply to Antony Flew: 'People are What You Meet,' " *Brain and Mind,* pp. 29-31. Quoted from p. 29.

12. See P. F. Strawson, *Individuals* (Garden City: Doubleday, 1959).

13. Casimir Lewy's attempt (*op. cit.*) to show a sentence like (B) to be false is based on clearing up what he calls the confusion of the proposition, "French began to feel pain at 8:50 last night but there has never existed a body" (which he claims is not self-contradictory) with the sentence, " 'French began to feel pain at 8:50 last night' expresses a proposition and there never existed a body," which is a contradiction. Lewy's reason for saying this is that if there never had existed a body at which a man could have pointed and truthfully uttered, "This is French," then any sentence of the type "French began to feel pain at 8:50 last night" could not express a proposition. The first part of (B), however, Lewy argues, is not claiming to express a proposition; therefore the proposition (B) is false. That is, only the proposition, "The sentence 'French began to feel pain at 8:50 last night expresses a proposition' entails 'A body has existed at some time or other' " is true.

This seems to me, however, to import a sense of "French" which Lewy does not stipulate. I doubt that we could imagine circumstances of its use, i.e., sentences using "French" as a name that do not express a proposition of any sort. Again, I think that Lewy's error is his failure to extend the (his own) analysis of "I am French (Lewy)" as synthetic to all statements containing reference to "French" ("Lewy").

14. See Annis Flew, "Images, Supposing and Imagining," *Philosophy* (1953): 246. See also J. M. Shorter, "Imagination," *Essays in Philosophical Psychology,* pp. 154-170.

15. Annis Flew, *op. cit.,* p. 251.

MYSTICISM AND THE PARADOX OF SURVIVAL

J. J. Clarke

Some Current Accounts of Personal Survival

The idea of survival after death has itself survived, as least as a logical possibility, the death of many other metaphysical notions. It is not difficult to see why, for it is possible to imagine many things in connection with one's survival of death: one can picture oneself watching's one's own funeral, reuniting with one's deceased friends and relatives, reflecting, dwelling on memories, and so forth. Such imaginative pictures can be painted in various thicknesses of color. One of the most richly colored portraits in recent years has come from John Hick.[1] His resurrection world, though sequestered from our own stretch of space and time, appears to be as richly detailed as our own. Though no longer made of physical matter, resurrected bodies are to all intents and purposes indistinguishable from our present unregenerate ones, and resurrected people therefore have no special difficulty in identifying their own or other people's bodies. The portrait is as easy as can be on our imaginations, so lifelike indeed that one might sometimes wonder whether one is in this world or the next. As an example of a more sparsely drawn picture of survival one might take the notion sketched by Strawson in *Individuals*.[2] It is possible to conceive of one's survival of bodily death, he thinks, but it would be a solitary and unenviable existence, for though one could have experiences, thoughts, and memories as at present, there would be no means of communicating with others, embodied or otherwise, and no way of initiating changes in the world.[2]

One of the persistent problems with the notion of survival is that of understanding how an individual *person* can pass through the needle eye of death and yet still sensibly be called the same person or even a person at all. Obviously this problem becomes more acute as the detail of the picture becomes more sparse. Thus Strawson's account is not merely, as he admits, "unenticing," but borders on incoherence for it is not intuitively obvious that the survival of my bare capacity to remember and to contemplate constitutes the survival of what could properly be called "me." The shadows he allows to pass are, one would suppose, attenuated beyond recognition. Hick's more fully drawn portrait probably has the advantage of avoiding such lines of criticism as these, but while he is more skilful in conveying persons whole and entire into the netherworld, there is one very serious deficiency in his account which has not to my knowledge been noticed and on which I propose to focus attention in this paper: his survivors remain human, all too human. It is not that we expect them for a

---

This selection is reprinted from the *International Philosophical Quarterly*, Vol. 11, No. 2 (June, 1971), 165ff. Used by permission of the editor.

priori reasons to be radically changed by this traumatic experience—though I think we would so expect—but rather that strictly speaking they do not appear to have survived death at all but merely *a* death.

Certainly from the point of theology such demisurvival can be of little interest. As I understand the matter, people who have wished for and believed in the soul's survival of death have found both justification for and comfort in this belief because of some kind of change that would thereby be wrought in the soul. Whether in the context of popular theology or metaphysics, the doctrine of immortality has featured not simply as an attractive hypothesis in itself but also as providing a necessary apotheosis for a life which would otherwise be without reason or justice. If life ended with bodily death then the pains and injustices of life would render it pointless, but eternal life hereafter not only compensates for present discomforts but also supposedly gives life a rational justification which it would otherwise lack. Hick's heaven offers neither justification nor comfort. To all intents and purposes it is a replica of our present unhappy estate, without even the prospect of eternal sleep to assuage its unending course. He has in effect merely redescribed the situation from which the problem originally sprang.

There might appear to be some unfairness to Hick in this argument. It is true that his resurrection world is remarkably like our own, but he does make note of two distinctive features: firstly it is situated in a different space from our own such that it has no spatial connections with our world, and secondly its occupants are housed in bodies that are exact replicas of their pre-resurrection abodes with the one difference that they are no longer constituted of physical matter. But it is not very clear in what sense his world is really qualitatively different from our own, for the claim that our bodies are identical with our former ones except in the one respect that they are not made of physical matter, is not an obviously meaningful one. "Being physical" is not a property that can be added to or subtracted from entities like a coat of paint. However, one may suppose that Hick, were he to elaborate his picture a little more, would insist on further important differences, and in particular he would probably want to claim that in his resurrection world pain and death no longer have dominion. This would certainly be an improvement from the point of view of the believer, and appears to be perfectly conceivable.

However, on both points—pain and death—there are difficulties. As far as the elimination of death is concerned, an unending existence is not necessarily an improvement on our present one and might even, due to its unconscionable length, represent a considerable deterioration. Nor is it any more self-justifying, for the eternal perpetuation of life as we know it is open to as many of the pessimist's objections as our present finite existence. And as far as pain is concerned, "being painful," like "being physical," is not a property that can be added to or subtracted from the world while leaving everything else as it is. There is some sort of case here for physical pain, for while this undoubtedly serves the important biological function of a warning system, we can easily stretch our imaginations to inventing a more congenial arrangement. But on the other hand nonphysical pain—what we could more usefully call "suffering"—cannot be eliminated without incurring disastrous side-effects. What

I have in mind is something like this: suffering does not have a function relative to well-being in the way that physical pain does, for the concept of suffering is *logically* tied to various sorts of typically human activities, unlike pain which is contingently tied. Minimally, and roughly, we can say that being human involves the capacity to make rational choices, and these in turn combine the capacity to assess states of affairs and to assess one's attitudes, desires, needs, wants, and so forth in relation to these states of affairs. But to have choices open to one, and to be able to deliberate about these choices in the light of what one wants and what is the case, necessarily implies the following three possibilities: firstly that one's beliefs about what is the case may be mistaken, secondly that one's chosen course of action may fail to achieve its end, and thirdly that having got what one wanted one may find that it is no longer satisfactory or satisfying. In other words at least *some* forms of suffering are necessary for beings who make rational choices in a world more or less like our own.

Hick's model clearly cannot accommodate this difficulty. There is nothing in his account of the resurrection world which allows us to think of it as being free from suffering and hence as being in some way more acceptable than our present life. The mere elimination of pain, happy enough in itself, is inadequate, for when people have sought in an afterlife an assuagement of their condition, they have sought a much deeper transformation. Cosmic engineering, tinkering about with details here and there, leaves the fundamental facts of the human condition unchanged, and hence the problem for which immortality is the supposed solution is left untouched. Furthermore, those who have found earthly life a matter of anguish and regret have often discovered the source of their dissatisfaction at an even more fundamental level, namely in the fact that we live in a world in which things are transitory and which therefore cannot give us any grounds for complete and permanent satisfaction. Such satisfaction, it has been thought, can only be gained in a world where time does not cheat us of the goals of our activities and where the very striving for the satisfaction of our needs and wants has been stilled.

Whether this represents even a coherent fantasy cannot be decided here, but at any rate it is a viewpoint which appears to underlie the Christian "heaven" and the Buddhist "nirvana," and it does at any rate point to those features of our earthly existence which have underlain many people's dissatisfaction with it, features which remain unredeemed in Hick's resurrection world. To sum up, then: while Hick's model does not, on the face of it, at any rate, strain our notion of personal identity, he achieves this at the expense of merely reiterating the human condition for which presumably the resurrection world is a sketch of an answer.

These deficiencies are to some extent remedied in the more economically drawn portraits of survival. Thus, in Strawson's version, suffering as a factor necessarily involved in the transactions of human persons in a spatio-temporal world has largely been removed. There are no longer any things or persons to block my choices, and indeed very few choices that are still open to me to make. But on the other hand, as we have already noted, such an existence is not exactly an enviable one. Being able to dwell on one's memories presumably allows one to regret deeds one has done and also to regret that one can do nothing about the regret except simply to dwell upon it. At any rate, the possibility of suffering remains, as in the case of fully bodied existence, even if confined within narrower limits. In addition to this it is a singularly pointless existence, not one that could be considered in any way an apotheosis of earthly life, and it remains as unregenerate as the embodied life it has succeeded. One can imagine a ghostly Strawson longing for redemption from his memories and his passive experiences. But whether or not Strawson's account offers justification and comfort, there still remains the difficulty which must beset all thinly drawn portraits of survival—whether in terms of a pure ego, memory traces, stream of consciousness, intellect, will, or whatever—namely that they demand the bending to breaking point of our usual criteria of personal identity. Whether or not it can be shown that a set of disembodied faculties represents an improvement on their previous embodied form, it is not at all clear that we can speak of a human person experiencing, remembering, deciding, choosing, desiring, and perceiving unless he is endowed with a mobile and sensitive organism.

In considering the notion of survival after death we are therefore presented with the following paradox. Either we survive with our full kit of mental and physical characteristics in more or less the same kind of world as our own; or we carry over with us a flexible list of mental characteristics only. In neither case is the problem for which survival has been offered as a solution—the problem of providing a meaningful and happy apotheosis to a supposedly miserable and senseless existence—in neither case is it solved. The first solution merely restates, in a large measure, the problem; the second dissolves, in varying degrees, the being for whom it is supposedly a solution. Is there any *tertium quid*? Can we offer an account of survival which takes care of both prerequisites, which allows for *persons,* not shadows or memories, to survive, and which makes such survival worthwhile? In the next section we shall explore one such possible account.

Mystical Experience as a Model

The tentative solution that I shall put forward here is in terms of a certain kind of mystical experience. First it is necessary to explain how this notion is to be employed.

It might be tempting to propound a solution to the paradox of survival on the basis of the obvious flimsiness of the concept of a person, for is it not the case that at the boundaries of the concept we are accustomed to enjoy a certain amount of freedom of maneuver? Where fetuses, for example, or idiots, or split personalities are concerned, we do not have a readymade decision procedure for the application of the concept, and it might be argued that even though disembodied persons are not central cases of persons they are sufficiently close to such central cases to allow us to assimilate them to the class of persons. But clearly this will not do, for by implication it would allow us to extend quite arbitrarily any concept in any direction we wished. In general what is required for the proper extension of an empirical concept beyond its wonted domain is something like what Kant called a "schema." According to Kant—though we do not need to borrow the notion from him in all its details—a concept remains vacuous and empty until we produce in our imagination a schematic representation of it, thereby providing rules for the application of the concept. To mention one analogy, if Freud's only reason for extending the concepts of "motive," "intention," "desire," and so on, was that these concepts had no fixed boundaries, then his theory of the unconscious would rightly have been rejected as arbitrary. Clearly in order to justify his extended use of these terms it was necessary for him to describe, or at any rate to provide imaginary descriptions of, examples of human activity to which these concepts, hitherto not found to be applicable, could now properly be applied, and indeed much of his work is devoted to precisely this task. What is required in our present case is something similar to this. Obviously we cannot point to actual cases of disembodied persons in the way that Freud could (in a sense) point to cases of unconscious desire, but what we can do is to point to cases of an experience, familiar at least to some earthly denizens, which, though itself not that of a disembodied person, can provide a schematic image of it. It is in this role that I have cast mystical experience.

We must next specify what we mean by "mystical experience." Certainly a wide variety of types of experience has been denoted by this term, but as far as the present paper is concerned there is no need to mention any other feature of them than their variety, for we are here interested in only one sort, namely that which is typically described in terms of *oneness and harmony with the universe.* This kind of experience, which is reduplicated in a variety of different contexts, religious and nonreligious, Oriental and Western, takes its rise initially perhaps from a sense of alienation and separation of the individual from the world and from the sense of pain and anguish that arises therefrom. The type of mystical experience in question comes as a radical assuagement of this sense of alienation. The rift between the self and the world is sealed, the sense of separation along with its accompanying anguish and regret is attenuated, and the very multiplicity of the physical world itself appears to the mystic to be dissolved into oneness. In particular it is the sense of the separateness of things including oneself that disappears, to be replaced by a feeling of total unity, harmony, and tranquility. There are of course varying degrees of oneness and serenity. At its lowest level it can be seen in experiences that can hardly be termed "mystical" at all and which are probably enjoyed sometimes by everybody and frequently by some, namely the kind of experience that involves a close unity with other persons either through love or through some form of absorbing group activity. A more specifically mystical experience—though we would not always describe it as such—can arise in the context of aesthetic contemplation, when we may become so absorbed in listening to a piece of music or in contemplating an art work that all sense of time and of involvement in real life is momentarily lost. Most typically, of course, aesthetic mysticism is associated with the contemplation of and absorption in nature. So-called "nature mystics" are not difficult to find, and one could cite the names of Wordsworth, Rimbaud, and Proust as examples of men who, without benefit of religion, have enjoyed and subsequently described states of blissful absorption in nature. In such states it is quite common that the individual ceases to experience himself as a being separate from the world and imagines that in some way he is dissolved into the object of his contemplation. Thus Tennyson describes an experience in which, as he says,

> ... out of the intensity of the consciousness of individuality, individuality itself seemed to dissolve and fade away into boundless being, and this is not a confused state but the clearest beyond words ... where death was an almost laughable impossibility—the loss of personality (if so it were) seemed no extinction, but the only true life.[3]

The absorption of the self into nature and the loss of a sense of the multiplicity of things is frequently accompanied by a sense of timelessness, an experience that is sometimes described as the "timeless moment." For example, much of the *Four Quartets* of T. S. Eliot appears to be devoted to the attempt to capture this feeling in words. Thomas Mann in his novel, *The Magic Mountain*, was similarly preoccupied and attempts in the following passage a "description" of the timeless moment:

> We walk, walk. How long, how far? Who knows? Nothing is changed by our pacing, there is the same as here, once on a time the same as now, or then; time is drowned in the measureless monotony of space, motion from point to point is no motion more, where uniformity rules; and where motion is no more motion, time is no longer time.[4]

And in case these examples should appear to be contrived for the sake of art rather than accurate reportage of an experience, here is a quotation in which a nineteenth century nature mystic, Richard Jeffries, claims to describe one particular such experience:

> It is eternity now. I am in the midst of it. It is about me in the sunshine; I am in it, as the butterfly floats in the light-laden air. Nothing is to come: it is now. Now is by this tumulus, on earth, now; I exist in it.[5]

There are several strands that connect together experiences of this type. They involve an experience of oneness and a corresponding loss of a sense of multiplicity in space and time, an attenuation of the sense of dualism of subject and object, the lessening or loss of one's sense of one's own separate existence, a feeling of bliss and harmony that arises from the loss of all desires and regrets, and in particular a sense of detachment which nullifies all fear of pain and death. So far I have related these experiences only to nonreligious and nonmetaphysical contexts, but this collection of interconnected characteristics aptly describes also the experiences of certain religious mystics and saints. Let us take Buddhism as an obvious example. The so-called Buddhist path of enlightenment, which represents an attempt to nullify craving and desire, is seen as necessarily involving the overcoming of the sense of the multiplicity of things and a loss of the sense of one's separate existence in space and time. As long as the world appears to exist externally to oneself it will inevitably constitute an object of desire and hence of suffering, and only through the obliteration of this sense of mutual externality can desire and suffering be attenuated. Such a state of desirelessness and of oneness is termed by the Buddhists *"nirvana,"* a condition that is to be understood, not in terms of a cosmological theory, but rather in the light of certain meditative practices along with the mental and physical discipline required to achieve the appropriate contemplative state. It is a state that can be described as one of complete and blissful detachment both from a sense of one's own self and of the external world, achieved in the first place by sustained concentration on a particular object and later by the complete removal from one's mind of all particular thoughts and ideas. The mysticism of the Upanishads moves in a similar direction. Its famous dictum, "tat tvam asi" ("thou art that") sums up its denial of the reality of the self and the world and its affirmation of the ultimate oneness of things, knowledge of which is similarly the fruit of ascetic contemplation rather than of discursive thinking. Similar too is the Taoism of Lao-tze and Chuang-tze which developed independently of the Indian mystical tradition. Here too the central feature is the attainment of harmony and unity with the world through withdrawal and contemplation, "an inner experience," as one commentator has described it, "through which man and the universe interfuse as one."[6]

The West too has produced religious mystics who have given accounts of monistic experiences of a similar kind, but in the interests of economy I shall limit myself to two quotations, the first from Plotinus and the second from Meister Eckhart:

> The man is changed, no longer himself nor self-belonging; he is merged with the Supreme, sunken into It; only in separation is there duality ... no movement now, no passion, no outlooking desire; ... reason is in abeyance and intellection and even the very self; ... all the being calmed he turns neither to this side nor to that, nor even inwards towards himself; utterly resting he has become rest itself ...
>
> So long as the soul beholds forms ... or herself as something formed: so long is there imperfection in her. Only when all that is formed is cast off from the soul, and she sees the Eternal One alone, then the pure essence of the soul feels the naked unformed essence of the divine unity.... What a noble endurance is that where the essence of the soul suffers no suggestion or shadow of difference.... There she entrusts herself alone to the One, free from all multiplicity and difference, in which all limitation and quality is lost and is one. This One makes us blessed.[7]

Here, then, we have our schematic model. Its advantages are twofold. In the first place it allows us to speak of the unknown in terms of the known. It has always been a problem for metaphysicians to give sense to talk about matters which are in principle beyond direct empirical observation, and the suggestion I have put forward is that mystical experience does provide us with an imaginative schema, a "via analogica," by which we may come to understand some of this talk. We are therefore not quite at the extreme disadvantage that St. Paul imagined us to be when he lamented that "the eye hath not seen . . ." etc., for even though we have not seen the real stuff, we have—or some of us have—seen something like it. In this respect, of course, it is no better than the models of Hick and Strawson, for they too have tried to describe the unfamiliar in terms of the familiar, but, as I have suggested, this familiarity turns out in their cases to be a large disadvantage, for they either offer us the same course again, or a similar course with the spices removed. The latter point may appear also to work to the disadvantage of our *tertium quid,* for it too, though not standardly a repetition of a previous course, lacks spice. It is certainly not what many of the faithful look forward to in the afterlife, and here perhaps J. S. Mill was for once in tune with popular opinion when he admitted that the only reason for hoping for an afterlife lay in the possibility of being united with one's loved ones.

But herein lies the second and perhaps most important feature of our model for if, to put it crudely, the afterlife looks like a mystical experience, and if therefore it is devoid of all sense of space and of separate existences in space, and of all sense of before and after, and if therefore there can be no sense of hope or regret, no desiring or wanting, then all possibility of regretting or lamenting one's estate ceases. Not only are the conditions eliciting regret no longer present, but the very possibility of regretting anything at all has been removed. However pleasant the prospect of being reunited with Harriet, Mill has no guarantee that their love will last for all eternity, for even though their happiness might persist, the conditions for unhappiness must remain. The comfort of our new model, therefore, lies in the impossibility of discomfort, and its justification in the impossibility of ever requiring one. As Wittgenstein remarked: "The solution of the problem of life is seen in the vanishing of the problem."[8]

Objections

It is now time to consider some difficulties that the proposed model inevitably runs into. The first concerns the *language* of mystical experience. This can be approached at several levels, but undoubtedly one of the first criticisms to be voiced against the foregoing remarks is that the argument relies on a spurious similarity between a multitude of reported experiences. It is absurd, the critic might continue, to imagine that the reports of so-called mystical experiences are "pure" and objective. In fact, the language of such reports is thoroughly soaked in the doctrinal presuppositions of the reporters. There is something in this criticism that must be taken seriously, for if our *schematism* turned out to be wholly or even largely metaphysical or religious doctrine, then we would simply be begging the very question we set out to answer; it is necessary for our case that these reports should be as objective as such reports can be. But in fact they pass this test adequately enough. In the first place, as far as the Oriental examples cited are concerned, it is quite wrong to separate doctrine from experience, as if the one is learned intellectually first, as it were, and only subsequently confirmed by esoteric experience. In a sense the doctrine *is* the experience, for the experience is a necessary and a sufficient condition for understanding, the understanding itself not being *of* anything, but simply a state of tranquil detachment: there is nothing beyond that to know. It is true that cosmological theories have developed alongside the mystical tradition, but again it is probably a mistake to suppose that the mystical experiences came as a result of the cosmological theories. It is at least highly likely that the doctrines themselves were developed to explain the experiences and that the universal similarity of the latter helps to explain in turn the remarkable similarity between cosmological theories in diverse cultures. It should also be noted that we are relying not only on the reports of religious mystics but also on nature mystics who, though they may have no doctrinal baggage to carry along, nevertheless tell us stories which strikingly resemble those of their religious counterparts.

But still it might be urged that the argument goes wrong at a more fundamental level. Since mystical experience is not available to everyone there is no way for the detached observer to check the reports of mystics, and indeed in the last analysis the mystic appears to be going beyond the limits of what can meaningfully be said. This is a large issue and only a few brief remarks must suffice in reply. It is indeed true that the language employed by mystics to describe their experiences is pushed well to the edge of meaningfulness—as Eliot says, echoing the sentiments of many mystics themselves, "Words strain / Crack and sometimes break, under the burden."[9] But it would be incorrect to claim that their remarks were totally meaningless. No doubt we cannot appreciate fully what the mystic is trying to tell us unless we have trod the same path ourselves, but enough of what he is saying comes through to us to enable us to be tolerably certain that we would recognize the experience if it came our way. Not everything that he says is totally foreign to us, and as has already been pointed out there is no clean break between fairly common experiences of harmony and integration with the world at the one extreme and full-blown mystical experiences at the other.

For this reason the mystic's words contain a core of meaning for us. Of course his descriptions do not function in quite the way that ordinary empirical descriptions do, but what he has to say does enable us at least to *pinpoint* the experience, to place it in a certain framework and to relate it to others. This is borne out by the fact that there is a remarkable superficial resemblance between descriptions of esoteric experiences from radically diverse sources, and it would be odd if not contradictory to refuse to allow a corresponding resemblance between the experiences themselves. In other words, it is reasonable to conjecture that we are dealing here with a fairly universal feature of the human mind, namely the desire for peace, harmony, and the identification of oneself with the world, a desire which finds its highest expression in the feeling that all differences are illusory, that there is no time, no multiplicity, but that all things are really one. My claim is the minimal one that something answering to, or pinpointed by, this sort of description has been experienced by a representative collection of people.

Objections along the foregoing lines are not, I believe, particularly strong, and though they have been dealt with briefly we can now pass on to some more powerful ones. It will no doubt have struck the reader that the mystical model is remarkably thin and sketchy by our own standards, and that therefore it ought reasonably to succumb to the same criticisms that were leveled at the Strawson model. For is it not the case that we too are allowing mere shadows—if that—to pass through death's needle eye, rather than anything that could recognizably be called a "person," let alone the "same" person who existed in a previous life? No doubt we have described a condition which represents a considerable improvement on our earthly existence. It is a state which could plausibly be called blissful (mystics have certainly thought of it as such), in which death, suffering, and indeed any vicissitude whatsoever can be of no consequence, and hence provides the comfort and justification lacking in the other models. But at the same time it looks as if we have so described this blissful condition that *persons* can no longer be sensibly described as participating in it, for one of the necessary conditions for the enjoyment of this blissful state is the attenuation of one's sense of separate existence and the feeling of absorption into some larger whole. A somewhat drastic solution to life's problems!

There are several answers that we can sketch to this objection. The first, and perhaps least telling, answer is that, typically, mystics themselves do not look upon suicide as an alternative to "nirvana," for there would be little point in undergoing a long and difficult process in self-discipline if the same result could be achieved in a moment by means of a bare bodkin. As Schopenhauer once remarked in this connection, "The cool shades of Orcus allure him only with the false appearance of a haven of rest." More telling than this, though, is the fact that in his descriptions and reports a mystic usually ascribes his experiences to *himself,* and is grateful for the favor done to *him,* rather than to the One, or to the World Soul, or to a corpse. And further they are not only described as *his,* but as his *experiences,* and this would make no sense unless we suppose them to be the experiences of someone, and this "someone" must surely be the person describing them. When a man sets himself the task of acquiring a state of indifference and absorption, he looks forward to achieving this state for *himself,* not for someone or something else.

But there are more important considerations that can be brought in defense of our argument. It is true that the vocabulary of mystics sometimes suggests extinction both of the self and of the world, and for this reason *inter alia* mysticism has often been stigmatized as "negative" or "nihilistic." But this attitude rests on a mistake. The Zen Buddhists, for example, who have frequently had the "nihilistic" label attached to them, have considered the attainment of what they call "self-sustaining independence," not as a weary escape from a life of pain and evil, but as an attempt to experience life more abundantly. The Taoist mystics have likewise believed that in our ordinary everyday attachments to ourselves and to the objects surrounding us we become dead to the value and beauty of things, and that this value and beauty only becomes a reality for us when we have achieved tranquil unity with nature. Furthermore, only in such a state, according to the Taoists, when a man is totally emptied of himself and of his sense of the separateness of things, only then can the full powers of artistic creation in a man be released.

These do not of course reflect the views of all mystics by any means, but it is at least one representative view that mysticism is not a negation but rather some kind of affirmation of the self, the development of one's "real" or "true" self rather than its destruction. The whole vocabulary of "release," "enlightenment," and so forth, which is so typical of this form of mysticism, helps to confirm this view. To the outsider, indeed, the mystic may appear to be as good as dead, but from his own point of view the mystic has moved not from life to death but in the reverse direction. As he now sees the world, it is in ordinary experience, with its "enslavement" to the self and to particular objects, that we live a kind of twilight existence, not in the state of mystical transport where, on the contrary, he claims to have found a more fully real life. This is a view that has been maintained, as we might expect, by Christian mystics as well. Meister Eckhart, for example, who explicitly compares the mystical experience with the beatific vision, maintains that such an experience involves at one and the same time a kind of identification with God and also an affirmation of the life of the individual.[10] We can ignore the fact that this is skating over very thin logical and theological ice, for our only concern here is to show that, as far as the quality of the mystical experience itself goes, the sense of oneness of all things does not appear to exclude the sense of one's own personal identity. Rather, on the contrary, in certain forms of mysticism the two appear to be necessary concomitants of one another.

There is one final problem, which has already been mentioned in passing. It has been argued that an immortal existence, conceived in accordance with the model of a certain kind of monistic experience, not only allows us to talk sensibly of personal survival, but also offers a plausible solution to the "problem of life" with which the doctrine of personal survival has traditionally been closely tied. But one might well wonder whether the faithful, on being proffered the hope of an afterlife that resembled the athletic and forbidding heights of asceticism, might no longer regard it as worth the effort. John Stuart Mill probably speaks for the average believer when he imagines the life to come as a continuation of all that is best in the present one. However, what the foregoing argument has tried to show is that such a conception of survival is misconceived on two counts: firstly that it must necessarily contain the suffering which it was designed to expel, and secondly that it does not represent any rational apotheosis of earthly existence. The only model which fulfills these requirements, and at the same time offers some semblance of a solution to the personal identity problem, is the one wrought from the materials of monistic experience. No doubt the believer will believe what he likes, but this model represents the only account which is fully consistent with the requirements of the problem for which it has traditionally been the solution.

Of course, it could still be argued that I am simply offering a solution to a problem of my own making, and since the believer's problem may be a different one—for example he may not be concerned about what I have called a "rational apotheosis"—he need not be concerned with my solution. In addition, the philosopher who has considered this question may also wonder whether he needs to tie down his discussion to problems concocted elsewhere: like the believer, he may surely set his own tasks. As far as the believer's objection is concerned it could be replied that if his notion of survival is to be anything more than blithely mythological then the problem as well as the solution must meet up to certain requirements. If the problem is posed simply as one of survival, then something like Hick's resurrection world will do, but such survival, which largely reduplicates earthly life and offers no fundamental transformation of the human condition, would represent an amusing fantasy but hardly anything of importance for philosophy or religion. And similarly for the philosopher's objection, obviously he can set his own problem and proceed to solve it, but if he deals with it as simply a question of logical possibility and nothing more—and this often *is* the manner of treatment—then his problem has no more claim on our attention than any of the other infinite number of questions of logical possibility that could be raised. If philosophical questions are in any obvious sense of the term "serious" ones, then the problem of personal survival of death must be treated as part of a more general issue that has been at the heart of religious and metaphysical thinking.

NOTES

1. "Religious Statements as Factually Significant," in *The Existence of God* (New York: Macmillan, 1964).
2. *Individuals* (London: Methuen, 1959), pp. 115-16.
3. Quoted from R. C. Zaehner, *Mysticism Sacred and Profane* (Oxford, 1957), pp. 36-37.
4. From the chapter "By the Ocean of Time." Translation by H. T. Lowe-Porter.
5. Zaehner, *op. cit.*, p. 47. F. C. Happold has collected together a number of descriptions of the experience of the 'timeless moment' in his book, *Mysticism* (London, 1963).
6. Chang Chung-yuan, *Creativity and Taoism* (New York, 1963), ch. V.
7. Quoted from C. J. Ducasse, *A Philosophical Scrutiny of Religion* (New York, 1953), p. 283; and Rudolph Otto, *Mysticism East & West* (New York, 1957), p. 59, respectively.
8. *Tractatus*, 6.521.
9. T. S. Eliot, from *Burnt Norton*, said about the problem of describing an atemporal state.
10. Otto, *op. cit.*, p. 210-11 and ch. IV.

EIGHTH SYMPOSIUM

PHILOSOPHY, SCIENCE AND PSYCHICAL RESEARCH: OPENING NOTE
  Peter A. French

RATIONAL ACCEPTABILITY OF THE CASE FOR PSI
  J. B. Rhine

SCIENCE AND THE SUPERNATURAL
  George Price

"Why sometimes I've believed as many as six impossible things before breakfast"

PHILOSOPHY, SCIENCE AND PSYCHICAL RESEARCH: OPENING NOTE

Peter A. French

We have come full circle back to the problem which opened this book: what is the status of psychical research and what relationship should it have to the recognized disciplines of science and philosophy? We have seen that many of the phenomena investigated by psychical researchers can only be accounted for if we suspend some of our basic certainties—*C-2 certainties*—and that such a suspension seemingly suspends us as well over a canyon of doubt and indecision because our life line conceptions of truth and falsity and rationality are tied to our certainties. There seem to be only two alternatives. First we may attempt to explain all forms of psychical phenomena in terms of our traditional categories of rationality and in so doing the field of psychical research will eventually be subsumed into the recognized sciences. There might, of course, remain a few ragged edges, but the hope would surely prevail that someday they will also fit nicely into our conception of normal science.

The second alternative is a revolutionary one. If the evidence is unimpeachable (albeit a rather big "if"), then we must squarely face the need to replace some of our traditional certainties with others more consistent with experience, certainties which we have been discussing as the philosophical concepts which underlie the wonderland world in which psychical researchers work. It is to this latter alternative that the following comments apply. They are made in a Presidential Address to the Society for Psychical Research in 1913 by the famous philosopher Henri Bergson:

> Behind the prejudices of some, the mockery of others, there is, present and invisible, a certain metaphysic unconscious of itself,—unconscious and therefore inconsistent, unconscious and therefore incapable of continually remodeling itself on observation and experience as every philosophy worthy of the name must do,—that, moreover, this metaphysic is natural, due at any rate to a bent contracted long ago by the human mind, and this explains its persistence and popularity....
>
> Just because "psychical research" cannot proceed like physics and chemistry, they conclude it is not scientific; and as the "psychical phenomenon" has not yet taken a simple and *abstract* form which would make it accessible to the laboratory, they are pleased to declare it unreal. Such, I think, is the "subconscious" reasoning of some men of science.[1]

NOTES

1. Reprinted in *Mind-Energy*, translated by Wildon Carr (New York: Henry Holt and Co., 1920), pp. 77 and 82.

RATIONAL ACCEPTABILITY OF THE CASE FOR PSI

J. B. Rhine

In the establishment of scientific discoveries in natural science there are discernible stages. Even though the process as a whole may well be one continuous development from original question to accepted conclusion, the character of the procedure changes sufficiently in its course that it can profitably be subdivided for discussion and better understanding.... We have already discussed two broad divisions of this general procedure of scientific investigation. The first of these was the exploratory stage characterized by the search for trial answers or working hypotheses to solve the problem in hand. The second stage was identified with the devices of testing the reliability of the working hypotheses developed in the earlier probings. It was shown that this verification division of the larger program of research is featured by the effort to design crucial experiments, to establish and confirm factual relations against the possibility of all alternatives relative to the problem.

At the end of the discussion..., a third stage in the scientific acquisition of knowledge was introduced. This stage involves the task of clothing the new discovery with a proper and presentable rationale adequate to making it acceptable to scientists in general. To leave a newly found fact on the doorstep of science without any evidence of the relationship it may have to already familiar knowledge of Nature is not enough at this stage of confidence in scientific method to win consideration for it by the average scientist. He is likely to regard the stranger as illegitimate and to use one of the numerous devices of the mind for avoiding recognition of it.

The preceding stage of verification should, it is true, develop an adequately controlled and really crucial experiment; and when, in addition to this, there is also independent confirmation of such an experiment, the confirmed finding should ideally be regarded by all as an established fact. But when a basically new advance is made that comes into conflict with prevailing theory, a further step of *rational* confirmation is always needed for eventual acceptance of the conclusions.

The reason for this third stage in the establishment of a fact is that the whole procedure of science is made up of a series of observations, judgments, and interpretations that are human and potentially subject to error. It is very reassuring, therefore, if the new result is consistent with logical expectation. On the other hand, the more the new conclusion seems to contradict current thinking, the more important and prolonged becomes the third stage of making it rationally understandable. While experimental confirmation eliminates most of the uncertainty associated with the personal conduct of the research concerned, it still leaves to rational synthesis the need to remove whatever intellectual blocks confront the new conclusions.

It is a function of the problem-solving operation of science, then, not merely to introduce and verify a new fact but to install it, as it were, in the rational setting in which it must work harmoniously with the other facts of Nature to which it is related. This does not mean that the new fact must conform to the old beliefs, opinions, and untested doctrines of the professional group concerned. To require the squaring of empirical facts with existing beliefs is a rank violation of the scientific way of inquiry. It is, however, a very different matter to buttress the new discovery with a supporting rationale of internal self-consistency and to stabilize its unsteady novelty with interrelationships with the groundwork of surrounding knowledge.

Any rational approach to the phenomenon of psi should first take account of the important historical fact that the psi researches arose out of no mere speculative claim promoted by a professional group or philosophical cult. The psi hypothesis grew out of reports of spontaneous human experiences coming from various cultures and from a wide range of types of individuals within a culture. These personal experiences of psi, when collected and classified, clearly justified serious consideration and study. In almost any other field of research such evidence would be given great weight and credibility. The present argument is that scientifically psi has a much stronger case because it rests on the experimental verification of a hypothesis derived from the study of widespread reports of human behavior than it would have had if a purely speculative invention had been the subject of investigation.

Parapsychology is, in fact, unique in the dual character of its method of investigation; that is, in the degree to which it has developed from parallel and mutually supporting lines of evidence—the case study line on the one hand and experimental tests on the other. It has thus been possible to make comparisons back and forth from one method to the other and acquire an added measure of reassurance from this type of confirmation. The same types of psi phenomena, for example, that have been verified experimentally are precisely those which have been manifested in the collections of case reports. Thus telepathy, clairvoyance, precognition, and psychokinesis as types of psi occurrences have a double order of support.

The case studies and the experimental tests have also supported each other with regard to some of the general characteristics of the psi phenomena. Both, for example, show independence of psi from time and space, both indicate unconsciousness of the psi operation, and both suggest a similar relationship of psi to motivation. For the most part, it is true, the use of case studies has been limited to the exploratory stage of the investigation. It was mainly from them that the hypotheses originated which later received experimental confirmation, but this will not likely be as much so in the future as the experimental work advances.

The experimental evidence itself divides easily into a number of main types, and this further diversification of the supporting material introduces new angles of relationship and very considerably reinforces the total impressiveness of the case. (All this is, of course, in addition to the great accumulation of just plain evidence of high scoring in the tests.) For example, it turns out to be quite common in psi experiments that the scoring rate declines in the run or in some other unit of the subject's performance. Statistical examination of these declines shows extrachance effects produced in this declining tendency alone. In other words, here is a secondary effect supporting the primary one, a phenomenon within the principal evidence of the phenomenon. These declines, moreover, lend themselves to rational explanation quite as well as do those of general psychology (memory curves, learning gradients, and the like) though the explanation is not necessarily the same.

When by the evidence a secondary discovery concerning psi is forced upon the experimenter and when it comes as a complete surprise, it has added value in making the phenomenon seem more objective and convincing. We may take the psi-missing tendency as an example. This tendency of some subjects under certain conditions to miss the target to a significant degree came as a wholly unexpected experimental result. It was, however, not difficult to find plausible explanations for such a tendency once it had been recognized and especially once it was also realized that subjects are wholly unconscious of the functioning of the psi process. It was understandable that a subject could direct his effort toward the card sequence serving as the target order without always being able to exercise enough control to keep from consistently giving the wrong responses to the target cards. In such a case, the more effectively he used psi the more consistently he missed the target. This curious evidence of "psi perversity" peculiarly well meets the rational need felt by some skeptics for test results to counteract the possibility that motivated errors on the part of the experimenter could account for the results.

Other variations of this unconsciously misguided aim of the psi function could be listed. The most conspicuous evidence of this is to be noted in the work of Soal and Goldney on displacement; that is, on the tendency of the subject to give a response corresponding to the target preceding or following the one intended. The consistent way in which this displacement occurred—for example, the fact that it was limited to one direction (forward or backward) with a given agent or sender and the fact that with one and only one sender did it spread both to forward and backward directions—gives a distinctly lawful appearance to the aberration. A number of other features and variations extend this concept of the orderliness in the working of ESP in the tests. No better example of this could be given than the regular way in which displacement, in the Soal and Goldney experiment just mentioned, extended to the second card ahead and the second behind the intended target when the speed of testing was accelerated. Such variation of performance with test condition provides a high grade of rational confirmation of the experimental results. The displacement effect, too, was as much of a surprise to the experimenter as it was unintentional on the part of the subject.

It adds a great deal to the reasonableness of the case for psi that there have been a number of persistent individual peculiarities of performance which were characteristic of special subjects. The peculiar limitation of the displacement effect to certain individuals constitutes a case in point. On this principle of individual differences it should be expected that a difference great enough to show significance should be found in scoring rates between the different personality classifications if the personality characteristics of the subject could be measured and correlated with performance in psi tests. Accordingly, it has now been well established that certain roughly measurable attitudes and personality traits and states have some connection with the subject's performance in the tests. It does appear that these personality correlates largely exert their effect, not in determining how long at a time or how effectively psi will function, but rather in determining whether or not a subject's response will be one of psi-hitting or psi-missing. At least there is evidence of a significant relation between personality measurements and success in psi tests. Moreover, this evidence indicates that psi interoperates in some way and degree with the more familiar elements of personality. This evidence adds a firmer rational quality to the case for psi as well as a better understanding of its role in the total personality.

Perhaps for many inquirers who look into parapsychology the effect of introducing interferences into the test situation will carry a supplementary measure of rational conviction. The drug experiments (for example, those with sodium amytal) will be especially to the point, but of closely similar bearing are those in which distracting psychological conditions were introduced, such as the effect of boredom or deliberate distraction of attention. It should be no less important, however, to consider along with these interfering states all that is known about the conditions especially favorable to high scoring, such as the use of rewards and playful competition.

Along with the evidence of individual peculiarities and the special conditions, there are certain more general features to be considered as a part of the rational concept of psi. Some of these, such as the unconsciousness of the function, we have already mentioned. The very consistency of this characteristic is remarkable, particularly if one considers the frequency of exceptions to generalizations about nature, especially in psychology. Psi has remained thus far an irrecoverably unconscious process and the research has revealed no exceptions. There is the same extraordinary consistency, too, in the evidence of the nonphysical character of psi. There simply has not been found any limiting relationship between the physical conditions and the test performance. This nonphysical quality becomes, then, a defining feature and the unexceptional lawfulness indicates that the boundary is no mere arbitrary one, as so many academic divisions of nature are. There is, therefore, a comparatively deep and important division between the phenomena on the two sides of the boundary. This distinction must be made, however, without any implication that the division is an absolute one.

The spontaneous, elusive, and uncontrolled character of the psi function is another of its most consistent features. In fact, this is probably more invariable than has been realized generally among parapsychology students themselves; it has been a difficult fact to accept. It is doubtful, however, if within the period of recorded history of the human species psi has ever been anything but elusive and uncontrolled. If any individual ever lived who could control psi, he surely would have been so elevated above the level of his fellows that a record of his unusual life story would have become a familar part of human history. Not even any of the great religious leaders lived lives that suggest anything approaching an unlimited control of psi capacity. As has often been pointed out, however, the suggestion is that they may either have had an unusual range of exercise of it, or a special ability to use it wisely and to advantage.

It adds greatly to one's appreciation of psi to know the weakness of its real antagonist, the philosophy of materialism. The situation is actually not a little preposterous since that philosophy is based on no factual evidence whatever. There has, of course, never been any crucial experimental test of the hypothesis of materialism other than the experiments of parapsychology and they have conclusively disproved it. Consequently there is no evidence for the other side of the issue which the psi hypothesis would have to refute. The case for materialism simply collapses in the face of the evidence against it from parapsychology.

The opposition of common sense to the case for psi is on similarly shaky ground, even in confronting that most puzzling problem, precognition. The fact is, practically all of the main discoveries of science have been in violation of the common sense of their day. Common sense catches up only as new discoveries themselves become converted into general knowledge and opinion. It is true, if causation properly applies to psi at all, the researches have produced results that seem to call for causation of a wholly new kind. In precognition it would appear that the order of causation is reversed and the perception precedes the event. This is not the first instance, of course, in which science has produced conflicts that seemed at the time to be unresolvable. The proper procedure in such cases is to suspend judgment until further knowledge is acquired by which to see the problem in a setting that will permit understanding.

The amount of internal consistency within the evidence for psi is of great importance to any appraisal of its entire value or meaning. On this aspect the case is especially strong. There has been found, for instance, no peculiarity of ESP of the telepathic type (except individual subject preferences and differences) that does not hold for clairvoyant ESP as well—that is, beyond the mere difference of targets, which distinguishes the two phenomena. Nothing has been discovered about precognition except the aspect of time that is not correspondingly true of contemporaneous ESP. Even in PK, except for a lower level of scoring rate and the nature of the test itself, there is nothing essentially peculiar. So the parapsychologist is naturally led to the working hypothesis that there is but one basic psi function underlying all the effects. It is even difficult and almost impossible sometimes to distinguish sharply and finally between these aspects of the manifestation of psi, so well-integrated is all of the experimental evidence. Neither do the various kinds of secondary evidence show any distinction between types of psi. All stand equally clear of physical involvement, all are equally unconscious, and all require subject motivation in a similar degree. The psychological conditions affecting one kind of psi affect all others similarly. This internal harmony of relationship is shown already even at this early stage of development of the field.

The supreme rational test for a new discovery consists of the success attainable in fitting it into the structure of related knowledge. Psi has passed this test as far as it has been possible to apply it. There is no real conflict between psi and the science of physics simply because physics has no franchise on the kind of phenomena with which parapsychology deals. Physicists, fortunately, have been the first to recognize this fact. That psi phenomena and physical phenomena are both a part of a larger universe it is hardly necessary even to state. If there were not some larger unity, one could not conceive how there could be interaction and the interconversion of causal influence that is involved in the subject-object reaction with which experiments in parapsychology deal.

It is entirely conceivable therefore that new and as yet unsuspected ways of looking at the relationship between physical and psi processes will have to be found. It is possible even that current ways of reasoning may have to be amended. It seems wise, in the meantime, to continue with the logical course that has been most useful in the study of nature at least until it is clearly necessary to leave it; and thus far in dealing with psi phenomena it has been rationally possible to use the concept of causality most of the way. Doing so requires the assumption for the time being of a cause, an active principle or energy, operating between subject and object, even in the extremely puzzling case of precognition. The supposition of a psychic energy, however, has often been made by general psychologists before, but until parapsychology demonstrated the presence of an extraphysical function in man, the assumption of a mental energy was never a *necessary* one. The materialist could always argue that perhaps some combination of the physical energies of the brain would suffice. Now it is known that the hypothesis of a mental energy is required.

The reasoning at this point must necessarily still be speculative, but it is pointing a way that empirical test can and will have to follow. Moreover, once a causal but nonphysical operation underlying psi effects is assumed and once a psychic energy is inferred, a theoretical basis for a tentative discussion of the place of psi phenomena in the natural order is available. Psi evidently is a mediating, energetic operation between the subject and his environment, one that supplements the sensorimotor system. Assuming a causal relation then, it is logical to invoke the Law of Reaction and, given the fact of a subjective perception of an object by ESP, to "predict" the psychokinetic effect upon an object by a properly motivated subject. And that effect the PK research has demonstrated in the case of moving objects (dice, etc.). Thus, even while leaving some first-rate problems still to be solved, the integration of ESP and PK as phenomenal aspects of an underlying causal subject-object relation is made considerably more understandable by the psychic energy hypothesis.

For the rational critic of psi, the most difficult phenomenon to cope with is that of precognition. It will help a great deal to remember, however, that natural science grew up on the basis of sense data and their derivatives, and those data are sensorially mediated experiences of the physical world. In the very nature of the case the laws of physics limit the operation of sense perception; and in this circular nature of the whole development of science the scientist has fallen into the habit of thinking that the world derived from sense data represents the total universe. That world is defined in terms of time, space, and mass. Sense data would have to depend on energies thus conditioned; ESP data would not. Precognition is, therefore, a *reasonable* aspect of psi function, just as it seems quite unreasonable to the physicalistic habit of mind which all students of science have acquired.

When we attempt to integrate psi with general psychology there is only one major distinction to be made. Psi, in both its ESP and PK aspects, is fundamentally different from the sensorimotor system of the organism in the fact just mentioned: that the sensorimotor functions are physically limited and intermediated. The operations of ESP and PK are not. Psi phenomena are unconscious. Sensory functions are primarily conscious, at least in man, and though often only marginally conscious or even subconscious, they are apparently never unrecallably unconscious. ESP, on the other hand, seems to be unconscious beyond recovery. There are, of course, many other sensorially imperceptible and unconscious operations in nature, some of them that actually affect the organism. Thus far all that are known are recognizedly physical, but possibly no other kind would have been recognized.

If, now, we assume the existence of a psychic energy that is not subject to the limitations of space, time, and mass, it is logical to assume further that unlike the known physical energies, it would not be sensorially perceptible or capable of producing directly conscious effects. It should be expected, rather, to have its own distinctly peculiar principles of operation and conditions of functioning. We may well inquire about the properties and functions of such an energy, how it interconverts, for example, to effects that are capable of crossing the threshold of the consciousness of the subject, and how it interoperates with an object that is the target of ESP or PK. But these are questions for the experimental researches of the future, for general psychology, for physics, for neurology, as well as for parapsychology.

The greater share of the mystery of the nature of psi is still left, to be sure. So far as showing consistency in what is already known is concerned, however, parapsychology does comparatively well—as well, it is safe to say, as any other frontier branch of the natural sciences. If psi is not inhibited by material barriers, if a thought as well as an object will serve as the target, if a present object as well as a future one can serve as the target to be perceived, and if an object can be perceived as well as influenced in its fall, then all of these operations at least take place within a consistent rational framework of nonphysical causation. Since they do not follow physical law they could not be expected to be sensorially perceived; if they do not follow spatial limitations they ought not to be expected to follow time; but since they do interoperate with the physical system they can be studied not only by objective methods but with quantitative measures as well.

More than half of the rational difficulty of the average student of science facing so new a phenomenon as psi is caused by sheer unfamiliarity with an unconventional concept. This effect of familiarity can best be appreciated if one starts inquiring into the explanation of his own simplest everyday experiences. Let him begin with the moment he awakes in the morning. Let him ask himself, what does it mean that he is awake? What really is sleep itself? Not physiologically but psychologically. If he answers that it means he is conscious, he is only rephrasing the question. He may go on describing his mental activity as that which constitutes being conscious. His words, however, are mere translation. He can never get far beyond the initial unanalyzed fact that he is conscious and knows it. He will remain unable to put it in any more elemental or original explanatory terms. Such a rational inquirer, then, coming back to a psi phenomenon, can comfort himself that familiarity, which is at least partially attainable through study and practice, will dissipate a large share of what appears at first to be a more serious difficulty.

It prepares the anxious skeptic very considerably for a better appreciation of the evidence for psi to recognize that, after two thousand years of the philosophy of materialism and a good century and a half of the popular promotion of it, it has still not been deliberately and systematically applied to social institutions, except through the arbitrary force of a communist dictatorship. It is valid to argue that if there be an essential truth in a philosophy, then to allow it to flow into the educational currents of the time should permit it to find its way to justification through use. But in spite of the preponderance of materialistic thinking in connection with the science of the last two centuries, this philosophy has never taken hold in any culture except through enforcement by military power and political intrigue. Thus, in blocking the acceptance of the psi discoveries as it has, this philosophy of physical monism has not had the support either of experimental fact or of practical experience.

In brief, then, psi appears to have a strong, supporting rationale. Its only opposition comes from an untested assumption. It is based on a system of evidence of varied, complex, and consistent character. Its lawfulness has been revealed in many facets of its study, showing interrelationships that reinforce its reliability. It supplements, rather than conflicts with, the science of physics; and with an inferred psychic energy to account for its effects, it integrates with the nature of the universe and of man with no difficulties which would seem insurmountable to future research. The essential mystery of psi, which should not be minimized, is the great mystery of all mental life as such. What, indeed, is this conscious (and unconscious) willing, thinking, feeling system of operations, this mind that is pursuing the question of psi itself? Whatever that mind may, in all its rational ramifications, turn out to be, psi is an integral part of it firmly united now by the strong network of interrelationships that makes a science sound and reassuring.

SCIENCE AND THE SUPERNATURAL

George Price

Believers in psychic phenomena—such as telepathy, clairvoyance, precognition, and psychokinesis—appear to have won a decisive victory and virtually silenced opposition. Many other times during the past century such victory has seemed close, as evidence for the supernatural has been produced that has been found convincing by some of the world's leading scientists. But always on previous occasions, other investigators have made criticisms or conducted new tests, thereby demonstrating flaws in the evidence. What is unique about the present is that, during the last 15 years, scarcely a single scientific paper has appeared attacking the work of the parapsychologists.

This victory is the result of an impressive amount of careful experimentation and intelligent argumentation. The best of the card-guessing experiments of Rhine and Soal show enormous odds against chance occurrence, while possibility of sensory clues is often eliminated by placing cards and percipient in separate buildings far apart. Dozens of experimenters have obtained positive results in ESP experiments, and the mathematical procedures have been approved by leading statisticians.[1]

I suspect that most scientists who have studied the work of Rhine (especially as it is presented in *Extra-Sensory Perception After Sixty Years*[2]) and Soal (described in *Modern Experiments in Telepathy*[3]) have found it necessary to accept their findings. Concerning the latter book, a reviewer has written: "If scientists will read it carefully, the 'ESP controversy' will be ended."[4] Against all this evidence, almost the only defense remaining to the skeptical scientist is ignorance concerning the work itself and its implications. The typical scientist contents himself with retaining in his memory some criticism that at most applies to a small fraction of the published studies. But these findings (which challenge our very concepts of space and time) are—if valid—of enormous importance, both philosophically and practically, so they ought not to be ignored.

Practical Application for Extrasensory Perception

A common belief concerning ESP experimentation is that the results are interesting but are of small importance because of the great inaccuracy of perception. For example, Boring writes in a discussion of Soal's work: "You see a 'brilliant' performance in telepathy is not so very striking after all. It is only 7 out of 25 instead of 5 out of 25. When people ask why these able percipients do

This selection is reprinted from *Science*, Vol. 122 (1955), 359-67. Used by permission of the editor and George Price.

not get rich by telepathing directors' meetings and playing the stock market with their superior knowledge, they do not know how small an advantage the best available telepathy of the modern age provides."[5]

But card guessing by ESP, inaccurate though it is, nevertheless is a communication system by which information is transmitted. In the terminology of Shannon's "Mathematical Theory of Communication," it is a case of a *discrete communication channel with noise*, "noise" representing whatever it is that causes errors.[6] Information theory is unequivocal in showing that any system that has a finite capacity for transmitting information can (if we employ proper coding) transmit with any degree of accuracy we may desire—say, as accurately as by telegraph, or more accurately—although it may take a long time to transmit a small amount of information with high accuracy.

In an ESP experiment where 6 hits are made in a run of 25, the channel capacity is about 0.0069 bits per trial; while 7 hits corresponds to 0.026 bits per trial, or 0.66 bits for a run of 25 trials.[7] This means that (if each trial takes only a few seconds) information can be transmitted at a rate of several bits per hour and as accurately as by telegraph. Thus this appears to be a solution to problem No. 449 of the National Inventors' Council, which involves "the development of a revolutionary new method of transmitting intelligence." Since ESP is independent of distance and requires no equipment (except possibly a watch for synchronization), it should be a most convenient means for transmitting information from an espionage agent in the Soviet Union directly to Washington or London.

Soal considers that there must be a selected human "sender" to aid in transmitting information, in addition to a selected percipient; but Rhine believes that a good percipient can percieve by clairvoyance in the absence of any sender as well as receive telepathically from virtually any person. Therefore, according to the findings of either Rhine or Soal, the suggestion made in the preceding paragraph is a fully practical one; but if Rhine's work is valid, then there are additional applications of enormously greater importance. In particular, while Soal has evidence that ESP may penetrate a few seconds into the future, Rhine has performed experiments of considerable ingenuity that show (in his opinion) that information concerning ESP cards can be received from as far as 10 days in the future.[8]

The general means for transmitting information accurately over a noisy channel is to send messages of high *redundancy*; that is, the information is repeated over and over again (in properly coded form) within the message. But events of great importance may be thought of as messages of high redundancy. Thus a nuclear bomb explosion would tell its story with enormous redundancy in terms of each of the hundreds of buildings destroyed and of the thousands of people killed (in excess of normal mortality). This suggests that ESP can be used for such purposes as accurate forecasting of a major catastrophe—assuming that Rhine's findings are valid. And this will be especially true if it is possible to use many percipients working simultaneously to increase accuracy.

Let us design a procedure to give a ten-day warning of a nuclear bomb explosion. ESP card designs are used, to make conditions closely similar to those

Rhine employed in his precognition experiments. Cards are prepared that will react to the thermal flash of nuclear explosion, so that the initial design will be bleached and a second design will develop. The cards are placed inside cameras with open shutters, surrounding a likely target area and directed upon various portions of the area. The cards are guarded and their symbols are kept secret. Each day several thousand selected percipients try to guess card symbols ten days ahead. Guesses are analyzed in terms of each of the two possible correct symbols for each card.

If card symbols have been properly randomized, then, in the absence of ESP, there will be no statistically significant pattern in the relationship between guesses and possible correct symbols. Thus, it will be virtually impossible to have a false alarm if ESP is not operating. Therefore, there will be strong presumption that there should be prompt evacuation, if some day, for cards corresponding to some contiguous area, guesses show a statistically significant relationship involving the initial symbols.

Does this suggestion seem absurd? No. If information theory and Rhine's conclusions are both valid, this is a practical suggestion of high importance. Such a warning system would be far more effective and less expensive than radar. To be sure, it is true that Rhine's evidence for precognition is not so much in the form of large numbers of correct guesses, but rather it depends on certain statistical abnormalities in the pattern of correct guesses. But in general, any relationship between cards and guesses that is so highly improbable that it constitutes evidence for ESP can be made use of for transmission of information. And even if there is only ten-percent probability that Rhine's findings are valid, it is still the clear duty of appropriate government officials to investigate this possibility promptly and thoroughly.

Furthermore, contemporaneous clairvoyance can also be put to work in many ways. For example, the arrangement of ore in a vein provides a form of redundancy plus a means of checking against guesses not based on ESP—provided that we exercise a little ingenuity in the way we set up the guessing procedure.

In short, it appears that wherever parapsychology can yield extrachance results, we can find a way to put it to practical use.

Improbability of the Supernatural

Now it happens that I myself believed in ESP about 15 years ago, after reading *Extra-Sensory Perception After Sixty Years*, but I changed my mind when I became acquainted with the argument presented by David Hume in his chapter, "Of miracles," in *An Enquiry Concerning Human Understanding*.

Hume's argument runs as follows: "A miracle is a violation of the laws of nature; and as a firm and unalterable experience has established these laws, the proof against a miracle, from the very nature of the fact, is as entire as any argument from experience can possibly be imagined.... No testimony is sufficient to establish a miracle, unless the testimony be of such a kind that its falsehood would be more miraculous than the fact which it endeavours to establish...."

Hume illustrated as follows the spirit in which he thought his argument should be employed: "You would in vain object to me the difficulty, and almost impossibility, of deceiving the world in an affair of such consequence . . . with the little or no advantage . . . from so poor an artifice: all this might astonish me; but I would still reply that the knavery and folly of men are such common phenomena, that I should rather believe the most extraordinary events to arise from their concurrence, than admit of so signal a violation of the laws of nature."

And also: "Where shall we find such a number of circumstances, agreeing to the corroboration of one fact? And what have we to oppose to such a cloud of witnesses, but the absolute impossibility of the miraculous nature of the events which they relate? And this, surely, in the eyes of all reasonable people, will alone be regarded as a sufficient refutation."

Long before Hume, a similar point of view was taken by the Greek writer Lucian: "To defend one's mind against these follies, a man must have an adamantine faith, so that, even if he is not able to detect the precise trick by which the illusion is produced, he at any rate retains his conviction that the whole thing is a lie and an impossibility."[9]

And Tom Paine, a little after Hume, stated the same argument succinctly: ". . . is it more probable that nature should go out of her course, or that a man should tell a lie?"[10]

My opinion concerning the findings of the parapsychologists is that many of them are dependent on clerical and statistical errors and unintentional use of sensory clues, and that all extrachance results not so explicable are dependent on deliberate fraud or mildly abnormal mental conditions.

The first step in applying Hume's argument would preferably be to make a numerical estimate of the a priori improbability of ESP. But unfortunately, it appears that scientific philosophy has not yet developed to the point where this is possible. This is regrettable, yet we should consider that if the problem were so simple as to permit numerical calculation, then this controversy would perhaps never have arisen.

Since I cannot prove, all I can do is try to convince by showing that ESP is incompatible with current scientific theory. It is sometimes asked: with what scientific laws does ESP conflict? But the conflict is at so fundamental a level as to be not so much with named "laws" but rather with basic principles. C. D. Broad has presented an excellent analysis showing that the psi effects are incompatible with nine "basic limiting principles" involving our fundamental concepts of space, time, and causality.[11] I accept his analysis and incorporate it as part of the present argument.

Broad's discussion is too long to summarize here, so instead I shall list several incompatibilities of psi phenomena, described in a less fundamental manner. (i) ESP penetrates the future even in situations where rational inference is powerless. (ii) ESP is apparently unattenuated by distance. (iii) Psi effects are apparently unaffected by shielding. They come from matter and interact with matter (control of dice in psychokinesis), so why do they not interact with matter in a shield? (iv) Dye patterns on cards are read in the dark: how does one detect a tract of dye without shining light on it? (v) Patterns on cards in the center of a pack are read without interference from other cards. (vi) We have found in the body no structure to associate with the alleged functions. (vii) There is no learning but, instead, a tendency toward complete loss of ability. (So far as I know, there is for this type of behavior no parallel among established mental functions.) (viii) Different investigators obtain highly different results. For example, Soal requires a telepathic sender, but Rhine finds this unnecessary.

The parapsychologists themselves have agreed almost unanimously that psi phenomena are completely incompatible with modern physics. The situation has been analyzed in detail and with excellent logic by both Rhine[12] and Soal.[13] And Rhine has correctly stated that "nothing in all the history of human thought—heliocentrism, evolution, relativity—has been more truly revolutionary or radically contradictory to contemporary thought than the results of the investigation of precognitive psi."[14]

To be sure, some scientists have argued that there may be no incompatibility. For example, see a recent paper on "Parapsychology and Dualism" by Walker.[15] And Boring writes: "All you have got yet for extrasensory perception is an observed difference between two frequencies, between hits and misses, and a great deal of ignorance as to what causes the difference. Ignorance does not overthrow old concepts."[16] But it seems to me that this is equivalent to arguing: "So you have seen a man turn into a small bat and fly away, and you think that this is evidence for the existence of vampires? Nonsense. All you have got is a difference between two patterns in which photons strike the retina, and a great deal of ignorance as to what causes the difference. Ignorance is not evidence." I feel that R. H. Thouless describes matters aptly when he says: "I suggest that the discovery of the *psi* phenomena has brought us to a ... point at which we must question basic theories because they lead us to expectations contradicted by experimental results."[17]

If, then, parapsychology and modern science are incompatible, why not reject parapsychology? We know that the alternate hypothesis, that some men lie or deceive themselves, fits quite well within the framework of science. The choice is between believing in something "truly revolutionary" and "radically contradictory to contemporary thought" and believing in the occurrence of fraud and self-delusion. Which is more reasonable?

But the parapsychologists usually reply that we should accept both science and the supernatural. Although these may not fit together within a single scheme of things, we can imagine two separate systems, each compatible within itself. Why should we not accept dualism? To answer this here, I must try to compress a complex argument into a minute space. The answer is: because past experience shows that dualistic reasoning has usually been comparatively unsuccessful in making predictions concerning observable phenomena.

Experience is all we have available as a guide to the future. As Reichenbach has pointed out, even when we consider magic phenomena, we must still base our expectations on inductive reasoning from past experience.[18] From our experience we have derived certain generalizations concerning observable phenomena. (Some of these we term *laws of science*, while others are so fundamental that we rarely name them.) In addition, we are able to make other generalizations concerning these first generalizations, for an enormous amount of pertinent data has accumulated. Thus, experience shows that scientific laws often fail when they are extended to a new range of size, like atomic size, but scientific laws do not fail in association with particular people.

For example: Suppose a physics student reports that he has found the wave-length of the red cadmium line to be 2 millimicrons greater than the accepted value. Now we cannot in any way at all prove that there do not actually exist some human beings whose presence can cause real, experimentally verifiable changes in physical constants—just as we cannot prove that the universe will not come to an end tomorrow. But our past experience suggests that the most profitable attitude for us will be to assume that the student made an error.

The Essence of Magic

We now imagine a new critic, who speaks to us as follows: "This is all very well, and I concede that psi phenomena appears to me most strange and improbable, but a half century ago I would have felt the same way concerning relativity. Does not any radically new complex phenomenon appear as baffling and improbable as ESP?"

What is required is a test to separate reported findings toward which we should be receptive. What is the fundamental difference between the natural and the supernatural? What is the essential characteristic of magic?

Let us compare scientific and magical methods of table levitation.[19] A scientist sits in his living room and says: "Table, rise." His speech pattern is portrayed on the screen of a visible speech apparatus. Phototubes observe the pattern through masks of appropriate shapes. A switch is closed, turning on an enormous electromagnet on the floor above. This attracts an iron plate concealed within the table top, and the table rises to the ceiling.

Similarly, the magician says: "Table, rise." And the table rises. The difference is that there is no iron plate, no electromagnet, no switch, and no speech interpretation apparatus.

Now a scientist can accept the absence of the iron plate; it is conceivable that there can exist sharply localized forces attracting wooden objects. He can even accept the absence of the magnet. What he cannot accept is the absence of the speech interpretation apparatus and the switch. New forces can be fitted into a scientific scheme of things. What cannot be made to fit is the *intelligent* manner in which the force is turned on and *directed* to act upon the table.

In the scientific process, each successive detail is provided for. In the magic process, there are just the wish and the result, and all intermediate steps are omitted. The essential characteristic of magic is that phenomena occur that can most easily be explained in terms of action by invisible intelligent beings.[20] The essence of science is mechanism. The essence of magic is animism. The way of science is to build a television system and a radio-controlled robot manipulator and have the manipulator cut a pack of cards at the twelfth card and hold it up to the television camera. The way of magic is to sit in a chair with eyes closed and vaguely wish to know the identity of the twelfth card down in a certain pact 100 miles away; and then the answer pops into one's mind.

Suppose that some extraordinary new phenomenon is reported: should we be narrow-minded or receptive? The test is to attempt to imagine a detailed mechanistic explanation. Whenever we can imagine any sort of detailed explanation without introducing incorporeal intelligences, we should be prepared to regard the phenomenon open-mindedly. For this test it is not necessary that our explanation be simple, reasonable, or usable in making predictions. For example, any nuclear physicist could postulate a score of new forces, transition rules, and such, and so produce a complete theory of the atomic nucleus. Such a theory would be scientifically worthless, yet it would still satisfy the proposed test.

But with the phenomena of parapsychology, the situation is entirely different. Suppose that we attempt to describe mechanisms. Let us start with ESP tests at a distance of 100 miles or so, and let us feel free to imagine strange, fantastic forces without limit. Assume that we have under our control an invisible observation device that we can send in any direction at the speed of light. How do we go about locating a pack of cards 100 miles away? Would we guide ourselves by landmarks—or what? And would we not have to perceive with great accuracy in order to find the target? But how can we be accurate in perception of landmarks when we are grossly inaccurate in reading the target card? And how do we go through this locating process without any consciousness of it?

The special linkage that seems to exist between a percipient and the proper target card or telepathic sender is the sort of linkage that is characteristic of magic. In Greek mythology, the life of Meleager was linked to a piece of wood, and when his mother threw it on a fire, he perished far away. Or an African witch doctor makes a clay image and buries within it nail parings and bits of hair, and when the image is destroyed a man dies in London. Or a curse is uttered, and some magic influence goes to seek a distant victim.

Next, consider the process of "reading down" through a pace of ESP cards. How do we accurately locate the twelfth card? How do we tell that we are reading the pattern on the face of card twelve and not confusing it with the back of card thirteen? How do we detect dye molecules in the dark? Do we subject the electrons to the same transitions that they would undergo in light, or do we employ different means of analysis? And how do we analyze just the dye and not the paper? Imagine anything you wish. Feel free to invent a new topology and a dozen different types of fields. But just describe the process in detail.

For other mental processes, conscious or subconscious, we can describe (or at least imagine) successive steps. We can describe in detail the steps involved in the creation of a great poem[21] or a mathematical theory.[22] We can explain subconscious processes such as the regulation of our heartbeat. Where information is missing, we can guess. But with the supernatural, all is different.

Moreover, how does the information get into a brain? How is it converted into electrochemical changes within neurons? And suppose that translation into neural impulses is already accomplished; then how are these signals to be interpreted? Pitts and McCulloch have suggested neural patterns in human brains for interpretation of visual and auditory stimuli,[23] but can anyone describe a conceivable nerve network for interpreting the raw data of ESP?

And finally, what conceivable way is there to explain precognition?

There is no plausible way to explain these details except in terms of special intelligent agents—spirits or poltergeists or whatever one wishes to call them. The proper target card is selected by a spirit. A spirit implants information in the brain in proper electrochemical form. The ability disappears when the spirit tires of working with a particular person. In short, parapsychology, although well camouflaged with some of the paraphernalia of science, still bears in abundance the markings of magic.

To be sure, the world of magic is a lovely world. To make a silent wish, and mysteriously influence the fall of dice; to sit with closed eyes while knowledge of the future strangely floats into the mind—these possibilities have for us the charm of childhood days, when we could fall asleep on Christmas Eve and in the morning find a tree hung with presents, like some Arabian Nights adventurer who fell asleep in a hovel and awoke in an enchanted palace. But the way of science is different. To construct a building, each brick and board must be fitted into place by human beings—not by jinn who answer the rubbing of a lamp. If our soldering is careless, our circuit will certainly be noisy; and if we make our seals poorly, our vacuum system will assuredly leak—and no incantation will help.

Fraud and Error

Following the publication in 1935 of Rhine's first book,[24] numerous papers appeared in American psychological journals pointing out possibilities of clerical errors and sensory clues and criticizing the statistical methods. These criticisms have been reviewed in detail by Pratt, et al.[25] Later attacks of this sort were made by Nabours,[26] Skinner,[27] Rawcliffe,[28] Brown,[29] and—most recently and authoritatively—by Soal himself.[30]

I believe that many of these criticisms were justified, but I am also completely convinced that some of Rhine's work and most of Soal's can be accounted for by no conceivable combination of such explanations.

What about fraud?

The parapsychologists speak of that possibility with utmost scorn: "We have done all that we can when the critic has nothing left to allege except that the investigator is in on the trick. But when he has nothing else to allege he will allege that."[31] The hypothesis of "extensive and collusory fraud has yet to be responsibly suggested."[32] "The notion of such wholesale conspiracy would be to most students more fantastic than the ESP hypothesis."[33]

Surprisingly, it is not only believers who are reluctant to imagine fraud, but virtually all skeptics as well will prefer almost any other type of explanation. It would be tedious for me to cite statistics to show that "the knavery and folly of men" are indeed "common phenomena," for everyone is aware of this—in an intellectual way. But when we try to imagine knavery and folly in connection with a particular individual, we encounter a surprising emotional blockage, and the possibility seems unreasonable. And thus we find skeptics searching for every other conceivable sort of explanation—proposing absurd systems of involuntary whispering, or indulging in the metaphysical acrobatics of arguing that ESP cannot occur because it involves a "negative hypothesis"—while the one explanation that is simplest and most in accord with everyday experience is dismissed as inconceivable. It is almost as though we give this answer to Pain: "We detest the thought that nature would go out of her course, but we will not believe that a man would tell a lie."

It is particularly difficult for us to conceive of dishonesty in any situation where fraud would have to be complex and daring. For example, most people find it easier to imagine that some assistant may have occasionally cheated in an ESP experiment, than to suppose that a chief investigator could have deliberately designed an entire investigation fraudulently. Similarly, in the field of the "confidence game," the victim might be capable of suspecting one or two of his new "friends" as crooks, except that he cannot imagine that the entire stock exchange or gambling club to which they introduce him is an artifice, with the manager, employees, and even patrons all "in the trick."

A good antidote against our curious mixture of credulity and incredulity is to become acquainted with some of the elaborate deceits of the past. Books that describe fraudulent production of supernatural phenomena have been written by Houdini,[34] Podmore,[35] Dunninger, Jastrow, and Rawcliffe. Confidence games involving expert understanding of the psychology of credulity are described by MacDonald.[36] And MacDougall discusses the history and psychology of hoaxing.[37]

There is a literature of the supernatural, just as there is a literature of chemistry and physics, and the scientist who ignores this literature and depends on his pure reasoning powers in evaluating reports of psychic phenomena is at a disadvantage. A little acquaintance with the careful studies of men like Podmore and Houdini will give one a broader point of view and a clearer understanding by which to evaluate modern parapsychology. For example, the man who knows that the Davenport brothers employed as many as ten confederates in a single seance[38] should not think it unreasonable when I presently suggest that I would want seven or eight confederates in order to imitate 170 Soal sittings. And the reader who finds that he cannot conceive of the possibility that any leading modern parapsychologist could be fraudulent should compare his attitude with certain earlier judgments concerning the honesty of mediums. Consider, for example, Houdini's report that Arthur Conan Doyle told him that "he did not believe any of 'the nice old lady mediums' would do anything wrong and it was just as unlikely for some old gentleman, innocent as a child unborn, to resort to trickery."[39] Or consider William Crooke's opinion of Daniel Home: "To those who knew him Home was one of the most lovable of men, and his perfect genuineness and uprightness were beyond suspicion . . ."[40] (Home was the most brilliant and successful of all mediums, and his patrons included the rulers of France and Russia. He could elongate his body by eleven inches, levitate himself and float around seance rooms near the ceiling, and perform numerous other miracles.)

History shows numerous men of great intelligence victimized by the simplest and most transparent trickery. Therefore, it is wisdom on our part to be aware that the rules by which we actually protect ourselves against dishonesty are little more than rules-of-thumb telling what to do in particular situations ("Don't gamble with strangers," "Know your endorser," "Always have a lawyer read the contract"), while our general principles for detection of dishonesty are mostly prejudices with little value. The courts, as a result of vast experience and utter necessity, have worked out a moderately satisfactory system of rules of evidence; but the psychological theorizing by which in daily life we judge innocence or guilt is valueless when it is applied to the work of a clever deceiver.

There is a certain stereotype of appearance and behavior that we associate with honesty, and a second stereotype that we associate with dishonesty—and successful swindlers are wise enough to imitate the former stereotype. "O what a goodly outside falsehood hath!" And so it is folly for us to survey the actions of a brilliant man and say: "This looks honest. If he were a charlatan, he would have done thus and so." Let us remember that those who seek to deceive us possibly are smarter than we are and probably have had more practice in simulating honesty than we have had in detecting dishonesty.

The wise procedure, when we seek to evaluate probability of fraud, is to try to ignore all vague, psychological criteria and base our reasoning (i) on such evidence as would impress a court and (ii) on purely statistical considerations. And here we must recognize that we usually make a certain gross statistical error. When we consider the possibility of fraud, almost invariably we think of particular individuals and ask ourselves whether it is possible that this particular man, this Professor X, could be dishonest. The probability seems small. But the procedure is incorrect. The correct procedure is to consider that we very likely would not have heard of Professor X at all except for his psychic findings. Accordingly, the probability of interest to us is the probability of there having been anywhere in the world, among its more than two billion inhabitants, a few people with the desire and the ability artfully to produce false evidence for the supernatural.

Has There Been a Satisfactory Test?

What is needed is one completely convincing experiment—just one experiment that does not have to be accepted simply on a basis of faith in human honesty. We should require evidence of such nature that it would convince us even if we knew that the chief experimenter was a stage conjurer or a confidence man. Has there been any single ESP experiment that would stand up if it were examined from this point of view?

Had I but space enough, I would analyze here all the major experiments of all the major investigators. But I do not have. I might select Rhine's work for discussion, but it apparently has not impressed critics nearly so much as Soal's. In fact, there are some indications that it has not impressed Soal himself very much.[41] But Soal's own work has been found convincing by eminent men of great intelligence. G. Evelyn Hutchinson wrote concerning the Shackleton experiments that "they appear to be the most carefully conducted investigations of the kind ever to have been made," and that "Soal's work was conducted with every precaution that it was possible to devise."[42] C. D. Broad wrote: "There was already a considerable mass of quite good experimental evidence for telepathy, e.g., in the work of Dr. Rhine and his colleagues at Duke University, but Dr. Soal's results are outstanding .... The precautions taken to prevent deliberate fraud or the unwitting conveyance of information by normal means are described in great detail, and seem to be absolutely watertight."[43]

So in the next two sections, I shall describe and analyze Soal's experiments. But I hope that readers will not search in these sections for psychological clues with which to bolster skepticism or belief. For example, one may note that Soal was originally himself a partial skeptic and from this conclude that he must be honest. Or conversely, one can reason: "The fact that for the Stewart series Soal altered the position of the screen aperture, raising it to eye level, suggests that he arranged conditions so that he could observe cards reflected in eyeglasses." But the wise course is to try to avoid such ethereal speculation. At best they may be treated as hunches to guide detectives but not as evidence to be presented in court. Such trivia would hardly be considered in a trial of a pickpocket, so they should not be offered as evidence for deciding profound cosmological questions.

This is the type of testimony that impresses a court: "On April 17, 1910, at a seance given by Eusapia Paladino in New York City at the home of Professor H. G. Lord, I crawled under some chairs and lay with my face on the floor within eight inches of the leg of the table at the left side of the medium, and a foot came from underneath the dress of the medium and placed the toe underneath the left leg of the table, and pressing upward, gave it a little chuck into the air."[44] Since I know of no evidence of this nature showing that Soal did or did not cheat, all that I am trying to do in the next two sections is to demonstrate that Soal *could* have cheated if he wanted to, and that therefore we should demand better evidence than his before we believe in the supernatural.

Soal's Experiments

In his early work as a psychic investigator, Soal published excellent papers reporting negative findings and showed himself to be a meticulous and ingenious experimenter, expert at uncovering trickery[45]. Then, allegedly, in 1939 He recalculated some old data and found that two people he had tested unsuccessfully for contemporaneous telepathy had actually been making highly significant precognitive scores.[46] These were Basil Shackleton and Mrs. Gloria Stewart. Shackleton was then studied in 40 sittings dating from January, 1941, to April, 1943.[46] Mrs. Stewart was investigated from August, 1945 to January, 1950, in 130 sittings.[47]

The complex experimental procedure devised by Soal is most conveniently described as a cryptographic process (although Soal himself does not employ this terminology). An original number sequence of 50 terms (randomly selected from the digits 1 to 5) is enciphered by use of a key to yield a letter sequence. The latter is transmitted telepathically to a percipient, who records his guesses. This received letter sequence is deciphered by use of the key to yield a second number sequence, which is compared with the original. The cipher system is simple, one-digit substitution, and the key is a permutation of the letters E G L P Z (or other symbols). The total process is illustrated in Table 1, as it might occur with the following key:

$$\begin{array}{ccccc} 1 & 2 & 3 & 4 & 5 \\ L & P & Z & G & E \end{array}$$

The steps in the process are carried out by (i) the "EA" (the *E*xperimenter *A*ssociated with the *A*gent), who shows the original sequence, one digit at a time, to (ii) the *Agent*, who performs the enciphering and then telepathically transmits to (iii) the *Percipient*. At the close of a sitting, all received sequences are deciphered and then scored for "hits," as is shown in column VI, which indicates postcognitive ("-2" and "-1"), contemporaneous ("0"), and precognitive ("+1" and "+2") hits.

Table 1

An example of the transformations involved in a typical telepathy experiment of the Soal type.

I Trial number	II Original sequence	III Enciphered sequence	IV Received sequence (guesses)	V Deciphered sequence	VI Type of "hit"
1	3	Z	G	4	
2	5	E	E	5	0
3	1	L	E	5	-1, +2
4	4	G	P	2	
5	5	E	L	1	-2, +1
6	1	L	Z	3	
7	2	P	P	2	0, +1
8	2	P	G	4	+1
9	4	G	Z	3	+1
10	3	Z	P	2	-2

The EA and Agent sit on opposite sides of a small table, separated by a screen with a three-inch square aperture. (The center of the aperture was thirteen inches above the table top in the Shackleton sittings and eighteen inches above the table in the Stewart sittings.) Resting in a rectangular box on the table on the Agent's side is a row of five *code cards* bearing animal pictures or initial letters (for example, Elephant, Giraffe, Lion, Pelican, Zebra). The open face of the box is toward the Agent, so that the code cards are shielded from the EA and others. The Percipient is in another room.

In a typical experiment, at each trial the EA displays at the aperture the digit indicated by a Random number list (column II), and then he calls out to the Percipient the serial number of the trial (column I). Then the Agent briefly raises and glances at the code card in the indicated position, and the percipient writes his guess. For example, at trial number 8 in Table 1, the EA displayed the digit 2 at the aperture and called out "eight." The Agent then raised the card in position 2 (second from the left) and glanced at the picture of a pelican. The Percipient wrote down the letter G, which was a "+1" precognitive hit.

Sittings were usually composed of eight runs of fifty trials. At "normal" rate of calling, each trial required between two and three seconds. At the start of each run, the Agent or an observer shuffled and arranged the code cards out of sight of the EA, thereby changing the key. After each fifty trials, the code-card order was recorded. Following the last run, the Percipient's guesses were deciphered by the appropriate key, and hits were counted.

There were a number of variations. In most experiments the original sequence was taken from a list provided by Soal, but occasionally lists were computed by outsiders and were given directly to the EA at the start of the experiment. At a few sittings the number sequence was generated by the EA during the run by drawing colored counters from a bag or bowl. Usually the sitting was in the Percipient's home, but occasionally other locations were employed; and in six sittings Mrs. Stewart made her guesses in Antwerp, with Agents in London.

In the Shackleton series, almost all the extrachance results were produced with either "R. E." or "J. Al." as Agent. With the former, most successes were "+1" precognitive hits. In 5367 "+1" trials at "normal" rate of calling with R. E. as Agent, Shackleton scored 1540 "+1" hits, for a mean of 13.77 per run of 50 trials.[48] Usually, with J. Al. as Agent, both pre and postcognitive guesses yielded more than thirteen hits per run; hits were ordinarily "-1" and "+1," but changed to "-2" and "+2" when the calling rate was doubled. Thirty-one sittings yielded extrachance results, and at all of these both Soal and Shackleton were present, plus at least one of the following: Mrs. Goldney, J. Al., and R. E. In addition, at twenty-three of the thirty-one sittings, one or more additional persons were present. Usually these took the roles of EP (*E*xperimenter watching the *P*ercipient) or EA, or watched the Agent; but two worked successfully as Agents.

In the Stewart series, thirty persons were tested as Agents, and fifteen were successful. Total score for 37,100 trials by standard procedure was 9410 "0" hits, for a mean score of 12.68 hits per run of 50. In these experiments Soal usually took the role of EA. The usual procedure was for the Agent to shuffle the cards and then arrange them face up and stare at them for thirty seconds. Then they were turned over, and during the run the Agent tapped the indicated card on the back instead of lifting it. The cards usually bore initial letters about two inches high instead of animal pictures.[49]

Analysis of Soal's Work

Before I continue, it should be clearly understood that I am not here stating that Soal or any of his associates were guilty of deliberate fraud. All that I want to do is show that fraud was easily possible.

I do not claim that I know how Soal cheated if he did cheat, but if I were myself to attempt to duplicate his results, this is how I would proceed. First of all, I would seek a few collaborators, preferably people with good memories. The more collaborators I had, the easier it would be to perform the experiments, but the greater would be the risk of disclosure. Weighing these two considerations together, I'd want four confederates to imitate the Shackleton experiments. For imitating the Stewart series, I'd probably want three or four—although it is impossible to be certain, because the Stewart sittings have not been reported in much detail. In recruiting, I would appeal not to desire for fame or material gain, but to the noblest motives, arguing that much good to humanity could result from a small deception designed to strengthen religious belief.

The next step would be to devise procedures. Like a competent medium, I would want several alternatives available, so that any skeptic who suspected one procedure could be confronted by a repetition performed under conditions making the suspected procedure impossible. One main group of procedures would involve matching a prepared random number sequence to a letter or number sequence previously memorized or written out by the Percipient. At about ninety percent of my sittings, the original sequences would be taken from lists provided by me. Here are a few of the possibilities:

Procedure 1. The Percipient and the Agent are "in the trick." The Agent arranges the code cards as previously directed by me, and the Percipient writes down a memorized sequence or takes a list from a drawer if no outsider is watching him. (This would be a preferred procedure in most experiments except when an outsider determined the order of the code cards. It could succeed with outsiders as EA and EP.)

Procedure 2. The Percipient and the Agent (or the EA or an observer) are "in the trick." The code card order is determined by an outsider. The Agent (or the EA or an observer) notes this order, classifies it into one of six groups, and signals the group number to the Percipient before or after the run. Only 2.6 bits of information are needed to designate a choice of one out of six. For example, the Agent glances at the backs of the cards and then says: "Ready," "All ready," "Yes, I'm ready," "Yes, ready," and so forth.[50] The percipient then takes from a drawer the designated guess sheet, which is already filled out in his handwriting.[51] (If the Agent is an outsider, the EA or an observer can note the card order when it is recorded at the end of the run and signal it in the conversation then.)

Procedure 3. The Percipient and the Agent are "in the trick." The Agent notes the card order and signals it (6.9 bits for the 120 possible permutations) before the start of the run. The Percipient has memorized a number sequence, and he uses the card order to encipher each number sequence, and he uses the card order to encipher each number mentally. (This can work with outsiders watching both the Agent and the Percipient and shuffling the code cards; or if the Agent is an outsider, the signaling can be done by an observer who shuffles the cards.)

Next consider some of the procedures that could be used even when the number sequence was not known to me in advance:

Procedure 4. The percipient and the Agent are "in the trick." They have copied or memorized the same lists of letter symbols. During the run the Agent records (concealed by the box) the numbers corresponding (precognitively) to the letters that he knows the Percipient is guessing, and at the end he rearranges the code cards to give the desired degree of success. For example, with a record like that shown in Fig. 1, the Agent could see that card arrangement LEGZP will yield a large number of hits. (This procedure would be particularly useful when the EA was an outsider.)

	1	2	3	4	5
E	//	////	//	//	/
G	//		///	//	////
L	///	///	//	/	/
P		//	//	/	///
Z	//	//	/	///	

Fig. 1. Type of record to be kept by an Agent employing Procedure 4 for simulating telepathy. If the number sequence "12345" is replaced by the letter sequence "LEGZP," it will be seen that arranging the code cards in this order will result in 16 "hits."

Procedure 5. The Percipient and the EA are "in the trick." The EA learns the order of the code cards and signals information to the Percipient during the run. The Percipient has memorized a random sequence of letter symbols. The EA, in calling out the serial numbers, slightly alters his voice or timing a few times during each run (five times per fifty trials to give fourteen hits). Ordinarily the Percipient is to guess at random, but at each signal he writes down the next letter in the memorized sequence. (I would use this method particularly in experiments when an outsider who wore glasses served as Agent. Then the preferred experimental arrangement would be that in which the cards are turned face up for thirty seconds, the screen aperture would be located as it was in the Stewart sittings, and the lighting would be so arranged that the EA could see the cards by reflection in the Agent's glasses.)

Procedure 6. The Percipient plus the EA, the *Recorder*, or the Agent are "in the trick." In runs where the number sequence is generated by counters, I would have the EA draw counters of the needed color at particular points, or the Recorder could keep false records of counters drawn. And in some experiments, Procedures 1, 4, or 5 could be used.

The procedures that could give the highest degree of success, and that thus would be chosen when I wanted simultaneous "-1" and "+1" or "-2" and "+2" successes, are Procedures 1 and 3. Any of the others would be more than adequate for scores of 12.68 hits per run of 50, or 13.177 hits in 48 trials. For long-distance experiments, Procedures 1 and 4 would work. Or I could employ Procedure 2 by telephoning the Percipient after the sitting to tell him which lists to mail in.

Many other procedures are possible. The six chosen for description were selected as samples of what can be done by simple means. Mental abilities required are similar to those needed for playing bridge competently, except that some collaborators would need a little memory training. Use of special apparatus or of collaborators with the abilities of a good stage conjurer would open up numerous new possibilities. Thus it should be clear that Soal's work was *not* conducted "with every precaution that it was possible to devise." The work would have been enormously more nearly fraudproof if Soal, instead of employing his highly complex arrangement, had simply had many different Agents "send" directly from lists prepared by outsiders and given directly to the Agent at the start of each run. And the examples to be given presently will show what precautions can be devised if one really wants to devise precautions.

Why Has There Been No Satisfactory Test?

Both Soal and Rhine have demonstrated ESP before intelligent "open-minded" outside observers, but what is needed is something that can be demonstrated to the most hostile, pig-headed, and skeptical of critics. Why has there been no such demonstration? Because when onlookers are hostile, "sensitives" allegedly lose their paranormal abilities. This excuse is an old one, long employed by spiritualist mediums, but contemporary parapsychology has modernized it with a touch of poetry. Thus Rhine asks: "Would you expect, if we had a young poet here, that we could send him up to your university to write some poems for you while your committee sat staring fixedly at him to see that he did not slip them from one of his pockets?"[52] And Soal argues: "But one would not expect even a poet to produce a good poem if he were surrounded by people who, he felt, viewed his activities with half-concealed scorn or humorous contempt. The best he could do would be to churn out a few passable verses from which the informing spirit of poetry would be absent."[53]

There are two replies to this excuse. The first is that it is false. It appears plausible to us because nowadays we tend to regard poets as rather erratic, neurotic beings. But in other periods, when it was expected of every educated man that he be able to write competent poetry, such reasoning would not have seemed convincing. Of course there are poets who require solitude for work, just as there are bridge players who are upset by kibitzers; but one would hardly imagine, say, Sidney or Raleigh or Byron suddenly starting to write like Edgar Guest because people were staring at him.

Poetic creation, as analyzed by John Livingston Lowes in his monumental study of Coleridge, *Road to Xanadu*, is strikingly similar to mathematical creation, as described by Jacques Hadamard in his brilliant little book on *The Psychology of Invention in the Mathematical Field*. We expect a young mathematician to be able to do creative mathematical thinking before a hostile examining committee, and a poet or any other kind of thinker can do as well. Rhine writes: "All the fickleness and skittishness of ESP and PK will find their counterparts in the fine arts, in the realm of the Muses."[54] But this is not correct. There is no established human ability whatsoever that shows the fickleness of ESP.

Such is the first reply to the excuse of Rhine and Soal. And the second reply is that it is perfectly possible to set up fraudproof tests permitting "sensitives" to work anywhere they wish, completely alone or with whatever company they desire, and yet with the experiments subject to the most searching scrutiny at all essential points.

In other days, numerous "sensitives" willingly demonstrated their marvels before critical examining committees. In the 1870's Daniel Home submitted to painstaking investigation by William Crookes. In the 1880's, a number of mediums appeared before the Seybert Commission of the University of Pennsylvania. Later, the British and American Societies for Psychical Research continued the type of investigations that had been started by the Seybert Commission. And from about 1880 to 1910, the great Eusapia Palladino made a specialty of holding seances before committees of scientists.

But a change came. Although scientists were often easily fooled, conjurers proved to be able foes of mediums. Houdini devoted the last years of his life to exposing mediums, and then this work was continued by Dunninger, who for many years defended the *Science and Invention* awards of $21,000 for psychical spirit manifestations that he could not duplicate by scientific means.[55] So effective has such work been that nowadays we hear very little of archaic wonders like materializations or elongations, levitations or transportations. Such tricks are too risky, too easily exposed by skeptics with flashlights. Instead, today we are expected to marvel at vague statistical effects, minutiae that a conjurer would scorn to imitate on a stage. So little is claimed, and this little is demonstrated only to such restricted audiences and under such carefully controlled conditions and with so many excuses for failure available that it is quite difficult to prove that the little is actually nothing. Yet this can be done, I think.

As scientists, what sort of evidence for ESP should we demand? This sort: one test of such nature that fraud or error would seem to us as improbable as the supernatural. Let us somewhat arbitrarily think of a committee of twelve and design tests such that the presence of a single honest man on the "jury" will ensure validity of the test, even if the other eleven menbers should cooperate in fraud either to prove or disprove occurrence of psi phenomena. Assume that the committee includes two experimental psychologists, two experimental physicists, one statistician, and three conjurers or other experts on trickery—all prominent men and all strongly hostile toward parapsychology, with that "admantine faith" that Lucian recommended.[56] Then probably most scientists would have confidence in the committee and would be prepared to believe psi phenomena in preference to believing that the entire committee was dishonest or deluded. In addition, so that results would be acceptable to parapsychologists, the chairman of the committee should be a person with a record of successes in psi experimentation, for it is claimed by West[57] and Soal[58] that the personality of the chief experimenter may in some psychic manner determine success or failure in a psychic experiment.

To test Rhine's "sensitives," the simplest procedure is to prepare sealed packages of cards and mail them to Duke University to be examined by clairvoyants at any time and place they select, and then have them mailed back along with records of guesses. In preparing the packages, cards would be shuffled automatically by a series of machines and placed within opaque containers in such manner that no one could possibly have seen any card from the beginning of the shuffling. A good procedure for insuring against opening would be to place each set of cards in a small metal container, weld on a cover, and take photomicrographs of the weld—for it is probably impossible to counterfeit microscopic details. When the cards were returned, first the seals would be checked, and then packages would be cut open and cards fanned out by machine, with the jury watching and with a motion-picture camera recording everything.

For the type of findings made by Soal, the simplest and most fraudproof type of test would make use of the precognitive ability that Shackleton allegedly showed most of the time and that Mrs. Stewart allegedly showed for a brief time. With precognition, the only safeguards needed are that the "message" be generated in a way not subject to ordinary human control or prediction, and that guesses be recorded before the message is displayed. Imagine a radioactive sample of high activity, plus a scintillation counter with ring-of-five scaling circuit and indicator lamps corresponding to Soal's five animal symbols. An accurate timing circuit turns off the counter at set intervals. The circuitry is wired in such open fashion that inspection is easy. The apparatus is battery-powered and is placed in a shielded case, with nothing penetrating through the shield except windows to show the indicators. The percipient and the telepathic sender can be wherever in the world they wish, together or far apart, in the same room with the apparatus or across the ocean from it, alone or with whatever company they want. The guesses of the percipient (transmitted via radio or cable, if necessary) are indicated in some visible form, and a single motion-picture camera records both guesses and subsequent "calls" of the number generator.

It is also simple to test psychokinetic control of dice. While a motion-picture camera records everything, one or more dice are placed at the top of a chute or in a throwing machine. Then a ring-of-six random number generator tells the psychic controller what number to wish for, and a few seconds later the dice are automatically released. The psychic controller can be in the same room, or anywhere in the world where telephone or radio can reach him.

For testing contemporaneous telepathy, symbols to be transmitted should be controled by a random number generator, and the percipient could be anywhere in the world except close to the sender. However, it is exceedingly difficult to guard against all known communication means, especially since only a few bits of information need be transmitted per twenty-five trials in order to give extrachance results. For example, the sender might signal to a member of the committee by means of slight motions of his body, and the committee member could use a pocket radio transmitter to relay the information. I have worked out several procedures that appear to be reasonably fraudproof, but the required precautions are quite elaborate, and I am not sure that others cannot think of much simpler procedures, so I prefer not to take the space to describe my ideas here. No doubt clairvoyance, precognitive telepathy, and psychokinesis should be examined first, since it is so easy to test them. Then—if anyone is still interested in the question—contemporaneous telepathy can be tested.

Even now (in 1955) paranormal findings continue to be published in England[59] and America,[60] so it is reasonable for us to expect that both the British Society for Psychical Research and the Duke University Parapsychology Laboratory will gladly offer "sensitives" to be tested.

Conclusion

What sort of reply will the parapsychologists make to these criticisms? I have read answers they have made to others, and on that basis I might expect some of the following:

1) "Some interesting suggestions for further demonstrations of ESP have recently been made, but we consider that ESP was demonstrated beyond any reasonable doubt many years ago, and it is a waste of time to keep proving the same thing over and over again. However, there is much need for additional workers in the field, so we hope that Price will try his suggestions himself."

2) "Standards of experimentation in psi research are already far higher than those in most fields of science, so it is absurd to seek further improvement. Science would have made little progress if every chemistry and physics experiment had had to be performed before witnesses and with numerous other precautions."

3) "A foolish attack has recently been made by an incompetent man who, to the best of our belief, has never published a single experiment in the field of parapsychology."[61]

4) "Unfortunately, I can furnish no one right at present for demonstrating ESP. However, I proved everything conclusively, with odds against chance of 10^{237} to 1, back in 19—."

But the only answer that will impress me is an adequate experiment. Not 1000 experiments with 10 million trials and by 100 separate investigators giving odds against chance of 10^{1000} to 1—but just one good experiment. And until such a demonstration has been provided, I hope that my fellow-scientists will similarly withhold belief.[62]

• • •

My paper is extremely unfair to J. B. Rhine and S. G. Soal because I simply assumed, without making any slight attempt to find evidence to support my assumption, that they had faked ESP results for the purpose of promoting Christianity; and I suggested this in a way that made clear what I meant while cleverly avoiding libel. During correspondence with Rhine in 1971 it became obvious to me that he really was, after all, concerned with the scientific question of whether ESP occurs, and not at all seeking to promote religious belief through fraud. Undoubtedly the same is true of Soal. And as for the question (asked by several correspondents) whether I now believe that ESP occurs, I'm afraid the answer is that I have myself become guilty of accepting and trying to follow (in a rather radical way) that strange system of beliefs that I accused Rhine and Soal of trying to promote, and consequently I now believe in much worse things than ESP.

NOTES

1. See, for example the press release by B. H. Camp, president of the Institute of Mathematical Statistics, quoted in the *New York Herald Tribune,* January 16, 1938, sec. II-IV, p. 6.
2. J. G. Pratt, J. B. Rhine, B. M. Smith, C. E. Stuart, J. A. Greenwood, *Extra-Sensory Perception After Sixty Years* (New York: Holt, 1940).
3. S. G. Soal and F. Bateman, *Modern Experiments in Telepathy* (New Haven: Yale University Press, 1954). I cite this book as "Soal," rather than as "Soal and Bateman," since large portions of it are taken almost unchanged from papers by Soal alone or by Soal and Goldney.
4. R. A. McConnell, *Journal of Parapsychology,* Vol. 18 (1954): 245.
5. E. G. Boring, *American Scientist,* Vol. 43 (1955): 108.
6. C. E. Shannon, *Bell System Tech. J.,* Vol. 27 (1948): 379-423, 623-656.
7. Channel Capacity is given by:
bits/trial $= \log_2 5 + (N/25)\log_2 (N/25) + 4[(25-N)/100]\log_2 [(25-N)/100]$ where N is the mean number of "hits" per 25 trials ($N \geq 5$). (This formula applies strictly only to cases where in each trial there is equal probability of selecting any of the five symbols; thus it applies strictly to most of Soal's work but will be slightly in error for most of Rhine's work.)
8. J. B. Rhine, *Journal of Parapsychology,* Vol. 6 (1942): 111; Vol. 9 (1945): 264. Rhine, *The Reach of the Mind* (New York: Sloane, 1953), pp. 73-75. *The New World of the Mind* (New York: Sloane, 1953), pp. 95 ff. B. M. Humphrey and J. B. Rhine, *Journal of Parapsychology,* Vol. 6 (1942): 190.
9. Quoted by J. Jastrow in *Wish and Wisdom* (New York: Appleton-Century, 1935), p. 25.
10. T. Paine, *Age of Reason*; the quotation comes a few pages before the end of part I.
11. C. D. Broad, *Philosophy,* Vol. 24 (1949): 291.
12. *The New World of the Mind,* chpt. 4; also *The New Frontiers of the Mind* (New York: Farrar and Rinehart, 1937), chpt. 12.
13. *Op. cit.,* pp. 303-305.
14. *New World,* p. 94.
15. R. Walker, *Sci. Monthly,* Vol. 79 (1954): 1.
16. *Op. cit.*
17. *Ibid.,* p. 357.
18. H. Reichenbach, *The Theory of Probability* (Berkeley: University of California Press, 1949): 476.
19. I refer here to genuine magic, not the deceptions of mediums and stage conjurers. Five methods of table levitation employed by mediums are disclosed by J. Dunninger in *Inside the Medium's Cabinet* (New York: David Kemp, 1935).
20. I am using *magic* in a particular sense, defining it in terms of what *can* be explained in a certain way—without regard to how those who attempt to practice it actually do try to explain it. Actions that overtly resemble magic ceremonies and yet are based on mechanistic reasoning (like much of alchemy), I would call not magic but gropings toward science.
21. J. L. Lowes, *The Road to Xanadu* (Boston: Houghton Mifflin, 1927).
22. J. Hadamard, *The Psychology of Invention in the Mathematical Field* (Princeton: Princeton University Press, 1945).
23. W. Pitts and W. S. McCulloch, *Bull. Math. Biophys.,* Vol. 9 (1947): 127.
24. J. B. Rhine, *Extrasensory Perception* (Boston: Humphries, 1935).
25. *Op. cit.*
26. R. K. Nabours, *Philosophy of Science,* Vol. 10 (1943): 191.
27. B. F. Skinner, *Am. Scientist,* Vol. 36 (1948): 456, 482 ff.

28. D. H. Rawcliffe, *The Psychology of the Occult* (London: Ridgeway, 1952). I think that most of Rawcliffe's ideas are correct, but that his explanation of Soal's work in terms of involuntary whispering is implausible.

29. G. S. Brown, *Nature*, Vol. 172 (1953): 154. I think that Brown's criticism has been adequately refuted by Soal in reference 3.

30. *Op. cit.*

31. H. Sidgwick, *Proc. Soc. Psychical Research*, Vol. 1 (1882): 7.

32. W. W. Carington, *Ibid.*, Vol. 46 (1940): 265.

33. Soal, *op. cit.*, p. 166.

34. H. Houdini, *A Magician among the Spirits* (New York: Harper, 1911).

35. F. Podmore, *Modern Spiritualism*, 2 vols., (London: Methuen, 1902); *The Newer Spiritualism* (New York: Holt, 1911).

36. J. C. R. MacDonald, *Crime Is a Business* (Stanford: Stanford University Press, 1939).

37. C. D. MacDougall, *Hoaxes* (New York: Macmillan, 1940).

38. Sidgwick, *op. cit.*, p. 23.

39. *Ibid.*, p. 142.

40. W. Crookes, *J. Soc. Psychical Research*, Vol. 6 (1894): 341. Dissenting opinions concerning Home have been written by Podmore, Houdini, and R. Browning. Houdini (*op. cit.*, p. 49) states that "His active career, his various escapades, and the direct cause of his death all indicate that he lived the life of a hypocrite of the deepest dye." (Houdini does not name the cause of Home's death, although he does quote this sentence from Madame Blavatsky's *Key to Theosophy*: "This Calvin of Spiritualism suffered for years from a terrible spinal disease, brought on through his intercourse with the 'spirits,' and died a perfect wreck.") And Browning, in "Mr. Sludge, 'the Medium,' " gives this picture of Home: "Now, don't sir! Don't expose me! Just this once!/This was the first and only time, I'll swear,—/ Look at me, —see, I kneel,—the only time,/I swear, I ever cheated,—yes, by the soul/Of Her who hears—(your sainted mother, sir!)/All, except this last accident, was truth—"

41. S. G. Soal, *J. Proc. Soc. Psychical Research*, Vol. 50 (1953): 67; especially 84, 94; and *The Experimental Situation in Psychical Research* (London: Society for Psychical Research, 1947): 25 ff.

42. G. E. Hutchinson, *American Scientist*, Vol. 36 (1948): 291.

43. C. D. Broad, *Philosophy*, Vol. 19 (1944): 261.

44. Paraphrased from a report by J. F. Rinn, published by J. Jastrow in *Colllier's Weekly*, Vol. 45. No. 8 (14 May 1910): 21.

45. S. G. Soal, *Proc. Soc. Psychical Research*, Vol. 40 (1932): 165; *Journal of the Society for Psychical Research*, Vol. 30 (1937): 55; *Preliminary Studies of a Vaudeville Telepathist* (London: University of London Council for Psychical Investigation, Bull. III, 1937).

46. Soal, *Proc. Soc. Psychical Research*, Vol. 46 (1940): 152.

47. *Modern Experiments*. pp. 199-337; Soal and K. M. Goldney, *Ibid.*, Vol 47 (1943): 21; F. Bateman and S. G. Soal, *J. Soc. Psychical Research*, Vol. 35 (1950): 257; S. G. Soal and F. Bateman, *J. Parapsychol.*, Vol. 14 (1950):168.

48. Since there was a pause at the middle of each run, and pre- and post-cognitive hits occurring across this gap were not scored, there were 48"+1" trials per run of 50.

49. This description of Soal's experiments omits details not relevant to my argument. For example, I have said nothing concerning precautions taken against tampering with the records. Therefore, readers previously unfamiliar with Soal's work should be cautious in deciding that they have found a flaw in it.

50. Houdini states: "Regarding the possibility of using codes and cues before others without being detected I can say positively that it is not only possible but simple and practical" (*op. cit.*, p. 259). And Soal in several different places discusses

auditory codes and other signaling means: for example, in *Modern Experiments,* pp. 104, 117.

51. A variety of ways are available for setting up such a system. In one of these, 22 prepared guess sheets can suffice for a sitting of 8 runs, and simple, short-cut methods are available for quickly preparing the lists of guesses.

52. *New Frontiers,* p. 246.

53. *Modern Experiments,* pp. 52 ff.

54. *Reach of the Mind,* p. 141.

55. Of the $21,000, $1,000 was offered by *Science and Invention* magazine, $10,000 by the same J. F. Rinn who observed Palladino's footwork at close range. Further details are given in reference 19, and in J. Dunninger, *Houdini's Spirit Exposes from Houdini's Own Manuscripts, Records and Photographs* (New York: Experimenter Publ., 1928). Of course, no medium ever won the $21,000. No doubt, if any one of them had been clever enough to devise a trick that Dunninger could not duplicate, that person would not have been a medium, for he would probably have preferred to make an honest living as a conjurer.

56. Strong hostility toward supernaturalism is desirable as a safeguard, even though it is not absolutely essential. To be sure, Houdini had strong yearning to find evidence for the supernatural, and yet he was a most effective exposer of psychic fraud, but such a combination is exceedingly rare.

57. D. J. West, *J. Soc Psychical Research,* Vol. 37 (1954): 323.

58. *Modern Experiments,* p. 388 ff.

59. G. W. Fisk and D. J. West, *Ibid.,* Vol. 38 (1955): 1.

60. G. L. Mangan, *J. Parapsychol.,* Vol. 19 (1955): 35; Forwald, p. 45.

61. Soal, *Proceedings,* Vol. 50, in replying to criticism by Rawcliffe, *op. cit.,* writes: "All Mr. Rawcliffe's knowledge is derived from books; to the best of our belief he has never in his life published a single experiment in the field of parapsychology." Also, Soal writes: "It would be interesting to meet the psychiatrist or psychologist who has perused every page of the 49 volumes of the *Proceedings* of the Society for Psychical Research, and who remains a complete sceptic..." (*Modern Experiments,* pp. 23 ff.). It would be interesting indeed.

62. For reading early drafts of this paper and making numerous helpful suggestions, I am greatly indebted to Herbert Feigl, Bernard Gelbaum, Gerhard Kalisch, Leo Mars, Paul Meeh, and Michael Scriven, all of the University of Minnesota, and to Clause Shannon of Bell Telephone Laboratories. However, this must not be taken as implying that these men or the Department of Medicine, University of Minnesota, necessarily endorse my views.